Taxes on Knowledge in America

Taxes on Knowledge in America

Exactions on the Press from Colonial Times to the Present

Randall P. Bezanson

University of Pennsylvania Press

Philadelphia

Library of Congress Cataloging-in-Publication Data
Bezanson, Randall P.
  Taxes on knowledge in America: exactions on the press from colonial times to the present
/ Randall P. Bezanson.
    p. cm.
  Includes bibliographical references (p.   ) and index.
  ISBN 0-8122-3212-7 (acid-free paper)
    1. Stamp-duties — United States — History.   2. Censorship — United States — History.
3. Press law — United States — History.   I. Title.
KF6645.B49   1994
343.7305'7 — dc20
[347.30357]   93-44447
                                                                                    CIP

Contents

Preface

When an author undertakes a work of broad scope there is a solemn obligation to inform the reader of exactly what is covered and what is not. This is particularly true with the subject of knowledge taxation, for the very words connote concepts of uncertain and exceedingly broad reach. The term "knowledge tax" has its more or less fixed historical meaning, but even that meaning is deceptive to the uninitiated. Given the paucity of material that has been written on the American experience with such taxes, and the hazy and often romanticized recollections of the English experience, it is perhaps safe to assume that virtually everyone qualifies as uninitiated.

For my purposes in writing this book, I have defined the term "knowledge tax" to mean economic exactions on the modes of publication and distribution of current public information. From a historical perspective, this seems the most accurate representation of the concept. From a practical standpoint as well, this is happily an apt definition, for sufficiently insurmountable problems of scope present themselves even within this framework. The definition connotes, in more mundane terms, a principal focus on taxation of the press — taxation of the various media for the dissemination of news, including newspapers, magazines, pamphlets, and the like, as well as their newly emerging technological equivalents. Taxation, for these purposes, includes direct and indirect governmental exactions on the publication, distribution, and sale of periodical publications, including postal exactions. It includes, as well, taxation of books, which are today becoming an increasingly common medium for dissemination of current information, and the "taxation" of the new technologies of communication such as broadcasting, cable, computer-based storage and distribution of information, and satellite transmission, to name but a few. The definition does not include general income taxes and the like, nor does it include the economic costs associated with satisfying general business regulations imposed by government (such as minimum wages, aesthetic requirements, zoning regulations, and the like).

This scope, while broad, excludes many important subjects that might logically fit within the general concept of knowledge taxation, such as the taxation of such forms of knowledge as art, literary works, entertainment, and the like, as well as the regulation of the distribution systems for these and other media. I do refer to many of these subjects during the course of the book, but without pretense of exhaustive coverage. What can be learned from the history of knowledge taxes has implications for these other subjects, and it is noteworthy that the implications have hardly surfaced, much less been explored, elsewhere. But I confine myself to identifying those implications without probing them deeply.

Finally, I must make two quite explicit confessions. First, I am not a historian, and it is with no small measure of trepidation that I even use the term "history" to describe this work. I hope the reader will forgive my failings, have patience with my "lawyerly" penchant for drawing conclusions when a historian might not, and be understanding (though surely impatient) when my own view gets mixed in with the historical record. I have tried to avoid such errors (or to be explicit about their commission when unavoidable), but I have surely fallen short of the mark.

Second, I confess to falling short of an exhaustive historical account even within the defined scope of this work. Here the English experience is not a problem, for while I set it out by way of background only, there are ample and rich resources upon which to draw. Principal among them are the works, all cited profusely, by Messrs. Siebert, Clyde, Frank, Herd, Wickwar, Morrison, and, most recently, Professor Hamburger. I omit from this incomplete list, only to give it special attention, the quite remarkable little book entitled *History of the Taxes on Knowledge* by Collet Dobson Collet, a participant in and in many ways philosopher of the later stages of resistance to the stamp and related exactions in England. I make no pretense of original research on the English history; it is enough to attempt a synthesis and to draw broad conclusions from the rich material that these scholars have bequeathed to us.

As this history moves beyond the colonial and early ratification period into the nineteenth- and twentieth-century experience, however, the problems posed for a history of knowledge taxation in America over a two-hundred-year period and in all jurisdictions become increasingly onerous, if not insuperable. The problems involve the sheer volume of material, most of which must be discovered because it has never been collected in an organized way, and the practical inaccessibility of contemporaneous materials, such as newspaper accounts, in all of the states and local communities throughout the stretch of time. They involve, as well, the issues raised by new technologies, which I explore but with a firm awareness that the pace of change is now so rapid that today's "new" technologies may well be commonplace if not obsolete even before the publication of this book.

As the reader will see, I have adapted the research, albeit imperfectly, to these problems by studying selected jurisdictions in depth, sometimes ignoring all other states and jurisdictions, sometimes only hitting the surface of material from other jurisdictions. I have attempted to select jurisdictions in a way that would reflect differences on geographic, economic, and cultural levels, but I do not claim that the materials drawn from selected jurisdictions paint a representative picture of the national experience. Judgments about generalizability and utility for specific purposes must, by necessity, be left to the reader subject, hopefully, to further probing of the history by future scholars.

*   *   *

Let me turn finally to the most important subject, that of acknowledging and expressing appreciation for the efforts of many other persons. First and foremost, of course, is my wife, Elaine, who put up with my frequently peculiar work habits over the many years of labor on this book, and who expressed nothing but affectionate bemusement at my interest in old books, in dusty documents, and, indeed, in the obscure and unfathomable subject of knowledge taxation. I must thank, also, many colleagues at both Iowa and Washington & Lee for their ideas, suggestions, and critical judgments. At great risk I single out three of my colleagues at Washington & Lee for particular thanks: Louise Halper, David Millon, and Brian Murchison. Each of them labored through the manuscript from beginning to end, and with great care, attention to detail, and insight.

Many students and former students worked on the book over the years, and their contributions are legion and indispensable, ranging from original research to tracking down obscure sources to final cite-checking. The students from Iowa are Janet Lyness, Janet Peters, Charles Williams, and Michael Zeller. The students from Washington & Lee are Amy Balfour, David Giles, Julie Hottle, Robert Howie, Jim Lake, and Moira Roberts.

Last but anything but least are Diana DeWalle, Carole Shorter, and Carolyn Tappan. Diana DeWalle and Carolyn Tappan ably managed the work and prepared early parts of the manuscript while I was at Iowa. For them, loyalty meant doing yet another draft . . . and another. . . . But the prize goes to Carole Shorter, my secretary and assistant at Washington & Lee, who kept everything organized, smiled at the prospect of each new revision, and did so while also running the rest of the Law School, cleverly covering for the Dean who was often occupied with taxes and knowledge.

Introduction

> When the King of the Tonga Isles, in the Pacific Ocean, was initiated by Mr. Marriner, the missionary, into the mysteries of the art of writing, he was alarmed at the idea of his subjects learning to read: "I should," he said, "be surrounded with plots."
> — Collet Dobson Collet, *History of the Taxes on Knowledge*

From a historical perspective, the subjects of taxation and freedom of expression are inextricably linked. Indeed, the history of freedom of the press in England during the eighteenth and nineteenth centuries is dominated by the use of taxation as a means of press control. "Knowledge taxes" became, in important respects, the rallying point in the struggle to free the emerging forms of mass distribution of information from control by the Crown and Parliament. The most dangerous and insidious forms of censorship and control of the English press prior to and during the early, formative years of the American republic were not direct and overt censorship, but rather control through the economic force of taxation.

The struggle for freedom of expression in England represented the intellectual heritage from which our American concepts of freedom of speech and of the press evolved. This heritage shaped the very concept of press freedom in America and represented the accumulated experience from which Americans drew in defining the specific safeguards necessary to the establishment and survival of a free press in America. In view of this it is remarkable, and indeed quite puzzling, that the subject of taxation of the press, or knowledge taxes, was rarely mentioned in connection with the ratification of the First Amendment. Even more rarely was the subject discussed with any thoroughness or care.

At the time the First Amendment was ratified, the English struggle against taxation of the press was ongoing, but it was far from over. Resistance to the English taxes on publications and awareness of their impact on the broad availability of political information were increasing, although the apex of the taxes had yet to be reached and the turning point in the struggle for their repeal would not be reached until the 1830s. For Americans, the concept of prohibited taxes on knowledge was not so clear, nor its contours so obvious, that the subject could be taken for granted by the framers of the First Amendment guarantees. The ongoing struggle in England was too obvious to be ignored, but the text of the First Amendment and the historical materials surrounding its drafting and ratification are strangely silent and unenlightening on the limits to be placed on government control of the press through taxation. The English experience, it seems, was remote and clouded by the more general "taxation without representation" controversies with the Crown. And, perhaps, in a government "of the people," concern with knowledge taxation was simply less pressing, or even incomprehensible.

A similar absence of serious attention to the knowledge tax question appears to have persisted throughout the nearly two hundred years since the Bill of Rights was adopted. Except for occasional and isolated events, the "problem" of taxation of expression rarely arose in the public dialogue. Yet the historical silence seems not to have been caused by an absence of such taxes, for, upon examination, it appears that taxation of the press has been rather common throughout this country's history. Indeed, the history of taxation in nineteenth- and twentieth-century America witnesses the evolution of an intricate and complex web of increasingly sophisticated mechanisms of knowledge taxation. And on those infrequent occasions when voices were raised against such taxes, the connection with our English heritage was not lost. The historical references, however, have almost always been to the English antecedents, for the lack of public attention to the knowledge tax problem has been accompanied by an almost utter lack of historical research focusing on knowledge taxes in this country.

If the subject of knowledge taxes in America consisted of little more than these curiosities and puzzles, the field could be left dormant. This is not possible, however, for not only is the subject a conceptually and technically complex one, but it is of theoretical importance to our understanding of liberty, and it has taken on very practical and pressing importance in light of the attention recently given it by a trilogy of Supreme Court decisions exploring the constitutionality of state taxes on publications under the First Amendment.[1] If it was not relevant or obvious before those decisions, it is both relevant and obvious now that the very concept of taxes on knowledge needs definition, and that the limits on government's increasingly pervasive exercise of the power of taxation must be explored. And the need is of pressing relevance today as we enter into a new era of communication in which technology will force us to reexamine many of the most basic assumptions we hold about the role and, indeed, the *meaning* of the press.

My purpose is to address these very issues, beginning with a brief, but essential, discussion of the English history and experience with knowledge taxes, turning then to a discussion of knowledge taxes in America from colonial times to the present, and concluding with a review of the common threads, or themes, that run throughout the history of knowledge taxation in America. It is the common threads that may help us in our effort to define the concept of free expression in the taxation setting and to chart the operative limits on the exercise of governmental power to tax the press.

The general conclusions that I draw from this historical review are fivefold.

- First, we should treat separately the problem of the use of taxation to censure specific ideas or editorial content and the more general problem of knowledge taxes; the former should not be viewed as a "knowledge tax" problem, but rather as censorship in but one of its many forms.

- Second, the "knowledge tax" issue should be understood to focus specifically on governmental imposition of direct economic exaction on a publication — generally periodical in nature — or on the publishing or distribution of a publication. This excludes, for analytical purposes, various forms of direct and indirect exaction on the press through general corporate taxes, such as income taxes, and the cost of compliance with governmental regulations that fall on the press as a part of the regulated business sector.

- Third, while there is ample historical support for the conclusion that government censorship is inadmissible, whether effected through taxation or other devices, there is no historical warrant for a corresponding presumption against taxation of the press. If anything, the historical record serves to validate many, if not most, taxes on the press. The important question, instead, is how to distinguish the bad taxes from the good, or the prohibited from the permitted.

- Fourth, our principal concerns with knowledge taxes should be their impact on the diversity of expression and on the broad and general availability of information and opinion to the general populace. Here there are two separate points to be emphasized. The "knowledge" to which the label knowledge tax relates concerns primarily current information we often think of as "news." In the

English struggle the phrase was knowledge about "politics and political economy." The principal concern should be the *effect* of taxes on public access to that knowledge, not simply or even primarily the purpose of the tax or the surrogate measure of purpose, discrimination. Yet "purpose" and "discrimination" are presently the twin standards by which knowledge taxes are judged by the United States Supreme Court.[2]

- Finally, and most importantly, discrimination in the application of taxes is not, historically, the chief evil of knowledge taxes, nor should it be the principal basis upon which we judge them. Indeed, history teaches that it is the imposition of a tax on the press itself, coupled with the economic and public consequences of the exaction, rather than discrimination in its incidence, that should occasion most suspicion. As often as not, discrimination can serve, as it frequently has served, to promote the interests of diversity and availability of information and opinion, therefore justifying rather than condemning a tax. Conversely, nondiscriminatory taxation may often suffocate diversity and foreclose access to important sources of current information by the general public. This has been true from the very earliest times, as we shall see;[3] it remains equally if not more true today in our increasingly diverse and technologically sophisticated marketplace of information and ideas. In assessing the advisability, much less constitutionality, of "knowledge taxes" today, we should look first to their impact on the diversity of ideas and broadened availability of information throughout society, subordinating questions of differential exaction and purpose to that larger question.

These are but a few of the conclusions that history suggests. Others are interspersed throughout the book. History does not, of course, govern our current approaches to today's problems. It does, however, provide a larger perspective in which to view problems that seem pressing in the present. It is with a view toward providing such a perspective that this book is written.

Notes

1. The three decisions are Arkansas Writers' Project, Inc. v. Ragland, 481 U.S. 221 (1987), in which certain aspects of the Arkansas sales tax were declared uncon-

stitutional because an exemption from the tax for certain magazines was content-based; Minneapolis Star & Tribune Co. v. Minnesota Comm'r of Revenue, 460 U.S. 575 (1983), in which the Minnesota use tax on newspapers was stricken because it imposed a differential *form* of tax on the press, and because of its differential application to large and small papers; and Leathers v. Medlock, 111 S. Ct. 1438 (1991), sustaining the constitutionality of portions of the Arkansas sales tax that taxed some, but not all, cable television and radio services, but exempted other forms of broadcast and print (newspaper) publication. See Randall P. Bezanson, "Political Agnosticism, Editorial Freedom, and Government Neutrality Toward the Press," 72 *Iowa L. Rev.* 1359 (1987). Many years earlier, the Supreme Court had stricken down a Louisiana newspaper tax on grounds of illicit purpose in Grosjean v. American Press Co., 297 U.S. 233 (1936).

2. The most recent Supreme Court decisions are Leathers v. Medlock, 111 S. Ct. 1438 (1991); Arkansas Writers' Project, Inc. v. Ragland, 481 U.S. 221 (1987); and Minneapolis Star & Tribune Co. v. Minnesota Comm'r of Revenue, 460 U.S. 575 (1983).

3. See Chapter 1.

1. Knowledge Taxes in England

Control of public information about the affairs of government is an age-old phenomenon, and in England such efforts were made from the very earliest times. The problems associated with control of information, however, took on a new complexion with the advent of the printing press. As the economics of printing made it profitable to publish and distribute information to a public audience, and as the audience to which such information could be disseminated broadened, the threat posed to government by mass dissemination of information became obvious. No longer could government's position as the possessor of most information guarantee its control of the distribution and use of that information. Now others who knew of important information could publish it free from the government's control. Perhaps more significantly, false and damaging, as well as embarrassing, information and opinion could be disseminated, and the government's position as the principal source of information was effectively irrelevant to the control of such false information or damaging opinion.

The history of the Crown's efforts to exercise control over the dissemination of information in this new environment can be divided roughly into two parts, or periods. The first period involved the earliest steps taken by the Crown in response to the threat posed by the printing press, and included relatively direct restrictions on publication. The second and more important period, for our purposes, involved the use of indirect means of control, which were more pervasive in application but less discrete in impact. Taxation was the centerpiece of control in the second period.

We will turn first, and briefly, to a review of the principal methods used in the early period, as they provide an important background for the subsequent and more extended discussion of the broader controls that followed, which included, most notably, the knowledge taxes. Our purpose is to lay the background for the American experience. No pretense of original research is intended. Instead, the discussion that follows will draw heavily, in chronology and emphasis, on the able and profusely cited works of Professor Hamburger and Messrs. Siebert, Wickwar, Herd, and Collet.

Early Methods of Press Control

The first systematic efforts to control general publication of information by the press in England began prior to the twelfth century. Their precise character varied over time, particularly as the Crown adapted its mode of regulation to changing circumstances and to the increasing availability of economically profitable means of publication. The early methods of control, however, had a common theme: they all focused on controlling discrete and specific types of information. They all, in other words, represented forms of direct censorship.

By the late sixteenth century, the government in England, no longer dominated by the Crown but acting through Parliament, had developed three basic forms of press control. The first form of press control was the law of treason. The use of treason was advantageous for the government because of the procedural ease with which it could be employed. As with most felonies at the time, defendants had few rights at trial. They were not given a copy of the indictment, a list of jurors, or counsel. There were few protections against perjury by government witnesses, and there was no right to an appeal.[1]

There were some difficulties associated with the use of treason as a means of press control, however. Under the relevant statute,[2] treason was limited to three categories: imagining the death of the king; making war against the king; and aiding the king's enemies.[3] To obtain a conviction, the prosecution had to prove an overt act associated with one of the forms of treason, and since most publications, even though highly critical, did not incite rebellion, it was difficult to prove treason in cases involving publication alone.[4] Treason, therefore, was at best a blunt-edged, and often ineffective, means of exerting strong and specific control over publication in the press.[5] According to one historian, "[n]o sixteenth century printer is known to have been convicted and executed for treason under . . . the original Act of Edward III."[6]

The ineffectiveness of the general law of treason as a means of press control led to a broadening of the scope of the treason statute. A 1534 statute made it possible to commit treason by "words or writing."[7] With this change, the requirement that an overt act be proved was effectively eliminated, or at least greatly weakened. The potential of a broadened treason law effectively to control the press, however, was never really tested, as the Crown was loath to use treason too frequently as a means of censorship and control for fear that the harsh punishment attending conviction for treason would provoke public reaction and make martyrs of the publishers.[8] Treason was principally used, therefore, as a threat to frighten and control printers.[9] It never formed a major systematic element of the press control enterprise.

The second form of press control, which was mainly directed at preventing criticism of government officials and policies, was the group of statutes called *Scandalum Magnatum*.[10] These statutes created a form of defamation action under which it was illegal to speak or write untruths about the king or other important persons of the realm.[11] The statutes were the historical precursors of the infamous Sedition Acts around which the earliest and most famous controversies about the meaning of the First Amendment arose.[12] Despite its apparent usefulness as a means of censorship and its procedural advantages, the *Scandalum Magnatum* posed at least two problems.

The first problem was that the statutes forbade only the spreading of "news."[13] While they could therefore be used effectively against some forms of communication, they could not be used to censor discussion or writing on the subjects of political or theological doctrine or opinion. The restriction to news, which was defined rather narrowly to encompass the reporting of events, was easily circumvented through a recasting of the publication.[14] More significantly, the very publications that presented the greatest threat to the Crown, and against which censorship was most desired, were the political and religious tracts, and these quite clearly fell outside the ambit of "news."

The second obstacle to use of the *Scandalum Magnatum* as a means of censorship and control was that, unlike the law of libel at the time, the defense of truth was permitted.[15] The law of libel, which was then principally aimed at preventing breach of the peace caused by defamation, did not permit truth to be set up as a defense, for the wrong was the inflammatory consequences of the offending words, and those consequences, if anything, would be greater if the published statements were true.[16] In contrast, the *Scandalum Magnatum* was premised on the need to avoid dissemination of scandalous falsehood, and therefore the truth of the publication logically constituted a defense or justification. The availability of truth as a defense posed a significant obstacle to the statutes' use as a means of censorship, for prosecution under them presented the real risk that the defense would use a trial as an occasion to establish the truth of the embarrassing facts. There were, of course, other criminal actions tied to the libel action which avoided this possibility and could be employed to prohibit certain types of dissent, but these offenses were capital felonies, and the government was reluctant to treat the crime of holding and expressing antiestablishment views as a capital offense for fear of the public reaction that might be provoked.[17]

With the failure of the treason and sedition actions to provide an effective, systematic form of censorship, an alternative means of control was required. The means that was finally selected was licensing. During the sixteenth and seventeenth centuries the ministries of the English government developed and employed systems of licensing publishers in order to afford the Crown an opportunity to censor and prevent publication before the fact, thereby effectively reasserting the control over dissemination of expression that the Crown had enjoyed before the advent of the printing press.[18] In furtherance of the licensing system, rules for printers were established, such as those decreed by the Star Chamber in 1586.[19] The licensing system was also supplemented with the use of felony prosecutions in those situations that warranted a higher punishment than that afforded for violation of the licensing requirements, or at those times when higher punishment would serve as an effective deterrent, such as during the Essex Rebellion. After Elizabeth's death, however, the felony statutes lapsed, and licensing became the primary method of controlling the printed word. During the period of Cromwell's rule, also known as the Commonwealth, licensing continued as a chief means of press control, and it was employed with success even during this difficult period.[20]

Control over the printed press was firmly reasserted in 1662, during the Restoration period, by the new government, which enacted "a series of identical licensing acts, each of which was limited in duration and required re-enactment by successive Parliaments."[21] The first of these, the 1662 Regulation of Printing Act, established a system of censorship by requiring that the church or special licensors (depending on the subject matter of the material) be given two copies of the publication by the printer, in advance of publication.[22] The Regulation of Printing Acts remained in force until 1694, with a hiatus between 1679 and 1685 in which the Acts lapsed, but in which licensing was sustained through application by judges. The Acts were finally allowed to expire in 1695, and they were never renewed.[23]

Although the licensing acts "provided a practical means of convicting printers" for having printed antigovernment materials, "the licensing system was not entirely successful" in achieving the aims set for it.[24] Licensing was designed to permit censorship prior to publication, and therefore to give the government effective control over the dissemination of important information and opinion. By the early 1690s, however, this objective could not be achieved in practice.[25] Printers often ignored the censor, if they submitted the material at all. Technology was advancing to the point that the cost of printing was low and the availability of presses great.[26] No matter how pervasive the licensing system, the government simply could not keep track of all of the printers and all of the publications.[27] After the tumultuous upheavals following the English Civil War, the demand for antigovernment literature was high, and the number of publications increased greatly.[28] Censorship — even censorship established by the device of a pervasive licensing system — proved ineffective in the face of this economic and political pressure.[29]

Additional economic forces also worked against the licensing system. Licensing enforced large and profitable printing monopolies, such as the Stationers Company, which generated resentment by other printers who were economically unable to bear the cost of the licensing system. The nonfavored printers, who made money (when at all) through the unlicensed publication of cheap pamphlets, opposed censorship, for their pamphlets frequently failed the censors' tests. Delays in obtaining licenses for even the shortest and most innocuous publications were a source of widespread discontent. Concomitant with unrest on the part of printers, especially the more numerous small printers whose publications were often critical and were widely read, there existed a growing public tolerance for divergent opinions at this time, particularly in the Protestant religious community.[30]

In view of this combination of discontent, spotty enforcement, and liberalizing public attitudes, the Crown became willing to let licensing drop as soon as an alternative means of controlling the press was developed.[31] For a short time, the government attempted again to turn to the law of seditious libel. Seditious libel became an independent form of action, rather than a subcategory of defamation.[32] As a result, important changes in the action occurred. Chief Justice Holt held in *King v. Bear*[33] in 1699 that to reduce a libel to writing was to make it, and neither publication nor intent to publish was necessary to constitute a libel.[34] Thereafter in Tutchin's case,[35] Holt held that bringing scandal upon the government constituted a crime, in contrast to the narrower rule that a defamation must concern particular persons in government.[36] The new action was used to prosecute members of the printing trade who did not agree with the government's policies.[37] Sedition, however, could never substitute for licensing and fell far short of affording the Crown an effective and systematic means of controlling the press, for it remained difficult and cumbersome to use and engendered a great deal of criticism against the government.[38]

It is widely agreed that the period following expiration of the licensing acts in 1695 was one of "comparative freedom for publishers."[39] New regulations to replace licensing had not been devised. The power of the monopolies had effectively been destroyed with the expiration of licensing. Even seditious libel failed as a means of effective control, for while the action was greatly broadened in its reach, its use was cumbersome and public attitude was often against it.

At the same time, government attitudes toward censorship and particularly toward the highly public and often loathed forms of press control changed, although the change represented more of a difference in strategy than in objective. Government efforts were accordingly made to "disguise all unpleasant facts, to achieve ends by indirectness, and to keep public business" out of the hands of the public.[40] The direct methods of control of the press, so effectively used in the sixteenth and seventeenth centuries, were discarded in the eighteenth century. As Siebert notes, "[t]he rhetoric of the times called for tactical expressions of political belief in the freedom of the press, that is, in freedom from the Tudor and Stuart types of control; but in actual practice, it was universally recognized by political leaders that the stability of government as well as their continuance in office demanded some form of control over the media of communication."[41] What was needed were more subtle and indirect, yet effective, methods of control of the press. What was discovered was control through taxation.

The Taxes on Knowledge

THE STAMP ACT OF 1712

The movement toward taxation as a central feature of press control resulted from a strange combination of forces. The first of these was the ineffectiveness and, ultimately, the political cost associated with the earlier forms of licensing. Licensing lapsed in 1695, and efforts to revive it failed. Attempts to reinstitute licensing in the parliamentary sessions of 1695 through 1698 met with opposition in the House of Commons.[42] In 1698–99 the House of Lords tried to pass a bill requiring that all presses register with the Stationers Company, and that each printed item identify the printer and publisher, but the Commons would not concur. Similar bills were attempted in 1702 and 1703, and again in 1713. These, too, were rejected, this time by both houses of Parliament.[43]

The demise of licensing was a product of its ineffectiveness. The problem is perhaps best captured by Collet:

> Though Milton had rated far too highly the statesmanship of his British Areopagus, his appeal was by no means without effect. The Licensing system broke down fifty years after his appeal was made, and, in all probability, because the credit of the book was augmented when it was seen that his predictions, various as they were, all came true, and showed that no satisfaction could be obtained from a law which, while it oppressed those who conformed to it, could not silence those who defied it.[44]

Little was it appreciated at the time that the problem of which Collet spoke was perhaps inherent in efforts at press control, and that knowledge taxation, too, would serve largely to oppress those who conformed to it, but not to silence those who defied it.

The failure of efforts to reenact licensing and similar systems of control of the press was due to a lack of political will, but the lack of will resulted from the ineffectiveness and political discord caused by licensing, not from any idea that control of the press was unnecessary. Both houses agreed that a suitable method of controlling the press was needed; if anything, feelings on this score became more pronounced with increasingly bitter political feuds in Parliament. The problem was the inability of the two houses to agree on the proper method.[45]

The other force contributing ultimately to Parliament's resort to knowledge taxes was, strangely enough, the press itself, or at least certain quarters of it. The printers had been subject to regulation for more than two centuries, and the more powerful and established printers, in particular, enjoyed and benefited from the competitive protection afforded by government control. Even the small printers and publishers, however, perceived a certain amount of self-interest in some form of continued government regulation, as foreign printers — particularly the Dutch — posed a threat to everyone.[46] In 1703 a group of printers requested that restrictions on the number of printing houses and apprentices be reinstituted. But while they wanted to retain the security and stability provided by the then-existing monopolies, they were not interested in reviving the full licensing system with its aspects of prior submission and censorship.[47]

The government, however, was the main driving force behind efforts to replace the Printing Act. According to Siebert, following the expiration of the Regulation of Printing Acts, "the queen [Anne], the ministry, and the clergy were continuously scandalized by the flood of pamphlets and newspapers meddling in matters of state and church."[48] Proclamations of the Crown proved ineffective. The first proclamation, issued in March 1702, ordered that the increasing tide of seditious and scandalous publications "is to stop."[49] The order "had little effect," a predictable fate that also befell similar proclamations issued over the course of the next ten years.[50]

Ultimately, Siebert reports, it was Whig criticism of Queen Anne's foreign policy that led her to appeal to Parliament in her efforts to control the press.[51] As a result, a series of bills to regulate printing were introduced in 1712 and 1713. They appear to have been met, at first, with both indifference — as matters of peace and the succession were occupying Parliament's attention — and resistance. The resistance came from both the Whigs and from London printers, who "opposed . . . the clause requiring the author's name to appear on every piece of printing."[52] In the midst of an apparent stalemate, Anne's ministers and Parliament came upon taxation as a potentially effective — *and revenue-producing* — means of exerting press control.

Two years earlier, in the revenue act of 1710, a one penny tax had been imposed on calendars and almanacs in order to raise funds to support Marlborough's foreign wars.[53] With this precedent, it was not difficult for the ministers and Parliament to conclude that its extension to publications would serve not only to raise revenue, but also — and perhaps more importantly — to provide a means for controlling the press.[54] From this beginning, taxes on publications were to serve, in varying degrees, both revenue and regulatory purposes, and to do so on a permanent basis, even though the first stamp taxes were only to be imposts for thirty-two years, designed to pay for the war of the Spanish succession.[55]

The beginning, of course, was the Stamp Act of 1712.[56] While we cannot know for certain what the predominant objectives of the original Stamp Act were, it seems clear that control of publications was a significant factor.[57] Given the prior experience with the Regulation of Printing Acts, it was no doubt known that further arbitrary efforts to suppress journals whose contents were offensive to the government would not sit well with the public. But a tax imposed on all periodical publications would accomplish a large measure of the same result, for while the tax would fall equally on all publications, the most offensive ones tended to be the most financially vulnerable.[58] The tax was viewed at the time as "the most effectual way for suppressing libels."[59] This was suggested even by the arguments made against it. Daniel Defoe asserted that instead of suppressing criticism of government, the tax would drive it underground.[60] Jonathan Swift observed that the government seemed to be primarily concerned with "those weekly and daily papers and pamphlets reflecting upon the persons and management of the ministry."[61] Notwithstanding these criticisms, the government ministers and Parliament concluded that the tax best achieved their objectives. As Siebert put it, "If the Stamp Tax produced revenue, well and good; if it discouraged periodical publications, so much the better."[62]

The inclination to view a stamp tax as "an expedient substitute for the lapsed Regulation of Printing Acts,"[63] with revenue purposes that were secondary, at best, was shared by the Queen. Siebert reports that in her speech to Parliament in January 1712, the Queen, with the support of the Ecclesiastical Convocation, lamented the "great license . . . taken in publishing false and scandalous Libels such as are a reproach to any government. This Evil seems too strong for the Laws now in force: it is therefore recommended to you to find a Remedy equal to the Mischief."[64] A significant impact on circulation was anticipated, as a similar proposal for a newspaper tax had been offered in 1711, and it had been estimated that it would reduce newspaper circulation from 45,000 to no more than 30,000 per year.[65]

The final resolve to enact the stamp tax, however, may have been provided by Samuel Buckley's publication of an article on the conduct of the Dutch in the war.[66] According to Siebert, Parliament was "incensed" and, after conducting an inquiry into the license of the press, within two weeks reported twelve resolutions that ultimately formed the Stamp Act of 1712.[67] Control of scandalous and licentious publication was a prominent consideration in the passage of the Stamp Act one month later. As Collet Dobson Collet said in his *History of the Taxes on Knowledge*,[68]

> Was there no way by which, without the necessity of constant contention, private men might be prevented from using the Press to make their opinions public? . . . If these sheets could be taxed their distribution might become difficult, and when any one attempted to evade the tax he could be punished, not as a libeller, but as a smuggler, and the character of what was printed would not come under discussion, as it generally would under a trial for libel. At the time we are recording, 1709, these considerations appear to have very much occupied the minds of the members of the House of Commons.

While printers and publishers had previously found occasion to seek reinstitution of selected features of press regulation—particularly the assurance of monopoly position and protection against Dutch competition — the stamp tax met a hostile reception from all quarters, including the printers, the publishers, and the paper manufacturers. The principal objection, of course, was that the tax was not, in reality, a revenue measure, but a means of suppressing publications. As Defoe stated, "to tax any Trade so that it cannot subsist under the payment, is not a means to raise the Money, but to destroy the Trade."[69] The printers reinforced the point by observing that if the true object of the Stamp Act were prevention of libels, that end could be directly achieved by a requirement that the publisher be identified in all publications.[70]

The argument was also made, with some basis in history and with remarkable foresight, that the tax would increase rather than diminish the quantity of uncontrolled libel.[71] By imposing unsustainable costs on publishers, printers either would go underground, continuing to print outside the stamp system, or would attempt to reduce other costs to offset the tax, and would do so by printing "whatsoever shall be offer'd them" out of desperation for cheap material.[72] As we shall see later, evasion did, in fact, occur on a large scale. Moreover, the economic burden of the stamp system was clearly substantial, and the economic costs were not limited to the stamp duties themselves. Following passage of the Stamp Act, "cart-loads of paper and bales of news-sheets had to be taken to the Stamp Office for each sheet to be stamped separately by hand,"[73] and the printers and publishers had to bear this cost. Perhaps more significantly, the requirement that sheets be separately stamped, which continued well into the nineteenth century, meant that the economic burdens of the tax would be manifested as well in the structure and technology of the industry. The stamp system prevented publishers and printers from using continuous reels of paper and rotary presses in the printing process, and thus foreclosed significant production economies in the publishing industry.[74]

Notwithstanding the objections from printers and publishers, which were notable because they were principally economic in nature rather than based on any clear sense of freedom of the press, the first tax on newspapers was passed on May 16, 1712, "without a division in the House of Commons,"[75] and agreed to without amendment in the House of Lords on May 22.[76] The Stamp Act, which embraced not only the "stamp" tax but also an advertisement and paper tax, took effect on August 1, 1712. Drawing on Siebert's able summary, the sections pertaining to publications can be briefly outlined.[77]

   1. *The Tax on Newspapers and Pamphlets.* A tax was imposed on news-

papers and pamphlets "for every printed copy" at various rates dependent on length. Newspapers and pamphlets printed on a half sheet or less were taxed one halfpenny sterling; those larger than a half sheet and not exceeding a whole sheet were taxed one penny sterling. Newspapers and pamphlets larger than a whole sheet and not exceeding six sheets octavo (or twelve sheets in quarto, or twenty sheets in folio), however, were taxed three shillings for every sheet in "one printed copy."[78]

The tax was imposed on all publications meeting the size criteria; no distinction was made, and therefore no definitions given, among newspapers, other periodical publications, and single issue publications such as pamphlets. Printed books larger than six sheets octavo, however, were exempted from the tax. It is clear from the limited application of the tax that the Act's primary purpose was suppression of the small, periodical publications that were highly critical of government policy. Other exemptions for educational and religious materials of any size also confirm the targeted objectives of the tax.[79]

2. *The Tax on Advertisements.* The tax on advertisements was imposed at the rate of twelvepence sterling for each advertisement. It applied to all newspapers published weekly or more often. In general, the number of advertisements in an edition was not great, ranging up to ten or so by 1712.[80] The effect, if not the purpose, of the tax was to exert economic pressure on periodical publications, thus putting the most marginal publications out of business, and making the rest more susceptible to control by the ministry through informal, though not always subtle, means. Books and, more notably, pamphlets were exempt from the tax, as were trade publications and separately published advertisements.

3. *The Tax on Paper.* Prior to the Stamp Act of 1712, duties had been imposed on imported papers pursuant to legislation enacted in 1696.[81] The 1712 Stamp Act thus extended the application of a tax concept already in place to domestic as well as imported paper.[82] The level of tax depended on whether the paper was imported or domestic, not on the quality of the brand.

4. *The Regulation and Enforcement Provisions.* Siebert observed that the true purposes of the tax system — the dominance of regulatory rather than revenue objectives — were most clearly revealed by the regulatory and enforcement provisions of the Act.[83] Newspapers and pamphlets printed in London had to be registered at the Stamp Office. The name and address of the publisher had to be included in all publications. These provisions permitted ready identification for enforcement purposes and, while offen-

sive to some, were an understandable feature of any tax scheme. Failure to comply with the regulatory requirements resulted in a penalty of twenty pounds; nonpayment of the tax resulted in loss of all copyrights.[84]

The regulatory and enforcement provisions gave the government a strong measure of control over all covered publications, and the penalties for noncompliance were sufficiently onerous as to require compliance, for they were exacted for every separate issue and therefore the cumulative penalties could effectively put a publisher in the poorhouse — as they did on more than one occasion.[85] They were intended, of course, to assure payment of the tax, which in turn would assure, because of the high tax rates, that the price of pamphlets and other printed materials was raised beyond the means of most persons. Through economic force, therefore, the government attempted effectively to control the publication of information to the people, and to eliminate the most economically precarious and obnoxious publications. It was this consequence that most accounts for the name given the taxes: taxes on knowledge.[86]

An examination of the actual effects of the Stamp Act of 1712 establishes that the apparent regulatory purposes were generally borne out in practice — but only generally. Here the exceptions are as revealing as the rule, for the effects of the Act establish, as well, the resiliency and creativity of the press and pamphleteers, who searched for and used every loophole and device *legally* to avoid the Act's application.

We begin with Siebert's exhaustive and very able review of the Stamp Act's effect, which led him to three general conclusions. First, "a sizable number of newspapers were immediately killed by the Act."[87] Second, about the same number of newspapers and periodicals "as were killed by the Act" were "able to survive the first year of taxation."[88] Third, "[w]ithin a year [after the Act became effective] publishers devised methods of avoiding the tax, and the government found it impossible to enforce collections."[89] A relatively brief survey of the experience with the Stamp Act provides insight into the general problems associated with taxation of the press, and places the later experience in America in its historical context.

Two notable observers at the time of the Stamp Act were apocalyptic in their predictions. Writing at the time of the Act's passage, Joseph Addison noted in the *Spectator* that "[t]his is the Day on which many eminent Authors will probably Publish their Last Words. I am afraid that few of our Weekly Historians . . . will be able to subsist under the Weight of a Stamp."[90] With specific reference to certain types of pamphlets, he stated that "the Necessity of carrying a Stamp, and the Improbability of notifying a Bloody Battle, will, I am afraid, both concur to the sinking of those thin Folios."[91] Addison's statements, made at the time of the Act's passage, represented his prediction of its impact — with a view, in all likelihood, to his own publication — not a report of its actual impact. In a similar vein, Swift wrote to Stella that "now every single half sheet pays a halfpenny to the queen. *The Observer* is fallen; the *Medleys* are jumbled together with *The Flying Post*; *The Examiner* is deadly sick; *The Spectator* keeps up and doubles its price — I know not how long it will hold."[92]

Swift's statement, while more specific, nevertheless represents an exaggeration of the tax's effects. He listed the periodicals that were, indeed, in serious trouble, but he did not mention the other newspapers that continued publication after the Act's effective date. A study of the available files of the newspapers at the time led Siebert to conclude that "at least five newspapers were suspended because of the Stamp Tax (*Observer, Medley, Plaindealer, Supplement,* and *Protestant Postboy*) and at least four newspapers were able to survive the Act (*The Examiner, Flying Post, Daily Courant,* and *Evening Post*). Also surviving were the official *London Gazette,* the monthly publications larger than six pages . . . and the commercial publications such as the *Weekly Pacquet,* all of which, with the exception of the *Gazette,* were exempted from the newspaper and advertising taxes."[93] Siebert notes that there were eight other journals publishing at the time the Act was passed, but existing files would not permit a definite conclusion regarding the fate of these publications.[94] Collet also suggests that some of the publications that went out of business after the Act may have done so for reasons unrelated to the tax.[95]

While the available evidence suggests that the tax had a destructive effect, it appears that its effect may not have been as great as the Tory ministry hoped for or expected. The tax appears to have driven a few publications out of business, and it was costly to most. It seems also to have occasioned a brief respite from the growth and power of the newspapers, but brief only, as it was not long before new papers appeared and growth in total circulation of papers was resumed.[96]

The effect of the tax on periodicals, as distinguished from newspapers, is even more difficult to measure. The three most influential periodicals were the *Tatler,* the *Spectator,* and Defoe's *Review.* While these periodicals were distinct from newspapers, they contained news as well as commentary on current issues. According to Siebert, Richard Steele discontinued the *Tatler* in January 1711, prior to the Stamp Act, because "he was tired of his original plan and had become interested in the production of a daily essay paper."[97] The effect of the tax on the *Spectator* is more difficult to discern. In response to the tax its publishers doubled the price of the periodical. At the end of 1712 the *Spectator* suspended publication, but it was resumed for six months in 1714. The precise reasons for the suspension are unclear. Some historians have suggested that publication ceased because the *Spectator* was no longer profitable, perhaps due not only to loss of circulation caused by price increases but also because of reduced advertising caused by the advertisement tax.[98] Siebert suggests that the tax contributed to the demise of the *Spectator*, but that the Act may not have been the sole contributing factor, and that unprofitability may have existed independent of the tax.[99]

In the case of Defoe's *Review*, uncertainty is equally great. In response to the tax, Defoe condensed his publication to a single leaf (two pages). In this condensed form, the publication appears to have been reasonably successful. Siebert suggests that publication of the *Review* most likely ceased in order to permit Defoe to start a new publication, and whether the profitability of the *Review*, even in the more successful condensed form, contributed to this decision is uncertain.[100]

The conclusion to be drawn about the effect of the Stamp Act is mixed. In the case of newspapers, the available information suggests that the Act had a demonstrable negative impact, but the consequences were not as widespread as contemporaneous observations would suggest. An impact was felt, as well, by the periodical publishers, but here the evidence is even sketchier and more ambiguous, for pamphlets were very personal undertakings that were almost always marginal from an economic point of view, and their continuation was often as much a function of the publisher's personal interests as of extrinsic economic forces. In any event, the true impact of the Act on newspapers and periodicals could never really be measured, for such a conclusion would have to be based on a longer period of time than one year. Within a year of the Act's effective date, however, means were found to escape its grasp or soften its impact.

Almost immediately upon passage of the 1712 Stamp Act, a number of loopholes in its provisions were discovered. By far the most important loophole was afforded by the phrase "in one printed copy" which appeared only in the section imposing a tax of three shillings on newspapers and pamphlets larger than a whole sheet and not exceeding six sheets (in octavo).[101] In contrast, the tax on smaller publications was imposed "for every printed copy" (those more than a half sheet but no more than a whole sheet). The publishers therefore concluded that the three shilling tax was to be imposed "*per impression* . . . [and] pointed out to the Stamp Office that whereas single sheets paid a penny *per copy*, newspapers and pamphlets more than a single sheet" in length were subject to a tax of only three shillings *per edition*.[102]

Largely because of this loophole, by 1713 evasion of the Stamp Act was widespread. Weekly newspapers quickly expanded to a sheet and a half, or six pages, with a large resulting reduction in, or complete avoidance of, the tax.[103] According to Siebert, "[e]ven the official *London Gazette* published six pages and omitted the stamp in its edition of May 5–9, 1717."[104] In order to fill the larger space, publishers used such devices as "larger type, deeper headings, heavier leading, wider margins, and more significant, began to include critical essays and feature material of the type made popular by the *Tatler* and the *Spectator*. The daily papers found it impossible to expand to six pages and continued to pay the tax."[105]

As a result, between 1713 and 1725 there occurred a tremendous growth in the influence of the weekly political review, and a corresponding decline of the daily and triweekly newspapers. There was also a corresponding expansion of the political essay or editorial in newspapers seeking to fill the larger space. Ironically, the political tract was one of the principal objects against which the stamp was directed, yet because of the tax it flourished, both in the newspapers where editorial opinion had not previously appeared, and in the pamphlets, which also expanded in length to take advantage of the loophole. The publications principally damaged by the tax were those that the government least wanted to regulate in the first place — the daily newspapers.[106]

Harris reports attempts made in London to adapt the then "well-established thrice-weeklies" to take advantage of the loophole.[107] The efforts were generally spotty and short-lived, however, as the difficulties of obtaining sufficient material for each issue, in light of the shorter deadlines, made the task impossible without substantial sacrifice of quality. An exception was the small-scale publisher who could cut the quality of paper and use secondhand material written in serial form. By this strategy some small-scale publishers were able to produce thrice-weeklies consisting heavily of republished serialized material that were long enough to fit within the loophole, and they were able to do so at an extremely low price.[108] The tax, therefore, permitted the smaller printers to compete, while the larger thrice-weeklies could not do so. Once again, the effect of the tax seems in material respects to have been to prefer the very publishers whose papers were viewed with greatest distaste.

The problems associated with the advertising tax were different from those experienced with the stamp tax, but they were no less difficult for the government. The tax was imposed on "all and every person and persons who shall print or publish, or cause to be printed or published, any advertisement or advertisements."[109] When the authorities tried to enforce this measure through exaction from the publisher, the publishers claimed that it was the author or the printer who was liable for the tax, not the publisher. The printers, in turn, argued that the tax should be collected from the publisher. The authors or editors insisted that liability should be borne by the printer or publisher. After coming full circle in its collection efforts, the Stamp Office often ended up not collecting the tax at all.[110]

Because of difficulties of collection and the unintended exceptions afforded by the language of the Stamp Act, widespread noncompliance with both the stamp and advertising taxes occurred after 1714. Siebert concluded that "[a]s many daily and weekly newspapers appeared after 1714 as were published before 1712."[111] By one count, sixty-five newspapers and periodicals were published in 1711, fifty-one were published in 1712, when the tax began, forty-five were published in 1713, fifty-four in 1714, and sixty-seven newspapers and periodicals were published in 1715.[112] Noncompliance with the Act was not uniform; it was uneven and differential. When the dust settled, the impact of the Stamp Act of 1712 fell predominantly on those publishers "who supported the government and who were therefore more or less compelled to pay the tax" because of loyalty or because they were unable to escape its grasp by restructuring their publication.[113] This was apparently viewed by the Tory party as an acceptable price to pay for the elimination of the opposition papers which, in the Tory mind, were spreading libel and scandal. But the bargain turned sour. The loyal journals, upon which the party relied for presentation of its views, bore the brunt of the tax, while the opposition publications escaped it.[114]

The consequences of this unintended and differential impact on the English press at the time are unclear. Some writers are of the opinion that the Stamp Act resulted in a purging in the press of those elements that lacked a serious cause to promote, and confined the management of the press to "men of character and respectability."[115] Others believe, as Swift did at the time, that the general lack of enforcement facilitated a healthy opposition "well versed in the topics of defamation," while those who would "draw their pens on the side of their prince and country, [were] discouraged by [the] tax."[116] Whichever view is adopted, it seems clear that the Act's effects were dramatically different from those intended, and that the Act fell far short of affording the government a renewed opportunity to exert systematic control over the flow of information to the public.

A final consequence of the Stamp Act of 1712 is noted by Siebert, and it is important because it reflects long term structural change in the English press. The provincial press developed and flourished under, and largely because of, the Stamp Act.[117] Before 1694 there had been essentially no country, or provincial, press in England. This was partly because of the economics of such enterprises, and more fundamentally because they could not survive the competition with the metropolitan newspapers, which provided daily news, a luxury the weekly provincial press could not afford. The first provincial papers began prior to 1712, but few, if any, survived the tax of 1712.[118] At the same time, however, the impact of the tax on the cost of the dailies and triweeklies soon became so high that the country readers, who at that point were getting their news from the weeklies, began turning to new provincial weeklies to meet that need. The number of such weeklies steadily increased, from perhaps twenty in 1725 to fifty in 1782.[119] The provincial papers operated much as the cheap, unstamped papers in London, and the Stamp Act encouraged their growth just as much.[120]

Perfecting the Imperfect: Enactments from 1724 to 1819

As might be expected, it was not long before the problems associated with the Stamp Act generated efforts to amend the Act. Having become aware of the loopholes in the newspaper tax, Robert Walpole, First Lord of the Treasury and Chancellor of the Exchequer, gave prompt attention to the problem. Walpole was an astute politician who was aware of the power of the press and its influence on public support, and thus of the importance of the issue.[121]

"As early as 1717," according to Siebert, "John Toland had called the government's attention to the loopholes in the tax on newspapers and pamphlets,"[122] observing also the differential burden that was placed on the loyal papers, as well as the loss of revenue occasioned by nonenforceability. He proposed that the six-page newspapers be fully subject to the tax, and that evening papers that simply appropriated news from the morning journals without paying tax be prohibited.[123] A complete census was taken of the London newspapers, including an assessment of their sympathy to the government. The census indicated that in 1723 thirty-four presses were favorable to King George, three were neutral, four were Roman Catholic, and thirty-four were "High Fliers" opposed to the existing government.[124]

The latter number resolved all doubt, and Walpole proposed that the loopholes be closed.

The effort to amend the Stamp Act and close the loopholes was concluded with the passage of a new bill in 1724.[125] While it has been suggested that the reason for amending the original act and closing the loopholes was solely revenue-related,[126] the uneven impact of the original act, coupled with the realization after the census that the opposition newspapers in London were as numerous as those friendly to the government, no doubt also contributed to the decision, and may well have dominated it. In February 1724 a committee of the House of Commons presented a bill which was subsequently enacted. Its preamble recited the various loopholes employed to evade the Stamp Act of 1712. The new Stamp Act imposed on all journals, mercuries,[127] and newspapers a tax of "one penny for every sheet upon which it was printed, and of one halfpenny for every half sheet thereof."[128]

The principal feature of the new Stamp Act was its specific focus on newspapers, as distinguished from pamphlets. At the time of the original act the greatest irritation to the government, and therefore a principal object of the stamp duties, was the political pamphlet, which was subjected to a three shilling tax. The purpose of the Stamp Act of 1712, however, was frustrated by its failure to impose the three shilling tax on each copy, rather than on each edition. As a result, the tables were completely turned when newspapers, which were not separately taxed as such, expanded to six pages to escape tax on each copy. Newspapers expanded and became more profitable; they also became a greater source of irritation.

The Stamp Act of 1724 left pamphlets alone, but closed the loophole for newspapers which by then (and largely by virtue of the 1712 loophole) were better described as political periodicals. Newspapers, regardless of size, were treated separately as a class under the new act, hence they could not escape through a loophole available to another form of publication, such as pamphlets. So, while the first Stamp Act was aimed principally, although counterproductively as it turned out, at pamphlets, the 1724 Act made no effort to close the loopholes for them, but instead was aimed directly at newspapers.[129] Newspapers were to be subject to the tax as a special class; pamphlets were left alone, and therefore largely exempted.[130]

Siebert reports that the effects of the 1724 Stamp Act were even more obscure and complex than those of the 1712 Act. The number of periodicals and newspapers decreased for a time, from eighty-two in 1724, to seventy-six in 1725, to sixty-four in 1726. The number did not reach the 1724 level again until 1734.[131] The number of new periodicals followed a similar pattern.[132] Journals that suspended publication because of the tax do not appear to have been the established ones, which were able to survive by increasing price and reducing cost by decreasing the number of pages from a six-page folio to a four-page quarto (since there was no longer any reason to publish more than six pages).[133] The more marginal journals whose survival was more directly dependent on the economic advantage afforded by the loophole in the 1712 Stamp Act seem to have been the ones that folded. In these respects the objectives of the 1724 Stamp Act seem to have been realized.

But beneath the surface other forces were at work. While compliance with the new Stamp Act was at first widespread, within a few years of enactment, stampless newspapers were again being sold due to evasion and loose enforcement of the Act. Evasion of the new Stamp Act was only partly a result of imperfections of drafting. Some periodicals avoided the tax by predating a series of issues, permitting multiple issues to be considered as one serialization, thus qualifying as a pamphlet and escaping the newspaper tax. The dominant form of evasion, however, appears to have been wholesale noncompliance, especially at the "lower end of the trade." These papers simply evaded the Act, and the authorities seem to have been unable or unwilling to deal with the appearance of a whole new level of unstamped publications and therefore left them alone.[134] During the late 1730s, the market was flooded with unstamped newspapers. Although the illegal press was operating at the direct financial expense of the legitimate press, nothing was done to protect the interests of the legitimate press until 1743.[135] In that year, "the hand of the law descended upon the unfortunate street-sellers."[136] Parliament made the selling of unstamped newspapers a crime subject to a three month jail sentence.[137] Informers were rewarded with twenty shillings.[138] Even with the addition of these sanctions, however, unstamped newspapers remained available in London.[139]

With the exception of the provision in the 1724 Stamp Act closing the loopholes for newspapers, the rates of the various taxes (stamp tax, advertising tax, paper tax, and pamphlet and almanac tax) continued unchanged from those established in 1712. It was not until 1757 that the first change in rates occurred, and with it, perhaps, a shift toward revenue as a more significant, although not dominant, basis for taxation of the press. The government found itself in need of new revenue to finance the Seven Years' War, and it was determined that increased rates would be willingly paid by a public that was eager for news about the war.[140] The 1757 act increased the stamp tax by one halfpenny, to three halfpence, on all newspapers of four or fewer pages. Advertisements in daily and weekly newspapers were taxed at two shillings each, up from twelvepence sterling.[141] Siebert reports that "[s]ome fifteen periodicals ceased publication in 1757 and six in 1758," an apparent result of the increased tax levels,[142] and that between 1758 and 1763 the tax yielded "approximately 43,000 pounds annually,"[143] a sizable increase from the 16,500 pounds he reports collected in 1749.[144]

In what was by now becoming almost a sacred tradition, the publishers managed to find a way to avoid paying the tax imposed in the newest act. The 1757 act imposed no tax on "newspapers" larger than one sheet, just as the original 1712 act had failed to do, but this time the newspapers had been singled out as a separate category under the 1724 Stamp Act. The result of this, quite remarkably, was effective reinstatement of the original loophole. The publishers were therefore able to expand their newspapers to six pages and pay only three shillings for an entire edition.[145] Because of the loophole, Parliament some sixteen years later passed a new act[146] applying the 1757 tax rate to all newspapers regardless of length. Thus newspapers were fully covered as a separate category of publication with a graduated duty of one penny for a two-page newspaper, three halfpence for a four-page paper, and two pence for a six-page newspaper.[147]

The next increase in the stamp tax on newspapers occurred in 1776. Once again, war was the occasion, and revenue the purpose. This time it was the American Revolution. The 1776 act increased the tax on newspapers by an additional halfpenny except for the six-page newspapers, which continued at the old rate.[148] The stamp tax was increased by a halfpenny again in 1789 to two pence and two and a half pence, respectively, on the two- and four-page papers. The tax on larger papers again remained unchanged at two pennies.[149] The advertisement tax was also increased, to two shillings, sixpence.[150]

Following the 1789 increase Siebert reports that "the newspaper publishers immediately raised the price to four pence per copy."[151] But this time the price increase was not so easily passed on and sales decreased. The ever-resilient publishers, of course, were not ready to give up, and they adopted new practices to defeat the tax or reduce its burden. The most notable tactic was renting newspapers. By renting the same copy to multiple readers, publishers could increase revenues, yet they would only have to pay the tax once.[152] Another practice that predated the 1789 act was that of returning unsold copies of the newspaper to the Stamp Office for a refund, thus reducing the tax paid and effectively converting the stamp tax into a sales tax. While this practice was halted by the 1789 act, in its place publishers were granted a four percent discount on the tax for overprinting and spoilage.[153]

From 1789 until 1819 the stamp tax continued essentially unchanged in its structure, but with upward adjustments in rate,[154] and its impact appears to have stabilized, although it was not a stability to be desired. By 1815 the rate was set at four pence per copy. According to Siebert, "[t]he stamp tax continued to be one of the most effective fetters on the periodical press of England during the late years of the reign of George III."[155] Between 1789 and 1815 rates were regularly increased.

The next wave of change occurred with the modifications enacted in the Publications Act, one of the "Six Acts" of 1819, which also included significant and onerous changes in seditious libel laws.[156] The focus of the Publications Act was the cheap weeklies, which were made subject to a high stamp duty if they sold for less than sixpence. The undisguised purpose was to drive the cheap (and scandalous) pamphlets out of business by forcing them to charge more than the market would bear (sixpence) to escape the stamp, or to tax them out of business if they kept their prices low.[157] Onerous sureties and bonds were also required.[158] As with most previous attempts at regulation through the stamp device, this one was only partly effective. Enforcement was lax; the Act's principal effect was to transform the size and frequency of publications; and it bore hard on friends as well as foes.[159]

The rigor of the "Six Acts" of 1819 was not without exception, however, as "judicious" exercise of discretion, according to Collet, could be wielded with politics in mind. Collet's account of the *Penny Magazine* and the *Saturday Magazine* is worth repeating here:

> [T]he Liberal school (it had not yet been amalgamated into the Liberal party) founded the Society for the Diffusion of Useful Knowledge, which . . . published a great number of works. . . . Many of Lord Grey's Ministry were members [including Henry Brougham, Lord Chancellor]. Among its publications was the *Penny Magazine*, and the *Saturday Magazine* was started soon afterwards by the Society for Promoting Christian Knowledge.
>
> The *Penny Magazine* was published once a week . . . , a number which does not exceed twenty-six days, and therefore [it] ought to have been stamped. Being the *penny* magazine its price was only a sixth part of the orthodox price — sixpence. The superficies of the *Penny Magazine* instead of being 714 square inches (the smallest superficies reckoned as two sheets) was only 308 inches. It is true that the news contained in the *Penny Magazine* was not the news of the day, but it was fresher than that of the *Spectator* [which was

stamped]. . . . There were not many remarks about matters in Church or State . . . , and the few such remarks it did contain were not contentious. . . . But the 60 George III. cap. 9, sections 1, 4, 5, 8, prohibits *any* such remarks at intervals of less than twenty-six days. [It] was not one of the papers which Lord Sidmouth or Lord Castlereagh would have wished to prohibit, . . . [but] the publication of blasphemy was *not* one of the necessary ingredients of an illegal paper. . . .

. . . [T]he *Saturday Magazine* was started [on July 7, 1832, about three months after the *Penny Magazine*], "under the direction of the Committee of General Literature and Education appointed by the Society for Promoting Christian Knowledge." . . . The *Penny Magazine* went in for being useful; the *Saturday Magazine* was pious. . . . Its news was not fresher than that of its rival, but it more frequently contained remarks on matters in Church and State. Being orthodox, it had nothing to fear on the special ground of any offence likely to be taken on account of such remarks.

Both publications escaped the ban of the 60 George III[,] cap. 9; presumably because the Chancellor of the Exchequer administered a judicious hint to the Commissioners. . . . The Commissioners of Stamps could . . . make it safe for any paper to come into existence, if they thought it did not come under the true intent and meaning of the Act. . . .

. . . Meanwhile the hand of the law descended heavily, though capriciously, on the many unstamped newspapers that abounded at this time.[160]

AFTER THE APEX: THE PATH TO ULTIMATE REPEAL, 1836–61

With the "Six Acts" of 1819, the apex of knowledge taxes came and, after a time, passed. One suspects that the combination of onerous provisions and undisguised motive in the 1819 acts provided, along with other economic forces, the straw that broke the camel's back. In the face of rising press and public sentiment against the taxes, the trend was reversed. We shall focus shortly on the political forces that emerged after passage of the "Six Acts" and ultimately led to the dismantling of the knowledge taxes, as well as on the underlying principles of freedom that animated that struggle. But before turning to that subject, the course of enactments, culminating in the final repeal of the paper duties in 1861, should be briefly recounted.

In 1836 the newspaper tax was reduced to one penny,[161] and, while a certain amount of mischief continued and enforcement was tightened, a measure of peace prevailed. The 1836 act was a compromise: the tax was lowered, but partisan interests (in this case, of the Whigs) were also served.[162] The Act combined a reduction in the level of the stamp to one penny, with free postage (but the stamp was due whether posted or not), and in return the provisions for application of the stamp and enforcement were tightened.

The impact of the 1836 act, beginning with its origin in 1832, is worth recounting. According to Collet, a Mr. Edward Bulwer had, "by repeated motions, . . . taken to himself the Parliamentary representation of the advocates of the repeal of the Stamp."[163] This had been the original purpose in raising the matter. Ultimately, the compromise struck was different, with retention of the stamp, and this occurred in part because Mr. Bulwer proved weak, and partly, as Collet says, because "the habit of mixing with 'practical' men is apt to lead enthusiasts, as they grow old, to think that there is something childish in demanding exactly what is right."[164]

In general, the 1836 act repealed all previous stamp acts insofar as they affected newspapers, except for the security system. In their place it imposed a tax of one penny on newspapers, per sheet, with newspapers being broadly defined and therefore catching most everything, including those papers not previously covered under the more oppressive Publications Act of 1819. Printers, publishers, and so forth had to register, therefore perpetuating the monopoly. A twenty-pound fine was imposed for publishing or possessing an unstamped newspaper. Names of printer and publisher had to be printed on the paper. According to Collet:

> The object of the Act was, for a considerable time accomplished. This object was to bring a whole trade of newspaper-proprietors, publishers, and printers under the supervision of the Commissioners of Stamps, who, though not compelled to do so, did to a considerable extent protect the trade against interlopers, and, by a judicious indulgence, collected a considerable amount of revenue from this newly-established trade, under the heads of Stamp, Advertisement, and Paper Duties.[165]

After the 1836 act some measure of peace prevailed, largely because, it seems, the interests of the "established" publishers had been well served. According to Collet:

> Mr. Spring Rice [Chancellor of the Exchequer] had consolidated into something like a Guild, a Press which gave, to a great extent, what the people wanted, though it gave it only to those who could, in one way or other, afford to pay fivepence for a newspaper. The members of the Guild were protected by the Stamp Office in their monopoly of news; but the Stamp Office gave this protection in order to preserve the revenue, not in order to enforce the law.[166]

The unstamped publisher posed little danger. Under previous acts, "[t]he unstamped publisher whose presses and whose newspapers were seized, found it only too easy to pile up the agony and to fill his columns with denunciations of 'the blasted tools of an infernal Government.' But when he was left to his own devices, this very necessary sauce to the slender meal he provided for his customers would require a good deal of care in its preparation."[167] In administering the 1836 act,

> the Commissioners of Stamps . . . never confessed that they had any difficulty in separating the news from the commentary. If at this time Somerset House examined any unstamped newspaper, it did so, not to decide whether the commentary contained any news, but to decide whether there was news enough to establish a competition with the stamped Press. If the paper was a monthly one, it was safe, whatever its contents. The newspaper reader likes his news fresh. Its truth is valued but as a secondary consideration.[168]

The 1836 Act provided free post for those papers which were stamped and which needed postage — the stamp applied whether posted or not. The converse, although not clear from the face of the Act, was that *in its administration* papers not needing to be stamped — those with no news content, published less often than every twenty-six days — had no right to the postal system. Collet remarks:

> It [postal carriage] was part of the reward to be given to those newspapers which, by registration and bonds of security, had become "responsible to their king and country." It was a privilege earned only by those who, under this responsibility, published news and observations on news. It was part of the plan for a newspaper guild that should support the Government. In utter forgetfulness that the words "public news, intelligence, or occurrences" originally included events of past centuries, and even events that were fictitious, Somerset House took up the notion that news must be something about the Government, and that nothing else constituted a newspaper entitled to go through the post, and finally, the smallest quantity of this would carry this privilege.[169]

Therefore, small papers attempting to escape the tax may have thus succeeded, but at the cost of the post, as was the case with a weekly paper, the *New Moral World*. Others of a literary or otherwise nonqualifying character that wanted the privilege of the post would "insert a chapter an inch and a half square headed 'Politics,' and were allowed to stamp as much as they pleased of their impression and no more."[170] By this device they got the post.

"[T]he Acts of Parliament," according to Collet, "were drawn so that nothing was legal to which the Commissioners objected, and nothing was illegal if they chose to permit it."[171] Papers that could have been subjected to the stamp but escaped it through the discretion of the Stamp Office died nevertheless because they could not compete with the stamped and higher priced papers with current news in greater quantity.[172] As Collet put it: "The policy of the Government had changed. Its object in 1831 was to suppress the cheap newspaper; in 1842 it was to promote the sale of a dear one."[173]

The peace that followed the 1836 act was not, of course, necessarily a "peace" to be desired, for it was worked not simply by lower rates of tax, but also by a healthy measure of "judicious" (calculating may be a better word) exercise of discretion by the Stamp Commissioners.[174] Judiciousness, one suspects, may have resulted partly from ambivalence, for the tide had turned and the ultimate outcome became clearer with the passage of each new year. The peace, in short, was also a prelude to repeal. The stamp duty was finally abolished in 1855.[175] Advertising duties met the same fate and were repealed in 1853.[176] The final remnant in the form of the paper duties was abolished in 1861,[177] and with its repeal the taxes on knowledge in England were ended. With the abolition of the taxes came the rise of the great national dailies headquartered in London.[178] Ironically, these had been the principal *and unintended* victims of the taxes from the beginning.

THE TIDES OF POLITICS AND PRINCIPLE:
A CAPSULE VIEW OF ANIMATING FORCES
The story of the English knowledge taxes, and particularly of their successful repeal, would be incomplete without an understanding, even if abbreviated and general, of the larger political forces that permitted their growth and, thereafter, fostered their repeal.[179] Discussion of this subject can most easily be organized by breaking the period of knowledge taxation into two parts, with the first covering the period up to and through the 1819 acts, and the second spanning the period from 1819 to 1861, when the last of the taxes were repealed.

During the period from 1712 to 1819, when the apex of English knowledge taxation was reached, resistance to the taxes was not widespread but was, instead, largely internecine.[180] As a general rule, objections to the taxes were limited to those voiced from within printing and publishing trade circles, and even there, consensus was far from complete. From the very beginning of the knowledge taxes in 1712, some quarters of the publishing business were advantaged by the taxes, or at least relatively so, even as others were harmed. And many of the "legitimate" or established publishers, while not necessarily pleased that the stamp and other taxes had been imposed, were nevertheless desirous that their burden be fairly and fully distributed, and that the papers escaping through loopholes in the taxes, or those simply publishing without a stamp, be brought within the system.[181] Finally, as revenue imperatives began to play an increasingly important role with each new (and usually more onerous) provision enacted over the course of the first century of the taxes, the objections expressed about censorship and illicit motive at the time of the 1712 act may have been muted, or at least less persuasive.

This is not to say, of course, that the taxes were successfully expanded simply because of the opposition's ineffectiveness. The government remained genuinely devoted to controlling the press, particularly with respect to its "libelous" and "irresponsible" (that is, unsupportive and bothersome) quarters. And as time progressed the stamp had the effect, though unintended, of making freer those publishers who by choice had declared freedom from the duty by noncompliance, creative or not. This brutal fact hardened the government's resolve, as it was not yet realized that the stamp itself had contributed to — and perhaps even produced — the problem. And the "hardening" of resolve was assisted by the "respectable" publishers whose "vicious enmity . . . to the hawkers . . . who did not keep a publishing office, but sent out their papers by unknown persons and kept themselves out of harm's way," yielded "vigorous complaints" that the stamp should be enforced against the miscreants.[182] Add to this the French Revolution, which "naturally roused the Parliament of the day to place fresh fetters on the Press,"[183] and one has ample evidence of the forces that perpetuated the tax, even in the face of principled opposition within the printing and publishing circles.

But it seems clear as well that over time the revenue needs came to play a more important role in sustaining and increasing the knowledge taxes. And it is for this reason that over the course of the first hundred years the very definition of the evil associated with the knowledge taxes became transformed from one of censorship, which the publishers were perhaps in a unique position to voice, to one of more systematic (and more revenue-based) choke holds on the widened distribution of information. The latter concern was one that the publishers, of course, could (and did) express.[184] Doing so without contemporaneous support in the broader public, however, made their case more difficult; without public support the publishers' cries may well have appeared as simply self-interested grumbling.[185] And even the self-interested grumbling was muted by the fact that it was far from universal. The perpetuation of monopoly power and economic advantage was not far from the minds of those in the established or "patriotic" partisan quarters who often benefited from the regime of taxes and, more importantly, from the combination of enforcement provisions and well-placed administrative discretion.[186]

The need for a strong and broadly based public effort geared not to "trade interests" but to a larger principle was nicely illustrated by Collet's story of an attempt to achieve repeal only of the paper and advertising duties. The effort was made, not in the name of knowledge, but by the papermakers and other trade interests on grounds of the taxes' oppressive impact on industry. Their deputation met with the Prime Minister to make the argument against the advertisement duty, at the completion of which they were reported to have said, with likely satisfaction for their representation of trade interests, "I trust we have succeeded in convincing your Lordship that we have a very strong case." According to Collet, the Prime Minister, Lord John Russell, "thanked them, but added with a smile, 'I have heard many other strong cases as well.'"[187] Their effort failed, and one suspects that too much self-interest and too little public interest had much to do with it.

This brief and incomplete summary of the main forces at work in the ineffectual resistance to the stamp and other taxes as they were consistently increased and expanded from 1712 to 1819 leaves out much that could be said. But incomplete as it is, the distillation will have to do, for our principal purpose here is to set the background for the American experience, and on that score the more interesting story is that which occurred in the relatively short period from 1819 to 1861 when the taxes were reduced and, ultimately, repealed. And there the interesting question is how and why, in view of the ineffective resistance during the first hundred years of the taxes, the course of events changed.

The answer, not surprisingly, involves a complex of factors. The first was revenue-related. By the early nineteenth century a greatly expanded array of sources of revenue had made the government's financial stake in the revenues generated by the knowledge taxes—particularly the stamp and advertising taxes—relatively less significant.[188] This was not because revenues from the taxes were falling off (though it was argued that they could be increased by a reduction in the tax),[189] but rather because in proportion to the totality of revenue sources they assumed a relatively minor place.[190] Coupled with this was the fact that the taxes had always been, and were continuing to be, sources of political distraction and infighting, and in any event the administrative apparatus for enforcement was cumbersome and expensive, as well as productive of strife. Indeed, one wonders whether by

1819 the whole venture was any longer worth the effort. The second factor was the continued development of the postal system, and with respect to the stamp, specifically, the tension that was developing between it and the rates of postage.[191] It may well have been deemed much more straightforward simply to eliminate the stamp and to address the issues directly through the postage rates. This is, of course, the solution ultimately arrived at in 1855.[192]

These first two factors are practical in character, however, and in the end it appears that politics, not practicality, played a decisive role in achieving ultimate repeal of the taxes. And on this question it is important to understand, from the outset, that the face of the politics of resistance to knowledge taxes changed after 1819. It changed from an internecine struggle largely waged from within the "club" of printers and publishers to one animated by a much more widely supported public appeal for the broad, *and cheap*, availability of information on "politics and political economy." The credibility and political momentum that the publishers could not garner during the first hundred years, because they lacked a broad base of opposition to the taxes and a broader theory of resistance, developed through a combination of sheer persistence, political coincidence, political savvy, and pure luck in the years following 1819, ultimately becoming a fairly widespread political movement.

The movement, however, did not emerge overnight, and its "platform" was not limited to the cause of freedom from knowledge taxation alone, or even to the egalitarian principle of wide availability to the body politic of diverse information free of government control or influence. Instead, the movement against the knowledge taxes, which ultimately took the organizational form of, among others, the Association for the Repeal of Taxes on Knowledge, seems to have been fired in the larger kiln of the Charter Movement.[193] Its political evolution is worth recounting, even if only cursorily.

Generally speaking, the political movement began with the Act of 1836, which was but the first step in the ultimate dismantling of the taxes. The Act's principal effect was at once to reduce the stamp and to broaden and consolidate its enforcement. The Act was not the product of broad-scaled political opposition but reflected the combination of a peculiar set of factors, only one of which was the beginning of a group of individuals devoted to the repeal of the knowledge taxes.

Between 1819 and 1836 there had developed an increasing hue and cry from the printers and publishers about the onerous provisions and undesirable effects of the Publications Act of 1819.[194] This was combined with the happy coincidence of a chancellor of the exchequer, Mr. Spring Rice, who may on principle have thought it wise to reduce the tax, but who also, and more importantly, believed it a politically expedient move to make.[195] To these circumstances was added the Whig party's appetite for partisan control of the press. The 1836 act became the last gasp in the effort to consolidate political authority over the press through taxation. In this case the Whig government was the victor, with the intended vanquished being the unstamped or otherwise exempt publications, or those who found it both expedient and economically rational simply to ignore the tax.[196] While the rate of tax was reduced by the 1836 act, the universe of affected publishers was broadened, and compliance was better assured by a variety of apparently effective enforcement measures, a happy fact, as it turned out, for the "privileged" papers.[197]

Collet Dobson Collet described the situation following the 1836 act as follows:

> For thirteen years the demand for the repeal of the Newspaper Stamp ceased. The causes of this calm were various. In the first place, Mr. Spring Rice had consolidated into something like a Guild, a Press which gave, to a great extent, what the people wanted, though it gave it only to those who could, in one way or other, afford to pay fivepence for a newspaper. The members of the Guild were protected by the Stamp Office in their monopoly of news; but the Stamp Office gave this protection in order to preserve the revenue, not in order to enforce the law. The quantity of news contained in the fivepenny paper, which he read at the public-house, seems to have indicated the amount which the working man expected to obtain. . . . Mr. Spring Rice had defended the prohibition of remarks and observations on news, as necessary to enable the suppression of news itself. This reason passed muster in the House of Commons, not because it was logical, but because it was put forward as a reason for doing something the House liked to do.[198]

If the 1819 act was the apex of the knowledge taxes, the 1836 act may well have been their partisan low point.

The 1836 act was not only followed by a period of "calm," as Collet reported, but indeed by a decline in the agitation for repeal of the knowledge taxes. This was not due to a lack of ardor on the part of those who sought, above all else, complete repeal; rather, it was due to the intervention of other issues that required "the diversion of reforming energies to other objects."[199] To this should be added the fact that much of the press had been patronized by the 1836 act and its provisions had been geared to the elimination of unstamped papers.[200] But it was the "other objects" to which "reforming energies" were directed that played the most important role in the decline of agitation, although in the end they also led to ultimate success in repeal.

The other objects included the repeal of the Corn Laws, a rising demand for universal male suffrage, growing interest in parliamentary reform, and "getting rid of the Bread Tax."[201] In one degree or another all of these objects, as well as others, coalesced into the Charter Movement and related efforts. "The repeal of the Newspaper Stamp," according to Collet, "had been [prior to 1836] looked to as the most probable measure to lead to the repeal of the Corn Laws and to a further measure of Parliamentary reform."[202] But the failure to achieve repeal, coupled with the growing agitation on the other objects noted above, momentarily swept the knowledge tax agitation aside, or at least made it but a small part of a larger political movement.

Notably, as Collet observed, the larger political movement with its broader objects of repeal of the Corn Laws, suffrage, parliamentary reform, and elimination of the bread tax garnered not only widespread support in the working classes but also brought the middle classes into the fray.[203] And the forces that were seeking repeal of the knowledge taxes joined in, becoming "actively engaged in the cause either of the Charter or of the Corn Law repeal."[204] Their involvement in this broader movement did not distract them from their interest in elimination of the knowledge taxes, but rather made them aware of the possibility of broadened support for future efforts at repeal. As Collet put it, in his characteristically amusing turn of phrase, involvement in the Charter and Corn Law efforts "had become, to [the knowledge tax opponents'] more mature years, not a blessing to enjoy but 'the heaven which we dream.'"[205]

Out of the Charter Movement, and one of its principal organizations, the People's Charter Union, established in 1848, emerged the subsequent support for the ultimately successful agitation against the knowledge taxes.[206] From the Charter Union evolved the Newspaper Stamp Abolition Committee, established in 1849, which gathered increasingly broad support from the middle classes. This support would prove ultimately critical to success in the efforts for repeal. Over time, and through efforts recounted in detail and quite delightfully by Collet, the Committee built support in literary quarters (originally mixed in their support), and developed support and sponsors in Parliament, beginning with a relatively few "radicals" but eventually embracing a broader array of interests. Public meetings focused on the need for repeal of the stamp, advertising, and paper taxes were held throughout England, all in what seems to have been a relatively well-conceived effort to portray a broad base of political opposition, especially in the middle classes, to those acts. Collet opined that "the number of public meetings for the total repeal of all the Taxes on Knowledge was much greater than that for any other relief from taxation except for the repeal of the window tax."[207]

The advertising tax was the first to go in 1853, and a critical factor seems to have been the acquiescence of Lord John Russell, the Prime Minister. Collet implies that he was less influenced by the arguments and reasoning in favor of broad dissemination of information than by the broadened political base with which he was confronted, as well, it seems, as the fact that elimination of the advertising duty would cost little in revenue.[208] The movement for repeal, particularly of the stamp, was further assisted in 1851 with the establishment of the Association for the Repeal of the Taxes on Knowledge.[209] The membership of the Association consisted of members of Parliament and other public persons — "an upper circle of public men," according to Collet.[210] The Association continued to gather public support through public meetings. The movement thus possessed the support of important men, of large numbers of citizens who would sign petitions supporting repeal, and of others whose sentiments for repeal of the knowledge taxes were as much a product of their dislike of other duties or of unrest directed at other objects. Thus the political mix that ultimately succeeded tapped many seams, including the Charter Movement, suffrage, trade interests, parliamentary reform, and even unhappiness with duties such as those imposed on "soap, hops, or malt."[211] Added to the mix, of course, were those whose motives were more exclusively and clearly fixed on knowledge itself.

For those who are interested in the details of repeal, Collet's book provides both a detailed and entertaining account. Our principal interest, instead, is the politics behind the success. And on this issue there is but one further, yet central, observation to make. The ultimate success of this untidy, and even at times unruly, political movement was based not only on its political acuity, but also on the fact that it provided a theme or principle that the publishers, during the first hundred years of the taxes, were not able to voice effectively. This theme, or message, voiced consistently throughout the period from 1836 to 1861, was the need for public knowledge that was cheap, not dear, and that was uninfluenced by the political wishes of the party in power.[212] The message was not permeated by the economic self-interest of the club of printers and publishers but was instead universal, and it garnered broad support for its straightforward injunction: the imperative of access to information on "politics and political economy" by the common citizen, and the availability of diverse and open opinion upon which the popular will would be freely shaped.

This was a message that the newspapers and publishers could not, alone, persuasively convey. And despite the apparent political sophistication of those involved in the movement for repeal of the knowledge taxes, and the happy coincidences of the publishers' economic interests, the government's willingness to forgo revenue, and other objects of popular discontent that enabled working and middle class support to be captured, it seems clear that without a unifying theme that struck a chord in the public mind no amount of political savvy would have achieved the end of the knowledge taxes, at least not as quickly. It is not, therefore, an overstatement to say — even while acknowledging a beneficent combination of political skill, economic forces, and companionable objects of public unrest — that the ultimate repeal of knowledge taxes in England was a product of high principle. And it is likewise not an exaggeration to say that the term knowledge taxes, embedded originally in the illicit and censorial motives of the Crown, was transformed in the nineteenth century into a symbol, instead, of the importance of practical and effective access by all segments of a self-governing society to knowledge about "politics and political economy." Its political force as a symbol and as a unifying theme for a popular movement is attested to by Gladstone's description of the final demise of the paper duty, as reported by Herd: It was "the severest Parliamentary struggle in which I have ever been engaged."[213]

CONCLUSION
A full grasp of the knowledge taxes and their impact cannot be obtained simply by a study of their provisions and chronology, no matter how fascinating that subject may be. For beyond the specific enactments, the particular means of avoiding them, and their immediate impact on particular segments of the press, the knowledge taxes had consequences that are best appreciated from a broader perspective. As a general matter, the stamp, advertisement, and paper taxes appear to have served as a fairly effective, although imperfect, means of control of the periodical press throughout the eighteenth century.

Control through taxation was exercised directly as well as indirectly. Direct control was achieved through the exactions themselves and served to limit the quantity and vigor of newspapers and periodicals. In this form, however, the controls were blunt-edged, often awkward, and even more often counterproductive. Direct control either hit everyone equally, a result not to be desired by a government bent on influencing rather than abolishing information for the public, or it hit the wrong parties.

In contrast, the indirect forms of control, largely exercised at the administrative level, were at once more subtle and more specific and effective. And, as it turned out, they proved (not surprisingly) thereafter to be more important. By squeezing the profitability of newspapers, the taxes forced the publishers to be more compliant and made both publishers and writers more susceptible to subsidies and political bribes.[214] With the ebbs and flows of partisan political control, the press was viewed as an important instrument for garnering and maintaining favorable public opinion, and economic insecurity was a device used to advantage by the parties in power[215] — a practice that would later take root in America.[216]

In the period following the Stamp Act of 1712, an increase in the number of papers, and in their circulation, occurred. Access by the controlling party to public funds as well as to the machinery of taxation gave a large advantage to that party in the fight for public support, and the developing press was a far-from-forgotten object of such efforts. Public money was used to buy up antiministerial papers, to start new newspapers which were produced or written by government employees, and to subsidize or buy off some of the more successful opposition writers and papers, as well as to bribe those writers to promote the ministerial cause in their articles.[217] The higher cost of printing and publishing which the taxes produced made it easier to buy or otherwise influence support for the government.[218] Control was heightened by the ultimate demise of the legitimate, or independent, small newspapers, which were squeezed by the impact of the taxes, and were ultimately put out of business by the added competition of the cut-rate stampless papers.[219]

The stamp tax also encouraged other corrupt practices in the government. The Post Office Clerks of the Roads, for example, exercised authority over newspaper distribution to the provinces. Their official authority made them susceptible to influence, both political and economic. Some clerks became shareholders in various papers that wanted to protect their commercial interests and were willing to submit to some ownership by the clerks as the price of unimpeded distribution of their product.[220] Parliament also passed a law permitting commercial concerns to use an M.P.'s franking privileges to send out newspapers. By this device, newspapers that pleased

Parliament could thereafter be sent out free, a further incentive to please the government and by so doing to save considerable expense, thus indirectly lifting the burden of the stamp.[221] In large measure because of the taxes, both the quality of news and the diversity of opinion in the press was wanting, notwithstanding the increasing availability of papers to the public during the time of the knowledge taxes.[222]

As imperfect in execution and often self-defeating in operation as the knowledge taxes were, they left an undeniable imprint on the press throughout the eighteenth century and until their demise. The imprint was not exactly what the government wanted, for the taxes fell far short of assuring close and effective government control of the distribution of information. Yet diversity was choked, and the capacity for indirect influence of the press was created. As Collet, the contemporary commentator, historian, and philosopher of press freedom during the later period of knowledge taxation, said, "[t]hose public-minded private men who were anxious to educate the people and to permit them to educate themselves were forbidden the only process by which their views could be carried out, the publication of cheap newspapers weekly. This was rendered impossible by the Stamp Duty."[223]

The English Heritage

The English history of regulation and taxation of the press is broad and diverse. It covers hundreds of years and spans profound changes in the form of government in England. It involves diverse forms of regulation, taxation, and control of the press, and these various practices were constantly being shaped by changing political circumstances and by the characteristics of a press that was rapidly evolving in technological and economic terms. Generalizations, therefore, should be offered with great caution, and any such conclusions should explicitly acknowledge the contribution that changing political and technological circumstances may have made to the shifting regulatory environment.

The English history, nevertheless, is instructive on a number of issues. At the most fundamental level, it can provide us with the basic understanding of the meaning of "knowledge taxes" — a term laden with implications, but of uncertain content. The term first arose in connection with the early Stamp Acts, and its meaning derives from the very particular historical setting in which those taxes were devised. Moreover, the history can provide insight into the various forms of "knowledge taxes," their impact, and the dangers they pose. Some forms of tax may, for example, be offensive *per se*, as they inescapably violate certain defined principles of freedom by their terms. Other forms of tax, however, may be condemnable only by virtue of the hands that wield them, and the historical circumstances surrounding the use and misuse of knowledge taxes in England can be highly instructive on this question. Finally, through the English experience we may begin to see the first manifestations of an evolving concept of freedom of the press — a concept that lies at the heart of any standards by which we might make judgments about the acceptability of various forms of knowledge tax. None of these issues, which we shall briefly explore below, governs the meaning of freedom of the press in America, or the circumstances necessary to its realization, but they represent the intellectual heritage from which the American versions of freedom emerged, and therefore constitute an essential perspective from which the later American experience with knowledge taxes should be understood.

The Meaning of Knowledge Taxes

The term and, indeed, the very concept of knowledge taxes arose from the English experience with regulation of the press. Its true meaning as a symbol of freedom and a principle of unimpeded access to information by a self-governing populace did not crystalize, however, until the ultimately successful efforts at repeal began to bear fruit in the nineteenth century. The term's meaning is therefore inseparable from its historical setting. Viewed across the landscape of nearly two centuries, the English history suggests that the concept of knowledge taxes means more than the particular types of tax imposed on the press or on publishers. Instead, the concept carries with it two central elements.

The first element is that a knowledge tax reflects, in its purpose or effect, a governmental exercise of control over the press. But the control is usually structural in character, in contrast to the then generally accepted and discrete imposition of liability for defamation or other private wrongs. The entire English experience with the Stamp Acts was infected by the obvious and often explicit purpose of using taxation as a means of bringing the press to heel. This was to be accomplished by exacting an economic penalty on publications that were disfavored, and by providing economic and regulatory leverage by which to control indirectly — through apprehension of unexercised, but available, power — the information and opinion communicated to the public.

This is not to say, however, that only taxes whose *purpose* was to control the press were objectionable. Particularly in the later stages of the English experience overt governmental purpose was less evident, yet taxes which visited significant burdens on the distribution of knowledge were still resisted, and such taxes were very clearly considered to be offensive "knowledge taxes." Such taxes carried the label of knowledge taxes because they had the effect (independently of their purpose) of controlling and limiting the availability of information, as such, quite apart from the information's specific content or point of view. On the other hand, taxes of broad application whose purposes, at least in their impact on publications, were purely revenue producing and whose effect, or actual administration, was benign were not, as a general rule, considered to fall within the offensive category of "knowledge taxes."[224]

The second element of the knowledge tax concept involved the incidence of the tax. Taxes so labeled tended to fall explicitly, and often uniquely, on the press. Of equal importance, their incidence fell squarely on the direct elements or components of publication, and therefore their economic impact on the cost of a publication was direct and immediate. Taxes on property, on transfers of property, and the like were not usually encompassed within the forbidden concept of knowledge taxes, for they were neither explicit in identifying the subject of the tax as "publications," nor were they differential, and their economic impact on the price of the publication was indirect and diffuse. In contrast, taxes on paper (at least when viewed in combination with accompanying stamp and advertising taxes) were largely restricted in incidence to publications, and this was more explicitly the case with the stamps. The advertisement taxes were also restricted, although in this case by the terms of the tax itself, to periodical publications. These three forms of tax — the paper, stamp, and advertisement taxes — also shared the other important characteristic. In each case the economic impact of the tax was felt directly and immediately on the cost of each finished product. Each form of tax, therefore, had the inescapable impact of requiring publishers to absorb a known cost per copy of a publication, or to pass that cost on in the form of an increased price per copy.

Two consequences of historical importance flowed from this economic impact. Depending on its amount, the tax endangered the publication's economic survival, and in any event reduced subscriptions and made the threat of economic disaster a real one. Of equal importance, by structuring the tax so as to require an increase in the price of the publication, and doing so with firm control of that price, government was permitted to limit distribution or exert leverage *and* at the same time to disguise its own role. The purchaser did not see the tax at all; all that was seen was a higher price for the newspaper. Government could therefore escape direct accountability to the purchaser, while still controlling price, much as a puppet is controlled by invisible strings.

The Dangers Posed by Knowledge Taxes

The second conclusion that can be drawn from the English history concerns the various forms of knowledge taxes and the dangers they pose. Here there appear to be three important observations. The first is that the danger of knowledge taxes, especially in light of their usual governmental purpose and their unique application to publications, is principally their confiscatory potential. Such taxes were dangerous, in other words, because they directly increased the price of knowledge to the populace, and therefore endangered the very availability of information. The problem of unequal access for the common citizen was not, from a historical standpoint, the principal concern; instead, the publications tended to be sufficiently precarious, and the level of potential tax sufficiently unconstrained, so that the tax would simply put the publications out of business, thereby denying information to anyone. This is the main legacy of the original Stamp Act of 1712, for in substantial respects that act was seen as a substitute means of recapturing complete and direct government control over political information. The absence of a privately controlled press would not result in an absence of information to the populace, but would instead permit the government to monopolize the information made available.

The second observation concerning the dangers of knowledge taxes is their potential for differential application among categories of publication. Interestingly, explicit differential imposition of stamp, paper, or advertising taxes was not the norm. When differential taxation occurred, it tended to be inadvertent, or to be disguised in the actual administration of the tax, and not reflected on the face of the tax itself. Some taxes, of course, did have a purposefully differential impact. The advertising tax, for example, differentially bore down upon those types of publications — generally newspapers — that relied heavily on advertising revenue, and such a tax could be and was used to tame a particular segment of the press. Such differential taxation tended, however, to be too blunt-edged, as it hit both friend and foe alike. For this reason, differential *administration* was the more effective device, but it was also the most dangerous, as explicit favor or forgiveness of the tax posed substantial political risks, even to the Crown and Parliament. This is borne out by the quite remarkable fact that while many of the disfavored publications were escaping the stamp through loopholes or simple civil disobedience, the tax continued to be imposed almost mechanically on the established newspapers that supported the party in power.

The differential use of knowledge taxes, therefore, usually took a much subtler form. The form of differential administration used was bribes and subsidy. By making publications economically precarious through taxation, the government could take advantage of their susceptibility, buying favor through subsidy in the form, for example, of favorable postal service. The taxes also made the writers and editors less secure and permitted the party in power to subsidize their writing through other employment or direct favor or payment. Through these devices discrete and content-based influence could be exerted in a fashion unattainable through even the most blatant and discriminatory application of a stamp tax. It should be understood, however, that this form of "influence peddling" was, in a sense, fair game. The press in eighteenth-century England — and thereafter in England *and* America — was overtly partisan. It was much more an open and partisan participant in the political process than it is today.

Finally, if there is a single and most important conclusion to be drawn from the British experience, it is that facially or overtly discriminatory taxation was not, in fact, the principal problem posed by knowledge taxes. In some instances overt discrimination served to enhance access to information and its availability. This was the result — although unintended — of the "loophole" in the original stamp exaction which fueled the political tracts and the smaller, often provincial, presses. More often discrimination was attempted, and with the worst of motives, but it consistently failed, either because of public reaction or because such means of press control were simply too blunt-edged and could not be framed in sufficiently discrete terms to avoid hurting friends as well as enemies. Instead, the most serious problem posed by knowledge taxes was their very imposition on the press as a unique tax category of itself, and the opportunity for employing the actual or threatened dependence such taxes caused as a means of exacting subtle and highly discrete control through means other than taxation, and as a choke on the availability of information, whatever stripe its source.

The Emerging Free Press Values

The final area of interest in the English history of knowledge taxes involves the general grounds — or principles of free expression — on which knowledge taxes, at least in the forms outlined above, were condemned. On this question history is quite revealing. While it was not until the later stages of popular disaffection with the taxes that the underlying principles of freedom emerged, two principles appear, in the end, to have won out. The first was that individuals must have the freedom to disseminate their views broadly, and people—all people—must be able to acquire them free of confiscatory governmental exactions—not free of exactions altogether, but free of exactions of such size that economical distribution to the ordinary citizen was impossible. The second principle was that government should not be able to employ taxation as a means of limiting availability of information and opinion to the body politic. As long as the information was accurate and the opinion within the range of fair play, free dissemination of diverse views was to be encouraged.

Equally interesting are the values or concepts of freedom of the press that were not generally voiced. While it became generally understood that the government should not be free to impose confiscatory taxation, relatively little concern with differential taxation was voiced. This was partly, it seems, because the fact of taxation was the main concern of the economically vulnerable publishers and partly because, as a general rule, differential taxation never worked, except against the government's interests. It is also noteworthy that, while government efforts to control the press were generally condemned, this condemnation did not extend to libelous or even seditious material. These were appropriate subjects of government concern and control, judging by both Parliament's attitudes and the publishers' outcries. Control of libel and seditious expression represented government efforts to cleanse communication and debate; they were generally accepted as proper and often tendered as preferable to the stamp.

In the context of knowledge taxation, the operative value was not an absolute freedom to publish anything on any subject, nor a freedom from all forms of government control over the content of publication. Nor, judged by what was said and what was not said throughout the English history of knowledge taxes, did freedom of the press imply freedom from taxation; even less was it meant to imply freedom from differential taxation within media of communication. Freedom of the press did, however, come to mean freedom to seek and to reach, in an open market, a broad audience with one's ideas, and the ability to do so free from the stranglehold of financial dependence on government.

Freedom of the press reflected a distinction between government regulation of the specific content of publications on the one hand, and government control of the availability of information on the other. False, libelous, and scandalous publications were generally acknowledged to be legitimate subjects of government control. Knowledge taxes, however, were not an effective means for reaching these concerns, at least at the level of specific publications; they swept more broadly, effecting more systematic constraints on the number and types of publications available to the public. With the knowledge taxes, it was the very availability of information — the facts and events and opinion "on the subjects of politics and political economy"[225] — that was at stake. It was in this setting that the knowledge taxes assumed great importance, for taxation became the chief instrument for the exertion of control over information itself, and resistance to the taxes was premised on the idea that the marketplace for information was to be substantially free of government control.

The history of knowledge taxes in England provides important perspectives on the full understanding of freedom of the press. The values of access to public audiences and freedom from government control over dissemination of information and opinion to the body politic emerged clearly from the struggle against the stamp. The history of English knowledge taxes and the principles of freedom generated in the struggle against them may also serve to fill out the more limited and relatively cramped Blackstonian view of press freedom which has been drawn from the Sedition Act debate and its historical antecedents.

Notes

1. See Philip Hamburger, "The Development of the Law of Seditious Libel and the Control of the Press," 37 *Stan. L. Rev.* 661, 666 (1985).

2. English Statute of Treasons, 1352, 25 Edw. 3, St. 5, ch. 2 (Eng.).

3. Hamburger at 666.

4. See Van V. Veeder, *Selected Essays in Anglo-American Legal History*, vol. 3, at 463 (1909).

5. *Id.*; see Hamburger at 666–67.

6. Hamburger at 667, citing Fredrick S. Siebert, *Freedom of the Press in England, 1476–1776*, at 90 (1952) (reporting on the execution for "high treason" of William Carter in 1580).

7. 26 Hen. 8, ch. 13. For a thorough account of the statutory and judicial developments in the evolution of treason during the sixteenth and seventeenth centuries, see Siebert at 264–69.

8. Hamburger at 667–68.

9. See Siebert at 265, 267–69.

10. The statutes spanned 3 Edw. I, (West.) c. 34 (1275) through l Eliz. c. vi (1558), according to Siebert at 118 & n.30.

11. *Id.*; see Hamburger at 668.

12. For an account of the Sedition Act controversy and its role in shaping the meaning of the First Amendment, see Leonard W. Levy, *Emergence of a Free Press* (1985); New York Times Co. v. Sullivan, 376 U.S. 254, 273–76 (1964); David A. Anderson, "The Origins of the Press Clause," 30 *UCLA L. Rev.* 455 (1983); Vincent Blasi, "The Checking Value in First Amendment Theory," 1977 *Am. B. Found. Res. J.* 521.

13. See Hamburger at 668; Siebert at 118. The exact language was "News or Tales." Siebert at 118.

14. In addition, the punishment was visited on the "original inventor" of the offending statement. Punishment could be escaped by one who merely repeated what had already been said by another and revealed the identity of the "original inventor" to the Crown. Siebert at 118.

15. *Id.* at 119 and authorities cited n.35; see Hamburger at 668–71.

16. See Van V. Veeder, "The History and Theory of the Law of Defamation," 3 *Col. L. Rev.* 546 (1903).

17. See Hamburger at 670–71; Siebert at 91–92.

18. See Hamburger at 672–73.

19. For a discussion of the decree, as well as other enforcement mechanisms surrounding the licensing system, see Siebert at 84. The Star Chamber was abolished by act of Parliament in 1641, and "the House of Commons took the regulation of the Press into its own hands." Collet Dobson Collet, *History of the Taxes on Knowledge: Their Origin and Repeal* 2 (facsimile reprint 1971) (1933).

20. See Siebert at chs. 10–11 (pp. 202–37); Joseph Frank, *The Beginnings of the English Newspaper, 1620–1660*, 236–68 (1961). The Commonwealth spanned the years 1649–60, following the execution of Charles I and the abolition of the monarchy and the House of Lords.

21. Hamburger at 680.

22. Act for Regulation of Printing and Printing Profits, 1662, 14 Car. 2, ch. 33 (Eng.); Hamburger at 680.

23. See Hamburger at 680–90.

24. *Id.* at 714–15; see Frank for a detailed and fascinating account of the experience with licensing and censorship between 1620 and 1660.

25. Hamburger at 715.

26. *Id.*

27. See Siebert at 249–63 for a discussion of the enforcement problems with the printing acts.

28. Hamburger at 715.

29. *Id.*

30. *Id.* at 715–16.

31. *Id.* at 716–17 and n. 169.

32. *Id.*; see Siebert at 269–75.

33. 90 Eng. Rep. 1132, Holt 442; 91 Eng. Rep. 363, 2 Salkeld 417; 91 Eng. Rep. 1175, Lord Raymond 414 (K.B. 1699).

34. See Hamburger at 728–34 for a thorough account of *King v. Bear*.

35. Queen v. Tutchin, 90 Eng. Rep. 1133, 1133–34, Holt 424 (Q.B. 1704).

36. See Hamburger at 735.

37. *Id*. at 724.

38. See Siebert at 273–75; Hamburger at 728–35, 746; William M. Clyde, *Struggle for Freedom of the Press* (1934). Licensing, however, was not without its own difficulties in public reaction and spotty enforcement. See Frank at 90–91, 99–102, 135–36, 158, 178, 197–98.

39. Siebert at 301; see Hamburger at 743–51.

40. Siebert at 305.

41. *Id*.

42. *Id*. at 306.

43. *Id*. at 305–6.

44. Collet at 3–4.

45. Siebert at 306–7.

46. *Id*. at 307. Siebert reports that in 1693 the printers submitted to Parliament a petition "[f]or reviving and continuing the act for the regulation of printing." The publishers stated that without the Act "the impoverishment and ruin of hundreds of English families, and the enriching of the Dutch printers and Booksellers" would result. *Id*. The printers made a similar proposal to the House of Commons in 1698. The printers' interest in preserving the Printing Act was selective, however, as they did not seek full restoration of the licensing system, but only selected protections it afforded. *Id*.

47. See *id*.

48. *Id*.

49. *Id*.

50. *Id*.

51. *Id*. at 308.

52. *Id*. at 308.

53. 9 Anne, ch. 23; see Siebert at 308. For almanacs printed on both sides of a sheet, the tax was twopence. For almanacs covering several years, the tax was to be paid for each year. The tax also applied to a large group of other consumer goods.

54. See Laurence Hanson, *Government and the Press* 11–13 (1936); Siebert at 308–9.

55. See Lucy M. Salmon, *Newspaper and Authority* 183 (1923).

56. An Act for Laying Several Duties, etc. (Stamp Act), 1712, 10 Anne, ch. 19, §§ 101–18 (Eng.).

57. Salmon at 183–85.

58. See Salmon at 182–84; 1 William Lee, *Daniel DeFoe: His Life and Recently Discovered Writings* 196 (photo. reprint 1968) (London, 1869); text accompanying notes 95–105 *infra*.

59. Harold Herd, *March of Journalism* 43 (1952).

60. Siebert at 309.

61. Salmon at 184.

62. Siebert at 309.

63. *Id*.

64. Quoted in Siebert at 309; see Collet at 4–5.

65. Siebert at 309.

66. *Id.* at 309. The article appeared in the *Daily Courant.*

67. *Id.*; see Collet at 4.

68. Siebert at 310, quoting from Collet, *History of the Taxes on Knowledge*, 7 (1899). The 1971 facsimile reprint of the 1933 edition of Collet's *History of the Taxes on Knowledge* at 4, omits the last sentence of this passage and contains other minor differences.

69. Lee, *supra* note 58, at 199.

70. Siebert at 310.

71. *Id.* at 310–11 (quoting Lincoln's Inn Collection, M.P. 102/305).

72. See *id.*

73. William H. Wickwar, *The Struggle for the Freedom of the Press, 1819–1832* 29 (Johnson reprint 1972)(1928).

74. *Id.*

75. Siebert at 311.

76. An Act for Laying Several Duties, etc. (Stamp Act), 1712, 10 Anne, ch. 19 (Eng.).

77. For a more complete description of the Stamp Act, see Siebert at 311–12; Collet at 5–13.

78. See text accompanying notes 101–8 *infra* for discussion of this statutory qualification and its impact.

79. Also exempted from the tax, regardless of size, were "school books, books of piety and devotion, daily accounts of bills and goods imported and exported, weekly bills of mortality, and single advertisements published by themselves." Siebert at 311.

80. *Id.*

81. 8 & 9 Will. 3, ch. 7 (1696).

82. The basis of the tax was also changed to the ream. See Siebert at 312.

83. *Id.*

84. See *id.*

85. See text accompanying notes 95–100, 134–39 *infra.*

86. See Dwight L. Teeter, Jr., & Don R. LeDuc, *Law of Mass Communications* 69 (7th ed. 1992); Siebert at 309; Collet at 7.

87. Siebert at 312.

88. *Id.*

89. *Id.* at 313; see Henry L. Snyder, *The Circulation of Newspapers in the Reign of Queen Anne*, 215, 217–18 (1968); J. M. Price, "A Note on the Circulation of the London Press, 1704–1714," 31 *Bull. Inst. Hist. Res.* 219 (1958).

90. *Spectator*, No. 445, August 1712, as quoted in Siebert at 313. H. R. Fox Bourne, *English Newspapers*, vol. 1, at 81 (reissued 1966) (1887), quotes the same passage with minor variations.

91. *Spectator*, No. 445, August 1712, as quoted in Siebert at 313. H. R. Fox Bourne, *English Newspapers*, vol. 1, at 81 (reissued 1966) (1887), quotes the same passage, dated August 7, 1712, with minor variations.

92. *Id.* at 82.

93. Siebert at 314.

94. *Id.*

95. Collet at 7.

96. Herd at 44; see Collet at 14–15.

97. Siebert at 314.

98. See Lawrence Lewis, *The Advertisements of the Spectator* 65 (1909); Siebert at 314–15.

99. Siebert at 315.

100. *Id.*

101. An Act for Laying Special Duties, etc. (Stamp Act), 1712, 10 Anne, ch. 19 (Eng.).

102. Siebert at 315 (emphasis in original).

103. See Stanley Morison, *The English Newspaper, 1622–1932*, at 84–86 (1932).

104. Siebert at 316.

105. *Id.*

106. See Morison at 85–88; Siebert at 317 (quoting Swift's conclusion that the stamp tax harmed only papers tending to be loyal to the Tory party).

107. See Michael Harris, "The Structure, Ownership and Control of the Press, 1620–1780," in *Newspaper History from the Seventeenth Century to the Present Day* 82, 84–85 (George Boyce, et al. eds., 1978).

108. *Id.* at 85.

109. An Act for Laying Several Duties, etc. (Stamp Act), 1712, 10 Anne, ch. 19, § 118 (Eng.).

110. Siebert at 316.

111. *Id.* at 317.

112. See R. S. Crane & F. B. Kaye, *A Census of British Newspapers and Periodicals, 1620–1800*, at 183 (1927).

113. Siebert at 317.

114. *Id.*

115. 1 Alexander Andrews, *History of British Journalism*, 109 (London, Richard Bentley 1859) (republished 1968).

116. Siebert at 317; Hanson at 12. Both Siebert and Hanson quote from Jonathan Swift's *History of the Four Last Years of the Queen*. However, Hanson uses the term "declamation" rather than "defamation" in the phrase, "well versed in the topics of defamation."

117. Siebert at 317–18.

118. Compare *id.* at 317 (none survived) with Donald Read, *Press and People, 1790–1850*, at 59 (1961) (about 50 provincial newspapers existed in 1782).

119. Read at 59.

120. Harris at 88.

121. Siebert at 318.

122. *Id.*

123. *Id.*

124. *Id.* at 318–19.

125. An Act for Continuing the Duties . . . and for Explaining a Late Act in Relation to Stamp Duties, etc., 1724, 11 Geo., ch. 8 §§ 13–15 (Eng.)

126. See Hanson at 13.

127. Mercuries, or newsbooks, were regular publications licensed as books that reported on the activities of government. They began as a means of escaping the scrutiny of the licensing officials through the device of obtaining "a license for the book proper and then . . . insert[ing] the questionable matter [such as political commentary] in a dedication or introduction." Siebert at 144.

128. Collet at 7; see Siebert at 319.

129. Siebert at 319.

130. The tax of three shillings per edition continued, but was *de minimis* in its economic impact. *Id.* at 319. It did, however, provide the *occasion* for regulation through associated regulatory provisions as well as the mere information obtained through the stamp.

131. See Crane & Kaye at 184–86.

132. See *id.*; Siebert at 319–20.

133. See Siebert at 320; Morison at 103.

134. See Siebert at 320; Harris at 85.

135. See Harris at 86.

136. Collet at 7.

137. An Act for Continuing Several Laws, etc., 1743, 16 Geo. 2, ch. 26, § 5 (Eng.); see Collet at 7.

138. An Act for Continuing Several Laws, etc., 1743, 16 Geo. 2, ch. 26, § 5 (Eng.).

139. Siebert at 320.

140. *Id.*

141. An Act for Granting to His Majesty Several Rates and Duties, etc., 1757, 30 Geo. 2, ch. 19, § 1 (Eng.).

142. Siebert at 321.

143. *Id.* at 321.

144. *Id.* at 320.

145. *Id.* at 321.

146. An Act for Explaining Two Acts, etc., 1773, 13 Geo. 3 (Eng.).

147. Siebert at 321.

148. An Act for Granting to His Majesty Several Duties, etc., 1776, 16 Geo. 3, ch. 34, § 7 (Eng.).

149. An Act for Granting to His Majesty Several Additional Stamp Duties, etc., 1789, 29 Geo. 3, ch. 50, § 1 (Eng.).

150. *Id.*

151. Siebert at 322.

152. *Id.*

153. *Id.*

154. An Act to Enable the Commissioners of His Majesty's Stamp Duties, etc., 1794, 34 Geo. 3, ch. 72 (Eng.); An Act to Repeal the Several Duties . . . and to Grant New and Additional Duties, etc., 1804, 44 Geo. 3, ch. 98 (Eng.); An Act for Repealing the Stamp Office Duties . . . and for Granting New Duties, etc., 1815, 55 Geo. 3, ch. 185 (Eng.).

155. Siebert at 322.

156. See Wickwar, William H., *The Struggle For Freedom of the Press, 1819–1832* (Johnson reprint 1972) (1928). Two of the "Six Acts" of 1819 are pertinent. The first was the Act for the More Effectual Prevention and Punishment of Blasphemous and Seditious Libels (60 Geo. 3, ch. 8), more commonly called the "Blasphemous and Seditious Libels Act," which clarified a broad concept of seditious libel and provided for more effective administration of the law and "frightening would-be offenders." Wickwar at 137. Judges were given broad powers of search and seizure for copies of articles, and second offenders were threatened with banishment, a measure designed to deter people from a first offense. *Id.* at 138.

The other of the "Six Acts" passed in 1819 directly related to knowledge taxation was An Act to Subject Certain Publications to the Duties of Stamps upon Newspapers, and to make Other Regulations for Restraining the Abuses Arising from the Publication of Blasphemous and Seditious Libels (60 Geo. 3, ch. 9), known as the "Publications Act." The target of the Publications Act was the cheap weeklies—"Pamphlets and Printed papers" on public matters which tended "to excite Hatred and Contempt of the Government and Constitution . . . , and also vilifying our holy Religion"—which were then being published "in great Numbers, and at very small Prices." *Id.* at § 1. The Publications Act made all pamphlets and papers newspapers for purposes of Pitt's Newspaper Act (1815, 55 Geo. 3, ch. 80 & 185) and the various stamp acts then in place (1815, 55 Geo. 3, ch. 80 & 185; 1816, 56 Geo. 3, ch. 56). In doing so, it provided that the duty so applicable, which was higher than that previously applicable to pamphlets, would apply only if the price of the pamphlet, etc., were less than sixpence exclusive of the duty. This represented an effort to force a sufficiently high price for the pamphlets not qualifying (i.e., sixpence or more for those not characterized as newspapers, a higher duty for those that did so qualify—a Hobson's choice) so that most people could not afford to buy the non-newspaper periodicals, especially those that were blasphemous, as the Parliament assumed (wrongly it turned out) that people would only pay a cheap rate for such drivel. Loopholes in paper size, etc., were also closed. Wickwar at 138–39.

Another apparently new and perhaps most important aspect of the Act was described by Wickwar at 139: "But this was not merely an Act for increasing the price of periodical pamphlets; it was also a periodical-producers' Liability Act, establishing compulsory insurance against the ever-present risk of conviction for criminal libel. Every person printing or publishing a periodical was to enter into recognizances before a Baron of the Exchequer at London, Westminster, Edinburgh, or Dublin, or enter into a bond before a Justice of the Peace in the country, along with two or three sufficient sureties, in the sum of [] 300 [pounds] if the periodical was published in or around London, or [] 200 [pounds] if published elsewhere, as a guarantee for the payment of 'every such fine or penalty as may at any time be imposed upon or adjudged against him or her, by reason of any conviction for printing or publishing any blasphemous or seditious libel, at any time after entering into such recognizance or executing such bond.'"

157. Wickwar at 138–39; see Collet at 9–14. Among the peculiarities of the Act's impact—which were many—was the effective exemption from onerous taxation of nonperiodical publications. As Collet notes, this "left the gentlemen pam-

phleteers at liberty to free their souls, though not to reach the masses of people." Collet at 14.

158. See *supra* note 156.

159. See Collet at 14 et seq. In summing up the Publications Act, Wickwar says: "Such is the collection of regulations in what is often very inadequately and superficially called the Newspaper Stamp Duty Act. [While] it did extend the [higher] Newspaper Duty from news to criticism; . . . as an alternative [for those periodicals escaping this duty] it increased the size and price of weeklies which continued to pay the light pamphlet-tax. It fixed a minimum frequency for monthlies which escaped from both these regulations. It prevented any person from publishing periodicals unless he could find sureties to the tune of several hundred pounds; and its augmentation of the power of magistrates to punish persons before trial referred to all publications suspected of libel and was not confined to periodicals." Wickwar at 140.

160. Collet at 15–17.

161. An Act to Reduce the Duties on Newspapers, etc., 1836, 6 & 7 Will. 4, ch. 76, § 1, sched. A (Eng.).

162. See text accompanying notes 165, 169–74 *infra*.

163. Collet at 27.

164. *Id.* at 28.

165. *Id.* at 33. It should be noted that (1) the act applied to all periodicals with news, but for those with commentary only, it applied only when publication intervals were less than twenty-six days; and (2) the Stamp Office had considerable discretion — which, according to Collet, it did not necessarily enjoy exercising. *Id.* at 33, 35–42.

166. *Id.* at 34.

167. *Id.*

168. *Id.* at 34–35.

169. *Id.* at 37–38.

170. *Id.* at 38.

171. *Id.*

172. *Id.* at 39–40.

173. *Id.* at 40.

174. *Id.* at 39.

175. An Act to Amend the Laws Relating to Stamp Duties, etc., 1855, 18 & 19 Vict., ch. 27, § 1 (Eng.).

176. An Act to Repeal Certain Stamp Duties, . . . the Duty on Advertisements, etc., 1853, 16 & 17 Vict., ch. 63, § 5 (Eng.).

177. An Act to Continue Certain Duties . . . and to Alter and Repeal Certain Other Duties, 1861, 24 Vict., ch. 20, § 4, sched. D (Eng.).

178. Interestingly, even with regard to the final and complete elimination of the stamp there were forces at work affecting the press and its power. The principal concerned party was the *Times*, which had broad circulation and substantial distribution in the rural areas beyond London. With the stamp came free postage. With its elimination the *Times* would have to pay postage for the outlying areas of distribution, and the rates, especially if dependent on weight (which turned out, for

a time, to be the rule), would put the *Times* at a disadvantage. The issue at stake for many, both in Parliament as well as in the news business, was the possible breakdown of the *Times'* power and effective monopoly. As events turned out, the *Times* remained strong, but no longer as dominant following repeal. See Herd at 152–55.

179. The following discussion draws heavily on Collet's account. Another valuable account is found in Herd at 147–59.

180. See Collet at 5–14.

181. *Id.* at 7.

182. *Id.*

183. *Id.*

184. See Siebert at 313–15; Collet at 14–15.

185. See Collet at 14–22, 77–78.

186. See *id.* at 66–71. The large papers, whose circulations Collet reports on page 67, had a large competitive stake in full enforcement of the stamp.

187. *Id.* at 78.

188. *Id.* at 56–58, 68–74, 132 *passim*.

189. The additional argument was made with the 1836 act that retaining, *but lowering*, the stamp tax would increase the revenue by building circulation and making taxation of the untaxed publications practical. *Id.* at 28.

190. *Id.* at 56–58.

191. See, e.g., Collet at 55.

192. An Act to Amend the Laws Relating to Stamp Duties, etc., 1855, 18 & 19 Vict., ch. 27; see Herd at 152–55.

193. Collet's account is both detailed and quite readable, and I recommend it to readers who wish to follow the winding course from beginning to end. See Collet at 48–79.

194. *Id.* at 14–33.

195. *Id.* at 26–27, 34–35.

196. *Id.* at 31–32.

197. *Id.* at 31.

198. *Id.* at 34.

199. *Id.* at 38.

200. *Id.*

201. *Id.* at 39.

202. *Id.* at 38–39.

203. *Id.*

204. *Id.* at 39.

205. *Id.*

206. *Id.* at 43–65.

207. *Id.* at 77.

208. *Id.* at 55–56.

209. *Id.* at 74. The actual title of the association was "An Association for Promoting the Repeal of the Taxes on Knowledge." *Id.*

210. *Id.* at 75.

211. *Id.* at 76.

212. I will not recount here the many petitions and public statements to this

effect made consistently throughout the roughly twenty years of successful agitation leading to repeal of the taxes. But they can be found quoted profusely throughout Collet's account.

213. Herd at 155.

214. Siebert at 322.

215. *Id.*; see generally Collet.

216. For an exhaustive account of newspaper patronage practices in the United States, see Culver H. Smith, *The Press, Politics, and Patronage: The American Government's Use of Newspapers, 1789–1875* (1977).

217. See Siebert at 323–45.

218. See Harris at 95–96.

219. *Id.* at 94.

220. *Id.* at 89.

221. *Id.* at 89–90. The availability of franking privileges for postal officials extended to the Colonies, as well, resulting in the free distribution of papers by printers who got themselves appointed to such positions. Perhaps the most notable beneficiary of the privilege was Benjamin Franklin. See A. D. Smith, *The Development of Rates of Postage* 148–49 (1917).

222. For accounts of newspapers during various periods of regulation, with information on coverage, quality, and editorial view, see generally Joseph Frank, *The Beginnings of the English Newspaper, 1620–1660* (1961); Laurence Hanson, *Government and the Press* (1936); Stanley Morison, *The English Newspaper, 1622–1932* (1932). Collet's book, *History of the Taxes on Knowledge* (facsimile reprint 1971) (1933), of course, is also a rich source of material on these subjects.

223. Collet at 14.

224. Perhaps the best example of this was the paper tax, particularly in the latter years of resistance to the knowledge taxes when it was decoupled from the other stamp and advertising taxes and continued alone. See Collet at 107, 132–33.

225. *Id.* at 45.

2. Knowledge Taxes from the Colonial Period Through Ratification of the First Amendment

We turn now to America, and to the beginnings of our nation's experience with knowledge taxation. The inquiry will begin in this chapter with the colonial and revolutionary experiences, continuing through the ratification of the Constitution and the Bill of Rights. As we explore the topic of knowledge taxation throughout this period, we will be simultaneously tracing the lineage of knowledge taxation from England, where the taxes were in full flower, to America, where they were first being introduced, and exploring the frequently different cultural, political, and social forces that surrounded such taxes and influenced their reception. In many respects we will discover that the lineage was direct, but that the response to knowledge taxation took on a very different complexion in America.

The Pre-Revolutionary Experience

The history of knowledge taxes in the Colonies prior to the Revolution consists of two parts. The first part involves the extension of the English stamp taxes to the Colonies in the form of a tax imposed by and collected for the Crown. Here, as we shall see, the "rub" was not taxation of expression, but taxation without representation. The second part involves colonial stamp taxes; that is, taxes imposed by and within certain of the Colonies. Notions of freedom of expression played a larger, although surely not a dominant, role in the resistance to the colonial taxes.

A full picture of the pre-revolutionary history of stamp taxation in England and in the Colonies cannot be obtained without viewing both forms of stamp tax. We will turn first to the English tax, for while it followed the colonial taxes, it flowed directly from the English stamp acts that have just been discussed. Thereafter we will turn to the taxes imposed by the colonies of Massachusetts and New York to fill out the picture. We will finally conclude with some tentative and general conclusions about the history of stamp taxation through both the English and colonial experiences.

THE ENGLISH STAMP TAX

In 1765, when the Crown extended the stamp tax to the American colonies, the ultimate demise of the English knowledge taxes was far from obvious, but revenue was by then coming to serve as a more significant (though not exclusive) object of the taxes. With the new taxes imposed on the Colonies, revenue seems clearly to have been the chief object. But an additional element was present as well: a challenge to the legal authority of the mother country.

The Seven Years' War, which had extended to the American continent, was not only responsible for increased stamp duties in England, it also provided the occasion for what would become in 1765 an act of Parliament establishing a stamp and advertising tax in the American colonies.[1] The stamp tax was set at one halfpenny on every newspaper and pamphlet of a half sheet or less, and one penny per sheet for each publication up to six sheets in size. Publishers of almanacs and calendars were required to pay a stamp duty of fourpence for every copy. The advertisement tax required that two shillings be paid on every advertisement appearing in a newspaper or pamphlet.[2] Stamp offices were established in each of the American colonies. While the tax lasted less than a year, the history of violent opposition in the Colonies which forced its repeal on May 1, 1766, is highly instructive.

The stamp tax of 1765 had a very different origin, and served very different purposes, than the Stamp Act of 1712 and its progeny. Unlike the English precedent, in which the revenue purposes were concomitant with, if not subordinate to, interests in regulating the press,[3] the colonial tax was principally revenue-related in purpose. Miller reports that a stamp tax for the Colonies was first considered as a means by which the colonists would help pay for the defense of their borders against the French and the Indians.[4] William Keith, the Royal Governor of Pennsylvania, supported by a "Club of American Merchants," proposed that a stamp tax be levied and that the proceeds be used to help the Colonies maintain an army. Such an action would, they asserted, "put the united strength of the colonies into the hands of the Crown."[5] Walpole refused to accept the plan, partly because he doubted the ease with which it could be accomplished, and partly because he was already well occupied collecting the stamp tax at home. In 1754 and 1757 a colonial stamp act was once again discussed, this time by the Treasury Board, but no action was taken in view of the then-ongoing Seven Years' War.[6] New York and Massachusetts, however, did impose stamp duties of their own. These quickly met with opposition and were dropped,[7] thus "serving notice on the Crown" that the tax was unpopular even when levied by the colonists' own government.[8]

In 1761 the idea of a stamp tax imposed by Parliament was raised again, and this time Grenville, then chancellor of the exchequer, agreed to it.[9] The idea met an even friendlier reception in Parliament, partly, one suspects, because by such a tax the members would not exact a duty on themselves or their constituents.[10] In larger part, however, it was well received because members of Parliament felt that the Colonies owed a debt to England for support in the war. When, almost at once, the question of the constitutionality of an internal tax within the Colonies arose, the challenge to England's authority to tax was framed in such threatening terms that passage by Parliament was not only inevitable, but necessary.[11] No member of Parliament disputed the sovereignty of England over the colonists, nor the right of Parliament to levy taxes in the Colonies as it saw fit.[12]

When a bill to establish the colonial tax was presented, a few members of Parliament spoke against it, but their objections went not to Parliament's authority but, as Miller put it, to "the inexpediency of taxing the colonies, exhausted and debt-burdened after a long and expensive war."[13] The proponents, on the other hand, thought the tax to be a modest one, at most, and one that would collect from the Colonies only a fraction of the costs of protecting the frontier.[14] But opponents and proponents alike, it appears, entertained not the slightest doubt that the colonists would realize that England was asking for no more than was rightly due it.[15]

Unfortunately for Parliament, the Stamp Act would represent merely one more in a long line of grievances which were seen as manifesting the British government's intention to interfere with the colonial prosperity and meddle in the colonists' way of life.[16] The uproar over the Sugar Act in 1764 would intensify with the Stamp Act of 1765.[17] Grenville was warned by colonial governors and others that England should clear up the problems that resulted from the Sugar Act and other incidents, including substantial economic dislocations in the Colonies because of the war, before moving forward with the stamp tax.[18] The warnings fell on deaf ears in Parliament, however, where the members simply could not conceive of colonial opposition to their right to tax. The Stamp Act was passed in 1765.[19]

Soon after the Stamp Act's passage, Grenville was replaced by Rockingham, and it was he who had to contend with the storm of opposition caused by the stamp tax — to accept, as Miller put it, the "poisoned chalice from the hands of George Grenville."[20] The Rockinghams, as well as Edmund Burke, their ally and close friend, were opposed to the British taxing policy toward the Colonies, but quietly so. As Connor Cruise O'Brien puts it in his recent and grand biography of Burke:

> Throughout this period [1768–73] the Rockinghams, including Burke, maintained their opposition to the policy of taxing the colonies, but they did not emphasize that opposition. This is not surprising because, as an issue for mobilising opinion against the Administration — which, after all, is what an opposition must try to do — the Rockingham policy on America was absolutely unsalable. The policy of raising revenue in America was as overwhelmingly popular in Britain as the resistance of the Americans was overwhelmingly unpopular.[21]

The groups alienated by the tax — lawyers, printers, merchants, and tavern keepers — were the backbone of British rule in America. The stamp measure hit hardest at the natural colonial leadership — groups which, "along with the clergy, formed the most literate and vocal elements of the population."[22] Part of the problem was that the Stamp Act was much more than a tax on newspapers, although it contained the familiar provisions of the English newspaper tax. Under its provisions, stamps were required in a broad array of settings: "Americans could not engage in commerce, exchange property with each other, recover debts, buy a newspaper, institute lawsuits or make wills, without paying for a stamp. Every diploma awarded by a college or academy required a stamp of two pounds and — what was more important to the common man — every tavern owner who retailed spirituous liquor was obliged to pay twenty shillings for his license."[23] Tavern owners, of course, were often also the leading politicians in their communities. The opposition, in short, came from many quarters, and the newspaper tax was only one aspect of the tax scheme, and only one source of reaction.

The substantive ground for colonial objection, moreover, was broad-based, not narrow. It was not based on an intention to revolt, or on a notion that the colonial constitutions or concepts of English authority overrode English "law." Rather, it was premised on the view that the colonial constitutions, as well as the "constitution" of the Empire — a concept based upon the distribution of authority in the Empire — were one with British legal or constitutional concepts, and foreclosed imposition of taxation by Parliament for Britain without representation in Parliament or without consent of the Colonies consistently with their constitution, which *was*, in the colonial mind, British law. In other words, "taxation without representation" as a rallying cry was not a revolutionary concept, but was instead viewed as a concept underlying British law and the terms of British rule. The objection was not to British rule, or to association with Britain, but to a perceived violation of the legal terms Britain recognized for its own rule.[24]

The colonists did not, as a general matter, dispute that they were subjects of Great Britain, but instead asserted that subjecting them to an internal tax levied by and for another subject — England, through the Parliament — violated the custom of the British rule. Stephen Sayre of Long Island expressed the essence of the problem when he stated that the tax "at a single stroke enslaved every Englishman in America."[25] As Edmund Burke told the Commons in 1775,

> It happened you know that the great contests for freedom in this country were from the earliest times chiefly upon the question of taxing. . . . [T]he people must in effect themselves, mediately or immediately, possess the power of granting their own money, or no shadow of liberty could subsist.[26]

The colonial objections to the stamp tax contained broader language than that of violation of the British Constitution, but the essence — that of representation as an element of taxation, and that one subject should not be able to impose an internal tax on another[27] — was similar to the views expressed by those voting against the tax in Parliament.[28] Other non-constitutional and nonlegal arguments against the tax were principally economic in nature. The cost was high and burdensome, and in the view of some fell unequally on the poor and common people. The latter view was held by Benjamin Franklin.[29]

Some historians have attributed the opposition, and the later revolution that grew out of it, to the economic cost of the stamp tax. While this may be an oversimplification, there is little doubt that economics played a large role, both in generating resistance to the stamp and also as an underpinning of the constitutional objection. It is clear, as well, that at a theoretical or legal level notions of appropriate British rule were paramount, and that the principal point of contention was *not* press freedom, at least as such.[30] As Edmund Burke expressed it in his speech on the Declaratory Resolution,

> This Practical Idea of the Constitution of the British Empire [must] be deduced from the general and relative situation of its parts. . . . "Govern

America as you govern an English Corporation which happens not to be represented in Parliament." Are Gentlemen really serious when they propose this? Is there a single Trait of Resemblance between those few Towns disseminated through a represented County, and a great [and] growing people spread over a vast quarter of the Globe[?][31]

But while notions of press freedom may not have animated the resistance, the press did play an important role in the resistance to the stamp, and a role that increased over time. The printers' initial reaction to the tax was indecision. Many printers feared a ruinous drop in circulation because of the stamp, but they were generally reluctant, at first, openly to defy the law. Instead, they were more likely to work vigorously to collect the tax than to protest it openly.[32] Some printers published notices to that effect in their newspapers. Others notified their readers that an increase in subscription rates was necessary (and hoped that circulation would hold).[33]

The rather flaccid response of the printers reflected the prevailing state of the craft in the Colonies — a subject that must be understood in order to place later steps in context. As Stephen Botein has put it[34]: "A colonial printer was not commonly expected to possess a mind of his own, and this expectation was likely to undercut whatever efforts he made to influence his neighbors."[35] The newspaper business was not competitive. A printer usually served a community alone, and even then was far from secure, "because local demand for his product was apt to be slight."[36] Printers were not ordinarily "able to rely for a living on the favor of any one group . . . , including those who wielded political power." Accordingly, they labored to serve diverse interests in their community.[37] According to Botein, "colonial America was a place for printers to be studiously impartial."[38]

Liberty of the press, in short, often meant a press that was "open to all parties" or, as Botein put it, one in which the printer "should offer everyone the 'liberty' of his press."[39] Forceful expression of opinion was most warranted, or at least most likely, when it comported with actual consensus in the community. When a highly controversial issue arose on which no consensus existed, printers would often try to escape the dilemma by ignoring the issue or toning down its expression.[40] For the majority of colonial printers, liberty of the press meant equality of access and, as often, a paper that was "dull and flat," a result that flowed more from business interests than from principled conviction.[41] While this observation should not reduce the history of the press's involvement in the Revolution to an exclusively cynical level, it nevertheless places the printers' initial indecision as well as the subsequent developments in a somewhat different light.

Not all of the printers were initially indecisive, however. Indeed, some of the bolder colonial newspapers were at the very forefront of the opposition to the tax. But even here one suspects that the lack of indecision was as much a function of constituent interest as of an independent conviction expressed freely by the printers. Nevertheless, the fear expressed by these printers — a fear which found parallel with the other constituencies — was that the Stamp Act threatened people's political liberty just as certainly as it took their money.[42] "Political liberty," however, bore the larger connotation of taxation without representation, at least in the public mind, if not in the printers'. The newspapers chronicled the mounting opposition to the tax, as well as its basis, in their pages, and they convinced the lawyers and merchants to join the attack.[43]

The challenge to the tax thus widened, but its rhetoric did not fully blossom nor did its proponents counsel outright disobedience until Patrick Henry's speech to the Virginia House of Burgesses in May 1765. His rallying cry, "Give me liberty or give me death," and the resolutions to the House of Burgesses favoring resistance to Parliament's taxes were printed in full in the leading newspapers. In what Schlesinger calls a "curious case of misreporting," all of the seven resolutions, known as the Virginia Resolves, were printed, even though only two of them ultimately passed the vote of the House, thus giving the impression that all seven had passed.[44] Henry's speech and the printing of the resolutions crystalized the rhetoric of freedom in relation to the taxes; they may have marked the start of the revolutionary movement in the Colonies.[45] As Miller has put it,

> In imposing the Stamp Act, Grenville departed from the time-honored British policy of ruling the colonies by taking advantage of their sectional and social divisions. Instead, he gave them a fundamental and well-nigh universal grievance which swept aside their petty jealousies in a mounting wave of anger against Great Britain.[46]

As the revolutionary movement started, groups such as the Sons of Liberty started to form, protesting the stamp tax and taxation of the Colonies in general. Occasionally printers became mob leaders. In a fashion reminiscent of the ironies occasioned by the taxes in England, the persons and groups actively engaged in the revolutionary movement throughout the Colonies effectively used the newspapers — the very items being subjected to the objectionable tax — as the principal channel of communication and as a means of coordinating the resistance movement itself.[47]

The demise of the stamp tax was perhaps preordained with the emergence of revolutionary fervor, but, as Reid suggests, it appears that the final blow was dealt by the convergence of commercial and ideological interests. After months of mob violence, the opposition to the tax organized a boycott of British goods that would continue until the Stamp Act was repealed. Significantly, British merchants too were a strong voice in favor of repeal of the Act, and this no doubt lent some political weight to the resistance efforts with Parliament. Notwithstanding a great deal of parliamentary disapproval of the idea that the colonists had any say in the way Britain ran her colonies, sufficient political forces had been set in motion to achieve repeal. Repeal came on May 1, 1766, less than a year after the Act's original adoption, but it was coupled with a Declaratory Act that proclaimed Parliament's complete authority over the Colonies, including the right to tax.[48]

For present purposes, the most important aspects of the stamp tax and the events that surrounded and followed its demise are those bearing on the role and evolving character of the press in America. In both the struggle for repeal of the Stamp Act and in the subsequent and more general movement to free the Colonies from all manner of British oppression, the press was a highly significant factor. The colonial press was in the hands of patriots from the outset of the revolutionary struggle. Schlesinger reports that as the movement caught hold, the press's indecision changed, and resistance solidified, with efforts to evade the tax becoming the norm. Some printers attempted to inflame public opinion against the tax by substituting a death's-head for the stamp. Others wrote editorial "farewells" that mourned the freedom to publish without the stamp.[49]

Observing that public sentiment was running their way, the printers escalated their tactics. Some openly defied the law — announcing their refusal to pay the tax. Others defied the law by subterfuge, or simply ignored the stamps, but in a manner calculated to avert the penalties for noncompliance. In some instances the printers retained the former titles of their newspapers but published them anonymously. A few journals, mostly Southern, suspended publication.[50] In all of these efforts, the newspapers sounded the alarm of loss of each citizen's liberties, repeating the theme for their readers in each edition.[51] The papers thus helped make the controversy over the Stamp Act "a great popular crusade in which every American could take part."[52] The popularization was made easier by the fact that the stamp duty covered so many facets of the average American's life. It was made easier, as well, by the fact that the press tended not to print articles which disagreed with the patriotic viewpoint.[53] The printers' involvement, and indeed their rhetoric, did not disguise the fact that freedom from rule without representation, not liberty of expression, was the principal source of concern.

In a different sense, however, the press's liberty was directly influenced by the stamp controversy. Many scholars, most notably Levy and Miller, have concluded that the stamp tax levied in the Colonies *caused* the emergence of a strong opposition press in America.[54] That this is so — and there seems ample support for the conclusion — is yet another of the peculiar ironies of taxation of knowledge. Unlike the pattern emerging in England with the 1712 Stamp Act, the Stamp Act of 1765 was not primarily or even significantly intended as a measure that would stifle opposition opinion. There is no evidence in the deliberations of Parliament that the law was intended to "shackle the colonial mind" or achieve greater Crown control over the press in America; the Stamp Act was, instead, truly a revenue-based measure.[55] The colonial press had not really presented a problem for England; it tended to be bland, compliant, and noncontroversial, although not without some help from the Crown.[56] To be sure, the press in the Colonies regarded itself as a free press, but not because it was blatantly partisan or given to libelous publication, but rather because in many quarters the printers proudly remained as nonpartisan as possible, accepting inoffensive articles that the different factions sent their way.[57] As Stephen Botein has noted, "Embedded in the prevailing colonial rhetoric . . . was a principle . . . that printers should be politically neutral in the conduct of their businesses, and publish whatever was submitted to them."[58]

Indeed, it may not have been until a few years after the Stamp Act, on the occasion of the controversy about the Townshend Duties, that the press really came of age. With the Stamp Act the press was swept into a running tide of opinion. Its role was important, but it is hard to conclude that the press was at the forefront or that the shape of the press as an independent agent of public opinion was really formed. With the Townshend Duties, the press first joined, and then exploited, the tide of opinion and took on a new and clearly defined identity.

The Townshend Duties were enacted in 1767. Charles Townshend, Chancellor of the Exchequer, levied duties on the import of glass, lead, papers, painters' colors, and tea as they entered the American colonies. Initial reaction to the duties by newspapers, which were directly affected through the paper duty, was again marked by some degree of indecision and uncertainty about the ground for objection. But with the publication in the *Pennsylvania Chronicle* of John Dickinson's "Letters from a Farmer in Penn-

sylvania to the Inhabitants of the British Colonies,"[59] newspapers throughout the Colonies took up arms and, as Arthur Schlesinger put it, "journalis-
tic warfare [was] touched off."[60]

Schlesinger's thorough and readable account of press activity from all
quarters and in all directions need not be recounted here.[61] Suffice it to say
that the newspapers very much took the lead in the dispute, and by their
editorial pronouncements as well as the opposing positions that arose
within the newspapers themselves, the press manifested by deeds as well as
words a fiercely independent role that was firmly to take root from that
point forward. As Arthur Schlesinger observed: "The newspapers had
waged a spirited fight against the Townshend regulations and in so doing
had asserted both by precept and example their freedom to criticize public
men and measures."[62]

It does appear that the immediate threat of financial ruin brought on
by the Stamp Act contributed to and perhaps sowed the seeds of the press's
radical transformation, even though this was occasioned by controversy
over the power to tax, not the freedom to publish. What the Stamp Act
began, the Townshend Duties completed. Unlike the rather compliant,
neutral, detached picture of the press painted prior to—and even for a time
following—enactment of the Stamp Act, a very different picture emerged
afterward. Throughout the Colonies printers ultimately defied the Act in
one manner or another—often openly, proudly, and defiantly. As Leonard
Levy notes, "partisanship and polemics became the vogue."[63] Under the
pressure of the times, an unpartisan press became unpatriotic and unprofitable. Neutrality hurt business.

There was, as well, even a certain degree of vigilantism about the press.
Printers who did not agree with the patriot cause were influenced to do so
either by persuasion to join the chosen method of defiance (usually nonpayment of the tax), or by outright intimidation.[64] The radical press became an instrument of ideology, mobilizing public opinion against Britain.
Fewer and fewer papers were able to support Britain or even to remain
neutral. A "free press," in the parlance of the time, could not, as Levy noted,
be distinguished from a "patriot press." Truth, it seems, was one-sided.[65]

As in England, the colonial Stamp Act gave the opposition press life.
Indeed, in America it gave birth to a veritable propaganda machine.[66]
Unlike England, however, the cause was not freedom from governmental
control of the press, but a very different idea of freedom of the Colonies
from taxation without consent. The Stamp Act, therefore, enlivened the
press—perhaps even led to its radical transformation—but did not provide

occasion for expressions of new concepts of press freedom. Throughout the period, the press was free in the Colonies — and freer than the press in England by a long shot.

THE COLONIAL STAMP TAXES

The colonial experience with stamp taxes was not limited to taxes imposed by England. Indeed, the first stamp taxes were imposed by the colonial governments of Massachusetts and New York. While these governments were agents of the English rule, they were nevertheless closer to the people, and the scope and purported advantages of the taxes were local. The experience with these short-lived colonial taxes is therefore instructive, both in view of the later English taxes, which have just been considered, but also to a fully rounded picture of the attitudes and values that took root in America prior to the Revolution.

Massachusetts

A colonial, or provincial, stamp and paper tax was enacted in Massachusetts in January 1755, fully ten years prior to the English tax. Under the Act a tax was imposed on "vellum, parchment, and paper,"[67] and a halfpenny tax was imposed for every printed news sheet. According to Duniway, whose remarkable book *The Development of Freedom of the Press in Massachusetts* contains a wealth of material on the colonial press, "there is no evidence that the provincial measure was meant to serve any . . . political purpose" of preventing the publication of libels or politically scandalous material, such as those underlying the English taxes.[68] The provincial tax did, however, share a heritage of more explicit efforts at censorship by previous provincial governors, efforts which had most often been similarly unavailing.[69]

The effect of the 1755 tax also followed the English pattern. It "bore hard" on newspapers, requiring increases in subscription rates.[70] One paper discontinued because of the tax, according to Duniway.[71] Another paper published articles on freedom of the press, borrowing from London papers, and argued that press freedom guaranteed the ability to publish one's sentiments in a manner calculated to reach the broadest public and that such liberty was implicit in free governments.[72] According to Duniway, the level of discord and agitation in the press apparently became so great, and the tax so unpopular, that it was abandoned on May 1, 1757.[73]

Duniway's conclusion that the demise of the Massachusetts tax resulted from newspaper opposition and general unpopularity is challenged by Professor Thompson.[74] Thompson notes that the tax was originally enacted to obtain needed revenue in the short term before a concomitantly enacted excise tax began producing revenue.[75] The stamp tax was retained for two years and expired by its own terms. Thompson found little evidence of general resistance to the tax; indeed, in some quarters it was viewed as an efficient source of revenue with few disadvantages when compared to other alternatives.[76] Thompson even suggests that the lack of general objection to the taxes "may very well have encouraged George Grenville and his colleagues to extend the English Stamp Act to all the colonies."[77] The most likely reason for the demise of the Massachusetts tax, he suggests, was that the occasion for its need passed as the excise tax revenues began to build, and in any event "revenue from the act was not large, and much of it was consumed by [the stamp commissioner's] salary, purchase of a stamp machine, and other expenses."[78]

The 1755 Act was not the only experience Massachusetts had with a stamp tax. In 1785, shortly after Massachusetts became a state, a stamp tax on newspapers and almanacs was enacted.[79] The tax met with considerable resistance from the newspapers (due in some measure, Duniway surmises, to its being called a "stamp tax"), and it was quickly repealed the next year.[80] An advertising tax was also levied, with the same revenue purposes as the stamp. This tax met the same fate, and for the same reasons (printers' objections coupled with marginal revenue production), but its repeal did not come for two more years, in 1788.[81] Enactment of these taxes tends to support Thompson's skepticism about the extent of outcry following the 1755 Act, but if he is right that the lesson was not learned in 1755, it seems to have been firmly reinforced following the 1785 acts.

New York

The New York stamp tax was enacted in 1756. Like the Massachusetts tax, the New York enactment was intended to raise money to support military expenditures. While there seems to be no reason to dispute this assignment of purpose, the New York tax generated significant opposition in the form of a campaign mounted by James Parker, a former employee of Franklin who published the *New York Weekly Post-Boy*.[82] According to Jeffery Smith, "[Parker's] campaign against the tax began in the *Post-Boy* with observations on the financial hardships it imposed on printers and culminated in a 1759 broadside asking 'British Subjects and Lovers of Liberty' to consider his plight and raising the possibility that New York politicians had passed the measure to put him out of business."[83] Parker's views did not go unchallenged even in the press, as Smith reports that the stamp enactment was commented upon with approval in the *New-York Mercury*.[84] In the end, however, the fate of the New York enactment was the same as that of Massachusetts, and the reasons were likewise the same. The tax ended by its own terms in 1759, having proved both controversial and productive of insufficient revenue to warrant the fuss.[85]

While the extent and impact of public objections to the Massachusetts and New York taxes are somewhat obscured, the colonial taxes and the issues they raised left their marks on the concept of a free press. The twin themes struck during the agitation were the liberty to communicate one's sentiments broadly, with the press as the most effective means of general distribution, and the freedom from government efforts through taxation to suppress the citizen's ability to effectively employ such means to reach the public. Whether these themes or more mundane economic facts accounted for the taxes' demise, the taxes represented America's first experience with knowledge taxation, and with them the themes of free expression began to take shape.

KNOWLEDGE TAXES IN THE COLONIES: CONCLUSIONS

The imposition of knowledge taxes in the Colonies marks an important turning point in the history of knowledge taxation in America, for it constitutes the transition between the English and American experiences. It represents, also, a prism through which the English experience was translated into American attitudes toward taxation of the press and freedom of the press. The conclusions that can be drawn, while limited, are therefore important to our understanding of future events.

The first and perhaps most important observation about the colonial experience is that the taxes imposed within the Colonies and by the Crown were revenue-related. The English taxes had their origin in the government's efforts to control the press. In marked contrast, the purposes behind the colonial taxes were benign. The ultimately successful resistance to the taxes, therefore, was of a different and far greater significance than the ultimate demise of ill-intended taxes in England, and the point of reference behind the resistance was of a different character.

The concept of press freedom that animated the resistance to the taxes—particularly the New York and Massachusetts taxes—was not, ultimately, dissimilar to that being contemporaneously voiced in England. But the cry for press freedom could not rest, as it did in eighteenth-century England, on the improper purpose and censorial effects of the taxes. Instead, the resistance had to rest more clearly and inclusively on the people's capacity to obtain information rather than on the publisher's right to express views free of censorship or control. The notion of free expression as the property of the body politic in a free society, which would not crystalize as a governing principle in England until the mid-nineteenth century, was starkly announced in the colonial period, most notably with respect to the taxes imposed at the colonial level rather than those imposed by England. But the voices were relatively solitary, and not without objection even from other quarters in the press.

It was, however, the tax imposed on the Colonies by England that ultimately generated widespread resistance and helped feed the fire of the Revolution. But resistance to the English tax was of a different character than that of the colonial taxes. While references were made to freedom of the press in the course of the resistance to the English stamp, their frequency and impact are uncertain, and in any event few clearly defined operative limits on governmental power were expressed. Instead, the resistance to the English stamp tax appears principally to have been animated by a broader resistance to English rule, the most recent manifestations of which had been the sugar tax. The stamp tax became a focal point as much through a coincidence of timing and expediency as because of a separable idea of freedom of the press, or a notion that the stamp tax was peculiarly offensive.

The stamp tax may have been the spark that ignited the fire, but it does not appear to have been the fire, or even an essential ingredient of the conflagration. It provided a useful, and perhaps necessary, expedient, however, because it affected a broad range of politically important colonial interests, and because through it the newspapers were motivated to join the fray in earnest. In the end, the newspapers appear to have played an important part in assisting and coordinating the mounting resistance and ultimate revolution, and their rallying cry of liberty and freedom, though largely couched in terms of freedom from taxation without representation, caught hold. But the fundamental problem in the Colonies was not one of freedom of the press, and the stamp did not genuinely endanger that freedom. In short, the English tax did little to elucidate *freedom* of the press; instead, it shaped the press whose freedom was later to be defined.

Yet the colonial experience with stamp taxation appears at least to have sowed the seeds of two strands that were to manifest themselves in later years. The first was the emergence, nascent to be sure, of concepts of individual liberty and freedom of the press, concepts that expanded beyond concerns with censorship to the larger idea of access to information as a political right of the body politic. The second and equally important strand was the distrust of English rule and its concomitant, the greater confidence in local legislation even as it taxed knowledge. We shall later see manifestations of this democratic concept in the enactment of taxes in the states and on the federal level.

Ratification of the First Amendment

It has been widely noted by modern writers that the Stamp Act of 1765 instigated both the revolutionary war and the radicalization of the colonial press,[86] and this view was shared as well by some historians writing at the time of the ratification of the First Amendment.[87] The United States Supreme Court has suggested an even more expansive role, concluding also that the framers' vehement opposition to foreign and indigenous taxation of the press animated the First Amendment.[88] While it is probably safe to suggest, as the Court has, that the "framers of the First Amendment were familiar" with the struggle of the English press to free itself from discriminatory and oppressive taxation,[89] and that they were familiar also with the "violent opposition"[90] that attended the attempts by Massachusetts to tax newspapers in 1785,[91] the Court's claim that these experiences "did much to bring about the adoption of the [First] [A]mendment"[92] is dubious.

As we shall see, the focus of debate on freedom of the press in the journalism trade and among editors at the time of the Revolution and Constitution was on seditious libel, and the need, according to Franklin and others, to guarantee a free press but to respect reputation, even of public officials.[93] The more radical Whigs proposed a more absolute liberty, but even here almost all discussion concerned censorship and libel. Essentially nothing was said about taxation.[94]

This might have been because the repeal of the colonial stamp acts was so recent that their evil, and the evil of taxation in any form, was patent, but there are ample grounds to doubt this conclusion. Unanimity of sentiment against the validity of the colonial stamp acts did not exist, little in the way of clear and principled objection to them ever evolved, and the English taxes, first enacted in 1712, were yet to reach their apex. The relative paucity of discussion about taxation of the press more likely reflected the fact that the objections to the stamp acts had much more to do with the limits of English colonial rule than with freedom of the press, and that with respect to the early English stamp and similar acts, the problem was the threat of censorship, or the imputation of such a purpose to saddle and silence the press, and therefore the focus even with taxation was on censorship and seditious libel rather than taxation itself. At least this was so in the eighteenth century, when the English taxes were still very much on the upswing. The same pattern of near-exclusive focus on seditious libel and libel appears with the state constitutions, as well, for their provisions focused on freedom of expression of views and the countervailing notions of responsible journalism, not on taxation.[95]

In challenging the breadth of the Supreme Court's conclusion, I do not mean to suggest that the English and colonial experiences were irrelevant, nor that taxation was not a part of the constitutional calculus. But the issue is more subtle and complex. My purpose is to bring some greater light to the role of the knowledge tax question in the framing of the Constitution, focusing on the knowledge tax issue directly rather than attempting a detailed historical chronology of the ratification of the Constitution and the Bill of Rights. The latter has been done ably by many others.

The following discussion shall therefore be limited to identifying and interpreting references to taxation of expression during the period, and to drawing limited conclusions about the contemporaneous understandings of the government's power of taxation as they might have been reflected in the purpose and language of the First Amendment. The review will disclose that the references to taxation were infrequent, at best, and usually unenlightening because of their generality. The only conclusions that they permit one to reach with confidence are that the problem of taxation of knowledge was acknowledged and discussed, but it was not paramount, at least in contrast to the questions of censorship and libel, and that while taxation was discussed, precious little analytical insight was brought to the issue by either the Federalists or Anti-Federalists.

We begin the inquiry, perhaps somewhat awkwardly, with a few general observations which, while perhaps redundant of conclusions later reached, provide a necessary context in which to survey the writings of the period. First, few of the Anti-Federalists, whose writings are generally considered "more influential" than those of the Federalists on the exegesis of the Bill of Rights,[96] used either the English or the colonial experience with taxation to buttress their contention that a specific reservation of liberty of the press was needed in the Constitution. Instead, the Anti-Federalists tended to express their fears in only the most general fashion. Second, some Anti-Federalists used the Bill of Rights issue solely to induce the rejection of the Constitution. It is far from clear that they were actually convinced that "mere" amendments were sufficient.[97] Third, the Anti-Federalists were infatuated with sophistic rhetoric, often employing a scattershot method of argumentation in the hope that one argument would hit the mark. It is hardly an exaggeration to say that for them, at one point or another, every enumerated power granted to the federal government caused alarm, and every clause of the Constitution threatened the press.[98] When viewed in isolation, therefore, their remarks appear more significant than when seen in context.

Finally, and on a more general note, it is unclear what kind of tax any given writer, Anti-Federalist or Federalist, would have found objectionable, since the writers do not discuss the various forms of taxation in any detail, much less those forms deemed offensive. If some of the statements are interpreted literally, one would have to conclude that some of the Anti-Federalists would have found nondifferential and indirect taxes offensive. While this is a possible position for someone to take, it would stretch the historical materials beyond a meaningful limit to claim any general support for it in the Anti-Federalists' writings, as it is equally obvious that what they meant by a "tax" on the press is unclear, and probably was unclear even in their minds.[99]

Notwithstanding these difficulties, the writings of the period are significant and provide important historical insight into the knowledge tax question prior to and at the time of ratification of the Constitution and, later, of the First Amendment. The historical materials, however, must be approached with a caution born of the historical context in which they arose. When approached in this fashion, the conclusion suggested by the historical materials is that the Anti-Federalists, and the Federalists as well, had precious little understanding of what was meant by freedom of the press, and even less when it came to taxation of the press.

Federalist and Anti-Federalist alike recognized the necessity of a free press.[100] They approached the question, and therefore voiced their concerns, differently. The Federalists opposed a specific declaration of press freedom in the Constitution on the ground that the federal government was granted no express power over the press, and therefore that such a declaration would be unnecessary.[101] As Hamilton expressed it in *The Federalist*:

> To show that there is a power in the Constitution by which the liberty of the press may be affected, recourse has been had to the power of taxation. It is said that duties may be laid upon the publications so high as to amount to a prohibition. I know not by what logic it could be maintained, that the declarations in the State Constitutions, in favor of the freedom of the press,

would be a constitutional impediment to the imposition of duties upon publications by the State legislatures. It cannot certainly be pretended that any degree of duties, however low, would be an abridgment of the liberty of the press. We know that newspapers are taxed in Great Britain, and yet it is notorious that the press nowhere enjoys greater liberty than in that country. And if duties of any kind may be laid without a violation of that liberty, it is evident that the extent must depend on legislative discretion, regulated by public opinion; so that, after all, general declarations respecting the liberty of the press, will give it no greater security than it will have without them. The same invasions of it may be effected under the State Constitutions which contain those declarations through the means of taxation, as under the proposed Constitution, which has nothing of the kind. It would be quite as significant to declare that government ought to be free, that taxes ought not to be excessive, etc., as that the liberty of the press ought not to be restrained.[102]

While Hamilton's statement, standing alone, is of exceedingly broad reach on the question of taxation and press freedom, it is important to note its context. The statement was part of an argument against inferring a power to regulate the press from the existence of a taxing power itself, and as such it was an argument against the *need* for specific press protection in the Constitution, as the press's freedom was secure without it.

Notwithstanding the Federalist position that a bill of rights was unnecessary because no powers to control such matters (including the press) were conferred, a remark by Hugh Williamson addressed quite directly his view of the basic historical understanding of press freedom, including freedom from taxation.

We have been told that the liberty of the press is not secured by the new Constitution. . . . There was a time in England, when neither book, pamphlet, nor paper could be published without a license from government. That restraint was finally removed in the year 1694 [the end of licensing, and the eve of taxation], and, by such removal, their press became perfectly free, for it is not under restraint of any license. Certainly the new government can have no power to impose restraints.[103]

What is notable about this statement is that it reflected an awareness of what had occurred in seventeenth-century England, though it evidenced little sensitivity to the contemporaneous growth of the English knowledge taxes in the eighteenth century. In 1788 the knowledge taxes were in their full bloom, and the discontent about them was well known. Yet his statement indicates that with removal of licensing, freedom of the press was achieved. The status of freedom from licensing, *not* freedom from the stamp, was what Williamson, drawing upon the English experience, was using as a definition of freedom. In view of the statements of Hamilton and Williamson, at least, it seems that the Federalist view of press freedom was either exceedingly narrow or, as likely, got lost in the zeal that they brought to the more general view of limited federal power.

The Anti-Federalist arguments were often equally zealous in decrying the feared federal powers. Their response to the Federalist view was illustrated by that of Melancton Smith, writing as "A Plebeian":

> The suggestion, that the liberty of the press is secure, because it is not in express words spoken of in the constitution . . . is puerile and unworthy of a man who pretends to reason. We contend, that by the indefinite powers granted to the general government, the liberty of the press may be restricted by duties, &c. and therefore the constitution ought to have stipulated for its freedom.[104]

The threat to the press flowed from the powers affirmatively granted to Congress, according to the Anti-Federalist position, since "where general powers are expressly granted, the particular ones comprehended within them, must also be granted."[105]

The Anti-Federalists expressed this view in a number of ways with respect to freedom of the press and the taxing power. The view that the imposition of taxes on newspapers would violate press freedom was stated succinctly and in absolute terms by Thomas Cogswell, Chief Justice of the New Hampshire Court of Common Pleas, writing as "A Farmer": "The liberty of the Press is essential to a free people, it ought therefore to be inviolably preserved and secured in the Bill of Rights, and no duty or tax to be imposed thereon, of what name or nature [what]soever."[106]

The Anti-Federalist view, however, was both abstract and often concerned primarily with the evils of taxation and only incidentally with the press. The most extreme view appears to have been taken by only one writer, Samuel Bryan of Philadelphia, who, writing as "Centinel," claimed that "the unlimited power of taxation" alone was "amply sufficient" to subjugate the people and the press.[107] Other writings based on the taxing power expressed two fears in relation to freedom of the press. The first, reflected also in the statements of Cogswell and Bryan, was that the power to tax was the power to destroy. As a Pennsylvania Anti-Federalist, who Leonard Levy identifies as "probably" William Findley, said: "The Liberty of the Press is not secured . . . as they may by a cursed abominable Stamp Act (as the *Bowdoin Administration* has done in Massachusetts) preclude you effectually from all means of information."[108]

The second fear expressed was that Congress could, pursuant to the taxing power, construct administrative machinery, thereby saddling the press with burdensome regulatory and accounting requirements and subjecting it to government influence. According to Richard Henry Lee, writing as the "Federal Farmer," the taxing power would give Congress the

> power to lay and collect all kinds of taxes whatever — taxes . . . on newspapers, advertisements, &c. and to require bonds of the naval officers, clerks, printers, &c. to account for the taxes that may become due on papers that go through their hands. Printing, like all other business, must cease when taxed beyond its profits; and it appears to me that a power to tax the press at discretion, is a power to destroy or restrain the freedom of it. . . . [and leave it subject] constantly to constructions and interferences.[109]

This statement implies a notable similarity to the English concerns of excessive taxation and the use of administrative discretion to exert control over publications.

Some Anti-Federalists built further on these concerns and focused on the dangers that arose from the taxing power when supplemented by some other constitutional grant, such as the Supremacy Clause. Centinel (Samuel Bryan) and the Federal Farmer (Richard Henry Lee) both struck this theme. Centinel wrote:

> Cannot Congress, when possessed of the immense authority proposed to be devolved, restrain the printers, and put them under regulation. — Recollect that the omnipotence of the federal legislature over the State establishments is recognized by a special article, viz. [the Supremacy Clause]. After such a declaration, what security does the *Constitutions* of the several States afford for the *liberty of the press and other invaluable personal rights*, not provided for by the new plan? — Does not this sweeping clause subject every thing to the controul of Congress?[110]

The Federal Farmer (Richard Henry Lee) similarly wrote:

> Should the printer say, the freedom of the press was secured by the constitution in which he lived, the congress might, and perhaps, with great propriety, answer, that the federal constitution is the only compact existing between them and the people; in this compact the people have named no others, and therefore congress, in exercising the powers assigned them, and in making laws to carry them into execution, are restrained by nothing beside the federal

constitution, any more than a state legislature is restrained by a compact between the magistrates and people of a county, city, or town of which the people, in forming the state constitution, have taken no notice.[111]

The conjunction of congressional authority to formulate fiscal policy and to impose upon the press any manifestations of that policy "notwithstanding the constitution of any state" greatly alarmed the Anti-Federalists, as in their view it eviscerated state constitutional protections afforded the press. An unknown essayist who used the pseudonym "An Old Whig" wrote:

> Suppose that an act of the continental legislature should be passed to restrain the liberty of the press; — to appoint licensers of the press in every town in America; — to limit the number of printers; — and to compel them to give security for their good behavior, from year to year, as the licenses are renewed: If such a law should be once passed, what is there to prevent the execution of it? . . . Suppose a printer should be found hardy enough to contravene such a law when made, and to contest the validity of it. — He is prosecuted we will suppose, in this state — he pleads in his defence, that by the constitution of Pennsylvania, it is declared "that the freedom of the press ought not to be restrained." — What will this avail him? The judge will be obliged to declare that "*notwithstanding the constitution of any state*," this act of the continental legislature which restrains the freedom of the press, is "the supreme law; and we must punish you — The bill of rights of Pennsylvania is nothing here. . . ." Such must be the language and conduct of courts.[112]

The foregoing writings of the Anti-Federalists, which were contradicted by the Federalists largely in relation only to the existence of the feared federal powers, suggest a number of things about freedom of the press and "knowledge taxes." First, there seems to have been general agreement in the writings that freedom of the press did extend to the context of taxation.[113] To be sure, there were exceptions to this view, the most notable of which was Hamilton's, quoted earlier. But many such objections were wrapped up in the tangle of Anti-Federalist fear of federal power and were based on a concern that express recognition of press freedom — including freedom from destructive taxation — would imply the existence of broad federal taxing power and federal authority over the actions of state governments.[114] The references to the issue of taxation and press freedom, moreover, were infrequent when judged by the totality of the writings of the time, and were most often so broad as to be unenlightening. And even the most absolute formulations of freedom from taxation were qualified by such terms as "unlimited" taxes, the "liberty" of the press, or excessive "discretion." But the connection between taxation and press freedom was made, with occasional references to the then-recent colonial experience. The English stamp, paper, and advertisement taxes, however, were rarely mentioned.

Second, the operative concepts of the press's freedom from taxation were obscure and variously expressed. Certain of the writings, however, mentioned the two central themes of the English experience: that the danger of taxation was that it would be confiscatory; and that while explicitly differential taxation was not of principal concern, the use of taxation as a means of exerting control through the tax's *administration* was a substantial problem inherent in taxation itself.

Third, the existence of supreme federal power was objected to because it could subvert the protections afforded by state constitutions. It is notable that in expressing this concern the Anti-Federalists understood that *state taxation* of the press — however that term might be defined — was likewise violative of liberty of the press. This is somewhat curious in view of the thesis advanced by some, like Levy,[115] who contend that the constitution merely divested the federal government of authority over the press in favor of state regulation and suppression.[116] At least in some circles it was believed that taxes imposed by state or federal government were antipathetic to freedom of the press — and, indeed, the state constitutions were generally quite protective of press freedom.[117]

Conclusion

As we look across the landscape of the English Stamp Act in the Colonies, the colonial stamp taxes, and the various references to the history of taxation and its relation to press freedom prior to and contemporaneous with the ratification of the First Amendment, the principal conclusions to be drawn from (and the difficulties posed by) the historical material surveyed here are threefold. First, while the cited references to taxation and press freedom are not, and do not purport to be, exhaustive, they nevertheless reflect the fact that, among the volumes of publications and statements at the time, such references were remarkably infrequent. From a strictly quantitative perspective, it would be hard to conclude, as the Supreme Court implied, that concerns about taxation of the press "animated" the First Amendment.

Second, those references that do exist leave open to substantial doubt exactly what was meant by the term "tax" when used in the often broad-ranging references to the press. Beyond a concern about a duty that might fall on the press's "liberty," that could be confiscatory, or the administration of which could be offensive, virtually no definition was given the word. Occasional allusions to stamps or advertising taxes were just that — occasional, and rarely analytically instructive. The qualities of differential imposition, direct impact on the price of publications, and the like are largely missing, perhaps because the nature of taxes at the time always contained these features. The historical record provides relatively little guidance for future legislatures and, as we shall see, the absence of guidance may have had an impact.

Finally, the chief concern expressed about press freedom seems to have been censorship, not taxation. In the context of the many statements made about the First Amendment and freedom of the press during the ratification of the Constitution (the period during which most direct reference to press freedom was made) and the drafting and ratification of the Bill of Rights, references to limitations on taxation of the press were few — indeed, rare — in comparison to the many statements made about licensing, libel, and the relation between press freedom and criticism of government.[118] And the references to taxation that were made almost always concerned fears of censorship or control, not the importance of access by citizens to current information about politics and political economy. Yet it was access to information, not censorship of it, that would later animate the English struggle and give meaning to the very concept of forbidden knowledge taxation. As David Anderson has concluded:

> [P]ress freedom was viewed as being closely related to the experiment of representative self-government. . . . The press was a "bulwark of liberty" "essential to the security of freedom in a state." It had to be protected, not for its own sake, but because it provided a necessary restraint on what the patriots viewed as government's natural tendency toward tyranny and despotism.[119]

That the focus of discussion was *not* on taxation, but was instead on censorship, libel, licensing, and criticism of government does not negate the relevance of the taxation question to the First Amendment. Nor does it suggest that no connection exists between a concept of the press as an independent source of constraint on government and the press's freedom from taxation, for such a connection was in fact drawn, if infrequently and ambiguously, and the English and colonial stamps were part of the experience that the framers and commentators brought to the issue of press freedom. But having said this, it seems also apparent that in the broader landscape of discussion and thought on the question of constitutional protection for the press, the question of taxation was genuinely incidental to the larger scheme of things.

Notes

1. An Act for Granting and Applying Certain Stamp Duties . . . in the British Colonies and Plantations in America, etc. (Stamp Act), 1765, 5 Geo. 3, ch. 12 (Eng.).

2. See Arthur M. Schlesinger, *Prelude to Independence* 68 (1958).

3. See Chapter 1.

4. See John Phillip Reid, *Constitutional History of the American Revolution: The Authority to Tax* 68–69 (1987); John C. Miller, *Origins of the American Revolution* 111 (1943).

5. Miller at 111.

6. *Id.* at 111–12.

7. See *infra* "The Colonial Stamp Taxes," this chapter.

8. See Miller at 112. But see Mack Thompson, "Massachusetts and New York Stamp Acts," 26 *Wm. & Mary Q.* 253 (3d ser. 1969), who expresses skepticism about the amount and impact of opposition to the taxes.

9. See Miller at 112.

10. An interesting bit of background is that one of the contributing forces behind the taxes on the Colonies may have been Parliament's concern with prerogative rule in Great Britain, and the increasing breadth with which the Crown was issuing instructions to the Colonies without involvement of Parliament. Taxation by Parliament, therefore, was in a sense a manifestation of Parliament's assertion of authority. See Reid at 13.

11. See *id.* at 9–11. The question of "constitutionality" was not, of course, predicated on a written document bearing that name, but concerned Britain's authority in the context of the constituted empire.

12. Forty members ultimately voted against the tax, but none on grounds of lack of authority. *Id.* at 21.

13. Miller at 112. In Parliament, the debates did not really ever concern the power or legal authority of Parliament to tax. They instead involved the issue of imposing an internal tax on the Colonies that would benefit England. Sir William Meredith, a member of Parliament from Liverpool, who would ultimately support Lord North against the Americans, perceived the American objections: "The safety of this country consists in this with respect that we cannot lay a tax upon others without taxing ourselves. This is not the case in America. We shall tax them in order to ease ourselves. We ought therefore to be extremely delicate in imposing a burden upon others which we not only share ourselves but which is to take it far from us." Sir William Meredith, Speech in House of Commons Debate (Feb. 6, 1765) quoted in Reid at 20.

Jared Ingersoll, reporting on the parliamentary debates and action, stated that the question was not the authority of Parliament to tax America, but that "[i]n short, altho [sic] there was about forty Members in the Negative . . . yet their Op[p]osition to it was not on account of its being Unconstitutional, but because they th[ought] the measure imprudent & perhaps burdensome." Letter from Jared Ingersoll to the Connecticut General Assembly (Sept. 18, 1765) quoted in Reid at 21.

14. See Miller at 113.

15. See *id*. at 113–14.

16. The Stamp Act was one of a series of "taxes" by Britain. As described by Reid at 28–32, they were (with relevant background):

a. *The Sugar Act*. Originally enacted in 1733, it was the "first tax laid upon the Americans to which they objected on constitutional grounds." The Sugar Tax was "instigat[ed by] Great Britain's West Indian sugar islands." An earlier law (6 Geo. II, ch. 13) had imposed a duty "on foreign molasses imported into the colonies," of sixpence per gallon, which was 100 percent of its value, and was therefore really a prohibition on imports, not a tax. It was difficult to enforce and predictably spawned a black market. The Sugar Act of 1764 replaced the 1733 Act (4 Geo. III, ch. 15), with duties reduced to three pennies per gallon, and enforcement tightened. The items covered by the Act were expanded to include, for example, certain wines, and the importation of foreign rum was prohibited.

b. *Townshend Duties*. Enacted in 1767 (7 Geo. III, ch. 46), the duties were formulated as an "external tax" — custom duties imposed, in this case, on imports of British goods into the colonies. Imposed on glass, painters' colors, paper, and tea, the duties were clearly intended to raise money rather than, as with the sugar duties, to regulate trade. They failed to raise much money, partly because of boycotts and resistance.

c. *The Tea Tax*. After most of Townshend duties were repealed (except the tea tax), the Tea Act of 1773 was passed (13 Geo. III, ch. 44). The original Townshend duty on tea was left intact, but the East India Company was permitted to "dispose of its surplus tea in the colonies by shipping tea on its own vessels and selling it through its own factors." The tax paid on importation into Great Britain (not a tax by the colonies) was rebated, and therefore the price in the colonies was low. Because the tea was cheap, the colonies would buy it and pay the tea tax to Britain, thereby generating revenue for Britain. But the colonies would end up with surplus tea. Reid quotes a New Hampshire writer as follows: "The East India Company have procured an act to ship their rotten and infected teas to America, which liberty they never could obtain before as a Company, nor would they now have done it, if it had not been by that means to support the British act of taxing America." Reid at 32 (quoting from *Gazette & Post-Boy*, Dec. 20, 1773, at 2).

17. Miller at 114–15; see Reid at 28–29.

18. See Miller at 115–16.

19. An Act for Granting and Applying Certain Stamp Duties . . . in the British Colonies and Plantations in America, etc., 1765, 5 Geo. 3, ch. 12 (Eng.).

20. See Miller at 117.

21. Connor Cruise O'Brien, *The Great Melody: A Thematic Biography of Edmund Burke* 126 (1992).

22. Schlesinger at 68; see Lawrence H. Leder, *America 1603–1789: Prelude to a Nation* 150 (1978).

23. Miller at 119.

24. Reid at 24.

25. Stephen Sayre, "The Englishman Deceived; A Political Piece: Wherein Some very Important Secrets of State are briefly recited, And offered to the Consideration of the Public," 12 (London, 1768), quoted in Reid at 21.

26. Edmund Burke, Speech in House of Commons (Mar. 22, 1775) quoted in Reid at 22.

27. The governor of Massachusetts wrote to a member of Parliament that "[t]he Stamp Act is become in itself a matter of indifference; it is swallowed up in the importance of the effects of which it has been the cause. The taxing of the *Americans* by the Parliament, had brought their very subjection to the Crown of *Great Britain* in question." Letter from Francis Bernard, Governor of Massachusetts, to Richard Jackson (Apr. 17, 1766) quoted in Reid at 212. Other reports were of the same import.

An exchange with Benjamin Franklin in the House of Commons concerning a proposed solution that would require colonies not to deny Parliament's authority illustrates the centrality of the taxation without representation issue.

"If the parliament should repeal the stamp act will the assembly of Pennsylvania rescind their resolutions [denying Parliament's authority]?"

BF: "I think not."

"If the stamp act should be repealed, would it induce the assemblies of America to acknowledge the rights of Parliament to tax them, and would they erase their resolutions?"

BF: "No, never."

"Is there no means of obliging them to erase those resolutions?"

BF: "None that I know of; they will never do it unless compelled by force of arms."

The Examination of Doctor Benjamin Franklin, before an August Assembly, relating to the Repeal of the Stamp Act, &c. 15–16 (Philadelphia 1776), quoted in Reid at 214.

The Pennsylvania resolution provided: "That the taxation of the people of this province, by any other persons whatsoever than such their representatives in assembly, is UNCONSTITUTIONAL, and subversive of their most valuable rights." Pennsylvania Resolves, (Sept. 21, 1765) quoted in Reid at 215.

28. See Reid at 14–16 (recounting the views of the colonies of Massachusetts, New York, and North and South Carolina).

There was, in a sense, representation of the Colonies in Parliament. The objection to taxation without representation was based on the American notion that "the only legal representatives of the inhabitants of this province [Pennsylvania], are the persons they annually elect to serve as members of assembly." Pennsylvania Resolves, quoted in Reid at 107. The representatives of the Colonies in Parliament were not elected by the citizens of the Colonies, and therefore representation did not exist under the stated principle. The Whig view, moreover, was a combination of two ideas. First, there was no representation in the sense of election by Americans in Parliament, and second and more basic, but quite distinct and more extreme, that the only representatives of the Colonies that could consent to taxation of the Colonies were the elected colonial assemblies, not Parliament, whatever its composition.

29. See Reid at 211.

30. See *id*.

31. These are excerpts of Burke's drafts of the speech, quoted in O'Brien at 113–14. The biography provides a fascinating account, from the British side and through Burke's writings, of the period from the enactment of the Stamp Act through and after its repeal.

32. See Schlesinger at 69–70.

33. *Id*.

34. Stephen Botein, "Printers and the American Revolution," in *The Press and the American Revolution* 11, 18–19 (Bernard Bailyn & John B. Heuch eds., 1980).

35. *Id*. at 19.

36. *Id*.

37. *Id*.

38. *Id*.

39. *Id*.

40. *Id*. at 20–22.

41. *Id*. at 19, 22.

42. Miller at 121–22.

43. Schlesinger at 70.

44. See *id*. at 71; Miller at 122–25.

45. Miller at 126.

46. *Id*. at 129.

47. *Id*. at 130; see Schlesinger at 71–76; Sidney I. Pomerantz, "The Patriot Newspaper and the American Revolution," in *The Era of the American Revolution* 305 (Richard B. Morris ed., 1939).

48. See Reid at 265–66.

49. See Schlesinger at 76–77; Miller at 127–37, 288–89.

50. See Schlesinger at 78.

51. Benjamin Franklin was often a object of scorn and criticism at the hands of radical publishers. Franklin, with others, generally took a nonviolent and non-radical approach to the Stamp Act. He was much maligned by the radicals, many of whom published newspapers and scurrilous articles alleging that Franklin and Co. were abetting the stamp. This was not the case, and the radical statements about freedom of the press were uniformly uninstructive on the specifics of why the stamp violated the press's freedom, except for the assertion that the press was to be completely free. Allegations of press control and favor, while perhaps true in isolated instances, were not generally true. See Jeffery A. Smith, *Printers and Press Freedom: The Ideology of Early American Journalism* 136–41 (1988).

52. See Miller at 289.

53. See Leonard W. Levy, *Emergence of a Free Press* 87 (1985) [hereinafter Levy, *Emergence*]; Miller at 289.

54. See Miller at 291–93; Levy, *Emergence* at 87–88.

55. See Schlesinger at 71.

56. This is not to say that a certain degree of influence by England was nonexistent, although it would be an overstatement to assert that the English influence accounted for the reported general blandness. The influence of England was present, however. Postmasters, who were often printers, were afforded personal franking privileges which could be and were used to distribute newspapers and periodicals free of charge. Perhaps the most famous beneficiary of this system was Benjamin Franklin. See Smith at 148–49. In calm periods, the conferral of the franking privilege may have helped keep the waters calm; in stormy periods the threat of its withdrawal (or its actual withdrawal, as occurred with Franklin) may have helped to keep matters in check. *Id.* Smith reports that "[a]s the friction [grew] . . . , the Crown postmasters became more and more active in their endeavors to hamper the distribution by port of newspapers which published improper intelligence, or proclaimed improper political doctrines." *Id.* at 149.

57. See Levy, *Emergence* at 86.

58. Stephen Botein, "'Meer Mechanics' and an Open Press: The Business and Political Strategies of Colonial American Printers," in 9 *Persp. in Am. Hist.* 127, 177 (1975).

59. The letters were published in 12 successive installments in the *Pennsylvania Chronicle* from Dec. 2, 1767, through Feb. 15, 1768. See Schlesinger at 88.

60. *Id.* at 90.

61. See *id.* at 85–128.

62. *Id.* at 129.

63. Levy, *Emergence* at 129.

64. *Id.* at 84–86.

65. *Id.* at 87.

66. See Pomerantz at 305–31.

67. Clyde A. Duniway, *The Development of Freedom of the Press in Massachusetts* 119, 119 n.3 (Franklin ed., 1969) (1906).

68. *Id.* at 120; see Thompson at 253–54.

69. Duniway at 121–22.

70. *Id.* at 120.

71. *Id.* at 120, 120 n.2. See Thompson at 256–57. Thompson disputes any clear relationship between the impact of the tax, and any opposition to it, and the tax's ultimate demise.

72. Duniway at 120.

73. *Id.* The tax apparently expired by its own terms.

74. Thompson at 253–58.

75. *Id.* at 254.

76. *Id.* at 256.

77. *Id.* at 257.

78. *Id.* (citing *Journals of House of Rep. of Mass.*, vol. 31 at 288, vol. 32 at 200–201, vol. 33 at 79, vol. 34 at 456–57).

79. See Duniway at 136.

80. See *id*.

81. *Id*. at 136–37.

82. Smith at 126, 130–31.

83. *Id*. at 130.

84. *Id*. at 131, n.14 (citing Hugh Gaine, *New-York Mercury*, Dec. 20, 1756).

85. *Id*. at 131; see Thompson at 256–57.

86. See Grosjean v. American Press Co., 297 U.S. 233, 246 (1936); Levy, *Emergence* at 86; William Stewart, "Lennox and the Taxes on Knowledge," 15 *Scot. Hist. Rev.* 322–27 (1918).

87. David Ramsay, for example, observed: "Opposition to the stamp act [of 1765] . . . assumed a bolder face. The fire of liberty blazed forth from the press; some well judged publications set the rights of the colonists, in a plain, but strong point of view. The tongues and the pens of the well informed citizens labored in kindling the latent sparks of patriotism. The flame spread from breast to breast, till the conflagration, became general. . . . The heavy burdens, which the operation of the stamp-act would have imposed on the colonists, together with the precedent it would establish of future exactions, furnished the American patriots with arguments, calculated to well move the passions, as to convince the judgments of their fellow colonists." David Ramsay, "The History of the American Revolution" (1789), reprinted in 2 Hyneman & Lutz, *American Political Writing, 1760–1805*, at 736 (1983). See also Simon N. North, *History and Present Condition of the Newspaper and Periodical Press of the United States* 32 (1884); 2 Samuel Miller, *A Brief Retrospect of the Eighteenth Century* 251 (1803).

88. Grosjean v. American Press Co., 297 U.S. 233, 248–49 (1936); see Arkansas Writers' Project, Inc. v. Ragland, 481 U.S. 221 (1987); Minneapolis Star & Tribune Co. v. Minnesota Comm'r of Revenue, 460 U.S. 575 (1983).

89. *Grosjean*, 297 U.S. at 248. As discussed at some length in Chapter 1, the resistance to the knowledge taxes in England neither succeeded nor, it seems, took on great force until the nineteenth century, and specifically until the period following the 1836 act.

90. *Id*. Whether "violent" opposition is the most accurate representation of the Massachusetts experience is, it seems, open to question. Compare Duniway at 136–37, with Thompson at 256–57. While instances of violent opposition may have occurred, the Court's suggestion that this opposition was the principal cause of repeal may be an overstatement. See *Grosjean*, 297 U.S. at 248.

91. *Grosjean*, 297 U.S. at 248.

92. *Id*.

93. Smith at 136–56, especially 152–56.

94. *Id*.

95. See Pa. Const. of 1776, Declaration of Rights, § 12, reprinted in *The Federal and State Constitutions, Colonial Charters, and Other Organic Laws*, at 3083 (F. Thorpe ed., U. S. Gov't Printing Off. 1909); Del. Const. of 1792, art. I, § 5, reprinted in *Federal and State Constitutions, supra*, at 569; Smith at 153–56.

96. 1 Bernard Schwartz, *The Bill of Rights: A Documentary History* 527 (1971). The Court's contention that taxes on knowledge contravene the First Amendment is

squarely predicated on the putative intention of the Anti-Federalists. See *Grosjean*, 297 U.S. 246–49.

97. See generally Robert A. Rutland, *The Ordeal of the Constitution: The Anti-Federalists and the Ratification Struggle of 1787–1788* (1966).

98. See, e.g., Centinel [Samuel Bryan], Letter 8 to the People of Pennsylvania (Dec. 29, 1787), reprinted in 2 *The Complete Anti-Federalist*, at 177–79 (Herbert J. Storing ed., 1981) (Tax Clause, Necessary and Proper Clause, Supremacy Clause, and Election Clause); Cincinnatus [Richard Henry Lee or Arthur Lee], Letter 1 to James Wilson, (*New York Journal*, Nov. 1, 1787), reprinted in 6 *Complete Anti-Federalist, supra*, at 7–10 (Treaty Clause).

99. One remark, however, does seem to suggest that visiting diverse pecuniary burdens on different publications, such as Huey Long attempted, would be viewed as an infringement of the press's liberty: "I confess I do not see in what cases the congress can, with any pretence of right, make a law to suppress the freedom of the press; though I am not clear, that congress is restrained from laying any duties whatever on printing, and from laying duties particularly heavy on certain pieces printed, and perhaps congress may require large bonds for the payment of these duties." Federal Farmer [Richard Henry Lee], "Observations Leading to a Fair Examination of the System of Government Proposed by the Late Convention; And to Several Essential and Necessary Alterations in It," Letter 4 (Oct. 12, 1787), reprinted in 2 *Complete Anti-Federalist* at 250.

100. 1 Schwartz at 454, 529.

101. *Id.* at 527; see *Debates in the Federal Convention of 1787 Which Framed the Constitution of the United States of America* 565 (Gaillard Hunt & James B. Scott eds., 1987) (reporting James Madison's *Journal*); Centinel [Samuel Bryan], Letter 2 to the People of Pennsylvania (1787), reprinted in 2 *Complete Anti-Federalist* at 146.

102. *The Federalist* No. 84, at 535n. (Alexander Hamilton) (Benjamin F. Wright ed., 1966).

103. Hugh Williamson, "Remarks on the New Plan of Government" (1788), reprinted in Schwartz at 551.

104. A Plebeian [Melancton Smith], Address (New York 1788), reprinted in 6 *Complete Anti-Federalist* at 145.

105. Cincinnatus [Richard Henry Lee or Arthur Lee], Letter 1 to James Wilson (*New York Journal*, Nov. 1, 1787), reprinted in 6 *Complete Anti-Federalist* at 9. Anticipating the Sedition Acts, Aristocrotis (identity unknown) conceived of a motive for suppressing printed matter. "[A]s there is no provision made for [the press's] security in the new frame of government, congress may abolish it at pleasure, which they will soon find it [in] their interest to do, and its own native licentiousness will furnish them with reasons plausible enough to form a preamble for the act." Aristocrotis [pseud.], "The Government of Nature Delineated, or An Exact Picture of the New Federal Constitution" (Carlisle 1788) reprinted in 3 *Complete Anti-Federalist* at 204.

106. A Farmer [Thomas Cogswell], Essay 1, (*Freeman's Oracle and New Hampshire Advertiser* Jan. 11, 1788), reprinted in 4 *Complete Anti-Federalist* at 206–7.

107. Centinel [Samuel Bryan], Letter 8 to the People of Pennsylvania (Dec. 21, 1787), reprinted in 2 *Complete Anti-Federalist* at 177.

108. Pennsylvania Antifederalist [William Findley (?)], *Independent Gazetteer*, Nov. 6, 1787, reprinted in 3 *Complete Anti-Federalist* 93 (H. Storing ed., 1981); see Leonard W. Levy, "On the Origins of the Free Press Clause," 32 *UCLA L. Rev.* 177, 209 (1984) (hereinafter "Free Press Clause").

109. Federal Farmer [Richard Henry Lee], "Observations Leading to a Fair Examination of the System of Government Proposed by the Late Convention; And to Several Essential and Necessary Alterations in It," Letter 16 (Jan. 20, 1788), reprinted in 2 *Complete Anti-Federalist* at 329–30. The entire relevant text of the Federal Farmer quote is: "All parties apparently agree, that the freedom of the press is a fundamental right, and ought not to be restrained by any taxes, duties, or in any manner whatever. Why should not the people, in adopting a federal constitution, declare this, even if there are only doubts about it? But, say the advocates, all powers not given are reserved: — true; but the great question is, are not powers given, in the exercise of which this right may be destroyed? The people's or the printers['] claim to a free press, is founded on the fundamental laws, that is, compacts, and state constitutions, made by the people. . . . No right claimed under a state constitution, will avail against a law of the union, made in pursuance of the federal constitution: therefore the question is, what laws will congress have a right to make by the constitution of the union, and particularly touching the press? By art. I sect. 8. congress will have power to lay and collect taxes, duties, imposts and excise. By this congress will clearly have power to lay and collect all kind of taxes whatever — taxes . . . on newspapers, advertisements, &c. and to require bonds of the naval officers, clerks, printers, &c. to account for the taxes that may become due on papers that go through their hands. Printing, like all other business, must cease when taxed beyond its profits; and it appears to me, that a power to tax the press at discretion, is a power to destroy or restrain the freedom of it. There may be other powers given, in the exercise of which this freedom may be effected; and certainly it is of too much importance to be left thus liable to be taxed, and constantly to constructions and interferences."

110. Centinel, Letter 2 to the People of Pennsylvania (1787), reprinted in 2 *Complete Anti-Federalist* at 146; see also *id.* at 152 (taxing power combined with the Necessary and Proper Clause).

111. Federal Farmer, "Observations Leading to a Fair Examination of the System of Government Proposed by the Late Convention; And to Essential and Necessary Alterations in It," Letter 4 (Oct. 12, 1787), reprinted in 2 *Complete Anti-Federalist* at 250.

112. An Old Whig [pseud.], Essay 3, (Philadelphia *Independent Gazetteer* 1787), reprinted in 3 *Complete Anti-Federalist* at 27–28.

113. A speech by James Wilson on December 1, 1987, to the Pennsylvania Ratifying Convention, to the effect that liberty of the press meant no more than that prior restraints may not be imposed and that prosecution of the common law libels would be permitted in federal courts, occasioned responses bearing on the taxation question. 2 *Documentary History of the Ratification of the Constitution* 455 (M. Jensen ed., 1976).

The first was a pamphlet by "A Federalist Republican" (identity unknown) who, as Leonard Levy describes it, "contended that the press faced real danger from

Congress' delegated power to tax; stamp duties could 'as effectively abolish the freedom of the press as any express declaration.' " "Free Press Clause" at 209 quoting "A Review of the Constitution . . . By a Federal Republican" (1787), reprinted in 3 *Complete Anti-Federalist* 81 (H. Storing ed., 1981).

The second was an essay by a Pennsylvania Anti-Federalist who Levy identifies as "probably" William Findley. "The Liberty of the Press is not secured, and the powers of Congress are fully adequate to its destruction, as they . . . may by a cursed abominable Stamp Act (as the *Bowdoin Administration* has done in Massachusetts) preclude you effectually from all means of information. Mr. W[ilson] has given you no answer to these arguments." Pennsylvania Antifederalist [William Findley (?)], *Independent Gazetteer*, Nov. 6, 1787, reprinted in 3 *Complete Anti-Federalist* 93; see Levy, "Free Press Clause" at 209.

These statements bear not only on the taxing power question, but also on the larger question pertaining to Leonard Levy's conclusion (probably correct notwithstanding much debate, in my opinion) that the animating view of freedom of the press at the time of the Constitution's ratification was essentially Blackstone's, and that the "Congress shall make no law" portion of the First Amendment reflected a purposeful effort to limit the federal legislative branch, as opposed to the executive and judicial branches. Without entering the debate surrounding these conclusions, it is noteworthy that, with respect to exercises of the taxing power to control the press, Congress, not the other branches, constituted the threat under the Constitution. Levy says as much, although he does not develop the point in detail with respect to the taxing power, when he concludes that the First Amendment was designed to "prohibit any Congressional regulation of the press, whether by means of a licensing act, a tax act, or a sedition act." Leonard W. Levy, *Freedom of the Press from Zenger to Jefferson* lvi (Introduction) (Leonard W. Levy ed., 1966) (hereinafter *Freedom of the Press*).

114. See note 98 *supra*.

115. Levy's basic point, however, is the more limited one that the First Amendment left in the hands of the states whatever level of protection, if any, the press warranted.

116. Levy does say that whatever the meaning of freedom of the press, the "Congress shall make no law" injunction was meant to prohibit all congressional "regulation" of the press, "whether by means of a licensing act, a tax act, or a sedition act." Leonard W. Levy, *Judgments: Essays on American Constitutional History* 136 (1972); accord, Benjamin A. Richards, "Historic Rationale of the Speech-and-Press Clause of the First Amendment," 21 *U. Fla. L. Rev.* 203, 214–15, n.66 (1968). The source of the inclusion of "tax act" in the statement is unclear, and without some operative definition of that which was encompassed within freedom of the press, or meant by "regulation," it would be difficult to interpret "make no law" to include taxation, at least in some forms. Indeed, even with respect to a sedition act, subsequent history places the proposition in some doubt, according to Levy.

It is also important to note that the focus of discussion was so permeated with concerns about libel and sedition — the practical problem then being faced in a partisan press — that references to taxation were virtually nonexistent and the core of concern — control of critical publications, scandalous publications, and libel — had no necessary relation to taxation, except in a limited form which was never well defined in the highly general references to taxes.

Indeed, the result of the Sedition Act controversy, according to Levy and others, was the ultimate emergence of a libertarian view of press freedom, a view that was directed to protecting criticism of government and government officials and had little direct relation to taxation as a general matter, or as a specific matter.

117. See Chapter 3, note 1, *infra*.

118. See Smith at 136–56, for an account of statements by journalists and editors at the time.

119. David A. Anderson, "The Origins of the Free Press Clause," 30 *UCLA L. Rev.* 455, 533 (1983) (footnotes omitted).

3. Federal Knowledge Taxes in Nineteenth-Century America

Discussion of freedom of the press — and particularly of the press's freedom from taxation — was sketchy at the time of the ratification of the Constitution and the First Amendment. Lofty statements were made about the press's freedom, and occasional reference was made to the types of concerns that might underlie a principle limiting the government's power to tax the press. On the whole, however, even the lofty statements were infrequent; discussions that explored the reasons against a power to tax even at the most abstract level were downright rare. If anything, the record is even more barren at the time of ratification of the Bill of Rights, which contained the guarantee of press freedom in the First Amendment. Perhaps it is because of the First Amendment's elegant and simple form, coupled with a focus on political licentiousness at the time, that very little of the discussion concerned the subject of press freedom from taxation.

The republic took shape through the Constitution and the First Amendment, therefore, with a grand and open-ended, but profoundly ambiguous (at least with respect to taxation), admonition, proclaimed by all as if self-evident, that the press should be free. The same was true of the states, whose constitutions assured freedom of the press in only the most general way.[1] When it came to taxation of the press, the subsequent history began with an essentially clean legal slate.

In the early years of the nineteenth century, of course, England was still to reach the apex of its knowledge taxes. The tide would not really turn until nearly mid-century. One might expect that the continued imposition of the taxes and, thereafter, the efforts leading to ultimate repeal in England would have received some attention in this country, not only around the time of ratification of the Constitution and the Bill of Rights, but particularly in the first half of the nineteenth century. This appears not to have been the case. Indeed, in a remarkable irony, it appears that the federal government in America was about to launch such a regime of taxes at the very moment of their final repeal in England. It is to this topic that we first turn as we begin to explore the subject of knowledge taxation in nineteenth-century America. Following a discussion of taxation at the federal level we will turn, in later chapters, to the use of taxation on the state and local levels.

The Federal Advertising Tax, 1862–67

The nation's first and, it appears, only experience with a national knowledge tax was occasioned by the Civil War. While the tax ultimately imposed appears to have consisted of an advertising tax and a little-known and apparently narrow and short-lived paper tax, various proposals were considered during the course of legislative deliberation. The legislative and public records are quite sketchy, and the debate limited, but the course of legislative consideration and the controversy surrounding the tax proposals can be at least partially reconstructed.[2] They provide an interesting and instructive perspective on the evolving American notions of freedom of the press in the taxation setting.

The federal knowledge tax began as part of a proposal to raise much-needed revenue to support the war effort. In January 1862 Schuyler Colfax, an animated representative from Indiana, who was chairperson of the House Committee on the Post Office and Post Roads and a former journalist, started matters off by introducing a bill, H.R. 215, that was designed to raise revenue by requiring that printed matter be conveyed only by mail.[3] This was to be distinguished from a requirement, which had previously been imposed, that newspapers using the mails pay postage.[4] The bill was reminiscent of similar legislation in England through which Parliament attempted to exert control over the country press. The connection was not lost on the major metropolitan newspapers, which had substantial distribution systems and which almost uniformly denounced the measure.[5] The *New York Times* editorial position was characteristic.

> MR. COLFAX, with less than his usual good sense, has just introduced a bill into the House of Representatives to prohibit newspapers from being delivered on post roads except by the Government mails. If the object of the measure is to increase the revenue, it must prove as bad an expedient as could well be devised. . . . This fiscal expedient would be extremely unpopular in this country, and would expose us to universal derision abroad. For it has always been the boasted policy of our Government to foster the circulation and promote the prosperity of the public Press. . . . And is it to be endured that, with the proud position of the United States, as regards newspaper enterprise,

we should resort to a prohibitory enactment which could be enforced, or would be endured, in no European country? . . . The British newspaper tax had its origin in an aristocratic jealousy of the people, and in a desire to prevent them from informing themselves on political subjects. But the impost was always odious. It has long been merely nominal, and was in 1840 repealed altogether. The use of the mails is now open to the Press as to other departments of public usefulness. But now, as always, it is optional to send papers by mail or by any other means. . . . The country now needs more than ever the influence of enlightened journalism. Shall we voluntarily recede from our position and without any benefit to the revenue, cause serious inconvenience to the public? If newspapers are to be taxed at all, let the impost be laid by some method which will be as little open as possible to the objections which must lie against all taxes on knowledge.[6]

While the *Times*'s objection was framed in terms of the maintenance of a free press in the United States, a theme expressed in the most abstract form, it was clear that increasingly valuable newspaper distribution systems would be placed in jeopardy, and that the statute would result in an immediate, but hidden, increase in costs. It was also clear that newspapers would be hard pressed to argue for a complete exemption from any taxation at a time when revenue was needed, and when the Colfax bill was simply one element of a comprehensive effort to raise revenue from all quarters of the nation.

To avoid the economic consequences of the bill, yet to do so on a politically palatable ground, the *Times* found itself advocating direct taxation of the press in lieu of mail regulation. On the following day, just before the House debated Colfax's bill, the *Times* suggested other means of generating the needed revenue from the press, which would, of course, do its own part:

Let [the government] require *postage to be paid* on newspapers thus conveyed, and at the same time require the railroads to carry them under their contracts with the Post-office Department. Let them impose, if they please, a stamp duty, or even a *direct tax upon every copy* of every newspaper issued, if this shall be deemed necessary as a means of revenue to the Government under the heavy expenditures of the war. A direct tax of *half a cent a copy* on the daily newspapers of this City would yield not far from $300,000 a year to the Government. Yet our City journals would much rather pay it than submit to a measure which would restrict their enterprise, and retard their prompt and rapid distribution throughout the country at large.

Indeed, we think that a direct tax on newspapers would be a perfectly legitimate and proper source of income. It is open to objection, doubtless, but so is every other tax. Newspapers have become necessaries of life, but so are tea and sugar. Taxes must be levied, and all classes of the community must be prepared to contribute their full share. The newspaper Press has suffered quite as severely as any other interest from the war, in its loss of advertisements; — but it is still willing to submit to whatever taxation may be required for the public good.[7]

While the paper's position seems plain, one might wonder about a possible ambush, especially in view of the reference to sugar and tea, the taxation of which sparked the Revolution.

A sentiment similar to that of the *Times* was expressed by Robert Bonner, publisher of the *New York Ledger*, in a dispatch to Representative Colfax:

I am aware, as you state in your communication in today's Tribune, that the Government sadly needs additional revenue; and so far as newspaper proprietors are concerned, I know of no class of men more willing to pay their share. But let it come in proper shape. . . . I would prefer to pay a tax of half a cent on every copy of that circulation rather than be compelled to conform to the requirements of your bill. It would be less onerous to give the entire profits of our business to the Government while the war continues than to have that business entirely destroyed. We are willing to be taxed; but in common with other newspaper publishers, we do not want the present well organized and satisfactory news agency system of selling and distributing papers broken up, which would virtually be the effect of your bill. If Congress considers it expedient to raise additional revenue off the circulation of newspapers, why would not a plan something like the following be a good one: Papers of one thousand circulation and less to be free from taxation; papers over one thousand and less than five thousand to pay a tax of one quarter of a cent on every copy published; and all papers of over five thousand circulation to pay a tax of half a cent on every copy published.[8]

Bonner's proposal is notable, of course, not only because it expresses a willingness to be subjected to a direct form of newspaper tax which better fits the historical mold of "knowledge taxes" than the postal bill, but also because it explicitly recommends a differential rate of tax depending on circulation, something the current Supreme Court would consider suspect, at best.[9] We do not know whether Bonner's views reflected those of other publishers, as well, but they represent an elaboration on the position of the *Times*, another New York paper. There is reason to believe, moreover, that his views were not uncharacteristic of the metropolitan press in general, for as we shall see later, there was an economic advantage to the newspapers in a half-cent tax, for it would permit them to raise the price of papers by a full cent at a time when a price increase on any other, nonpatriotic ground may have been untenable.

On January 21, 1862, Colfax's postal bill, H.R. 215, reached the floor of the House. After the bill's reading, Colfax noted the "general willingness of the people to submit to taxation for the purpose of renovating the country."[10] Taxes were being proposed for imposition on "all the various branches of industry in the country . . . for three purposes: first, to carry on the war energetically and successfully; second, to defray the ordinary expenses of the Government; and third, to wipe out deficits that exist in the various branches of the Government."[11] Since Congress had relinquished its franking privilege for the good of the fisc—a move the press had applauded—now the newspapers should do likewise and give up their own mailing privileges. He then stated the purpose of his postal bill. "I want the privilege of the newspapers to load down our mail trains free of postage abolished. . . . This bill is, as they conceive, striking at their interest. I regretted to have to do it; but it is necessary, in order to raise sufficient revenue, to legislate unfavorably on a great many interests of this country."[12]

Congress's constitutional authority to enact the bill was unquestioned, according to Colfax. The authority rested in the Article I power to establish post offices and post roads.[13] Moreover, Colfax argued that the framers of the Constitution had specifically sanctioned his bill. Until 1845, he said, it was the "universal rule" that newspapers were "prohibited from going outside of the mail."[14] In 1845, according to Colfax, Congress had created an exception for those newspapers which were immediately distributed, and publishers, he believed, were exploiting that exception.[15] Thereafter, the press relied increasingly on express companies for distribution, which resulted in an affirmative expense to taxpayers as well as a reduction of revenues. In contrast, Colfax asserted, his bill would raise some million dollars in revenue annually; moreover, he asserted, it would concomitantly benefit subscribers by reducing the cost of newspapers through use of the cheaper postal system.[16]

Colfax did not let the matter rest here, however, for he was skeptical of the press's avowed interest in direct taxation in lieu of the postal requirement. He addressed the issue straightforwardly:

> It seems that some of the New York papers are willing that a half cent stamp tax shall be laid upon them, because they will really make money by it. They have for several years been considering the question of raising the price of their daily issues from two cents to three cents, but they have hesitated about doing it for

fear their patrons would not justify them in it; but if we require them to pay a half cent stamp tax, they will then raise the price, and can afford not only to pay the tax, but will receive half a cent additional profit on every paper they sell.[17]

Representative Colfax did not truly believe that the papers would support a stamp tax, or at least that they would do so unless it served their economic interests directly. In this he was later proved correct, as the newspapers changed their tune when the alternative of direct taxation became a reality.[18]

Notwithstanding Colfax's arguments in support of the committee bill, and his cynicism about the direct tax alternative, his view did not prevail. Representative Blair of Missouri rose to the defense of a stamp tax, making three arguments. First, he argued that a half-cent tax would be administratively efficient, and more so than the postal requirement. Second, a direct tax would leave intact the current newspaper distribution system, in which the newspapers had a considerable investment. Finally, he estimated that a stamp tax would generate some three million dollars in revenue annually, much more than the million dollars estimated for the postal requirement.[19] Blair then introduced the following resolution:

> *Resolved*, That the bill now under consideration be recommitted to the Committee on the Post Office and Post Roads, with instructions to report a bill imposing a stamp duty upon newspapers in lieu of postage, upon the payment of which newspapers may be transported without charge for postage.[20]

After reiterating the advantages of a stamp tax, Blair outlined the general terms of a stamp tax that he would consider desirable, including differential rates.

> I desire to see some measure of taxation adopted in reference to newspapers which will bear less heavily upon newspapers which circulate in cities and within fifty miles of the place of publication, than upon those which circulate at a greater distance. Those might be charged one half cent each, while these might be taxed one cent each. That would greatly enhance the revenue.[21]

Colfax's reply took no issue with the differential aspects of Blair's suggestion. Instead, he argued that the cost of collection of a stamp tax in small towns would exceed the revenues obtained, and that his postal proposal was superior "because it is simple, and restores the practice which prevailed prior to 1845, which was, that such printed matter shall go in the mails, and if it goes outside it shall pay postage."[22]

The differential character of Colfax's proposal was also challenged. Representative Riddle demanded to know under what pretense Congress could force any article of commerce to be distributed in a certain fashion. "Why should you tax this particular branch of industry and production any more than any and all others? . . . [I]t does not follow that because exceptionally you carry printed matter in the mails, that gives you the right to seize upon this special and peculiar article of production, and tax it specially and peculiarly to supply this particular deficit."[23] Notably, the concern with differential application of the postal requirement appeared to have little, if anything, to do with a perceived constitutional constraint. Riddle moved to table H.R. 215. The motion was first denied, but after a series of amendments were rejected, H.R. 215 was finally tabled by a vote of 75 to 60.[24]

The newspaper taxation question did not disappear following the tabling of Colfax's bill; it was refocused and rechanneled. During the two months following the House action, amid reproach from abroad that the United States was fiscally irresponsible, the House Ways and Means Committee fashioned the nation's first comprehensive internal tax bill, which included an advertising and, later, a paper tax.[25] On March 3, 1862, the Committee reported its bill containing a three percent tax on newspaper and periodical advertisements, to be paid by the publisher.[26] After praising the wisdom of the proposal's authors, and adopting a generally laudatory tone, the *New York Times* stated:

> Nearly every class will probably find something to complain of. . . . But in the main, we have a right to assume, that the provisions of the bill have been justly balanced. . . .
> . . . The cause of popular or newspaper knowledge comes in for its burden in the shape of an excise upon all printing paper, and a tax upon the proceeds of newspaper advertisements.[27]

The paper tax mentioned in the *Times* article appears to have been enacted at a later date, in 1863, and little evidence surrounding its passage and its scope and impact is available. Before recounting the very sketchy record of the paper tax, the fuller record pertaining to the advertising tax—a direct descendant of the Blair stamp proposal—will be explored.

The *Times*'s support for direct taxation of newspapers, which earlier took the form of a suggested stamp tax and was later manifested in the positive statements about the advertising and paper taxes in the comprehensive tax bill of March 1862, quickly faltered. On March 5, the day after the above-quoted *Times* article, the *Times* ran its first and only criticism of the newspaper tax provision.

After a political existence of more than seventy years, we have for the first time been driven into a system of internal taxation as a permanent policy or measure — a system which will connect nearly every act or enjoyment with a contribution into the National Treasury. . . . But the spirit of discord that has been let loose has instantly brought our expenses up to those of a first class Power. . . .

. . . We should not tax the means for the extension or transmission of intelligence, as all wealth, and progress, and society itself, is based upon it. . . .

The greater part of the subjects presented for taxation in the bill reported are of course very proper; but it strikes us that several of them are palpable violations of the principles laid down. . . .

. . . So with a tax upon the diffusion of intelligence. It is certainly remarkable that republican America should impose a tax upon newspapers, the great educators in modern times, at almost the same moment it has been removed by monarchical England.[28]

The *Times*'s editorial objection fell on deaf ears, by all appearances. The portion of the bill that imposed a tax on newspaper advertisements was approved by the Senate less than three months later on May 24, 1862, without any debate.[29] The paper tax was not approved at this time, and appears not to have been proposed for approval. The advertisement duty took effect on August 1, 1862.[30] It provided for a three percent duty on the gross advertising receipts of all periodical publications. The penultimate provision exempted from taxation the first one thousand dollars of advertising revenue. The final clause also exempted from the duty "all *newspapers* whose circulation does not exceed two thousand copies."[31] The tax therefore singled out not only newspapers and other periodical publications, but also certain classes of newspapers in precisely the same way as did the statute stricken down over fifty years later in *Grosjean v. American Press Co.*[32] The tax remained in effect for only five years, and was repealed on March 2, 1867.[33] The reasons for repeal are not apparent, as there is no record of debates or other legislative history.

From a strictly economic point of view, the decision to impose an advertising rather than a stamp tax was curious, although we can only guess as to the reasons, for no explanatory material has been uncovered. There was, to be sure, a base of advertising revenues from which to derive taxes. In antebellum America, the space given over to paid commercial announcements in periodicals was constantly on the increase, as was the price charged for the space.[34] Even in the mid-nineteenth century, advertising receipts constituted a large portion of a newspaper's total revenue — usually forty to fifty percent.[35] Notwithstanding the steady increase in advertising revenues on which the tax revenues would be based, the advertising tax was a considerably inferior source of revenue when compared with either of the alternatives — a postage requirement or a stamp tax. The revenues produced from the tax represented only a fraction of the estimates for the other taxes, as the reported receipts disclose:

Advertising Tax Revenues, 1863–1867[36]

1863	$ 40,628.59
1864	$133,315.11
1865	$227,530.21
1866	$290,605.31
1867	$288,009.80

In contrast, Colfax estimated that his postal bill would have raised about one million dollars annually. Blair asserted that the stamp measure would have contributed up to three million dollars in annual revenue. While both estimates may have been optimistic, especially if various exemptions were taken into account, it seems clear that the revenue generated would have been significantly higher under either alternative scheme.

In view of the greatly reduced revenue from the advertising tax, it is surprising that one can only surmise the reason for Congress's choice of that tax, as no record of the basis for the decision could be found. It is possible that Congress imposed the advertising tax on grounds of ease of administration, a concern that had earlier been raised in the House debates about the postal bill. An advertising duty avoided the difficulty of taxing every single transaction between paper and customer.[37] Congress may also have believed that an advertising duty would affect readers the least, both because of its smaller cost to the papers and because it was less obvious in its impact on circulation, as such, and therefore might not as easily lead to an increase in subscription price. The tax could be passed to the advertisers rather than the consumers.[38] For related reasons, the tax might also have been viewed as less offensive to the sensitivities of the metropolitan press. At least in its nominal application to advertisements it could be asserted that the tax did not fall on "knowledge" — the news and intelligence about politics and political economy.

Beyond the questions pertaining to the chosen form of tax, there remains the more basic question about Congress's reasons for imposing any tax on the press at all. Here, too, we must speculate and draw inferences from the total course of events leading to the tax, for the advertising tax was ultimately passed with essentially no discussion and in the face of limited and relatively weak opposition by the metropolitan newspapers. The most obvious reason for enactment of the tax, of course, was that the nation badly needed revenues to enforce the war effort. This patriotic imperative conjoined with the press's weak resistance — indeed, their backhanded support of a newspaper tax which, in truth, they all but proposed. The press was undoubtedly deeply concerned about the postal bill, whatever the combination of reasons that contributed to this view, yet the newspapers were in the uncomfortable position of not wanting to appear unpatriotic to their readers.

It is also possible that the press was inhibited in its criticism of government policy, not so much out of a fear of government retribution, but out of a fear of public violence. It was part of the tenor of the times that feelings ran high, and scores of newspapers were literally attacked by mobs or by troops for the publication of "unpatriotic" views about the war. If free speech can be chilled, it surely was during the Civil War, as newspapers were forced to suspend by mobs and in at least one case a newsperson was tarred and ridden on a rail until he promised to quit writing.[39]

Finally, it is possible — indeed it appears likely in light of the editorials published on the postal bill — that the newspapers did not view the tax as a violation of press freedom. Simon North, writing in 1884 as the primary nineteenth-century chronicler of the history of newspapers and periodicals in America, did not appear to view the advertising tax as a "knowledge tax" or as in any way repugnant to a free press.[40] With the exception of the late and ineffective, as well as ambiguous, *New York Times* editorial against the tax bill, nothing discovered in the major public press indicated that a stamp tax would violate press freedom or be contrary to the free press guarantees of the various state constitutions, much less the clearly applicable federal one. At least with respect to the original Colfax proposals the newspapers seem to have been preoccupied with — indeed distracted by — their stake in the distribution system rather than with any possible loss of liberty to publish.

While this seems surprising today in light of the English experience as well as current ideas about the First Amendment guarantees, it may not have been surprising at the time. The mentality of constitutionality was not so prevalent then, and no nineteenth-century court struck down a tax on knowledge as violative of freedom of the press, even though there were at least five opportunities to do so, all of which occurred after the Civil War period.[41]

The Federal Paper Tax

As mentioned earlier, Congress also enacted a paper tax as part of its efforts to raise revenues for the Civil War. The legislative and public record of this tax, which was enacted in 1863, is very sketchy, and therefore the principal focus of attention has been placed on the postal bill and the resultant advertising tax. What little can be gleaned about the paper tax is instructive, however, and represents a part of the record of federal legislative efforts to tax the press during the Civil War period.

The paper tax was enacted in 1863, the year following enactment of the advertising tax. It appeared as a rather obscure section of an act "to modify existing Laws imposing Duties and Imports, and for other Purposes."[42] The paper tax provision was contained in Section 5 of the act, as follows: "*And be it further enacted*, That in lieu of the duties now imposed by law there shall be levied and collected upon printing paper unsized, used for books and newspapers exclusively, twenty per centum ad valorem."[43] The history and scope of the tax are obscure. No prior or subsequent versions of the tax have been uncovered, and no repealing statute has been discovered, either.[44]

The subject of a paper tax, however, had been earlier noted in connection with the work of the Ways and Means Committee when it undertook a comprehensive taxation scheme in 1862.[45] It appears that the tax had been part of that committee's work, although its passage was deferred or channeled differently than the advertising tax. Shortly after the Ways and Means Committee reported its tax recommendations — almost a year before the paper tax was enacted — the *New York Times* noted that "[t]he cause of popular or newspaper knowledge comes in for its [tax] burden in the shape of an excise upon all printing paper, and a tax upon the proceeds of newspaper advertisements."[46] The specific terms of the paper tax proposal then being referred to, however, are unknown, because by the time the Ways and Means Committee's bill made it to the floor of the House, no paper tax was included.

The paper tax was introduced as H.R. 779 and approved on March 3, 1863.[47] No substantive debate on the bill occurred in the House, and no stated opposition appeared. In December 1862, however, the omnipresent Representative Colfax had introduced a bill to reduce the rate of the duty on paper. His bill was read twice to the House, with no attendant debate, and was then referred to the Committee on Ways and Means, where it apparently died.[48] Colfax's bill may have related to an already-existing import duty on paper, and following its referral to the Committee it may have reemerged as Section 5. Indeed, Section 5 was enacted as part of an act modifying duties on imports "and for other purposes." The terms of the tax imply a general applicability, not one restricted to imported paper, and the *Times* reference to an earlier effort supports this view. It cannot be determined with certainty whether, despite its broad language, it was understood to have a more limited application to imported paper alone. This seems unlikely, however, given its application to paper "used for books and newspapers exclusively."[49]

Conclusion

The drawing of general conclusions from the federal experience with knowledge taxes must await the survey of experience in the states during the nineteenth century. The values, attitudes, and exigencies of the times are best understood in the broader setting of national experience on the local, state, and national levels combined.

It is worth noting here, however, that in the national experience with the advertising and paper taxes we see a theme that will be manifested, as well, on the state and local levels. The original distrust of knowledge taxes, it seems, was substantially if not principally grounded in suspicion of a distant sovereign whose interests were increasingly at odds with those of the new American colonies. On the other hand, when ideas emerged in the Colonies and in the new republic — new public imperatives, we might call them — and when those ideas were fueled by patriotism and legitimated by democratic government, there was surprisingly little hesitancy to employ the taxing power in their service. Diversity of thought was chiefly recognized when the source of "diversity" was local, and the threat external. In this respect it was not the lesson of the English struggle against taxation of knowledge that was recalled, even though its final stages were occurring contemporaneously with enactment of the federal taxes. Instead, the lesson recalled, if any, may have been that of the colonial taxes, and that lesson — freedom from taxation by a distant sovereign — posed no obstacle to taxation by the American government.

Notes

1. The language of state charters and enactments was cast in the broadest of terms, as illustrated by Virginia, Pennsylvania, and Delaware:

a. Virginia Declaration of Rights of 1776, apparently the first enactment to protect freedom of the press, provided: "That the Freedom of the Press is one of the greatest bulwarks of liberty, and can never be restrained but by despotick [sic] Governments." 1 Bernard Schwartz, *The Bill of Rights: A Documentary History* 235 (1971), citing 6 *American Archives* 1561 (P. Force ed., 1846).

b. Article XII of the Pennsylvania Declaration of Rights of 1776, the first constitutional enactment of freedom of the press and speech, provided: "That the people have a right to freedom of speech, and of writing, and publishing their sentiments; therefore the freedom of the press ought not to be restrained." *Id.* at 266, citing 5 *The Federal and State Constitutions, Colonial Charters, and Other Organic Laws* 3081–92 (F. Thorpe ed., 1909).

c. Section 23 of the Delaware Declaration of Rights of 1776 provided: "That the liberty of the press ought to be inviolably preserved." *Id.* at 278, citing 1 *Laws of the State of Delaware, 1700–1797* 79–81 (1797). The Maryland Declaration of Rights was identical in this provision to that of Delaware. See *id.* at 284.

The other state enactments were modeled after one of these three. See *id.* at 287 (N.C.), 300 (Ga.), 324 (Vt.), 335 (S.C.), 338 (Mass.), 378 (N.H.).

2. There appears to be no scholarly literature on the taxes. The principal component was a differential advertising tax on particular classes of newspapers, and the other component was an extremely obscure paper tax enacted in 1863. An Act to Modify Existing Laws Imposing Duties, etc., ch. 77, § 5, 12 Stat. 742 (1863). See *infra* notes 41–49 and accompanying text.

3. *Cong. Globe*, 37th Cong., 2d Sess. 419 (1862). The original version, to the extent that it differed from that reported from the Committee on the Post Office and Post Roads, is unknown. H.R. 215 was reported out of the Committee and debated on the floor, and provided in relevant part that: "from and after April 1, 1862, it shall not be lawful for any railroad company, express company, common carrier, or other company or person, to carry for hire, or for sale or distribution, upon or along any post road or postal route on which the mails of the United States are now or shall be transported, any newspapers or periodicals not contained in the mails of the United States, and on which, if carried by such mails, postage would be chargeable by law; and that any person or corporation so offending shall forfeit and pay to the United States for each offense the sum of $100, to be recovered by action of *qui tam*, one half for the use of the informer, and the other half for the use of the Post Office Department; but this prohibition shall not apply to any company, person, or agent who shall have at any time written authority from the Post Office Department to carry such matter outside of the United States mails upon specified routes; and such license may be granted by the Postmaster General, under regulations to be by him prescribed and conditioned upon the due observance thereof, providing thereby for the payment of rates of postage thereon not exceeding the rates now fixed by law; but this prohibition shall not apply to any mail route upon the seas to foreign countries; and any package carried otherwise than herein provided may be seized by any authorized agent or officer of the Post Office Department, and disposed of as

the Postmaster General shall direct." *Id*. A second section authorized the Postmaster General to provide and regulate the sale of suitable stamps or labels. A third section exempted from the mail requirement travelers who carried reading material "not intended for sale, distribution, or delivery to others." *Id*.

4. Newspapers, it appears, had been subject to postage (although at a reduced rate) since 1792. Prior to 1792, no mention was made of newspapers in the postal requirements, although the imposition of postage is implied during the colonial period by the valuable franking privileges which attracted printers to positions in the postal system. See A. D. Smith, *The Development of Rates of Postage* 148–49 (1917).

From 1792 until the Civil War, rates for newspaper and periodical postage were established. They were frequently modified, and from 1845 to 1847 small newspapers were allowed to pass through the post free of charge within a limited geographic range (30 miles). Again in 1851 free postage was given to small papers within the county of publication, and this practice appears to have continued until the 1860s. *Id*. at 150–52.

As to the actual practice of charging postage for newspapers under these regulations, we have little other than Representative Colfax's statement to guide us. He asserted that "[f]or the first fifty-six years of our national history, from 1789 up to 1845, the universal rule . . . was that all mailable matter should go through the mails. They prohibited from going outside of the mail, letters, newspapers, pamphlets, and periodicals of any kind, and they were properly transmitted by mail." *Cong. Globe*, 37th Cong., 2d Sess. 421 (Jan. 21, 1862) (statement of Rep. Colfax). There is some reason to believe, however, based on sentiment strongly expressed in Congress, that the actual practice departed from the strict letter of the rate regulations — possibly through the franking expedient. See Smith at 149–50, citing "Debates and Proceedings in the Congress of the United States," Dec. 16, 1791.

The history of the postal system and the rates of postage are summarized in Chapter 8.

5. On the floor Representative Colfax said, "I think I need not tell the house that this is an unpopular bill with the great metropolitan press of the country, and with the newsdealers who receive these papers comparatively free from all charge for carriage." *Cong. Globe*, 37th Cong., 2d Sess. 419 (Jan. 21, 1862). Colfax noted that the following newspapers opposed the measure: the *Boston Herald*, *New York Tribune*, *New York Times*, *Cincinnati Commercial*, *Cincinnati Gazette*, *New York Ledger*, *New York Evening Post*, and *Philadelphia Inquirer*. The *New York Herald* was the exception. *Id*. at 419–25.

6. *N.Y. Times*, Jan. 19, 1862, at 4.

7. *N.Y. Times*, Jan. 20, 1862, at 5. But see *N.Y. Times*, Mar. 5, 1862, at 4, for a withdrawal from this position, quoted at note 28.

8. *Cong. Globe*, 37th Cong., 2d Sess. 422–23 (1862).

9. See Minneapolis Star & Tribune Co. v. Minnesota Comm'r of Revenue, 460 U.S. 575 (1983); Arkansas Writers' Project, Inc. v. Ragland, 481 U.S. 221 (1987); Randall P. Bezanson, "Political Agnosticism, Editorial Freedom, and Government Neutrality Toward the Press," 72 *Iowa L. Rev.* 1359 (1987).

10. *Cong. Globe*, 37th Cong., 2d Sess. 420 (1862); see also *N.Y. Times*, Feb. 11, 1862, at 4.

11. *Cong. Globe*, 37th Cong., 2d Sess. 420 (1862).

12. *Id.*

13. U.S. Const., art. I, § 8, cl. 7.

14. *Cong. Globe*, 37th Cong., 2d Sess. 421 (1862); quoted *supra* note 4.

15. See *supra* notes 4–5.

16. It is unclear whether the mails would, in fact, have been cheaper. In any event, the newspapers' own distribution system was probably significantly quicker. Mr. Colfax's reasoning was as follows: "It is said that this [H.R. 215] will enhance the price of the papers to the people. I say that it will not, and I propose to give you my own experience on this subject. I propose to show that by receiving their newspapers through the mails the people will get them cheaper than they now do. . . . In my own town we get all our news from the Chicago dailies, which reach there about nine o'clock in the morning, and the people buy them by hundreds, paying five cents for a single number, or twenty cents a week for them, which amounts to $10.40 a year. The subscription to the highest priced of those papers, by mail, is $7.50 a year. The postage upon each paper, if carried within the State where printed, is a quarter of a cent, if paid one quarter in advance; if carried to another State outside of that where printed, half a cent. The postage on a newspaper, therefore, published in Illinois and carried to a subscriber in Indiana, Wisconsin, or any other State, being half a cent apiece, is $1.56 per year, making the cost of the paper $8.56 a year, instead of $10.40, which they now pay." *Cong. Globe*, 37th Cong., 2d Sess. 422 (1862).

17. *Id.* at 423.

18. See *infra* text accompanying note 28.

19. *Cong. Globe*, 37th Cong., 2d Sess. 424 (1862).

20. *Id.*

21. *Id.*

22. *Id.*

23. *Id.* at 425.

24. *Id.* at 426–27; see *N.Y. Times*, Jan. 22, 1862, at 1 (reporting parts of the debate).

25. See *N.Y. Times*, Feb. 11, 1862, at 4; Mar. 4, 1862, at 4.

26. See *infra* note 30.

27. *N.Y. Times*, Mar. 4, 1862, at 4; see *id.* at 8 (report of the tax abstract: "Printing paper, three mills per pound. . . . Advertisements, five per cent. on amount of receipts annually").

28. *N.Y. Times*, Mar. 5, 1862, at 4.

29. *Cong. Globe*, 37th Cong., 2d Sess. 2339 (1862).

30. An Act to Provide Internal Revenue, etc., ch. 119, § 88, 12 Stat. 432, 472 (1862). The text of the Act follows:

And be it further enacted, That on and after the first day of August, eighteen hundred and sixty-two, there shall be levied, collected, and paid by any person or persons, firm, or company, publishing any newspaper, magazine, review, or other literary, scientific, or news publication, issued periodically, on the gross receipts for all advertisements, or all matters for the insertion of which in said newspaper or other publication, as aforesaid, or in extras, supplements, sheets, or flyleaves accompanying the same, pay is required or received, a duty of three per centum; and the person or persons, firm or company, owning, possessing, or having the care or management of any and every such newspaper or other publication, as aforesaid, shall make a list or return quarterly, commencing as heretofore mentioned, containing the gross amount of receipts as aforesaid, and the amount of duties which have accrued thereon, and render the same to the assistant assessor of the respective districts where such newspaper, magazine, review, or other literary or news publication is or may be published, which list or return shall have annexed a declaration, under oath or affirmation, to be made according to the manner and form which may be from time to time prescribed by the Commissioner of Internal Revenue, of the owner, possessor, or person having the care or management of such newspaper, magazine, review, or other publication, as aforesaid, that the same is true and correct, and shall also, quarterly, and at the time of making said list or return, pay to the collector or deputy collector of the district, as aforesaid, the full amount of said duties.

(*Id.*) Fines were also provided in the statute. If failure to pay was not willful, the penalty was five percent of the amount due. If it was deliberate, a fine of $500 was imposed. The statute also permitted publications to add the duty to the price of advertisements "where the rate or price of advertising is fixed" by law. The final proviso read: "*Provided, further*, That the receipts for advertisements to the amount of one thousand dollars, by any person or persons, firm, or company, publishing any newspaper, magazine, review, or other literary, scientific, news publication, issued periodically, shall be exempt from duty: *And provided, further*, That all newspapers whose circulation does not exceed two thousand copies shall be exempted from all taxes for advertisements." § 88, 12 Stat. at 473.

31. § 88, 12 Stat. at 473 (emphasis supplied).

32. 297 U.S. 233 (1936).

33. An Act to Amend Existing Laws Relating to Internal Revenue, etc., ch. 169, § 34, 14 Stat. 471, 485 (1867).

34. See Isaiah Thomas, *The History of Printing in America* 16 (Weathervane Books 1970) (1874); Simon N. North, *History and Present Condition of the Newspaper and Periodical Press of the United States* 86–87 (1884).

35. North reported the following figures in his work for the United States Census Bureau in 1884: "*Dailies*: receipts from advertising, 49.17%; from subscriptions, 50.83%. *Weeklies & Other*: receipts from advertising, 38.95%; from subscriptions, 61.05%. *Combined*: receipts from advertising, 43.97%; from subscriptions, 56.03%." North at 85.

36. *Id.* at 86. It is interesting to note that North did not regard the advertising tax, Section 88, as a knowledge tax. In the course of his *History*, he proudly proclaimed that, with the unfortunate exception of Virginia during the first half of the nineteenth century, the American press has never been subjected to a knowledge tax. The only reason he produced the table in the text was for use as evidence of growth in advertising. *Id.*

37. See *Cong. Globe*, 37th Cong., 2d Sess. 424 (1862) (statement of Rep. Colfax regarding high collection costs of stamp tax in smaller towns).

38. See An Act to Provide Internal Revenue, etc., ch. 119 § 88, 12 Stat. 432, 473 (1862) (first proviso permitting press to pass cost of advertising tax on to its advertisers notwithstanding any contrary federal or state law).

39. See Harold L. Nelson, *Freedom of Press from Hamilton to the Warren Court* 223 (1967). Nelson reports: "On the same night [August 20, 1861], Ambrose S. Kimball, editor of the 'Essex County Democrat,' published once a week, at Haverhill, Mass., was violently taken from his house by an excited crowd, and refusing to give such information as was demanded of him, 'he was covered with a coat of tar and feathers, and ridden on a rail through the town.' He subsequently was made to take an oath that he would 'never again write or publish articles against the North and in favor of secession.'

"About the same time the printing office of the 'Jeffersonian,' a weekly paper, published at Westchester, Pa., was destroyed." *Id.* (no citations in original). Nelson says of press freedom during the period of the Civil War: "Through it all ran the gang or mob that threatened, manhandled, or tarred editors, required changes in editorial policy, burned print shops, and had its way. . . . [T]here were at least six cases of threats and violence against Northern newspapers and editors from angered citizens and soldiers during the war." *Id.* at xxvi–xxvii. John A. Marshall reports many instances of violence against the press, including the following: "On the evening of the 17th of April, 1861, Mr. [Archibald] McGregor was seized by a mob of several hundred excited and infuriated men . . . their excuse being that his paper [the *Stark County Democrat*] did not favor the war. . . . The mob were about to hurl him into the canal, when the Mayor . . . came to his rescue. . . . On the night of August 22, 1861, the newspaper and job office of the 'Stark County Democrat' was broken into by a squad of new recruits. . . . The maurauders did their work effectively, making a bonfire in the street, and burning wood, type, stands, cases, and all that was combustible. The destruction was complete." John A. Marshall, *American Bastille* 118–20 (16th ed. 1875). See also Leon Whipple, *The Story of Civil Liberty in the United States* 148–49 (1927).

40. See North, *supra* note 34.

41. See Preston v. Finley, 72 F. 850 (W.D. Tex. 1896); Baldwin v. State, 21 Tex. Crim. 591 (1886); Thompson v. State, 17 Tex. Ct. App. 253 (1884); *In re* Jager, 29 S.C. 438, 7 S.E. 605 (1888); City of Norfolk v. Norfolk Landmark Pub. Co., 95 Va. 564, 28 S.E. 959 (1898), discussed in Chapter 4.

42. § 5, 12 Stat. at 742.

43. *Id.*

44. It is possible that the provision was repealed as part of the codification of the United States Code in the 1870s, or as part of a general revision of the applicable import duty provisions.

45. See *supra* notes 25–27 and accompanying text.

46. *N.Y. Times*, Mar. 4, 1862, at 4.

47. See *Cong. Globe*, 37th Cong., 3d Sess. 1488, 1495 (1863).

48. See *id.* at 91 (1862).

49. § 5, 12 Stat. at 742.

4. State and Municipal Knowledge Taxes in Nineteenth-Century America

Following ratification of the Constitution and the Bill of Rights and throughout the nineteenth century, knowledge taxation was not uncommon at the state and local level. On reflection, and notwithstanding the history of the English taxes, including those imposed on the "unrepresented" colonies, this is not surprising. Sources of much-needed revenue were limited, the earlier colonial history of knowledge taxation, marked by concerns about taxation without representation, seemed inapt, and in view of the regional and cultural diversity of the states, state and local governments were viewed as closely aligned with the political will of the governed. State and local knowledge taxes predated and postdated the federal taxes imposed during the Civil War. More significantly, the knowledge taxes imposed at the state level, as well as those imposed at even more local levels, often had a very different and more censorial character. Such taxes, in short, were often more directly reminiscent in purpose, although not necessarily in form, of the early English taxes.

As time progressed, the censorial characteristics common to early state knowledge taxes became less prevalent, or at least less obvious, especially with the rise of sales and use taxation and the inclusion of periodicals within those taxing schemes. In its place, economic protectionism often became an obvious, although usually implicit, feature of the taxing schemes. We will accordingly attempt a rough division of the consideration of state knowledge taxation into two parts. In this chapter we will review examples of early state and municipal taxation in the nineteenth century, exploring the use of knowledge taxes to exert control over the press. In a later chapter we will turn to the twentieth century, when more mature, generally applicable, and apparently benign forms of state and local taxation evolved.

The nineteenth century review of state and local taxation will be illustrative, rather than exhaustive, in character. Four states have been selected for study, largely on grounds of geographic and cultural diversity, in order to determine the manner and extent to which the classic forms of knowledge tax were employed. The states are Virginia, a southern state and former colony; Massachusetts, an industrialized northern state and former colony; Texas, a western frontier state; and Illinois, a midwestern state with growing economic and political power. Experience in other states will be mentioned at various points, but no effort has been made to survey the experience in all states, nor is it claimed that the experience in the four selected states is representative of the nation as a whole.

Knowledge Taxes in Virginia

Perhaps the clearest example of knowledge taxation by a state is provided by Virginia. Virginia's history of knowledge taxes involves the widest variety of forms of taxation, includes the most diverse mixture of purposes and motives, and, with the exception of colonial taxes in Massachusetts, spans the longest period of time. Newspapers in Virginia were singled out to pay state duties on practically every aspect of their business at some point during the nineteenth century. The relatively constant stream of taxation included taxes on paper, taxes on printing presses, and taxes imposed on the dissemination of the completed publication. Perhaps as remarkable as the proliferation and variety of knowledge taxes is the apparent absence of literature on the subject.[1] For the most part, the only record we have is the texts of the statutes themselves.

Little if anything, of course, can be conclusively stated about the purposes and effects of the taxes from the statutory texts alone. There is, however, some historical background that may place them in context, although no direct conclusions about purpose and effect can be drawn from it.[2] In colonial Virginia the press had been prohibited from operating within the borders of the colony. As one author put it, "[t]he rulers in the colony of Virginia in the seventeenth century, judged it best not to permit public schools, nor to allow the use of the press."[3] The colonial heritage, therefore, was not adverse to the protection of the rulers and the body politic from the activities of the press. The extent to which this heritage was directly reflected in the actions of the Virginia legislatures and courts during the nineteenth century cannot be known, but, at least with respect to the slavery question, efforts to exert explicit and direct control over expression continued through most of the nineteenth century.[4] It is certainly clear that neither legislatures nor courts considered taxes on the press to be constitutionally defective, although they also purported to protect freedom of expression.

KNOWLEDGE TAXATION AT THE STATE LEVEL IN VIRGINIA

With the exception of peddler taxes, which are notable but are considered later, it appears that the first tax imposed on newspapers in Virginia was the Act of February 20, 1813.[5] Under the terms of the statute, a tax was imposed "for every printing press of newspapers, [in] the amount of four annual subscriptions to each paper." The precise operation of the tax is unclear. It appears from the text of the Act that the amount of the tax was calculated by adding the sum total of the cost of four subscriptions to every newspaper printed by the press. A press that printed three different newspapers, therefore, would pay a tax in the amount of four subscriptions to each of the three papers. While the price of subscriptions is not known with particularity, as the amount varied depending on the newspaper, and the circulation varied widely as well, the tax is unlikely to have represented a heavy economic burden for newspaper printers. It did, however, provide a mechanism by which the government was knowledgeable of the newspapers published throughout Virginia. It is noteworthy, as well, that the tax was specifically laid upon newspapers. It did not constitute an element of a more broadly applicable tax laid on other categories of nonprinted matter, and other forms of publication, presumably including at least some periodical publications, were not taxed.[6] Newspapers, alone, were subject to the tax.

The tax on newspaper printers apparently continued for about three years. The original tax, which seems to have expired after one year, was enacted again in 1814 and 1815.[7] After 1815 no record of reenactment by succeeding legislatures could be found, and it is therefore assumed that the tax expired by its own terms in 1816. No records have been discovered concerning the administration or effect of the tax, nor the amount of revenue raised by it. Likewise, no evidence of opposition to the tax has been discovered, although little should be inferred from this, for the records of legislative debate are nonexistent. It is interesting, however, that the historians of the period failed to make note of the tax or any reaction to it.[8]

It was not until March 1843 that another newspaper tax is found in the Virginia statutes, when a tax was once again imposed on newspaper printing presses. The Act of March 27, 1843, provided that "there shall be collected and paid . . . upon every printing press of newspapers, twice the amount charged per annum for a subscription to the highest priced paper that may issue from such press: *Provided, however*, That no press shall pay a higher tax than ten dollars."[9] As with the earlier tax, the incidence of the 1843 tax was on printing presses, and it singled out newspaper presses for taxation. By all appearances, however, the tax was nominal in amount, in no event exceeding ten dollars. Its impact, therefore, was likely negligible except, perhaps, to the very smallest, struggling newspaper printers. As with the earlier tax, the 1843 tax was limited by its own terms to one year. The statutes indicate that it continued in effect through 1848, as it was reenacted in each legislative session between 1843 and 1848.[10]

Licensing of sellers of newspapers and periodicals, as well as pamphlets, began in Virginia in 1852. In that year a statute was enacted requiring the "commissioners of the revenue" to "assess[] licenses . . . and the amount of tax to be paid by . . . all pedlars of pamphlets or periodical papers."[11] The license and tax were part of a more general set of licensing requirements. Virginia had previously taxed hawkers and peddlers, but the scope of the earlier acts in relation to newspapers and periodical publications, as well as pamphlets, books, and prints, is unclear. The earlier acts most likely included many and perhaps all of the periodical peddlers covered by the 1852 act, but without the specificity as to subject and at a higher rate.[12] With the 1852 act, any doubts about inclusion of peddlers of periodicals and pamphlets were resolved; the former tax continued, now apparently being made explicitly applicable to peddlers of periodicals and pamphlets, and a new license fee in an amount to be set by the commissioner of licenses (credited against the tax) was also imposed.[13] In 1854 the license fee was set at five dollars.[14]

In 1856 Virginia revised and expanded the license and tax on peddlers of periodicals and pamphlets, and in so doing increased the tax and differentiated between local and foreign peddlers. The 1856 act imposed a tax "[o]n every license to a person obtaining subscriptions to books, or to a person selling prints, or to a pedlar of pamphlets or periodical papers, each twenty-five dollars: provided, however, if the hawker, pedlar, print seller or person obtaining subscriptions to books taxed under this section has not been a resident in the state for two years and in the county one year, the tax shall in each case be two hundred dollars."[15] The license and tax scheme appears by this act to have been consolidated into a single tax on peddlers of periodicals and pamphlets, as well as peddlers of book subscriptions and prints, and out-of-state peddlers were subject to a non-negligible eightfold increase in license tax.

The 1856 act continued in effect by its own terms until 1860, when it was at least partially repealed. The 1860 act provided that a license was no longer required "to receive subscriptions for or to sell newspapers, books, pamphlets or other periodicals printed and published in this state."[16] It is noteworthy that the 1860 act specifically exempted the license tax on newspaper sellers, a term not employed in the previous acts, but which, by implication, seems to have been included in the definition of "periodical papers." It is also interesting, although of uncertain significance, that the exemption applied only to the receipt or sale of newspapers, books, pamphlets, or other periodicals "printed and published in" Virginia. By implication, the preexisting license tax continued on out-of-state books and periodicals, although there is no other record to confirm the actual continued application of licensing to such publications.

The hiatus in licensing — at least for Virginia printers and publishers — was short-lived. The next year, 1861, saw the licensing system reestablished and, through a series of enactments during the Civil War, "refined" to achieve less benign — or at least more explicit — ends. The first statute was enacted in April 1861 and reinstated the basic framework of the preexisting licensing.[17] The new act required that "a person obtaining subscriptions to books, maps, prints, pamphlets, or periodicals" obtain a license and pay a tax of twenty-five dollars for every county in which such subscriptions were obtained, as well as a flat license fee of twenty-five dollars. For persons who had not been residents of Virginia for two years, the license tax was two hundred dollars, with that amount being required both for the license itself, as well as on a county basis.[18] The license tax did not expressly mention newspapers, although it seems clear that it covered newspaper subscriptions by virtue of the breadth of language used. Unlike the original license tax, the 1861 tax applied to sale of subscriptions — perhaps a sufficiently ordinary form of distribution at the time to permit a distinction between single issue sales and subscriptions for periods of time. The term, however, is of ambiguous meaning in light of the tax's application to books as well as pamphlets and periodicals, and it may be that the coverage was not intended to be narrowed so as to exclude single sales. We can only speculate on this point, as the operation of the tax is unclear from other historical materials at the time. Finally, it is notable that, with the county-based assessment, and with the amount set at twenty-five dollars per county, the level of the tax burden became, with the 1861 act, non-negligible. In view of the average cost of newspapers and periodicals, which ranged in the pennies, twenty-five dollars per county would require a rather high level of sales to justify payment of the tax. For the out-of-state sellers[19] the tax was, almost surely, prohibitive, a result that was no doubt desired.

The already increased and nonnegligible license tax in the 1861 act was increased the next year from twenty-five to thirty-eight dollars per license and per county. The nonresident fee was increased commensurately to three hundred dollars, and was now applied to any person who had "not been a resident of the Confederate States" for two years.[20] The increase was no doubt attributable in large part to imperatives of the war effort: the desperate need to raise funds to continue the struggle; and the likely concomitant interest in restricting the influence of those not sympathetic to the Confederate cause (and their presumably Northern publications).

This inference is strongly suggested by two further amendments that followed closely on the heels of the tax increase. In October 1862 a provision was added requiring applicants for a license to take an oath "that he will not pay out within the limits of this commonwealth, notes of any denomination, issued by banks, corporations or individuals, without authority of law," or else pay four times the applicable license tax.[21] The relation to the Confederacy, reflected in the required medium of exchange, was further reflected in a subsequent enactment in March 1863, by which the twin objectives of exclusion of foreign (Northern) writings and obedience to the Southern cause may have been exacted. By an act dated March 28, 1863, the license tax on books, prints, pamphlets, and periodicals was raised from thirty-eight to sixty-five dollars for sellers who were Confederate State residents, and from three hundred to five hundred dollars for those not residents (of the Confederate States) for two years. Religious materials sold or distributed by Confederate residents were exempt from tax, and the entire license requirement was removed for any books, newspapers, or pamphlets "written by citizens of, or published in the Confederate States."[22] The same act imposed a new tax on paper. The act required that a license be obtained, and tax paid therefor, by "every person, firm, company or corporation, for the privilege of carrying on any of the occupations following, viz: . . . The manufacture and sale of paper of all kinds."[23]

It is quite remarkable, given the dramatic and even radical changes enacted in 1862 and 1863, that virtually nothing has been written or documented in connection with these license and paper taxes. With the advent of the war and the establishment of the Confederacy, a license tax in an almost confiscatory amount was enacted in Virginia, the taxing scheme became explicitly discriminatory, and a companion tax and license system for paper was imposed. The conjunction of these enactments can leave little doubt that their purpose was not strictly revenue-related; rather, they seem to have been overtly designed to exert government control through the sheer weight of economic burden, and to eliminate the distribution of publications deemed dangerous, because foreign, to the Confederate cause. They also provide an interesting, and disturbing, parallel with the federal knowledge tax, which was also enacted in the fever pitch of civil war, although it was not calculated to exert specific control over the printed word.

The lesson to be learned—beyond the general one concerning the types and dangers of knowledge taxes—is the age-old one: that liberties are most at risk in times of national stress, when the appearance of genuine consensus in the populace makes the value of diversity less apparent, and when the majoritarian or democratic processes are *least* equipped to protect that diversity, and therefore are least to be trusted with our liberty. Whether or not Justice Holmes had the Civil War in mind at the time,[24] the views he expressed more than fifty years later in *Abrams v. United States* apply here as well: "Persecution for the expression of opinions seems to me perfectly logical. If you have no doubt of your premises or your power and want a certain result with all your heart you naturally express your wishes in law and sweep away all opposition."[25]

Thankfully, the odious Virginia knowledge taxes were short-lived. They passed into history when the occasion of their creation passed. The paper tax and the vendor tax apparently were suspended on March 3, 1864, and repealed on March 3, 1865.[26] The former taxes were replaced in 1866 with a generally applicable licensing tax on merchant sales (in nominal amount), and a system for licensing and taxing sellers of religious books and periodicals published in other states was enacted.[27] While the tax on sellers of books and periodicals was differential, with Virginia publishers (including Virginia newspapers) being exempted, the tax was nominal in amount and, at least in comparison to the earlier regime, benign in appearance. Its principal purpose was most likely the protection of in-state merchants and control of door-to-door peddling. In this respect the subsequent enactment paralleled similar peddling laws enacted broadly throughout the United States.[28] Despite these later enactments, with the repeal of the pre-1865 taxes came the end of the most odious forms of knowledge taxes at the state level in Virginia.

MUNICIPAL KNOWLEDGE TAXES IN VIRGINIA
The imposition of knowledge taxes was not the exclusive function of state government in Virginia, and in this respect Virginia is most likely no different from other states. The use of local taxes and regulations on the

press has been noted by others,[29] and will not be recounted here. One municipal knowledge tax in Virginia is worthy of note, however, not only because it illustrates the use of such taxing mechanisms at the local level, but also because it reflects the then-prevailing judicial attitude toward the constitutionality of such taxes.

In April 1897 the city of Norfolk enacted an ordinance imposing a tax of one hundred dollars per year "on every person, firm, or corporation . . . engaged in the publication of a newspaper."[30] The circumstances surrounding passage of the tax, and its effect on newspapers, are not known. Shortly after its passage the ordinance was challenged by the Landmark Publishing Company, the New Pilot Publishing Company, and M. Glennan, owner of the Norfolk *Virginian*, in an action seeking an injunction against its enforcement. The grounds for the challenge included a claim that the tax constituted an abridgment of freedom of the press. Apparently agreeing with this line of reasoning, the district court issued the requested relief and enjoined enforcement of the ordinance.[31]

On appeal, the Virginia Supreme Court reversed, and in so doing expressed its views on the meaning of freedom of the press in the context of taxation. The court stated:

> A tax imposed upon the business of publishing a newspaper is not an abridgement of the freedom of the press. The guarantees of the Constitution and Bill of Rights in favor of freedom of the press, freedom of speech, and personal liberty, were never intended to restrict the right of taxation for the support of the government. If these guarantees did restrict the power of taxation, the government would soon be insolvent, and powerless to furnish the protection claimed.
>
> In the *Federalist*, p. 632, note, Mr. Hamilton says: "I know not by what logic it could be maintained that the declarations in the Constitution in favor of the freedom of the press would be a constitutional impediment to the imposition of duties upon publications by the State legislatures."[32]

The court, it appears, was making more than a point about the limited reach of the First Amendment, which by its terms applied only to actions of the federal government, and had not been otherwise construed at the time. This is clear from the reference to the government's insolvency in the absence of such taxing authority. The point is made clear, as well, by the court's quotation from *In re Jager*,[33] a South Carolina decision in which it was stated that "a tax on the business of publishing a newspaper is [no] more an abridgement of the liberty of the press than a tax on the office, type, and other material used in the business."[34] The Virginia court's view of freedom of the press was not uncharacteristic of other courts' views at the time,[35] and to the extent it reflected more broadly held perceptions as well, it would be difficult to conclude that taxation of the press, as a general proposition, and even a tax bearing down specifically on newspapers, was seen to pose serious threats to press freedoms.

Knowledge Taxes in Texas

The experience with knowledge taxes in Texas presents an interesting contrast with that of Virginia. Virginia was persistent throughout much of the nineteenth century in imposing taxes on the press, but more often than not the precise purpose and effect of the taxes were obscure and, with the exception of the taxes enacted in the early 1860s,[36] they were surely not blatant. In contrast, Texas very explicitly and blatantly employed its fiscal powers to injure unpopular newspapers.

In 1881 the Texas legislature enacted a statute that taxed "every person, firm or association of persons selling or offering for sale the illustrated Police News, Police Gazette, and other illustrated publications of like character, the sum of five hundred dollars in each county in which such a sale may be made or offered to be made."[37] In 1895 the legislature enacted a similar measure. This one provided as follows:

> There shall be levied on and collected from every person, firm or association of persons selling or offering for sale the "Sunday Sun," the "Kansas City Sunday Sun," or other publications of like character, whether illustrated or not, the sum of five hundred dollars in each county in which sale may be made or offered to be made.[38]

At the time the taxes were enacted, Texas had 226 counties.[39] Were the affected periodicals sold in every county, the total tax would have been $113,000 per year, an obviously confiscatory amount. By way of contrast, the tax liability of the American Press Company, addressed some fifty years later in the *Grosjean* case,[40] would have been only $1,652.26 per year.[41]

In view of the specific focus and confiscatory character of the taxes, it is not surprising that they were challenged. The first statute was challenged by a San Antonio newsdealer named Thompson, who was convicted for selling the *Illustrated Police News* and *Police Gazette* without a license. In *Thompson v. State*,[42] the newsdealer's conviction was affirmed by the Texas Court of Appeals. Although Thompson did not argue that the statute contravened freedom of the press, the court's answer to his vagueness claim provides useful information about the purpose of the statute and the court's expansive view of the taxing power, even as to newspapers. Quoting Cooley, the court stated:

> The power to impose taxes is one so unlimited in force and so searching in extent, that the courts scarcely venture to declare that it is subject to any restrictions whatever. . . . It is not for this court, therefore, to say whether this tax is oppressive. . . . It is to be conclusively presumed that the Legislature had good and sufficient reasons for imposing this tax.[43]

Under this view, the statute's purpose was effectively irrelevant, as it was "conclusively" deemed proper. Indeed, the court said as much, and much more as well, in the following passage:

> [The tax] is leveled at a well known class of publications which were regarded by the Legislature as immoral and pernicious in their tendency, and there can be no misunderstanding the class of publications intended to be embraced in the act. . . . It is a matter of notoriety that . . . these publications were of an indecent, immoral and pernicious character, and that many of the citizens of the State demanded some legislation that would prevent, restrict or regulate this class of publications. . . . The tax imposed by this law is not a tax upon property, but upon a privilege, and is a police regulation as well as a tax for revenue. . . . It was within the discretion and power of the Legislature to enact as many statutes upon the subject as were thought by them to be necessary to regulate, restrict or prohibit the evil which they were seeking to remedy.[44]

While the court's attitude toward the liberty of the press was only implicit (though surely not friendly) in *Thompson*, the issue was explicitly addressed in a later case. In *Ex Parte Neill*[45] a similar law, although not in the form of a tax, was challenged, and this time the liberty of the press was explicitly broached. Neill was a newsdealer in Seguin, Texas, who was arrested and fined for violating a local ordinance that forbade the sale of the *Sunday Sun*. The ordinance was almost exactly the same as the Minnesota Gag Law at issue in *Near v. Minnesota*.[46] The ordinance declared:

> [T]hat the Sunday Sun, a paper said to be published at Chicago, Ill., is hereby declared a public nuisance, and its circulation prohibited within the corporate limits of the city of Seguin. Any person or persons offering to sell, barter, give away, or in any manner dispose of the Sunday Sun in violation of above ordinance shall be punished in a fine not to exceed one hundred dollars.[47]

Neill's application for a writ of habeas corpus had been denied by the district court, and the appellate court reversed on grounds of freedom of the press. The court held that the ordinance violated the Texas Bill of Rights, explaining that "[t]he power to prohibit the publication of newspapers is not within the compass of legislative action. . . . [W]e understand liberty of speech and of the press to imply, not only liberty to publish, but complete immunity from legal censure and punishment for the publication, so long as it is not harmful in its character."[48]

Standing side by side, the *Neill* and *Thompson* decisions were subsequently viewed as delineating the scope of legislative authority over the press.[49] Both cases involved publications that could be considered pernicious; it would be hard to distinguish the cases in terms of the content of the affected publication. Instead, the rule that emerged from the cases was that government could not ban outright and in advance the sale of a newspaper, but it could, with the sanction of the courts and with apparent consistency with the guarantee of freedom of the press, crush the newspaper through the exercise of the taxing power. Indeed, this is precisely what Texas did on the heels of the *Neill* decision when it enacted just two years later a five-hundred-dollar tax on sellers of the *Sunday Sun*.[50] It is also noteworthy, and ironic, that the penalty for violating the prohibition in the *Neill* case was one hundred dollars. The tax approved in the *Thompson* case was five hundred dollars per county. Freedom of the press, it seems, was not viewed as much of a limit on the imposition of knowledge taxes, at least in Texas.

Knowledge Taxes in Massachusetts

Experience with taxation of the press in Massachusetts began during the middle of the eighteenth century. In 1755 duties were imposed by the colonial government on paper and parchment.[51] As discussed more fully in an earlier chapter,[52] the tax was not popular in at least some quarters—most notably one Boston newspaper—and it expired in 1757 by limitation.[53] Soon after the end of the American Revolution, the newly formed Massachusetts government passed a tax on newspapers and almanacs.[54] Although the purpose of the tax was to raise revenue, it, too, proved unpopular, as evidenced by its repeal the following year.[55] These attempts would be the last blatant attempts at taxing knowledge for more than a century in Massachusetts. But the issue of knowledge taxation was still present throughout the late eighteenth century and the entire nineteenth century, although it was manifested in somewhat different form. And it has arisen again in quite explicit terms in very recent times.

An appropriate place to begin our brief inquiry into the history of taxation of knowledge in Massachusetts is with its 1780 constitution.[56] In contrast to the First Amendment of the soon to be drafted United States Constitution, Massachusetts included one article devoted solely to the freedom of the press.[57] It provided that "the liberty of the press is essential to the security of freedom in a state; it ought not, therefore, to be restrained in this Commonwealth."[58] The apparently clear and concise wording of the clause was not so clear to those who would interpret it during the subsequent years. The major problem that was debated was whether the free press clause merely granted the Massachusetts press freedom from previous license, or whether something more substantial was comprehended within its language.[59]

Two early jurists in Massachusetts disagreed over the breadth of the sixteenth article. Chief Justice Cushing wrote to John Adams in 1789, observing that "[t]he words of our article [XVI] understood according to plain English, make no such distinction, and must include subsequent restraint, as much as previous restraint."[60] Chief Justice Parker, however, read the provision differently. He noted that "it is well understood, and received as a commentary on this provision for the liberty of the press, that it was intended to prevent all such *previous restraints* upon publications. . . . The liberty of the press was to be unrestrained, but he who used it was to be responsible in case of abuse."[61] By either interpretation, however, the New Declaration of Rights limited any restraint on the press prior to publication. And however narrowly or broadly the constitution was to be read, the actual legislative policy followed — at least in the tax setting — made the point moot.

Throughout the nineteenth century the General Court of the Commonwealth — the legislative branch of government — appears to have imposed no license or tax on newspapers directly.[62] No record could be discovered of any serious attempts — even unsuccessful ones — to enact legislation specially taxing the press or licensing newspapers or pamphlets during the nineteenth century. Indeed, when the issue of taxation of knowledge did arise in the context of general licensing and taxing regulations, exemption of knowledge was the rule.

Until 1846, Massachusetts law forbade the hawking or peddling of any "goods, wares, or merchandize" within the commonwealth.[63] A statute passed in 1846 expanded the laws on hawking and divided the merchandise that hawkers could sell into two categories: goods that could be sold only with a license and goods that could be sold without a license.[64] The statute specifically included "newspapers, books, [and] pamphlets" as goods that could be sold without a license.[65] A provision did permit town officials to restrain the sale of any goods — including goods for which a license was not required — by minors, but as of 1846 newspaper hawkers were not subject to any license fees or taxes.[66]

Despite many revisions in the laws pertaining to the procedure for licenses, there was no change for forty years in the ability of hawkers to sell newspapers without a license.[67] And even then the change did not pertain to taxation or licensing, but to regulation of sale. In 1883, the General Court enacted a law that allowed cities to regulate hawkers, even those who could sell without a license. The provision read: "Any city may by ordinance make such regulations respecting the exposing for sale [of newspapers and the like] as may be necessary and proper for preserving the public health and securing the peace and comfort of its inhabitants."[68] Although city officials could not charge for licenses, they could now regulate and impose fines for any violations of their regulations.[69] The scope of permitted regulation is unclear from the statute, but it presumably embraced the then-common restrictions on door-to-door peddling, location of street-corner sales, and the like. Regulations of this character were widely enacted at the state level in the late nineteenth century. While falling upon the distribution of knowledge, among other things, they were directed at ends of public tranquillity and privacy. The Massachusetts statute is notable because, unlike many others, the machinery of licensing and taxation widely employed in other states was explicitly made inapplicable to knowledge in the commonwealth.

As the nineteenth century drew to a close, Massachusetts had compiled a notable — indeed a remarkable — record of freedom from knowledge taxation. This freedom extended to books and pamphlets as well as newspapers. Only the ability to fine hawkers who violated local regulations existed as an explicit financial penalty. There were no taxes on printing presses, paper, or periodicals as there were in other states during the same time period.[70] At least as far as legislation was concerned, Massachusetts seemed to live up to the most expansive interpretation of Article XVI of its constitution, allowing a free and unfettered press.

This was not always to be so, as we shall see in a subsequent chapter recounting the twentieth-century Massachusetts experience with sales and use taxes, peddler taxes, and other forms of regulation. But that discussion must be deferred. For present purposes, Massachusetts exited the nineteenth century and entered the twentieth with a quite remarkable record of freedom from knowledge taxation, a record influenced, perhaps, by the bitter aftertaste of the two unsuccessful efforts at taxation in the late eighteenth century.

Knowledge Taxes in Illinois

Like Massachusetts, with its long history, Illinois, with its shorter one, serves as a useful vehicle for the study of knowledge taxation at the state level. The original colony and the frontier state provide both contrasts and parallels in their treatment of the press, differences and similarities that will prove instructive to our study of knowledge taxation.

Because it gained statehood in the early nineteenth century, Illinois laws can be traced from the time it gained territorial status to the present. The state's development from a remote outpost to a cosmopolitan center in just a century gives us a sort of time capsule in the history of taxation of knowledge. It is a capsule that contains all of the forms and varieties, all of the politics and principles, of knowledge taxation.

As with our extended treatment of Massachusetts, therefore, we will survey the history of Illinois in some depth, from territorial times to the present, from the era of hawkers and peddlers to the era of computers and electronic communication. In the present discussion we will trace the history of knowledge taxation through the end of the nineteenth century. In a later chapter we will follow that history to the present.[71]

PRE-STATEHOOD KNOWLEDGE TAXES IN ILLINOIS

Upon petition of the residents, Illinois was carved out of the Indiana Territory in 1809. The legislative body of the new territory held its first session in the summer of that year, and on July 21 adopted wholesale the Indiana Territory laws as its own and also enacted a few items of original legislation. The earliest incidence of knowledge taxation was enacted at this time.

One of the very first laws passed in 1809 by the "Governor and Judges of the Illinois Territory" was, not surprisingly, one to "enforce the collection of the county levies."[72] Revenues were the first imperative of government, and the taxing mechanisms were crude and limited. The act required that a fifteen-dollar fee be paid "to the sheriff as treasurer" by "every possessor of merchandize . . . previous[ ] to offering the same for sale."[73] The law contained no distinction between merchants, hawkers, or peddlers, resident or not, providing only that the fee must be paid by every "possessor" of merchandise before it could be sold. The fee applied to the seller, not to the wares, and it did not vary according to sales, but applied by its terms to sellers of all kinds, including sellers of written matter and newspapers, pamphlets, or books. The monies thus collected were used to defray the expenses of the territorial government.[74]

The act remained in effect until Illinois was granted statehood in 1818. It appears not to have attracted much attention, at least from those who sold publications subject to the tax. Fines and taxes imposed at the county level were the principal, if not exclusive, source of support for the government. The government was comparatively simple, and its financial needs were not great — nor were the taxes.

KNOWLEDGE TAXATION UNDER THE FIRST
CONSTITUTIONAL CONVENTION, 1818–47
The grant of statehood to Illinois in 1818 was followed by a flurry of activity from the new constitutional convention and state legislature. These bodies, charged with forging state policy, established by their actions a protective environment for freedom of the press. The press was the only real source of information at the time, and Illinois was very much a frontier state.

The Illinois Constitution of 1818 declared the basic principle of freedom of speech and freedom of the press in a form that remains unchanged in substance to this day. Section 22 of Article VIII of the constitution provided that:

> [t]he printing presses shall be free to every person who undertakes to examine the proceedings of the general assembly or of any branch of government; and no law shall ever be made to restrain the right thereof. The free communication of thoughts and opinion is one of the [invaluable] rights of man, and every citizen may freely speak, write, and print on any subject, being responsible for the abuse of that liberty.[75]

The free speech provision of the Illinois Constitution is framed in terms similar to those adopted elsewhere, and while the language is sweeping, its particular meaning is ambiguous. No records of the 1818 convention are available. Nor is there any case law from the period bearing on the meaning of Section 22 or on any of the statutes passed in regulation of trade which may have affected the dissemination of information promoted by the guarantee. Accordingly, the most significant source of information on knowledge taxation, especially as it relates to freedom of expression in the early days of Illinois statehood, is statutory law from the period, and it is that upon which we shall focus.

The new legislature's first act was to repeal all territorial laws, beginning lawmaking anew.[76] During the first legislative session in 1819, and as part of the initial set of laws enacted specifically by and for Illinois, the first act affecting the dissemination of knowledge was passed. The act required that any nonresident peddler obtain a license "to sell goods" from the county commissioners' court in any county in which goods were to be sold.[77] The tax was to be assessed at between ten and twenty dollars per county, and carried a fifty-dollar fine for selling without the required license.[78]

The act conferred substantial, if not excessive, discretion on county officials for its interpretation and enforcement. For example, the term "nonresident pedlar" was not defined; instead, its meaning was left expressly to the county commissioners' court.[79] This provision was subsequently repealed in 1823 and replaced with a definition of a nonresident peddler as one who had not resided in the state for six months.[80] The repeal may have been occasioned by problems in enforcement or interpretation, perhaps because of inconsistent interpretations from county to county, or even economic protectionism, but we cannot know for sure. The 1823 definition surely clarified matters, but it did not resolve all ambiguities, for the meaning of "pedlar" and "reside" remained far from clear.

More significantly, the act lacked a definition of the term "goods." Under the popular meaning of the term, one could assume that "goods" included clothes, food, supplies, and equipment, for example, but whether the printed word was included was not made explicit. It was common at the time to include newspapers, pamphlets, and books within such early hawker and peddler statutes, and the common meaning of "goods" would include them, so the safest assumption is that they were covered. But no further statutory clarification or judicial interpretation has been found to resolve the question.

While the amount of the fee — ten to twenty dollars per county — was not, in 1823, *de minimis*, it was likely not prohibitive either, and the purpose of the license fee was almost certainly revenue-related and not directed at certain ideas or forms of expression. In comparison to the similar tax on nonresident merchants in Civil War Virginia, assessed at five hundred dollars per county, the Illinois tax seems small.[81] Multiple-county sales may have resulted in a significant accumulation of fees, but a publication with a large enough readership to be so distributed would probably not be affected in its sales by the county fee, especially given that the fee would ordinarily have covered the peddler's sales of other merchandise as well. The county-by-county fee must have pinched a bit, however, at least after a time, for in 1845 legislation was enacted that gave peddlers the option of purchasing a statewide license for fifty dollars.[82]

The original peddler licensing act of 1819 remained in effect with only minor upward adjustments in fees for many years. Changes, reenactments, and amendments to the act were passed, with the most significant for our purposes being the exemptions. The first notable change, adopted in 1831, represented a wholesale modification of the earlier act, although it retained the same underlying fee and county collection and enforcement structure.[83] Unlike the original act, the licensing requirements of the 1831 act applied to all sellers of goods, not just nonresident sellers. And sellers subject to the license fee (five to fifty dollars per county) were more broadly defined to include the "merchant, auctioneer, pedler, or other person, or persons, company, or corporation." Goods were likewise defined more broadly to include "goods, wares, or merchandize."[84]

The nonresident character of the statute was not eliminated, however. Instead, it was recast as an exemption, although a substantially qualified one. The act provided that "any resident of this state may sell, without license, any articles not prohibited by law . . . if such articles shall have been produced, or manufactured within this state by the person selling the same."[85] While this provision was doubtlessly directed principally at local and domestic manufacture, it would, by its terms, exempt from the license fee the sale of local and state newspapers and pamphlets by direct subscription or by an agent of the publisher or printer. Out-of-state newspapers and pamphlets, however, and the sale of publications produced in Illinois but not sold directly by the publisher or printer, were subject to the license fee.

The act continued in effect until 1853, when it expired, replaced by a more significant and lucrative taxing mechanism first enacted in 1839. It had been amended again in 1841, however, largely in response to the emergence of that new taxing mechanism, which, until 1853, functioned in tandem with the peddler licensing act. In 1839 the legislature had passed an act that permitted counties to collect personal property taxes from merchants, based on the value of goods held for sale.[86] We will discuss this act and its successors fully in the following pages. But for purposes of the peddler licensing statute it is noteworthy that the existence of both a license fee and a property tax would fall doubly on merchants. And so, no doubt, it did, leading to an amendment to the peddler statute in 1841, which exempted from its requirements merchants "who pay an annual tax upon merchandize assessed according to the present revenue law [enacted in 1839]."[87] In all other relevant respects, the peddler tax remained in force until 1853, when it seems to have been left to a quiet death.

No record of any serious objection or resistance to Illinois's first peddler tax exists. While changes were made from time to time to address specific problems, neither newspaper publishers nor publishers of other written material seem to have registered concern. The tax was visited on the peddler, of course, and not the goods or their manufacturer, so publishers may have been largely unaware of or unaffected by the license requirement, which in any event was not, except perhaps in rare cases, visited on persons exclusively involved in the sale of publications. And the absence of objection may be explained also by the fact that the tax did not fall explicitly on the dissemination of knowledge, but fell on all merchants, whatever they sold, and by the undeniable fact that the tax was revenue-related.

Knowledge Taxation Under the Second Constitutional Convention, 1848–69

The second constitutional convention was held in 1848, and the language of the 1818 constitution's Article VIII, Section 22, which guaranteed freedom of the press and freedom of speech, was adopted once again without change.[88] The peddler act continued for a time, but without any apparent affect on the dissemination of knowledge, and in other respects the press seems to have been free, and valued, at the level of state policy. Indeed, in 1845 the legislature had passed a resolution "instruct[ing]" the Illinois representatives and senators in Congress to reduce postal rates on "letters, newspapers, pamphlets and periodicals," as the rate was deemed "oppressive" and a reduction would increase "the dissemination of useful information amongst those who are now deprived of such means by the present price of postage."[89]

The principal development in the taxation of knowledge during the 1848–69 period was the enactment of a personal property tax, a tax which, in respect to merchants and manufacturers, was really a precursor to a sales tax. The act, initially adopted in 1839 but enacted in comprehensive form in 1853, required the assessment of a property tax at a rate locally determined by counties adopting the township organization law.[90] Property taxed under the act included not only real property, but also personal property,[91] including average inventory held by merchants, and equipment and materials used in the manufacture of goods for resale.[92] "Merchant" was defined as: "[e]very person that shall own, or have in his possession, or subject to his control, any personal property within this state, with authority to sell the same, which may have been purchased in or out of this state, with a view to being sold at an advanced price or profit."[93] Merchants were required by the act to file a statement annually with the assessor containing the value of average inventory during the preceding year, and pay tax thereon.[94] The definition of personal property was suitably inclusive, comprehending "every tangible thing . . . whether animate or inanimate," and thus included newspapers, pamphlets, books and other writings, none of which were saved from tax by the spare exemption provisions.[95]

The act also taxed manufacturers by imposing the personal property tax on supplies, stock, and equipment or machinery on hand and used in the process of manufacturing.[96] With respect to supplies and stock, the tax applied to the value of all personal property "had on hand" during the year for the purpose of "adding to the value thereof" by manufacturing, net of debt on the stock and supplies.[97] The act was, it seems, a form of value-added tax, exacted through the property tax system. Equipment, defined as "all engines and machinery of every description, used or designed to be used in any process of . . . manufacturing, . . . including all tools and implements," was to be separately listed and taxed.[98] There seems little doubt that the manufacturers tax applied to publishers and printers of every description.

With the tax rates left to the counties, little can be said about the fiscal consequences of the merchant and manufacturer taxes to the publishers, printers, and distributors and sellers of newspapers, pamphlets, and books. No record of objection to the tax by publishers has been discovered, and one might surmise from this and from the fact that the tax remained in effect for many years that its impact was negligible. In any event publications and their manufacture were taxed equally with all other enterprises, both in the form of the tax and its rate, and the purposes of the tax were surely benign and closely related to the revenue needs of government.

Knowledge Taxation Under the Third
Constitutional Convention, 1870 Through Century's End
In 1870 a constitutional convention was again convened, and this time the earlier provision concerning freedom of speech and freedom of the press was eliminated.[99] In its place was added Article II, Section 4 of the Illinois Constitution, a provision allowing the defense of truth in certain libel actions.[100] The new provision, which afforded "[e]very person [the right

to] freely speak, write and publish on all subjects, being responsible for abuse of that liberty," was more concise, but it does not appear that any change in substance was intended. The second clause pertaining to the defense of truth in libel actions was later elaborated, in 1895, by an act limiting damages in libel actions against newspapers to actual damages if the publication was made in good faith and with reasonable grounds for believing the published facts to be true.[101] The act, however, was short-lived. It was unceremoniously repealed in the next legislative session, in 1897.[102] While there is no doubt an interesting story behind this, pursuing it here would, unfortunately, be an inadvisable digression.

Little else bearing directly on the knowledge tax question occurred prior to the turn of the century, so we will conclude this portion of the Illinois history with but brief mention of three developments bearing only indirectly on the principal focus of our inquiry. All three occurred after the turn of the century, but will be discussed here in order that our later discussion can begin with the emerging sales and use tax issues, and because they provide a suitable close to this phase of history.

The first development was a law enacted in 1917, titled the "Unlawful Exhibitions and Publications Act."[103] Promulgated as part of the criminal code, the Act made it

> unlawful for any person, firm or corporation to manufacture, sell, or offer for sale, advertise or publish, present or exhibit in any public place in this State any lithograph, moving picture, play, drama or sketch, which publication or exhibition portrays depravity, criminality, unchastity, or lack of virtue of a class of citizens, of any race, color, creed or religion which said publication or exhibition exposes the citizens of any race, color, creed or religion to contempt, derision, or obloquy or which is productive of breach of the peace or riots.[104]

The Act also prohibited any media portrayal of any hanging, lynching, or burning of any human being.[105] Violation of the law carried a fine of not less than fifty and not more than two hundred dollars.

In the same session the legislature passed the second item, an act making criminal the publication of anonymous material pertaining to a candidate for nomination or election.[106] In this case newspapers, magazines, journals, and official publications were specifically exempt from the act and from its penalties, which included fines of from one hundred to five hundred dollars and thirty days to six months in jail.[107] Each publication was a separate offense.[108]

The first of these acts was intended to protect the public from the hateful and inciting, as well as the tasteless, habits of public discourse at the time. The second was designed to protect against the analogously tasteless and mudslinging tactics in the elective political arena. Despite the stifling quality of the statutes, no challenge seems to have been brought to their constitutionality. This is no doubt due to the fact that their constitutionality seemed apparent; the Supreme Court had yet to recognize the First Amendment as a limit on the power of states to regulate speech.[109] It would not be until twenty-five years later that the constitutionality of legislation making "fighting words" illegal was challenged — and sustained — by the United States Supreme Court.[110] Both acts, however, reflected an increasing public awareness of the power, and danger, of speech, and an increasing inclination to regulate it.

The third development occurred at the local government level and involved one of the first efforts in Illinois to regulate the new technologies of communication — in this case telegraph and telephone. Pursuant to their delegated power, local governments, including the city of Peoria, began to regulate the use of public lands for transmission lines used by telegraph and telephone, and to assess fees on such use, all with the objective of protecting the public interest. Peoria decided to levy an annual license fee of one dollar each upon poles erected on city streets, alleys, or sidewalks. The city's authority was challenged in the 1916 case of *City of Peoria v. Postal Telegraph-Cable Co.*[111]

The telegraph company argued that the fee was, in reality, a tax, and that as such it constituted an unconstitutional tax on interstate commerce in violation of the Commerce Clause. The court, however, relying on a federal post road act of 1866,[112] which prohibited telegraph lines from interfering with "ordinary travel" on roads, viewed the exaction as a "fee" rather than a tax on the ground that the Post Road Act impliedly granted local governments certain regulatory authority in the interest of safe travel for the public.[113] That regulatory authority was broad enough to embrace licensing and to include, as well, a license "fee," which is what the city had advisedly called it in the ordinance. The constitutional challenge was therefore rejected. Whatever one might think of the court's decision — if not a tax, the "fee" was more akin to "rent" than to a fee for a license, given that it was levied on a per-pole basis (unless every pole was separately licensed!), and, if a fee, it certainly had the salutary potential for raising significant amounts of revenue — this is the first instance discovered in Illinois of an exaction visited specifically on communication.

But one should not expect too much of the court at the time. The First

Amendment was, after all, little more than inchoate even as a significant limitation on laws enacted by Congress, and its application to the states through the Fourteenth Amendment would not be recognized until almost a decade later.[114] And telegraph and telephone communication, which we now consider to be an everyday and inextricable part of the larger communication process, was then only developing. An argument that a fee — even a tax — on such transmission facilities was a tax on knowledge, I suspect, would have been met by laughter. We should not let this single instance of exaction (in whatever form) distort what seems otherwise to have been an exemplary record of evenhandedness toward taxation of the press throughout the nineteenth century in Illinois.

Notes

1. Of the sources that were reviewed, only one mentions taxation of the press. Howison notes that newspapers, along with horses and riding carriages and other articles of commerce, were subject to state taxation, but he says nothing more about the taxes. 2 Robert R. Howison, *History of Virginia* 506 (1848). Cappon's *Virginia Newspapers, 1821–1935* is completely silent on the subject, even though instances of Civil War suppression of the Virginia press are mentioned. Lester J. Cappon, *Virginia Newspapers, 1821–1935* (1936). Bryson does not list any pertinent articles. William H. Bryson, *A Bibliography of Virginia Legal History Before 1900* (1979). Equally remarkable, Howison mentions the taxes in passing, but does not report any opposition.

2. Notable among works that provide pre-revolutionary and revolutionary background, drawing heavily on Virginia history, is the exceedingly good recent book, Jeffery A. Smith, *Printers and Press Freedom: The Ideology of Early American Journalism* (1988).

3. Isaiah Thomas, *The History of Printing in America* 7 (Weathervane Books 1970) (1874) citing George Chalmers, *Political Annals of the Present United Colonies* 345 (1780), in which Chalmers states that Lord Effingham, who was appointed governor of Virginia in 1683, was ordered "to allow no person to use a printing press on any occasion whatsoever."

4. The tax and licensing laws in Virginia followed and were directly related to quite overt laws punishing abolitionist expression. In 1832 Virginia enacted a statute that provided for the lashing or, upon second offense, execution (if "a slave, free negro or mulatto") or imposition of a fine (if "the person so offending be a white person") for writing or publishing any book, pamphlet, or other writing "advising persons of colour within this state to make insurrection, or to rebel." Supplement to the Revised Code of the Laws of Virginia 246, 247 (1833). With the introduction of substantial quantities of Northern abolitionist propaganda into the South in the mid-1830s, Virginia, like many other Southern states, enacted legisla-

tion directed at prohibiting such publications. On March 23, 1836, Virginia passed a law making it a high misdemeanor punishable by fines and imprisonment for "any member of an abolition or anti-slavery society, or agent [to maintain in the state] by speaking or writing, that the owners of slaves have no property in the same, or advocate or advise the abolition of slavery" and providing also for the "burn[ing] in his presence" of such a writing, if mailed, by a justice of the peace. Act of Mar. 23, 1836, §§ 1–3, 1836 Va. Acts 44–45.

In 1848 another act was passed that replaced and consolidated the former ones. The act broadened the prohibition of statements that owners of slaves had no right of property in them to include statements to that effect by "[a]ny free person" rather than members of abolition or antislavery societies, and made the penalty imprisonment for up to a year or a fine of $500 or less. The prohibition on inciting slaves to rebellion, etc., was made applicable only to free persons, and punishment was set at not less than one and not more than five years in prison. The provision requiring burning of such materials by the justice of the peace was retained. Act of Mar. 14, 1848, ch. 10, §§ 24–26, 1848 Va. Acts 117.

The political and public excitement caused by the abolitionist material was widespread, although many newspapers freely (and bravely) published editorials and opinion sympathetic to abolition. See Harold L. Nelson, *Freedom of the Press from Hamilton to the Warren Court* 167–210 (1967). The mails, which carried much of the "objectionable" material, were very much in the midst of the fray, although here the politicians became directly involved and, at the urging of Postmaster General Amos Kendall, President Jackson, and John Calhoun, censorship of the mails prevailed in the South. *Id*. at 211.

5. An Act Imposing Taxes for the Support of Government, § 1, 1813 Va. Acts 4.

6. We are only able to surmise the precise reach of the tax, however, as the term "newspaper" was not defined in the Act.

7. Act of Feb. 10, 1814, § 1, 1914 Va. Acts 4; Act of Dec. 21, 1814, § 1, 1815 Va. Acts 6. The February 1814 act increased the amount of the tax from the cost of four subscriptions to that of five subscriptions. That rate continued under the December 1814 act.

8. See *supra* note 1.

9. Act of Mar. 27, 1843, § 6, 1843 Va. Acts 7 (1843).

10. Act of Jan. 26, 1844, § 7, 1844 Va. Acts 8; Act of Feb. 13, 1845, § 7, 1845 Va. Acts 8; Act of Feb. 28, 1846, § 7, 1846 Va. Acts 8; Act of Mar. 17, 1847, § 7, 1847 Va. Acts 8; Act of Mar. 31, 1848, § 7, 1848 Va. Acts 8.

11. Act of June 5, 1852, § 1, 1852 Va. Acts 11; reenacted as Act of Apr. 7, 1853, § 29, 1853 Va. Acts 15.

12. See e.g., 1808 Va. Acts 1 ("on every license to a hawker or pedlar, thirty dollars"); 1809 Va. Acts 26 (same); 1810 Va. Acts 1 (same).

13. Act of June 5, 1852, §§ 1–2, 1852 Va. Acts 11; reenacted as Act of Apr. 7, 1853, § 29, 1853 Va. Acts 15.

14. Act of Mar. 2, 1854, § 10, 1854 Va. Acts 6.

15. Act of Mar. 18, 1856, § 22, 1856 Va. Acts 14.

16. Act of Mar. 30, 1860, § 4, 1860 Va. Acts 41.

17. Act of Apr. 3, 1861, § 44, 1861 Va. Acts 14.

18. The statute is not without ambiguity. It provided in complete relevant part: "On every license to a person obtaining subscriptions to books, maps, prints, pamphlets, or periodicals, twenty-five dollars for each county. On every license to sell, or in any manner furnish the same, twenty-five dollars. If the person obtaining such license has not been a resident of the state two years, the tax shall in each case be two hundred dollars." *Id.*

19. Out-of-state sellers, of course, meant anyone not a resident of the state for two years.

20. Act of Mar. 27, 1862, § 45, 1862 Va. Acts 14.

21. Act of Oct. 6, 1862, 1862 Va. Acts 15 (specially called session).

22. Act of Mar. 28, 1863, § 51, 1863 Va. Acts 17 (adjourned session).

23. *Id.* § 71, at 21.

24. Holmes fought and was wounded three times as a member of the Union Army in the Civil War. The influence of the war on Holmes was profound. See Oliver Wendell Holmes, *Touched with Fire: The Civil War Letters and Diary of Oliver Wendell Holmes, Jr.* (Mark DeWolfe Howe ed., 1946).

25. Abrams v. United States, 250 U.S. 616, 630 (1919) (Holmes, J., dissenting).

26. Act of Mar. 3, 1864, § 1, 1864 Va. Acts 3; Act of Mar. 3, 1865, § 1, 1865 Va. Acts 48. Surprisingly, the 1864 act, passed by the General Assembly in Richmond, predicted that, under the 1863 act, tax receipts would be "ample for the support of the state government." Act of Mar. 3, 1864, 1864 Va. Acts 3. The General Assembly therefore suspended enforcement of the 1863 act through January 31, 1865. *Id.* Precisely a year after the Richmond legislature took that action, the General Assembly in Alexandria apparently eliminated the tax on paper and printed matter permanently by declaring that "no taxes [would] be imposed" except as provided elsewhere in the March 3, 1865, act. Act of Mar. 3, 1865, § 1, 1865 Va. Acts 48. That act nowhere mentioned a tax on publications. *Id.*

The distinction between the Alexandria and Richmond General Assemblies is not merely geographic. The Alexandria legislators constituted Virginia's so-called Restored Government, which consisted of opponents of secession and which Washington had recognized. See Richard G. Lowe, "Francis Harrison Pierpont: Wartime Unionist, Reconstruction Moderate," in *The Governors of Virginia, 1860–1978*, at 36–39 (Edward Younger & James Tice Moore eds., 1982); 3 Richard L. Morton, *History of Virginia* 63–74 (1924). The Richmond legislators, however, supported the Confederacy through March 1865. See Alvin A. Fahrner, "William Smith: Governor in Two Wars," in *The Governors of Virginia, 1860–1978*, at 28–29 (Edward Younger & James Tice Moore eds., 1982).

27. Book, periodical, and pamphlet sellers were subject to licensing in 1866 in the same manner as, and with the same tax as, other merchant sales. The fee was nominal, at $10. Act of Feb. 13, 1866, § 12, 1866 Va. Acts 37; Act of Feb. 28, 1866, § 29, 1866 Va. Acts 66. A "nominal" fee for the licensing of religious book and periodical sellers, based only upon evidence of good character and generally applicable regardless of state residence, was also enacted in 1866. Act of Feb. 13, 1866, § 12, 1866 Va. Acts 37. Publishers of books, pamphlets, or other periodicals in Virginia,

and newspapers published in the state, were made free of any licensing requirement. *Id*. § 1, at 32.

28. See Jones v. Opelika, 316 U.S. 584 (1942).

29. See J. Smith, *supra* note 2.

30. See City of Norfolk v. Norfolk Landmark Publishing Co., 95 Va. 564, 565, 28 S.E. 959 (1898).

31. The circuit court's decision is unreported, and therefore the basis for the court's decision must be inferred from the Virginia Supreme Court's opinion, which discussed, and rejected, the claim based on freedom of the press. 95 Va. at 565; 28 S.E. at 959.

32. *Id*.

33. 29 S.C. 438, 7 S.E. 605 (1888).

34. *In re* Jager, 29 S.C. 438, 445, 7 S.E. 605 (1888), quoted in City of Norfolk v. Norfolk Landmark Publishing Co., 95 Va. 564, 566 (1898). The exact quotation is: " 'We cannot see that a tax on the business of publishing a newspaper is any more an abridgement of the liberty of the press than a tax on the office, type, and other material used in the business.' "

While *In re Jager* did hold that a tax on the business of publishing a newspaper did not restrain the liberty of the press, it is fair to observe that the opinion is devoid of any reasoning in support of the conclusion. The statute in *Jager* was interesting. On December 31, 1887, Charleston adopted an ordinance "to regulate licenses for the year 1888." It deemed unlawful the business of "publishing a daily newspaper worked by steam" without a license. *In re* Jager, 29 S.C. 438, 439, 7 S.E. 605 (1888).

35. See *infra* notes 42–48.

36. See *supra* notes 17–23 and accompanying text.

37. Act of May 4, 1882, § 1, 1882 Tex. Gen. Laws 20.

38. Act of Apr. 16, 1895, § 1, 1895 Tex. Gen. Laws 78.

39. See Preston v. Finley, 72 F. 850, 852 (W.D. Tex. 1896).

40. Grosjean v. American Press Co., 297 U.S. 233 (1936).

41. J. Edward Gerald, *The Press and the Constitution, 1931–1947*, at 101 (1968).

42. Thompson v. State, 17 Tex. Ct. App. 253 (1884).

43. *Id*. at 257 (1884).

44. *Id*. at 257–58; see also Preston v. Finley, 72 F. 850 (W.D. Tex. 1896).

45. *Ex Parte* Neill, 22 S.W. 923 (Tex. Crim. App. 1893).

46. Near v. Minnesota, 283 U.S. 697 (1931).

47. *Ex Parte* Neill, 22 S.W. 923 (Tex. Crim. App. 1893); *Preston v. Finley*, 72 F. at 856.

48. 22 S.W. at 923–24.

49. See *Preston v. Finley*, 72 F. at 856.

50. See text accompanying note 38 *supra* for the text of the statute.

51. 1755 Mass. Acts 794, 834, quoted in Clyde A. Duniway, *The Development of Freedom of the Press in Massachusetts* at 119, n. 3 (Franklin ed., 1969) (1906).

52. See Chapter 2.

53. *Boston Gazette or Country Journal*, May 26, 1755, and June 2, 1755, quoted in Duniway at 120. See also *Fleet's Evening Post*, April 4, 1757, also quoted in Duniway at 120, n. 4.

54. See Chapter 3.

55. *Id.* See also *Mass. Centinel*, April–May 1785, quoted in Duniway at 136, n. 2.

56. The Massachusetts Constitution was enacted in 1780 and contained several parts. The first part contained provisions similar to the Bill of Rights to the U.S. Constitution. An earlier 1778 constitution was rejected because it contained no protection for personal liberties. See 1 Bernard Schwartz, *The Bill of Rights: A Documentary History* 337–44, 372 (1971).

57. Mass. Const. pt. 1, art. XVI, reprinted in 1 Schwartz at 342. The U.S. Constitution did not mention a free press, and even the Bill of Rights devoted only one portion of the First Amendment to a free press.

58. Article XVI has remained virtually unchanged to this day, although a 1948 amendment added the following sentence: "The right of free speech shall not be abridged." Mass. Const. pt. 1, art. XVI.

59. Although this debate has been resolved today, there appears to have been no consensus until well into the twentieth century.

60. Letter from William Cushing, C.J., to John Adams (Feb. 18, 1789), in *Mass. L. Q.*, Oct. 1942, at 12–15.

61. Commonwealth v. Blanding, 20 Mass. (3 Pick.) 304, 313 (Mass. 1825). This interpretation seems to have been popular as it allowed prosecutions for libel to remain unhampered.

62. The Massachusetts legislature, composed of the House of Representatives and the State Senate, is referred to as the General Court.

63. An Act Concerning Hawkers, Peddlers, and Petty Chapmen, § 1, 1821 Mass. Acts 491–92. The Act stated that "every hawker . . . going from town to town . . . within this Commonwealth, shall, on conviction thereof, forfeit and pay a sum not less than ten dollars, nor more than one hundred dollars for each and every offense aforesaid." The Act did provide that goods could be taken and sold "abroad." *Id.* at 492.

64. See An Act Concerning Hawkers and Pedlars, 1846 Mass. Acts 167–70 (approved April 16, 1846). There was also a small group of goods including liquor and playing cards that were prohibited from being sold even with a license. *Id.* at 167.

65. *Id.*

66. Information on licensing procedures is contained in the 1846 act, *supra* note 64.

67. During the intervening years a complex system of regulating licensing evolved. Persons paying local taxes were made exempt from licensing fees. Act of May 24, 1852, § 1, 1851 Mass. Acts 800. Licenses were restricted to one year terms. An Act Relating to Hawkers and Peddlers, § 1, 1864 Mass. Acts 95–96. See also 1870 Mass. Acts 243–44.

68. An Act Empowering Cities to Regulate by Ordinance the Sale of Certain Articles by Hawkers and Peddlers, 1883 Mass. Acts 462. The regulations were approved on May 5, 1883. A later amendment expanded the power to regulate to "towns" as well as "cities" in Massachusetts.

69. *Id.* This bill made clear that it did not expand a city's ability to license hawkers, but it gave the added power of regulation.

70. Texas and Virginia, of course, both imposed explicit taxes on printers, sellers, or on newspapers themselves.

71. See Chapter 6.

72. Act of July 20, 1809, Laws of the Territory of Illinois 1809–11, at 6–8 (Ill. State Hist. Library 1906). The law repealed and replaced a former Indiana law that would otherwise have been adopted as part of the receipt of Indiana laws by the territory.

73. *Id.* at 7.

74. *Id.*

75. Ill. Const. of 1818, art. VIII, § 22.

76. An Act to Repeal Certain Laws, § 1, 1819 Ill. Laws 351.

77. An Act to Authorize Non-resident Pedlars to Sell Goods in This State, § 1, 1819 Ill. Laws 352.

78. *Id.*

79. *Id.*

80. Act of Feb. 14, 1823, §§ 1, 2, 1823 Ill. Laws 145.

81. See *supra* text accompanying notes 21–23.

82. Act of Mar. 3, 1845, § 7, 1845 Ill. Laws 4.

83. An Act Requiring Merchants, Auctioneers, Pedlars, and Others Engaged in the Sale of Goods, Wares, and Merchandise in This State, to Procure a License for That Purpose, Under the Penalties Therein Prescribed, 1831 Ill. Laws 89–92 (adopted Feb. 16, 1831).

84. *Id.* at 89–90.

85. *Id.* at 90.

86. An Act Concerning the Public Revenue, 1839 Ill. Laws 3–23 (adopted Feb. 26, 1839).

87. An Act in Relation to Pedlars, § 5, 1841 Ill. Laws 179–80 (adopted Feb. 27, 1841).

88. Ill. Const. of 1848, art. XIII, § 23.

89. Resolution Concerning Postage, 1845 Ill. Laws 380.

90. 1853 Ill. Laws 3–20.

91. Personal property was defined as "every tangible thing, being the subject of ownership, whether animate or inanimate, other than money" or real property. *Id.* § 2, at 4.

92. *Id.* at 9–10.

93. *Id.* § 12, at 9.

94. *Id.* § 12, at 10.

95. *Id.* §§ 2, 3, at 4–5.

96. *Id.* §§ 14, 15, at 10–11.

97. *Id.* § 14, at 10.

98. *Id.* § 15, at 11.

99. 1818 Ill. Const., art. VIII, § 22; 1848 Ill. Const., art. XIII, § 23.

100. 1870 Ill. Const., art. II, § 4.

101. An Act in Relation to Libel, 1895 Ill. Laws 315. The Act also provided for exemplary and punitive damages, and for retractions.

102. Act of June 14, 1897, 1897 Ill. Laws 297.

103. Act of June 29, 1917, 1917 Ill. Laws 362–63.

104. *Id.*

105. *Id.*

106. Act of June 26, 1917, 1917 Ill. Laws 456–57.

107. *Id.* §§ 3–4, at 457.

108. *Id.*

109. See Gitlow v. New York, 268 U.S. 652 (1925); Palko v. Connecticut, 302 U.S. 319 (1937).

110. Chaplinsky v. New Hampshire, 315 U.S. 568, 571 (1942).

111. City of Peoria v. Postal Telegraph-Cable Co., 113 N.E. 968 (Ill. 1916).

112. Act of July 24, 1866, ch. 230, 14 Stat. 221.

113. 113 N.E. at 970.

114. See Gitlow v. New York, 268 U.S. 652 (1925); Palko v. Connecticut, 302 U.S. 319 (1937).

5. Knowledge Taxes in Nineteenth-Century America: Observations at the End of the Print Era

The history of knowledge taxes in America divides naturally into two stages, the first of which covers the eighteenth and nineteenth centuries, and the second of which covers the twentieth century. The first period spans the colonial taxes, the ratification of the Constitution and the Bill of Rights, and the nineteenth-century federal, state, and local taxes. During this period the types of knowledge taxes used, and the occasions in which they were used, represented a relatively straightforward extrapolation of the English forms of taxation—the paper, advertising, and stamp taxes. In short, a rather fixed and classic framework of analysis can be employed.

In the twentieth century, to which we shall turn in the next and succeeding chapters, the economic, political, and legal environment becomes a great deal more complex. As the forms and incidents of taxation become more diverse, new and often indirect types of "duties" on expression come into being, the political environment becomes more imbued with increasing government regulation of the economy, the press emerges as a more cohesive and powerful economic and political force, the courts enter an era of active judicial interpretation and interposition, and, ultimately, technology begins to break down the forms of taxation and the institutions of communication, even the very meaning of the "press," requiring a wholesale rethinking of the knowledge tax problem. It is important, therefore, to pause and take stock of the situation at the turn of the century—to synthesize the patterns of the eighteenth- and nineteenth-century historical experience—before we begin to explore the taxation of knowledge in the infinitely more complex environment of the twentieth century. For it is history that, ironically enough, will become our most important guidepost when next we move forward to the present day.

Our review of the eighteenth- and nineteenth-century knowledge taxes has been an illustrative, not an exhaustive, one. That is to say, we have not surveyed and discussed every enactment in every state, nor even the general experience of every state. Rather, against the background of the colonial taxes and the ratification debates, we have discussed in some depth the singular and important federal taxes, and we have surveyed the experience of selected states in order to ascertain the manner and extent to which the classic forms of knowledge tax were employed. This has necessarily led us to explore, to the extent possible on a limited record, the historical and economic circumstances in which resort to such taxes occurred, the purposes such taxes served, and their effect.

It is not easy to encapsulate the eighteenth- and nineteenth-century American experience with knowledge taxes into a neat and tidy set of conclusions. The widely disparate views expressed in the halls of government and on the editorial pages of news periodicals, and the many and varied — and often short-lived — forms of taxation employed at all levels of government make synthesis difficult. Instead of conclusions, therefore, it may be more apt at this intermediate point of historical review to venture some observations — some strands of history that lend perspective to our understanding of taxation of knowledge in America.

The first and most obvious observation to be drawn from the eighteenth- and nineteenth-century materials is that taxes were, in fact, imposed on paper, on advertisements, on printers, on publishers, and on distributors of periodical publications. Equally notable is the fact that relatively little objection was voiced to such taxes on grounds of freedom of the press, and when such objections were voiced they were relatively meek. In a real sense, it was as if the partly contemporaneous English experience[1] and the earlier colonial experiences never existed, or in any event failed to register.

The reason for this state of affairs can only be surmised, of course, as we have precious little historical record surrounding the taxes themselves, much less the grounds upon which the failure to object to them rested. Educated judgments about the reasons, however, can be ventured, and in this connection three contributing factors seem plausible. The first is the perceived differences between democratically self-imposed measures as contrasted with duties imposed by a sovereign perceived as distant, foreign, and nondemocratic. The struggle against knowledge taxation in England, which was winding toward its conclusion in the first half of the nineteenth century, began with the Stamp Act of 1712 and was followed by a century of onerous features designed to maintain government control over information to the populace. It was therefore essentially a struggle of the people, represented by the pamphleteers, the country newspapers, and to a lesser extent by some of the metropolitan papers, against the Crown and its remaining manifestations and a Parliament intent on limiting access to political information. In short, it was but part of the struggle of the governed against government. The colonial experience was no different; indeed, it represented an even more accentuated form of resistance of the wholly unrepresented "governed" against the "foreign" governors. The evil of knowledge taxes was perceived through the prism of disenfranchisement and oppression, and a press free of the burden of the stamp was important more for its instrumental and symbolic role in achieving freedom than it was valued as a virtue in and of itself.

When the question of taxation of the press arose in post-revolutionary America, therefore, the lesson of the English and colonial experiences may have been less than obvious. Taxation of the press in America involved taxation of the governed *by the governed*, not by a distinct or detached sovereign, and taxes were used to raise revenues necessary to the accomplishment of democratically established objectives. Indeed, this view represented a fair and accurate description of the taxes actually imposed in the first half of the nineteenth century; for the most part those taxes were levied in order to raise revenue for the accomplishment of important public purposes unrelated to suppression of expression. It is, therefore, perfectly understandable that even during the debates on the federal taxes the connection with the English and colonial experiences was rarely made. It was not until Virginia's use of taxation to control and silence expression during the Civil War that purposes more reminiscent of the early English taxes emerged, and even then the lesson of the English struggle was lost in the fever pitch of war.

The second reason that little resistance to knowledge taxes emerged in the nineteenth century may be that the English experience failed to yield any distilled principles of freedom of the press that could be translated into organized and coherent opposition in this country. In part, this is because in significant respects the English struggle represented at its core a struggle for political, rather than simply press, freedom. In America political freedom had been won. In larger part, however, the absence of any overriding principles of the press's freedom from taxation is simply a fact of the English struggle, at least until its successful conclusion in the second half of the century. And even then the principles which seem clear now may not have been so then. Resistance to taxation in England was not, in truth, animated by a single grand and principled concept of freedom. Instead, it was a series of skirmishes, more akin to guerrilla warfare than to a coordinated and

coherent battle, and it drew at different points on a complex matrix of political imperatives that included not only the free dissemination of knowledge,
but also trade interests, suffrage, and resistance to duties on "soap, hops, or
malt."[2] The means were not inappropriate, for the tactics had to be, perhaps, as insidious as was the enemy.

This is not to suggest that frequent and eloquent resort to principles of
freedom was not made in England, for it was. But it is notable that the
assertion of concepts of free expression were episodic, far from consistent
over time, and late to cohere. The press, itself, was often of two (if not
more) minds on the question of taxation.[3] Even Collet, a principal figure
in, and often the philosopher of, the later stages of the struggle against the
English stamp, bemoaned the more than occasional incoherence of the resistance and failed to express any coherent principles underlying the struggle once it succeeded. What resulted from the victorious struggle against
knowledge taxation in England was, in the main, the fact alone of political
victory; at least this may be how it appeared at the time, and this is what the
contemporaneous observers in America would have seen. With hindsight
and the longer perspective of history, we can detect some common strands
from the English history, but we might be mistaken to assume that even
those strands were obvious or discernible in nineteenth-century America.
More likely, they were at least as shrouded to American eyes as they were to
Collet and his contemporaries.

The final reason for the absence of principled resistance to taxes,
especially in late nineteenth-century America, is the passion of democracy
which, when called into play, obscured the senses and generated a compla-
cency born of self-governing consensus. It is no accident that the period of
most obvious and obnoxious knowledge taxation was during the Civil War,
when the purpose of taxation was service to the patriotic cause, both in the
North and in the South, for at that time "knowledge" was a fixed and
known commodity, and the shades of gray that represent diversity of
opinion were unperceived. This is manifest in both the federal and the
Virginia taxes. The confidence born of moral certainty, coupled with the
security of self-government, fully explain the failure of American institutions to perceive a threat to freedom and explain as well the reluctance of
those few who saw things more clearly to speak up.

A second observation to be drawn from the nineteenth-century history
concerns the pattern of taxation and the general forms into which taxes
levied on knowledge fit. Over the course of the century essentially four
different forms of taxation evolved. In the greater complexity of tax mecha-

nisms, the contrast with the more singular and straightforward English taxes stands out — and indeed the contrast may partly explain the discontinuity between the English struggle and the American experience.

The first form of tax consisted of taxes levied directly on the printed word, the brunt of which fell on only certain types of subject matters or certain identified ideas. Virginia's differential taxation of non-Confederate publications is one example, and Texas's taxation of certain offensive — and named — publications is another.[4] These are, without doubt, the most odious forms of knowledge taxation, although they may be the least dangerous because they are the most obvious and detectable. They tend also to be the most short-lived, even without the assistance of judicial intervention, for they are occasioned by passions of the moment and usually end when the passion subsides.

The second category of knowledge taxes included taxes levied expressly and only on the press or the printed word, although without explicit differential application based on content or point of view. While the nineteenth century witnessed such taxes, their number is small. Perhaps the most notable such tax is the federal advertising tax.[5] This form of tax, exacted upon publications alone, bears the closest resemblance to the English knowledge taxes, except for the very earliest overtly censorial ones. Here purposes or motives, censorial or benign, must generally be inferred, for none but the revenue-generating objectives are explicitly stated. I shall later refer to such taxes as differential in *form*, an important distinction whose constitutional significance remains inchoate until the United States Supreme Court's 1983 decision in *Minneapolis Star and Tribune Company v. Minnesota Commissioner of Revenue*.[6]

The third form of knowledge tax consisted of taxes imposed on the press or printed word but as part of a tax imposed generally on a more broadly defined category of activity of which transmission of knowledge is but a part. Many of the state taxes were of this type. The peddler taxes in Illinois are a fitting example, as the taxes were imposed on all peddlers of goods or merchandise including, but not limited to, publications.[7] A subset of this form of tax would include generally applicable taxes which, however, were imposed at a different *rate* on publications. Few examples of this subgroup are found in the nineteenth century largely, it seems, because the taxing structures were unsophisticated and blunt-edged and because the varieties of publications were limited.[8]

Taxes that fit this form, whether differential in rate or not, present fewer, yet often more substantial, knowledge tax concerns, for the equality of treatment seems to limit the likelihood of abuse, yet the indiscriminate imposition of taxes on all publications, including the marginal or struggling ones, can have quite discriminating consequences (including maintenance of the established media and the informational status quo). And the very imposition of additional costs on knowledge has consequences which are far from irrelevant, even though they may not be historically or constitutionally determinative. Little concern was expressed about such forms of knowledge taxation in the eighteenth and nineteenth centuries, however, and this is due in part to the clear and, in the context of early and crude revenue structures, compelling revenue justifications that existed, and in part because such evenhanded taxes represented in many respects the very end sought in the English struggle against taxation of knowledge.

The fourth and final form of knowledge taxation that evolved in the nineteenth century was the tax (whether general in application or limited to knowledge) that was imposed on some forms of knowledge and not on others, with the distinction often drawn in terms of subject matter. Such a tax is illustrated by the Virginia tax that exempted religious materials[9] or the English tax that, at first, exempted books and, later, did the opposite.[10] These forms of tax were relatively rare in the nineteenth century but would become increasingly common in the twentieth century.[11] With such taxes the purposes behind the exemption must, of necessity, be made explicit, as the exemption is openly carved out of a generally applicable tax. Both historically and for good reason these taxes have been treated differently from taxes visited uniquely on the press. As our discussion of their more common use in the twentieth century will reveal, it would be a mistake to presume from this that such taxes are improper or even generally to be discouraged.

There are two other types of tax that have been encountered during our survey of the nineteenth century, but, while they deserve mention, they are not, in truth, separate forms but simply extreme versions of one or more of the forms described above. The first is the utterly confiscatory tax best illustrated by the five-hundred-dollar San Antonio, Texas, "tax" challenged and approved in *Thompson v. State*.[12] It is worth separate mention here only to emphasize that such a tax *can* be enacted in America, and that it has been enacted on more than one occasion.[13] But it is equally notable that our survey, incomplete as it is, failed to disclose any *generally applicable* confiscatory taxes.

The second tax which deserves mention is the one that explicitly exempts knowledge from its reach, such as the early taxes in Massachu-setts.[14] This is, in a sense, not really a knowledge tax at all, but we shall see that tax systems that specifically exempt knowledge present important knowledge tax issues nevertheless, for the conferral of a benefit on knowl-edge through exemption can raise issues that lie at the heart of the knowl-edge tax problem, particularly for the press.[15]

Through the evolution of these various forms or generic groupings of knowledge taxes, the nineteenth century provides a more complex texture for the knowledge tax issues. The earlier English and colonial periods witnessed the emergence of knowledge taxation as a problem deeply con-nected to individual and political liberty, but the problem arose in the relatively simple and straightforward setting of stamp, paper, and advertis-ing taxes imposed directly on the printed word. The nineteenth century may have contributed little further insight into the underlying problems of knowledge taxation or to their ultimate solution, but it made evident that the issue of taxing knowledge could — and with American ingenuity, surely would — arise in a far richer array of settings. And the nineteenth century witnessed virtually every twist of form in which taxation of knowledge would occur, permitting us across the landscape of nearly two hundred years to chart the basic forms around which our later discussion will revolve.

Yet the issue of differential taxation of the press rarely surfaced in the eighteenth and nineteenth centuries. This is partly a function of the gener-ally receptive attitudes toward taxation of publications, but it is also a function of the relative simplicity (or crudeness) of the taxation mecha-nisms of the time. In nineteenth-century America the complex of taxes we now take for granted was unthinkable. Instead, taxes were raised by levying duties on commercial activity — producing, selling, and distributing. Taxing the production of paper or the sale or distribution of periodicals, therefore, was not remarkable in the general scheme of things. Such taxes were merely instances of taxes being levied on a broad array of similar types of commer-cial activity, and the concept of differentiality when such taxes were levied on publications would have been incomprehensible. Instead, a claim that paper or publications should not be taxed would have represented a claim for exemption, not for equal treatment, and such a claim, while made on occasion (but usually in disguised form), was not viewed as an essential feature of press freedom, notwithstanding the English experience.[16]

A final observation concerns the legal status of knowledge taxes in the eighteenth and, particularly, the nineteenth century. The most problematic of the nineteenth-century taxes (at least as judged by historical standards) lasted for only a short time. This is so, especially, with the federal and Virginia taxes. Their demise, however, was quiet and achieved politically, their invalidity tacitly rather than expressly acknowledged. Courts rarely became involved; when they did, they didn't help. Taxation of the press, as such, even confiscatory taxation aimed at specific publications, was not deemed problematic in constitutional or other "legal" terms.

Notwithstanding this, one can also detect from the political resolution of the most problematic taxes and from scattered judicial opinions relating largely to direct censorship, not taxation, the beginnings of an approach based largely on preventing censorship of specific ideas or publications through the device of taxation. That such a concept emerged is not surprising, as the one clear thread running throughout the history of knowledge taxation from its very beginnings was the use of such taxes to coerce and control expression. What is surprising is that the knowledge tax problem was not understood in more expansive terms, particularly in view of the recently successful English struggle based not on preventing censorship but instead on broad principles of access to information and diversity of publication. Yet it was not until the end of the nineteenth century that the limited idea that the power to tax should not extend to censorship took hold in America.

Notes

1. The dismantling of the English knowledge taxes was not "complete" until 1861. See Chapter 1.
2. See Collet Dobson Collet, *History of the Taxes on Knowledge: Their Origin and Repeal* 76 (facsimile reprint 1971) (1933); Chapter 1.
3. See Chapter 1.
4. See Chapter 4.
5. See Chapter 3.
6. 460 U.S. 575 (1983), discussed in Chapter 9.
7. See Chapter 4.
8. An example of differential rates on various publications would be the proposed federal stamp tax, discussed in Chapter 3.
9. See Chapter 4.
10. See Chapter 1.
11. See Chapters 6 and 7.
12. 17 Tex. Ct. App. 253 (1884).

13. Some of the Virginia taxes were similarly confiscatory in amount. See Chapter 4.

14. See Chapter 4.

15. For a full discussion of this issue, see Chapter 7.

16. The end result of the English struggle, of course, was largely the achievement of exempt status, a fact which may have made general principles difficult to extract from that history. See Chapter 1.

6. Knowledge Taxes in Twentieth-Century America

The Dawn of a New Age of Technology

With the advent of the twentieth century, America had entered a period of industrial expansion, a period marked, among other things, by increasing economic complexity and growth in governmental regulation at all levels. Significant shifts in population from rural to urban areas had already begun, and they accelerated during the early twentieth century. With industrial expansion came industrial concentration. The scale of business as well as the scale of cities increased; so also did the scale of government and the pervasiveness of its regulatory and fiscal presence.

The press was changing, too, and in ways that mirrored the economy as a whole. The rise of the penny press, begun in the mid-1800s, occasioned dramatic changes in the news business. With increasing concentrations of population in urban centers came the opportunity for truly mass distribution of information to new and relatively homogeneous audiences. And these facts ushered in an era of explosive technological change in the publication and distribution of information, an era in which the power of the press became highly concentrated in a few very large organizations. As Michael Schudson has observed:

> The new journalism of the penny press . . . ushered in a new order, a shared social universe in which "public" and "private" would be redefined. . . . With the growth of cities and commerce, everyday life acquired a density and a fascination quite new, "society" was palpable as never before, and the newspapers — especially the penny papers — were both agent and expression of this change.[1]

News became pervasive and powerful, as did the large, highly organized, and increasingly powerful news organizations. And journalism, as a profession marked by standardized processes, institutionalized norms of value and behavior, and even educational legitimacy, came of age. With the power and political influence that journalists and the news organizations exerted, the political dynamics of knowledge taxation changed. Along with the increasingly pervasive and intricate mechanisms for government funding came the highly *political* issues of exemption from taxation and of protecting markets and power through differential exactions.

Finally, as the twentieth century passed beyond its midpoint, yet another transformation began to manifest itself. This one was technological in nature, and its early signs were most evident, perhaps, in the field of communication. Thus, in the latter half of the century we began to witness great structural changes in communication and in the press, brought on by computer technology and the explosive development of technologies of distribution of information, including cable and satellite transmission, telecommunications, and the emergence of vast amounts of information in data bases, accessible to a wide array of persons and organizations. These developments in turn began to produce structural changes that are now only in their infancy. A communication industry that became highly centralized in the industrial period, especially with the press and publishing businesses, witnessed thereafter the beginnings of radical transformation toward *de*centralization, toward fragmentation of markets and audiences, toward specialization in function, toward economically viable publication on a smaller scale, and toward variety in editorial approach. Mass markets no longer dominated. Large-scale organizations operating under widely enforced rules of journalism became substantially displaced by small organizations employing more idiosyncratic rules.

In short, the texture of the knowledge tax problem in the twentieth century became infinitely more complex; so also with the range of our inquiry. Our study of knowledge taxes in the twentieth century will by sheer necessity, if nothing else, become even more illustrative, yet more specific in focus, holding to the threads and strands inherited from the nineteenth century. We will explore only briefly the ever-broadening modes of economic regulation of knowledge which, as the century progresses, have become increasingly difficult to distinguish from taxation of the press, even though they often differ in form. These new forms of exaction include, for example, the postal regulations and rate structures, which will be addressed in a separate chapter but in summary fashion only, regulation of emerging technologies of communication, direct regulation of distribution of information, and the ever more complex income tax structure.

In focusing principally on the more traditional forms of retail sales and gross receipts taxes, paper and ink use taxes, stamp (now postal) exactions, and their modern offspring, this historical analysis can be criticized for . incompleteness. Incomplete it is. But the criticism, I think, would be unjustified, for the purpose of this historical review is amply served by following the principal strands, incomplete as they may be, through the chosen period. More basically, the underlying forces of interest in the present work do not appear, upon review of the new and diverse forms of exaction, to be very different from those relevant to the sales tax, use tax, and postal exactions.[2] In this, of course, I may be wrong, and I hope that others will probe more broadly, and in the course of doing so shed additional light.

Introductions and qualifications now aside, we will turn our attention to the twentieth century. In the following pages this period has been divided into two basic parts, the first chronicling the historical developments during the present century, including a general discussion of state sales tax regimes between roughly 1930 and 1950, supplemented by an in-depth history of taxation in two states, Massachusetts and Illinois. This is a period during which the centralization of the press and of mass communication reached full bloom. The second section will address the knowledge tax issues in the context of expanded media of communication in the twentieth century. This section will focus principally on the second half of the century, during which mass markets began to break down, communication became increasingly *de*centralized, and new technologies began to develop at a radical pace.

Sales and Use Taxation to Mid-Century

The twentieth century brought with it a period of great economic expansion, the development of large-scale industry in urban centers throughout the country, and increased government intervention and its concomitant. increased demand for sources of public revenue. These developments did not much affect the press and the taxation of knowledge, however, until the Great Depression. This is especially so at the state and local levels where. with the exception of postal exactions, discussed generally in a later chapter, the brunt of knowledge taxes have been imposed. Our discussion of state and local taxation of knowledge, therefore, begins with the Great Depression and focuses on the principal mode of taxation and the principal chosen source of revenue, the sales tax.

Treatment of the Press in Early State Sales and Use Tax Structures

The widespread adoption of state sales and use taxes throughout the country was more a product of economic necessity than of free choice, at least at the beginning. And their application to the press and other instruments of communication was, quite frankly, only incidental to the adoption of broad-based tax schemes. It was the Great Depression and the concomitant need for substantial new revenue to support programs for the unemployed, measures to spur economic development, and the continuing costs of increasing governmental activity at the state and local levels, that required states to implement broad consumption taxes during the 1930s.[3]

In 1930, only two states levied sales taxes. The number rose to fifteen by 1933.[4] By 1938, more than half of the states had adopted a sales tax in some form.[5] The same pattern was generally followed with use taxes. Although specifically focused levies on the use, storage, or consumption of selected articles of personal property within a state were imposed occasionally before the Depression,[6] the general use tax came into being along with the sales tax.[7] The use tax complemented the sales tax, filling the gaps created by the states' inability to impose sales taxes on goods purchased outside their borders.[8]

Prior to 1937 it was generally believed that interstate transactions were immune from sales and compensating use taxes by virtue of the Commerce Clause of the United States Constitution, which was intended to foreclose barriers to trade among the states.[9] As a result, states restricted their sales taxes to only local transactions. Two inequities resulted from this. First, corporations avoided consumption taxes by structuring their transactions as interstate sales. Second, residents of taxing states circumvented taxation by purchasing goods in jurisdictions that did not tax sales or did so at lower rates.[10]

To vitiate the Commerce Clause impediment to sales taxes on interstate shipments, state officials sought federal legislation authorizing state taxation of the transactions.[11] The National Association of State Tax Administrators was formed in 1934 to lobby for such federal authorization. Bills were introduced in Congress, but none survived both houses.[12] During this period, the states of Washington and California enacted compensating use taxes to remedy the inequities caused by sales taxes restricted to purely local transactions.[13] The need for congressional action was eliminated in 1937, however, when the Supreme Court upheld Washington's use tax in *Henneford v. Silas Mason Co.*[14] In sustaining the tax against Commerce Clause challenge, the Court stated that because the tax on the privilege of using tangible personal property within the jurisdiction was imposed after the article had come to rest within the taxing state, its incidence did not fall on the stream of commerce protected against burdens by the Constitution.[15] As might be expected, other states quickly imposed similar forms of compensating use taxes, and the era of state sales and use taxes came of age.[16]

THE IMPOSITION OF SALES AND USE TAXES ON THE PRESS, 1935–50

Because the application of sales and use taxes to publishers was incidental to the larger revenue objectives of such tax schemes and indeed promised little in the way of marginal revenue, their application to publishers was hardly a make-or-break issue. From the beginning, therefore, most states specifically exempted newspapers and periodicals from sales taxes and from compensating use taxes, which normally would take the form of paper and ink taxes.[17] This pattern, begun at the very inception of state sales and use taxation following the Depression, continues to the present, though it is not a universal rule.[18] The pattern, as well as the variants on it, is reflected in the experience of six states whose consumption tax systems during the 1930s and 1940s are outlined below. The pattern is reflected as well in the experience of Massachusetts and Illinois, whose record is recounted more thoroughly from the beginning of the twentieth century to the present. The Massachusetts and Illinois histories are not only illustrative of the broad array of settings in which taxation and related issues have arisen in this century; they also serve as a useful transition to the increasingly complex and technological environment in which such issues will arise in the future.

New York

New York followed a common taxation scheme during the first half of the twentieth century. The state taxed activities involving enumerated articles whenever sold or used within the state. This is in contrast to a general sales and use tax, whose scope was reflected not in the articles subject to the incidence of tax, but was rather reflected in its exemptions. For example, in New York beer was taxed "when sold within this state or used for commercial purposes within this state." New York singled out three species of goods and taxed activities involving them to the limit of its constitutional power, visiting the tax on either the point of use or the point of sale.[19] Because the state taxed only specific goods or activities defined by statute and had no general sales or use tax,[20] newspapers were not objects of taxation even though not specifically exempted.

In New York City, however, a sweeping retail sales tax was enacted in the 1930s. As an emergency revenue measure, the city imposed a two percent tax on receipts generated from every sale of tangible personal property sold at retail.[21] Against the background of a general sales tax on tangible personal property, the code explicitly exempted, among other things, sales of newspapers and periodicals.[22]

Ohio

In 1937 Ohio promulgated a "use and storage" tax. The legislation imposed a sliding scale tax on the storage, use, or other consumption of tangible personal property within the state. The tax was coordinated in its provisions with Ohio's general sales tax.[23] Some, but apparently not all, newspapers were exempt from the use tax. The act exempted from taxation the storage, use, or consumption of tangible personal property that was exempt from Ohio's general sales tax.[24] Exempt sales, in turn, included the sales of newspapers and magazines shipped by second-class mail.[25]

The Ohio tax was notable for two reasons. First, it immunized only publications shipped by second-class mail, presumably subjecting newsstand purchases and carrier delivery to both the use and sales taxes.[26] Second, it carefully delineated what constituted a newspaper or magazine. The provision, contained in the revenue department regulations, is worth recounting in detail.

Sales of newspapers and magazine subscriptions shipped by second-class mail are not subject to the [sales] tax.

For purposes of this Act, a newspaper shall be: A publication bearing a title or name, published at a fixed place of business, regularly issued at fixed intervals as frequently as once a week and having a second-class mailing privilege, being not less than four pages of five columns or more each; the primary function of such a publication shall be to inform, instruct, enlighten and entertain; and to which the general public as a whole will and does resort for intelligence of passing events of a political, religious, commercial and social nature, local and general current happenings, editorial comment, announcements, miscellaneous reading matter, advertisements and other notices; circulated and distributed from an established place of business to subscribers or readers generally of all classes in the county or counties in which it is circulated, for a definite price or consideration for each copy or at a fixed price per annum, the circulation of which is proven bona fide by at least fifty percent thereof being paid for by regular subscribers or through recognized news dealers;

must publish in all editions an average of forty percent news matter which has sufficient merit to have created a following of paid readers; *provided*, such a publication must be eligible for membership in the Ohio Newspaper Association or the American Newspaper Publishers' Association, and if published daily it must be eligible to become a subscriber or member of one of the recognized news gathering organizations in the United States, such as the Associated Press, United Press, United News Service, and it must be a newspaper of general circulation.

This definition shall not be construed to include publications such as racing forms, shopping guides and similar publications devoted primarily to advertising or any other publications devoted solely to specialized fields.[27]

This remarkable definition literally bristles with verbosity. When all is said and done, it appears that Ohio exempted from sales and use taxation most daily and weekly "newspapers" as we understand that term in the traditional sense. Many periodicals of unconventional nature, whether by virtue of irregular publication dates or disqualification from membership in private news organizations, and periodicals not qualifying as magazines but published at intervals greater than one week, were subject to the taxes. Moreover, the exact definition of "magazines" that were exempted is unclear. The precise impact and administration of the scheme, however, is not known.

Colorado

Colorado's sales tax was, like most, a product of necessity. In 1935 the legislature enacted the Emergency Retail Sales Tax Act of 1935, a general sales tax. The Act levied a two percent tax on the purchase price paid or charged upon sales of tangible personal property at retail.[28] Exempted from the general tax were sales and purchases of "newsprint and printers ink for use by publishers of newspapers and commercial printers." Such transactions were treated as wholesale sales.[29] At the same time, the sales tax upon retail purchases exempted sales of newspapers, declaring that newspapers were not corporeal personal property and therefore were not subject to the tax.[30]

In 1937 Colorado supplemented the sales tax through enactment of a "use" tax imposed on the privilege of storing, using, or consuming in the state any articles of tangible personal property purchased at retail.[31] Consistent with the sales tax, the use tax exempted "the storage, use or consumption of printers ink and newsprint."[32]

Arizona

Arizona followed the New York pattern rather than that of Ohio and Colorado. Rather than enacting a general sales and use tax, Arizona imposed a use tax only on specifically identified items or transactions. For example, in 1941 Arizona enacted a Use Fuel Tax, which imposed a tax of five cents per gallon of fuel used within the state.[33] No express exemption from this or other similar taxes was enacted, nor was it needed, as no use tax was imposed on any article used uniquely or primarily by newspapers and periodicals.

Washington

Washington, of course, was one of the first states to enact a sales tax on articles coming into the state from interstate commerce. The State's Occupation and Sales Tax or Excise of 1935, which survived Commerce Clause attack in the *Silas Mason Co.* case,[34] exempted from a two percent retail sales tax the distribution and newsstand sale of newspapers.[35] The exemption was continued in subsequent reenactments of the law in the 1940s.[36]

Washington's compensating use tax seemingly applied to the instrumentalities of the press, however. The original act provided that a tax was imposed on the use of "every article of tangible personal property except as hereinafter provided."[37] Only five exemptions appear to have been granted, none of which encompassed newspapers.[38] While newspapers and other periodicals seem to have been subject to the use tax in Washington, through use of paper and ink, the tax, set at two percent, was low and perhaps of marginal interest to publishers. Unlike Washington's use tax on fuel oil and cigarettes,[39] the general use tax, imposed on the raw materials employed, not on the full cost or selling price of a paper, and set at only two percent, was probably not burdensome.

Pennsylvania

Pennsylvania's pattern of taxation began very early. In 1821 Pennsylvania enacted a mercantile tax, which originally applied to the sale of "foreign" (non-Pennsylvania) goods, and was later extended to the sale of all goods at retail and, ultimately, at wholesale as well.[40] The mercantile tax act imposed a license fee (in nominal amount) and a license tax the amount of which varied with sales. There were few exemptions, and no exemptions for sales of publications. The tax continued beyond the turn of the century and provided some base of experience for the state when, during the Depression, the first formal sales tax was enacted.

The Emergency Relief Sales Tax Act, Pennsylvania's first sales tax, was enacted in 1933 for the purpose of generating revenue to support the state's unemployment fund, and it was imposed only for a period of six months.[41] The Act levied a one percent tax on the gross receipts from the sale of tangible personal property which, in the absence of any further definition in the statute, was left to common law interpretation and included within its sweep the sale of periodicals and publications.

It was not until 1953 that Pennsylvania once again enacted a sales tax, this time to provide support for public schools in the state. Once again, the tax was of limited duration, expiring after two years. The tax actually consisted of two taxes, the Consumers Sales Tax[42] and a companion Use and Storage Tax.[43] The use tax specifically exempted newspapers, magazines, and other periodicals,[44] and the sales tax likewise excluded sales of newspapers, magazines, and other periodicals from the definition of "sale at retail."[45]

Shortly after the expiration of the 1953 sales and use taxes Pennsylvania adopted its first permanent sales tax law. Titled the "Selective Sales and Use Tax Act" and adopted in 1956, the Act imposed a sales tax on a long list of goods sold at retail and imposed a use tax on essentially the same items in order to compensate for revenue lost from the purchase of goods out of state.[46] The tax was complex, both in its definitions of goods subject to tax and in its exemptions. For our purposes the important point is that the Act exempted from tax the sale at retail or use of "periodicals and publications which are published at regular intervals not exceeding three months, circulated among the general public and containing matters of general interest and reports of current events."[47] Newspapers and magazines published at least quarterly were therefore exempt; other publications, including books, were not exempt from the tax. The terminology of the provision exempting newspapers and periodicals has been carried forward in future versions of the Pennsylvania tax.

The Selective Sales and Use Tax was superseded in 1963 by the Tax Act of 1963 for Education.[48] The structure of the 1963 act was similar to the 1956 act, although the exemptions were broadened. The exemption for newspapers and periodicals was retained in essentially identical form. In addition, exemption was provided for the sale at retail or use of tangible personal property or services used in "broadcasting radio and television programs by licensed commercial stations,"[49] and the sale at retail or use of "motion picture film rented or licensed from a distributor for the purpose of commercial exhibition,"[50] "mail order catalogs and direct mail advertising materials,"[51] and "religious publications sold by religious groups and Bibles and religious articles."[52] Once again, books were not exempt.

The 1963 act was technically repealed but in fact substantially re-enacted as part of the Tax Reform Code of 1971, an act which embraced within it all of the various tax provisions found in Pennsylvania law.[53] While the exemptions were essentially the same, two of them are of particular interest. The first was an exemption for the sale at retail or use "of textbooks for use in [accredited] schools, colleges and universities, either public or private when purchased in behalf of or through such schools, colleges or universities."[54] Because books were taxed under the act, it appears that the general tax exempt status of educational institutions had not proved adequate to protect such sales by those institutions. A specific exemption was therefore required.

The second noteworthy exemption was that for newspapers and periodicals, which was both expanded and made more specific. The provision excluded from tax:

> The sale at retail or use of periodicals and publications which are published at regular intervals not exceeding three months, and which are circulated among the general public and containing matters of general interest and reports of current events published for the purpose of disseminating information of a public character or devoted to literature, the sciences, art or some special industry. This exclusion shall also include any printed advertising material circulated with such periodical or publication regardless of where or by whom such printed advertising material was produced.[55]

The various purposes to be served by the expanded provision are unknown, but it appears that the added language concerning matter of a "public character or devoted to literature, the sciences, art or some special industry" had the effect both of making the inclusive nature of the exemption clear, and also of limiting it so as not to include, perhaps, sexually explicit or obscene publications. The final sentence seems clearly directed to advertising inserts which, by 1971, had become commonplace in newspapers.[56]

CONCLUSIONS ON THE SALES AND USE TAX EXPERIENCE, 1935–50

The experience with the imposition of sales and use taxes on publications in the first half of the twentieth century is reflected in the enactments of the six states, as well as Illinois and Massachusetts discussed below. While the states were not selected at random, they were selected with a view to obtaining a fair representation from a geographic, population, and cultural perspective. A review of other states, not discussed in detail here, suggests the representative nature of the experience in the eight chosen jurisdictions.

Indeed, it should also be observed that the experience reflected in the early stages of sales taxation continues, in general, to be borne out today. A survey of the current sales and use tax policies of the fifty states led to the following conclusions. Of the forty-six states with an applicable sales or use tax, fully forty states exempt newspapers. Sixteen states have fairly broad exemptions for both newspapers and periodicals, while twenty-four states broadly exempt only newspapers. With respect specifically to periodicals, many states provide limited rather than broad exemptions, and the limitations vary. North Carolina, for example, exempts only sales of magazines by door-to-door vendors,[57] Alabama exempts religious publications,[58] Arizona only exempts state travel magazines,[59] and Idaho exempts periodicals published and sold by tax-exempt charitable organizations.[60] Also interesting is the fact that at least forty states *impose* a sales or gross revenue tax on telecommunications, and as many as seven more states impose a tax different in form or title but functionally similar to a gross receipts tax.[61] The differential character of nearly universal exemption for newspapers and frequent exemption for other print-based current publications, when contrasted with the widespread taxation of nonprint telecommunication media which are now pervasively involved in the transmission of current information,[62] is striking. This raises issues that will be explored in some detail in the next chapter.

The conclusions that can be drawn from the sales and use tax experience in the first half of the twentieth century are limited, but interesting. The first concerns the near-unanimity of the states in exempting newspapers from the sales and use taxes.[63] This is remarkable primarily because of its apparent unremarkability. The exemption seems to have been almost second nature, and while little contemporaneous legislative and newspaper material has been reviewed, the fact of nearly unanimous exemption from the very first enactments in the states suggests that the exemption issue was hardly controversial. In part this might be traceable to the United States Supreme Court's denunciation of a discriminatory exemption in the *Grosjean* case in 1936,[64] but many of the statutes predated that decision. It is equally likely that the pattern of exemption had been set with the earliest statutes, like Washington's, and even earlier with the state and local sales and peddler taxes enacted in the nineteenth century.[65] The newspapers, of course, exerted considerable influence on the legislative process when it touched their domain, as newspapers were the principal way in which the general population received public information at the time, and they no doubt had a hand in the matter.

The second conclusion concerns the scope of the exemptions. At least in those states having a general sales and use tax, which required that exemptions be explicit, the scope of the materials excluded from taxation was often narrow. Ohio, of course, defined newspapers very narrowly. Washington appears to have exempted only the distribution and newsstand sales of newspapers and not to have exempted magazines. Only those states imposing focused sales taxes appear to have exempted publications in the broadest terms, and then by default rather than by deliberate design.

The specific terms of the exemptions, however, are not as important as their general thrust. Here there are two observations to be made. The first is that the focus of concern (or, to the skeptic, of political power) was on the traditional and principally daily or regular "news of the day" publications. At the time these were, and had always been, the principal instruments of broad public dissemination of public information. The rise of the special interest periodicals of *commercial* character had not really occurred. It is therefore understandable that the focus was more restricted. We shall see in a later section the impact on tax policies of the increasing fragmentation of markets, the growing specialization of publications, and perhaps most importantly the emergence of new technologies which have begun to re-place the newspaper as the principal source of daily news and information.

The second observation, noteworthy with the sales taxes but equally true before the advent of state sales taxes, as well as today, is the clear distinction drawn between periodicals on the one hand, and books on the other. This distinction has deep historical roots which appear not, even today, to have been reexamined. None of the sales taxes that have been examined exempt books from taxation. The exemption of paper and ink from compensating use taxation, which on its face would often apply to books, is of no significance, as the sales tax was imposed on books and therefore exemption from the use tax would be of no practical effect.

The principal focus of this book is on the "press," and therefore a complete exploration of the phenomenon of imposing sales taxes on books is beyond the scope of this work. Some thoughts on this peculiar situation, however, can be ventured. The origins of the distinction between periodi-cals and books may be traceable to the origins of copyright protection in the seventeenth century, the initial focus of which was on books.[66] Following the demise of the licensing system in England in the late seventeenth century, copyright afforded a necessary and ample means by which the

Crown could perpetuate its "control" of books; taxation was not needed. In the context of the subsequent system of "exactions," therefore, the distinction between current periodicals and books originated *sub silentio* in the stamp duty setting, where the focus was placed on exerting government control over the newer and less "manageable" sources of information on current political affairs, and therefore on periodical publications rather than books.[67]

This original pattern of exactions on "news" in the interest of government control has persisted since the first Stamp Act of 1712 and has carried over into the advertisement and paper tax settings. Because books were not originally of principal concern to the Crown from the perspective of government control—especially in view of the control then more directly exerted through the copyright system as well as the books' more limited availability only to the educated (and governing) classes—they were not generally subject to the exactions. This background makes it understandable but ironic that success in the English struggle against the stamp in the periodical setting has resulted, today, in frequent exemption of news from taxation, but nonexemption of books. In effect, the tables have been completely turned. While books were not originally subject to exaction and periodicals were, today periodicals are not but, largely by virtue of inattention, books are. "Knowledge" was news and current information, not history, religion, or philosophy, at least for purposes of the sobriquet "Knowledge Taxes."

It is hard to make sense of this state of affairs without the perspective of the knowledge tax problem. From any vantage point of timelessness and, ultimately, cultural impact and value, taxation of books but not of news can hardly be justified. On the other hand, if our perspective is that of the struggle against the stamp, it is historically accurate to say that the principal mode of *general* public access to information was the periodical press, and therefore from a purely "democratic" point of view the preference for access to news over books is consistent with the goal of broad dissemination of information to all parts of a society. The availability of information to the general citizenry was, after all, the animating goal of the English struggle. It is worth noting, however, that today the "book" is less the province of the privileged or educated classes, as the mass merchandising of the book chain stores attests, and it is more often a source of current information. We might, therefore, reexamine in today's world the justification for taxation of books even from the vantage point of the interest in broad dissemination of current knowledge to the public.

We will return once again to the subject of taxation of books and other sources of information in our contemporary communication marketplace in a later chapter, but for the moment our focus is on early state sales and use tax regimes. The state sales and use tax experience in the first half of the twentieth century is of interest because, while it reflects a pattern of relief from taxation of news and periodicals that had been set in England, it constitutes a departure from the hard edge of experience with knowledge taxes in the nineteenth century. The pattern set with state sales and use tax schemes, in other words, manifests both a quiet and natural acceptance of the order of things that emerged from previous struggles that were anything but quiet and natural, as well as a political solution assisted in no small measure, one suspects, by the political force of the news industry in the twentieth century. It is probably more than coincidental that the mid-nineteenth-century development of the penny press matured into the rise of the large—and powerful—metropolitan and regional newspaper at and after the turn of the century, just as the sales tax system (and the exemption issues it raised) blossomed.[68]

There is an additional reason for the exemption of news but not of books that should be mentioned, as it is at once technically important and also intellectually curious and complex, especially in its persistent influence to this day. From the beginning the sales tax structure was predicated on taxing *tangible* personal property. And the "product" of a newspaper— news—was most commonly viewed as intangible, and thus not subject to tax. Books, though, were tangible, both physically and in the purported durability of their value. The pattern of exemption of news, in other words, may also be traced to a sort of intellectual accident, not to conscious policy choice alone.[69]

With few exceptions, newspapers and periodicals were relieved from taxation in rather broad and categorical terms, and the discrimination sometimes reflected in the exemption provisions seems not to have caused trouble or concern. The distinction between periodicals and books—news and knowledge—was hardly noticed, if at all, and this state of affairs continues to this day. In this and other respects the strands from the past— resistance to censorship and the goal of broad dissemination of information to all levels of society—continued unabated, even if somewhat unintentionally. The new problems posed by a changing market in information and the explosive emergence of new technologies, posing very different problems to which the strands from the past would not as easily apply, remained dormant.

State Knowledge Taxation in a Changing Environment: The Massachusetts and Illinois Experiences

Use and sales taxation were, to a significant degree, symptomatic of larger forces at work during the twentieth century. These included, of course, industrial expansion and economic growth. But they included as well other forces bearing directly on the press and communication, such as greatly expanding government regulation of the private sector of the economy, shifting political attitudes toward the press, changing cultural definitions of the role of the individual in society, tendencies to resist change and toward protectionism for existing economic interests, and the related explosion of technology. Through a detailed chronology of knowledge taxation in Massachusetts and Illinois from 1900 to the present, we will trace the development of those larger trends and see the complex issues they pose for an approach to knowledge taxation in the present and the future.

MASSACHUSETTS

It will be recalled that after a brief period of taxation in colonial times and another brief effort to enforce a paper tax shortly after the Revolution, Massachusetts was essentially free of knowledge taxes throughout the nineteenth century.[70] Indeed, the almost complete freedom from taxation and accompanying regulation existed not only for newspapers, but for pamphlets and books as well. The twentieth century, however, brought great change, both social and economic. With great change came efforts at taxation and regulation of the press. While rarely successful in the end, the story of such efforts in Massachusetts is instructive.

Hawking, Peddling, and Vending Regulation

The first developments in the twentieth-century history of taxation in Massachusetts occurred in the law regulating hawkers. In 1928 the General Court, by resolution, convened a commission to reexamine the law regarding hawkers and peddlers.[71] That law, it will be recalled, had since 1846 exempted "newspapers, books, and pamphlets" from its provisions.[72] For reasons that are not fully explicated in the legislative record but likely arose out of a need to control the proliferation of door-to-door peddling of periodicals at the time,[73] the commission's recommendations included removal of the exemption for books and pamphlets, and in 1929 books and pamphlets were eliminated from the list of goods that hawkers could sell without a license.[74] Pamphlets and books could still be sold by hawkers, but they were subject to licensing fees by towns; only newspapers were exempt.[75] In order to obtain a license, the hawker had to obtain a certificate signed by the mayor or a majority of town selectmen. A local license could cost anywhere from four to twenty-six dollars depending on the town population. A special state license that would entitle the hawker to sell goods throughout the state cost fifty dollars.

A 1930 Massachusetts Supreme Judicial Court decision involving the 1929 act revealed little more about its background and purpose than that the longstanding exemption had been removed. The court cited a state senate document which noted: "Under present conditions it is felt that supervision is needed in the peddling of these articles (books and pamphlets), and no reason appears why the sale thereof should be permitted without a license."[76] There is no explanation why the "supervision" became necessary, although it was likely due to the continued growth of the door-to-door sales industry.

In 1931, the hawking laws were again amended, but this time the purpose was to expand the exemptions by adding religious publications in the list of goods and merchandise that could be sold without a license. This was effectively a partial reinstatement of the exemption for books and pamphlets that had been eliminated in 1929.[77] While specific legislative background is not available on the amendment, the exemption of religious materials was by then a common practice in many states, and it remains so to this day.[78]

The hawker statute experienced little legislative change from 1931 to the early 1970s, when litigation arose with respect to a local ordinance based, in part, on it. The town of Cambridge enacted an ordinance requiring hawkers selling newspapers to obtain a permit and badge before selling on Harvard Yard.[79] The ordinance was challenged in federal court, and on appeal the United States Court of Appeals for the First Circuit ruled in *Wulp v. Corcoran*[80] that the municipal attempt to license hawkers was unconstitutional even if it did not violate any state statute.[81] The court held, based on the First Amendment, that "the physical acts of registering and of procuring and wearing a badge" cannot be required of a hawker of a newspaper.[82] The town had also attempted to levy a small licensing fee. This appeared to violate the fee exemption for newspapers.[83]

In the years since the *Wulp* decision, the Massachusetts hawker statute has remained essentially intact. Towns are still permitted to regulate hawkers but may not require a license or fee.[84] Newspapers are exempted from licensing fees, but books and pamphlets — other than religious materials —

are not. The latter feature exempting religious publications is of uncertain constitutionality in light of the Supreme Court's recent, although not altogether consistent, decisions.[85]

In 1979 a new attempt at knowledge taxes occurred, and it contained a number of new twists. While also of doubtful constitutionality, it was, quite rightly, taken very seriously. State Senator McKenna filed two bills in the 1979 legislative session, one that would have required all reporters covering the General Court to disclose their financial assets, and a second bill that would have required investigative reporters to be licensed as private detectives.[86] The senator argued that he saw "no reason to put reporters in a special class."[87] McKenna also announced that "the First Amendment does not afford (reporters) the privilege they claim which they have been getting away with for 300 years."[88]

Unlike the early attempts at taxation of the press in Massachusetts, the primary purpose of these bills appeared to be a combination of retaliation and censorship.[89] McKenna had been the "victim" of unfavorable press coverage in the past.[90] While testifying before a joint judiciary committee, McKenna observed, "they'll [reporters] be more careful about what they say in the paper about legislators — or about anyone."[91]

The licensing bill was passed by the Massachusetts Senate, and Boston's largest newspaper, the *Globe*, editorialized strongly against it.[92] The *Globe* noted that the state senate had passed a bill that violated Article 16 of the Massachusetts Constitution and called McKenna's actions "an unconstitutional restraint on 'the liberty of the press.'"[93] The editorial observed that because of the $750 licensing fee, the press would be restrained by unfair taxation.[94] The bill (S. 1093) was eventually declared unconstitutional by a joint judiciary committee but not before it had gained passage in the Senate and preliminary approval in the House of Representatives.[95] Several state representatives expressed surprise that such a blatant attempt to tax and license reporters could gain approval, and the *Boston Globe* warned against the ignorance it reflected.[96]

McKenna's second bill, which would have required personal financial disclosure by General Court reporters, never made it to the governor's desk either. Instead, it was taken (by the *Globe*) to the Massachusetts Supreme Judicial Court for an advisory opinion on its constitutionality. In a 1979 *Opinion of the Justices*, the court told the state senate that the bill (S. 1308) would not be constitutional.[97] The justices admitted that neither the First Amendment to the United States Constitution nor Article XVI of the Massachusetts Constitution gave the press preferred status but concluded nevertheless that the bill "may tend to discourage some from covering State House activities."[98] That the bill's invalidity arose from its underlying purpose was revealed by the court's observation that "[i]mpartial coverage of State House activities cannot be compelled by statute," and that an attempt to do so, by whatever means, would be unconstitutional.[99] In the end neither of Senator McKenna's bills was approved, but that they were offered, that they received favorable votes in the legislature, and that they were taken very seriously, is itself notable.

The next episode in Massachusetts occurred in the 1980s with a series of controversies over newspaper vending machines. As the *Boston Globe* noted in its coverage of the issue, vending machines have largely assumed the place in the twentieth century of the hawkers and peddlers of the nineteenth century.[100] In 1983 three Massachusetts towns enacted regulations to license vending machines. The regulations appear to have been specifically directed at the brightly colored machines of *USA Today*.[101] The regulations required permits for each rack and left a great deal of discretion with town officials.[102] A federal district court struck down this local attempt at licensing as violative of the United States Constitution, largely on the ground that the regulations left too much discretion, subject to no clear standards, with those who were authorized to issue the permits.[103]

Two years later, in 1985, a state representative from the town of Lee introduced a bill in the General Court that would have allowed towns to ban newspaper vending machines from public areas.[104] The major purposes of the bill were to protect public safety by eliminating obstacles to passage, and to preserve aesthetic values.[105] The attempt at regulating vending machines by banning them was reminiscent of the 1883 provision which allowed localities to regulate hawkers and peddlers for public safety.[106] The 1985 bill was pronounced constitutional by Massachusetts Attorney General Francis Bellotti, but the opinion evoked sharp, and surely not unanticipated, criticism from the press.[107] The *Boston Globe* said that the key factor in locating vending machines was to allow "people to have access to them," a purpose that would be effectively thwarted by banning them from public areas.[108] The *New York Times* said the ordinance was "clearly unconstitutional."[109] The *Times* attorney also remarked: "That's not the sort of thing the great old towns of Massachusetts should be doing."[110] The bill did not pass.

While the attempt at regulation on a state level was unsuccessful, in 1987 another local attempt at licensing stirred up controversy. In that year the city of Boston voted, through the city council, to regulate the placement of vending machines as well as to require payment of a twenty-five-dollar permit fee for each machine.[111] According to city council members, the ordinance was designed for aesthetic purposes, but the fee aspect was troublesome to some.[112] Managers of several Boston papers responded angrily. The *Boston Herald* called the ordinance "excessive," while the *Boston Phoenix* general manager said he thought it was illegal.[113] The newspapers most affected by the fee were larger papers such as the *Globe* and *Herald*, but all papers were subject to the regulations on location and design.[114] In this instance, the newspapers did not prevail in defeating the ordinance, although its constitutionality, along with many other ordinances of similar character across the country, remains unsettled.[115]

The Sales Tax

While the regulation of hawking, peddling, and vending machines has received great attention in Massachusetts during the twentieth century, the major taxation issue regarding the Massachusetts press has been the sales tax. Interestingly, the sales tax issue did not arise until the 1960s in Massachusetts, in contrast to much earlier taxing regimes in other states. And the press has generally been free from the imposition of sales taxes in Massachusetts, but with some notable exceptions in recent years.

In 1966 the General Court of Massachusetts (the legislative body) first instituted a state tax on retail sales.[116] As part of the tax scheme, a series of exempt commodities and transactions was identified as not subject to the three percent (now five percent) sales tax. In one section newspapers, books, and magazines were all exempted from the retail sales tax.[117] In another section goods that were used in the production of newspapers, including machinery, were also broadly exempted.[118] The effect of these laws was that newspapers escaped the sales tax burden both in the production process and at the point of retail sale.

A 1971 amendment attempted to narrow the exemption for manufacturing resources to only those materials used "exclusively" in the publishing of a newspaper, but the Supreme Judicial Court interpreted the amendment differently.[119] In a 1986 opinion, *Lowell Sun Publishing v. Commissioner of Revenue*,[120] the court said that "[a] broad exemption for sales of certain property used in the 'publication,' and not just in the printing of a newspaper is consistent with the intent [of the sales tax chapter]."[121] Accordingly, the exemption in the use tax provision was not narrowed and, in effect, the new language in the 1971 amendment was given no effect.[122]

The General Court responded several years later, in 1990, by specifically removing the entire exemption for newspapers in the use tax stat-ute.[123] This legislation had large revenue implications and, as it turned out, large political ones, too. According to the Massachusetts Revenue Commissioner, the new legislation did not disturb the newspapers' exemption from use taxation of ink or paper, but other manufacturing materials and machines would be subject to taxation.[124] This would be true even though materials used by other manufacturers would still be exempt (even though, and indeed *because*, the end product *would* be subject to the sales tax), while use of such materials by newspaper publishers would not. The purpose of the tax did appear to be revenue-based.[125] But to newspapers, who viewed the issue in the context of the use tax alone and not in the larger context of the use and sales tax together, it seemed that this new tax was merely singling out the press for a special burden. In 1990, Massachusetts was suffering from a serious recession, and sources of additional revenue were being eagerly sought. In addition to removing the newspaper use tax exemption, the General Court also levied new sales taxes on many other services.[126]

The *Boston Globe* quickly brought a lawsuit against the Revenue Commissioner claiming that it was, as a newspaper, being singled out for taxation in violation of the First Amendment and Article XVI of the Massachusetts Constitution.[127] The *Globe* argued that the tax "single[d] out newspaper publishers for treatment different from that afforded to other manufacturers."[128] The *Globe* also contended that the tax "discriminate[d] unconstitutionally between newspaper publishers and publishers of other types of publications," such as magazines.[129] The Revenue Commissioner responded that there were no magazines manufactured in Massachusetts (as distinguished from the place of publication), so the argument about differential taxation was irrelevant.[130] The Commissioner also argued that the newspapers were benefited by the differential tax, for if the Commonwealth imposed the standard retail sales tax on newspapers rather than exempting them, the newspapers would pay more.[131] In its reply brief, the *Globe* responded that the very fact of a differential tax, even if less burdensome, could lead to a more burdensome tax in the future, for the principle of permitting different treatment of the press from all other taxpayers would be established and would be difficult to limit.[132]

Although the tax may have been less burdensome than a retail sales tax, it was estimated by several newspapers to be quite steep.[133] The *Globe*'s publisher, William O. Taylor, estimated the cost to be five million dollars annually.[134] The publisher of the smaller *Cape Cod Times* estimated that the tax would cost his paper $157,000, a "substantial amount," as he put it.[135] He also remarked that his paper might not be able to survive.[136] These estimates are much higher than those provided by the state. But whichever is closer to the truth, one might well suspect that something else was at work, and that the "something else" might have been that the machinery and equipment tax, unlike a sales tax, could not be passed on to the customer as easily as a tax imposed on the retail price.

Curiously, there was a surprising lack of editorial outcry from the *Boston Globe* itself, at least when judged by the *Globe's* earlier and more strident editorial positions on the other bills. Perhaps this was a result of the newspaper's previous editorializing in favor of an expansion of the sales tax.[137] Some saw a curious double standard at work, with the newspaper now turning around to sue the Commonwealth over a tax imposed on the *Globe* as part of a general tax that the *Globe* had encouraged.[138]

One final argument used by the *Globe* is illuminating on the way Article XVI of the Massachusetts Constitution is interpreted against the background of the First Amendment to the United States Constitution.[139] In its brief, the *Globe* cited a 1946 Massachusetts case, *Bowe v. Secretary of the Commonwealth*,[140] which acknowledged that "freedom from the need of previous license by no means satisfies the constitutional guarant[ee] [of a free press]."[141] In an ironic twist of fate, the 1979 opinion of the Supreme Judicial Court on the senate bill filed by Senator McKenna to force financial disclosure from reporters had hinted that the Massachusetts Constitution might provide more protection for the press than the United States Constitution.[142] There the court expressed "grave doubts that any asserted governmental interest would support a law such as this, that places a special burden on the press not imposed on the general public."[143] The *Globe* argued that this set up a "per se" rule against any differential taxes—a rule that would be even more strict than the *Minneapolis Star* standard.[144]

The Supreme Judicial Court decided the case on May 20, 1991, and ruled in favor of the *Globe*.[145] The court did not adopt the absolute position advanced by the *Globe*, but instead relied upon the United States Supreme Court's position in the *Minneapolis Star* case, holding that taxation of the press through a different form of tax than that generally applied to other taxpayers had to be justified by a substantial, nonrevenue-based, purpose. The court rejected the relevance of the Commonwealth's attempt to show that the tax was less burdensome and was not, in view of the sales tax exemption, discriminatory in its effect. The court stated that "[i]t is not within the expertise of the court to make such calculations."[146] The risk of erroneous calculation was considered to be too high,[147] and the court found no compelling state interest, even in the administrative burden of collecting a newspaper retail sales tax, to justify the differential treatment of the press.[148] The court did not address the arguments about the distinctions between newspapers and magazines because it had already struck down the tax based on the fact that newspapers were singled out from other manufacturers.[149]

Notwithstanding that the victory was, in significant respects, Pyrrhic,[150] the reaction from the *Boston Globe* was predictably joyous. The *Globe* was "pleased [that] the Supreme Judicial Court had judged this proposed tax to be unconstitutional."[151] The executive director of the Massachusetts Newspaper Publishing Association, William Plante, believed "the cost would have been horrendous."[152] He also remarked that "the newspapers are undergoing economic changes [they] haven't faced since the great depression."[153] The *Globe* largely refrained, however, as it had before the decision, from substantial editorializing about the victory. Fear of public perception of inconsistency, or even hypocrisy, one suspects, held sway in the councils of the editorial page. And given that the court's rationale allowed ample room for imposition of the retail sales tax on newspaper sales, a muted response seems appropriate.

Conclusion

The most recent striking down of the use tax on newspapers confirms a well-established pattern in Massachusetts. Massachusetts is a state in which, like many others, efforts at direct taxation of the press have been attempted. But unlike other states, such efforts have almost universally failed. Massachusetts possesses a longstanding devotion to education and a heritage of liberty and a history of free—even fiercely free—expression. It was the home, after all, of the Boston Tea Party, that most famous example of tax resistance.

The history of knowledge taxation in Massachusetts is therefore one with many attempts but few lasting results. From the short-lived stamp tax of 1755 to the even shorter-lived use and sales tax amendment of 1990, one might conclude that Massachusetts is a state that is willing to propose, but hesitant to dispose, taxes on the press. As we turn now to the state of Illinois, reviewing its history of taxation before venturing broader conclusions on the Massachusetts experience, we will witness a different, and in some ways opposite, pattern: caution in the imposition, but aggressiveness in the disposition, of taxes on the press.

ILLINOIS

Turn-of-the-century Illinois found a legislature increasingly inclined to legislate broadly on a wide range of subjects to protect the general welfare of its citizens. Significant population growth, economic development, and a streak of populism no doubt contributed to this phenomenon. Industrial development brought with it an increasing array of publications available to the population, and this, in turn, carried with it an increased potential for abuse. It also afforded occasion for legislative action, which was forthcoming. As the century unfolded, new occasions for legislation, including legislation taxing publications, were afforded by the difficulties associated with the Great Depression, which hit industrialized Illinois with particular force. And when the dust of the Depression had settled, technology became the occasion for legislative action, and for present purposes it was communication technology that gave rise to the development of tax policies affecting the press, the printed word, and communication in general.

The twentieth century, in short, provides a rich source of historical materials bearing on the knowledge tax question in Illinois. As we shall see, the policies pursued were, if not always laudable, both broad in their reach and surprisingly explicit on the subject of taxation of knowledge. And as the century progresses, the Illinois history provides a bridge from the traditional knowledge tax issues to those presented by emerging communication technologies. The history is instructive, therefore, on the difficulties that lie ahead as technology continues to develop.

Introduction: Knowledge Taxation in a Period of Evolutionary Change
In the pages that follow we will first trace the taxation and regulatory framework as it evolved in Illinois over the course of the twentieth century. This discussion will focus principally, although not exclusively, on legislative enactments, and as the century unfolds the discussion will increasingly concern the adaptation of the traditional sales, use, and occupation tax systems to new and emerging technologies for the production and distribution of news and periodical information. It will focus as well, particularly in the later stages of the century, on the broadening and increasingly elusive concept of news as it evolves rapidly toward a more generic idea of "information."

Following this chronological account of the Illinois experience, we will turn in the final section of this chapter to some general conclusions to be drawn from the Illinois and Massachusetts histories. We will also begin to identify, in light of those states' experience, the issues that will confront state legislatures and courts as they grapple with new forms and technologies of communication and new meanings of information. This is a topic that will carry forward into the next chapter, where it will become our principal focus.

In both discussions we will confront the breaking apart of the previously integrated production, editing, and distribution phases of communication of current news and information. What had been integrated and interdependent steps in a single process within a single organization will increasingly become discrete and isolated steps and enterprises operating within a highly specialized and fragmented "information industry."[154] We will see, as well, a radical change in the meaning of "news"—an increasingly expansive idea of information taking many forms, serving many new functions, and more often than not unaccompanied by the synthesis or selective judgments we have been accustomed to expect of news, and that we have traditionally called "editing."[155] We will assess, finally, the valiant but ultimately futile efforts of legislatures and courts as they attempt to address issues raised by the technologies of information (in the context of taxation) by analogy to past experience, to forms of publication that are increasingly becoming obsolete and that do not provide useful answers or policy guidance through the tight but distorted process of iterative reasoning.

We will be forced, therefore, to begin to think differently about the nature of the knowledge tax problem; to return, interestingly, to the basics and to the general perspectives, rather than to the strict examples, of history. It is from the animating purposes behind the struggle against the taxes on knowledge, and from the underlying principles of freedom that emerged, that we must draw in shaping legislative and judicial policy in a radically different technological future. We begin this complex and challenging undertaking in Illinois shortly after the turn of the century, when the print medium has reached its zenith, and just before the dawn of a new technological era.

Legislative Activism and the Beginnings of Change, 1920–70
Beginning in the early twentieth century, advances in communications technology permitted more widespread dissemination of information by more people, and this provided fertile ground for broadened legislative action in the service of the "general welfare."[156] The increased capacity for disseminating information necessarily brought with it greater potential for abuse, thus affording a rationale for the legislative action. The laws and

court decisions of the period from 1870 to 1917, discussed earlier,[157] reflected in the area of newspapers and periodical publications the early signs of what would eventually become a large body of legislation regulating communication, often through the devices of taxation.

The arrival of the 1920s brought the first of many in a series of sales, use, and service taxes aimed principally at large-scale businesses and retailers. The new laws reflected the growth of the state economy and the commensurate need to increase revenue in support of an expanding government. During the period from 1920 to 1970, legislation established franchise, sales, retailers', and message taxes, each of which we will consider in order.

THE FRANCHISE TAX ACT

As part of a broad Business Corporations Act enacted in 1919, the Illinois legislature enacted a franchise tax act.[158] The 1919 act provided that all businesses organizing themselves as corporations under Illinois law be subject to a yearly franchise tax. The annual tax was set at five cents on each one hundred dollars of the "proportion of its authorized capital stock represented by business transacted and property located in this State."[159] The method for computing the tax was very cumbersome, and this as well as other shortfalls of the tax were later addressed in the Sales Tax Acts and the Retailers' Occupation Tax Act. Because all corporations in the state were responsible for similar fees, the communications industry was not disadvantaged by the tax, and there were no distinctions drawn among media.

For our purposes the franchise tax act is notable primarily because for the first time it employed the term "tangible property." The act defined "tangible property" as corporeal property such as "real estate, machinery, tools, implements, goods, wares and merchandise, and [it] shall not be taken to mean money, deposits in bank, shares of stock, bonds, notes, credits or evidence of an interest in property or evidences of debt."[160] The distinction drawn between corporeal property and physical manifestations of interests or value that lay elsewhere than in the corporeal property itself (such as stock certificates) would become central to the taxation of news under the sales, use, and merchant taxes throughout the 1920–70 period — and beyond.

But in 1919 the "tangible" property issue remained inchoate, and the franchise tax generated little, if any, resistance. Perhaps this was because of its benign character; more likely it was because the cost was nominal. In a sense, however, the franchise tax was an opening salvo, leading soon to other taxes that were less benign, that produced a great deal of revenue, and that generated no small amount of controversy. The battle was first joined with the first attempt to impose a sales tax in 1932.

THE SALES TAX ACTS

The Sales Tax Act of 1932 authorized the levy of a county tax of one percent on retail sales. The Act established for the first time a definition of sale at retail and selling price.[161] The Act was short-lived, however. Its constitutionality was immediately challenged, and within a year of its original passage it was declared unconstitutional by the Illinois Supreme Court in *Winter v. Barrett*[162] because of the manner in which proceeds were distributed under the statute.

In the face of the failure of the 1932 act, the legislature passed the Sales Tax Act of 1933, a stopgap measure that modified the earlier act in light of the failed 1932 legislation. The method by which the proceeds were distributed was revised to comply with the state constitution. But this did not serve to avert controversy. From the very beginning it had in all likelihood been the tax itself, not the use of its proceeds, which *really* caused resistance.

The 1933 Sales Tax Act, like the 1932 act, imposed a tax on the sale of "tangible personal property," thus following a pattern employed in many states. It was the concept of "tangible" personal property that caused both immediate and long-term problems, especially for the media of communication. By its terms the tax appeared to apply to newspapers and all other forms of printed communication, though we shall have much more to say about that in the pages that follow. At the very least no specific exemption for newspapers was enacted.

The problems that lay ahead principally involved whether newspapers and other printed material constituted "tangible" personal property. Moreover, if newspapers could be classified as tangible items, while radio was intangible, could the resulting discrimination against the print media be justified? Because of the vague definition of tangible personal property under the 1933 Sales Tax Act, the precise scope of the Act, as well as its successors which drew on the same terminology, was and remained for many years unclear, affording fertile ground for litigation.

The new bill was vigorously protested by merchants of the day, though the protest was based on the idea of sales taxation itself, not on the impact of the tax on the press. But the 1933 Sales Tax Act withstood scrutiny and was passed into law.[163] It was soon to be revisited, however, in the Retailers' Occupation Tax Act, passed three months after the 1933 Sales Tax Act, which effectively modified the 1933 act.

THE RETAILERS' OCCUPATION TAX ACT OF 1933

The Retailers' Occupation Tax Act was enacted with the same purpose as the Sales Tax Acts of 1932 and 1933: to tax retailers rather than consumers.[164] The new act was much more procedurally sophisticated than the Sales Tax Act, but other than some differences in tax amount and distribution of proceeds the function of the two acts was similar. As in the sales tax, newspapers and periodicals were not specifically exempt from the tax and appeared, at least at first blush, to be treated just like all other forms of "tangible" personal property.[165] And indeed newspapers and other publications were taxed, as they had been under the earlier acts, but only for a brief period, as the discussion below reveals.[166] The tax rate was lowered from three percent to two percent by the Act, no doubt due to merchant objections.[167] Distribution of receipts remained in the hands of the state, as opposed to counties.[168]

With the flurry of legislative and judicial activity over the 1932 and 1933 Sales Tax Acts coming to an end, and with passage of the Retailers' Occupation Tax Act, the dust had finally settled. The controversy over the general question of a sales tax subsided, and the issue about the tax's application only to "tangible" personal property as well as the implications of this limitation for the various media of communication that were only beginning to develop lay dormant. But the issues were destined ultimately to arise, as indeed they did in the form of several important amendments to the 1933 Retailers' Occupation Tax Act.

The first amendment was adopted in 1941. A provision enacted that year stated that "sales of tangible personal property, which property as an ingredient or constituent goes into and forms a part of tangible personal property subsequently the subject of a 'sale at retail,' are not sales at retail as defined in this Act."[169] With respect to newspapers and periodicals the effect, if not the purpose, of this amendment appeared at first glance to be to allow an exemption for the sale of newsprint, ink, and paper because they were parts of a product that was later sold at retail. But it could also be argued that newsprint was not exempt because the subsequent sale of a newspaper was not to be considered a sale at retail under the Act[170] on the theory, later adopted, that a newspaper's value was not the paper and ink, but information, and information (at least current information, or news) was neither "tangible" nor of anything but fleeting value. If the sale of newspapers was not subject to tax, the argument went, then newsprint, ink, and paper were not ingredients of property later sold at retail, and they were therefore not, by the express terms of the amendment, exempted from the tax.

Indeed, this was the position ultimately taken by the state shortly after the Act's enactment in 1933 and prior to the 1941 amendment. The route taken to this end, however, was circuitous. As recounted in the Illinois Supreme Court decision in *Time, Inc. v. Hulman*,[171] it was apparently soon after the Retailers' Occupation Tax Act was enacted in 1933 that the Revenue Department adopted its first version of Rules 2 and 63. The rules provided that "receipts from sales of newspapers, magazines and periodicals, and receipts from subscriptions from Illinois subscribers were subject to this tax."[172] However, in the case of *Calumet Publishing Co. v. McKibben*, which arose in the Cook County Circuit Court, the collection of the tax from newspapers and magazines was declared illegal.[173] The Department of Revenue soon thereafter enacted a Revised Rule 2 which stated that vendors of newspapers, magazines, periodicals, books, sheet music, or phonographic recordations were *not* engaged in the business of selling tangible personal property at retail.[174] After the issuance of the rule, the Revenue Department made no effort to collect the retailers' occupation tax on sales of newspapers and the like until a further amendment passed in 1961, discussed below.[175] Sales of newsprint, ink, and paper, however, were taxable, as they were considered tangible personal property and were not exempt by virtue of the taxability of the later retail sale.

Before further probing the effect of the 1941 amendment, however, and before plumbing the depths of the meaning of "tangible" personal property, we will turn to other amendments. They, with the 1941 amendment, provide the necessary backdrop for what is to come.

The next important amendment was enacted in 1945. It required a registration certificate from the Department of Revenue to sell tangible personal property at retail.[176] A significant aspect of the 1945 amendment involved ways in which the certificate requirement was frustrated by an earlier 1940 Illinois Supreme Court decision. In *Village of South Holland v. Stein*, the court had ruled that with respect to books and pamphlets a local ordinance which prohibited the soliciting of orders for "goods, wares, and merchandise" without a permit was unconstitutional.[177] Although the court expressed uncertainty about whether the ordinance included selling books and pamphlets, it ruled that the ordinance was void with reference to solicitation of orders for books and pamphlets, and that books and pamphlets could not be included in the licensing of goods and merchandise. The *Stein* court observed that "[t]he constitution of Illinois is even more far-reaching than that of the constitution of the United States in providing that every person may speak freely, write, and publish on all subjects."[178]

In 1942 the Illinois Supreme Court expanded the *Stein* decision in *City of Blue Island v. Kozul.*[179] The *Kozul* case involved a city ordinance which required peddlers selling "goods, wares, or merchandise" to obtain a license and pay a license fee.[180] In its opinion the court acknowledged that the magazines sold by the defendants came within the definition of "goods, wares, and merchandise" earlier construed by the *Stein* court.[181] The court held, however, that the city ordinance could not lawfully be applied to sales of magazines and leaflets because to do so would conflict with the First Amendment.[182] The court cited *Grosjean v. American Press Co.*[183] and *Near v. Minnesota*[184] for the principles that even a small license fee could lead to a curtailing of freedom of the press and censorship, and that the First Amendment applied to both distribution *and* publication.[185] Although the *Kozul* court acknowledged that publishers and distributors were not immune from state taxation, it held that the licensing fee forced the publishers and distributors to pay for something to which they were entitled as a matter of right under the First Amendment.[186]

Both the *Stein* and *Kozul* decisions held that although magazines, books, pamphlets, and the like were included in the terms "goods, wares, and merchandise," they could not be subject to a license requirement, a conclusion that had clear implications for the validity of the 1945 amendment. Although a license to sell personal property is a valid requirement, and therefore a certificate for that purpose as required by the amendment was likewise valid, the courts had held that such licenses and the accompanying license fees could not be applied to the sale of newspapers, magazines, and pamphlets under the First Amendment. The press was thus freed from an obligation imposed generally on others, and the application of the 1945 amendment to publishers of newspapers and magazines was frustrated. But the related, yet distinct, question of the applicability of a sales tax (as opposed to a license or certificate) to newspapers and magazines, either as a matter of constitutional law or a construction of the term "tangible personal property," was not explicitly touched upon in *Stein* or *Kozul*, and was therefore left to the devices of the Department of Revenue.

It was not until 1961 that the underlying sales tax exemption question arose once again. It did so through a 1961 amendment to the Retailers' Occupation Tax Act which reflected the legislature's intent to exclude from the tax some facets of the publication process. Although the 1941 amendment had exempted from the tax sales of ingredients or constituent parts of goods that were to be sold (and taxed) at retail, it will be recalled that the Revenue Department's rule exempted newspapers and the like from the sales tax, and therefore the exemption for sales of newsprint, ink, and paper became unavailable because newsprint, ink, and paper were not constituent parts of tangible property sold (and taxed) at retail. In view of this, the 1961 amendment explicitly exempted the sale of newsprint and ink from taxation.[187] The legislature noted that the purpose of the amendment was to prevent discrimination against newspapers and in favor of competing "news-conveying agencies [such as radio and television] that do not transfer tangible personal property."[188] The legislature based its exclusion of newsprint and ink from the definition of tangible property on the previously expressed view[189] that the value of the ultimate product, a *newspaper*, lies in the information it conveys, not the materials which facilitate its conveyance. The information conveyed, so the argument went, loses its value if not read immediately, and, once read, the value of a newspaper expires.[190] It seemed now that ink and newsprint would be indisputably exempt regardless of whether newspapers were considered tangible property sold at retail, and on the latter point it seemed that the legislative intent (at least in 1961) was clear.

Perhaps so. But in other respects the effect of the amendment was to make an already murky situation murkier. The issue left unresolved by the explicit language of the amendment was, of course, its application to publications other than newspapers. This question was soon addressed in the 1964 case discussed briefly above, *Time, Inc. v. Hulman*, brought by magazine publishers claiming amnesty from the Retailers' Act under the 1961 amendment.[191] It appears that shortly after the 1961 amendment the Department of Revenue reversed its earlier position on the sales tax exemption for the retail sale of magazines and other non-newspaper publications. The department issued a Revised Rule 2 providing that sellers of "magazines, books, sheet music and phonograph records incur retailers' occupation tax liability when they sell any of these items to purchasers for use or consumption and not for resale. Sales of newspapers are not subject to the tax."[192]

Predictably, the magazine publishers objected, making two arguments for exemption from the retail tax. The first was that they were not engaged in the sale of tangible personal property. The magazine publishers relied on cases holding that blueprinters, photostaters, and commercial photographers were not retailers of tangible personal property.[193] The Illinois Supreme Court in *Time* disagreed, announcing pithily that "[t]he sale of a magazine is essentially not different from the sale of a loaf of bread."[194] The test, according to the court, looked to the substance of the transaction. In the court's view the sale of magazines involved the substance of the transaction and therefore constituted a sale of tangible personal property.[195] The court did not address the fact that prior to 1961 the Revenue Department had made no effort to collect a tax on *any* publications (whether newspapers or magazines and pamphlets) under the Retailers' Occupation Tax Act.

The second argument made by the magazine publishers was that even if they were engaged in the sale of tangible personal property, they were exempt under the 1961 amendment, which was applicable to newsprint and ink and was not, by its terms,[196] limited to newspapers. In response the Revenue Department argued that the value of magazines was more permanent than newspapers and therefore exemption of magazines would not be consistent with the legislative purpose behind the 1961 amendment, which was only to exempt publications that distributed news of fleeting value.[197] On this argument, however, the magazines prevailed, with the court expressing its view "that there is no real or substantial difference between newspapers and plaintiffs' magazines."[198] This was a conclusion that left the magazines victorious in court, but with little solace to be found in the rationale, as at base the conclusion rested on the lack of lasting value in their product. In fairness to the court it should be noted that its construction of the statute to exempt newsmagazines was also deemed necessary to avoid finding the statute unconstitutional on grounds of differential taxation of the press.[199]

It is noteworthy that the court in *Time* also held that newsmagazines were exempt, along with newspapers, from the Use Tax Act and the Service Occupation Tax Act, to which we will turn shortly. The reasoning was the same: the magazines were printed primarily for the purpose of conveying news; news was of fleeting value and not tangible personal property subject to the retailers' tax; and therefore the use of the newsprint, ink, and paper was likewise exempt under the use portion of the statute.[200] The important distinction drawn was between those media not considered to convey news, such as books and leisure magazines, and those that do, such as newspapers and newsmagazines. The former, non-news media were apparently still subject to the tax because their "value" did not lie in any immediate and evanescent message conveyed.

The final stage of the saga occurred in 1983. In that year the door to exclusions for the print media was to be further opened with the Illinois Supreme Court's decision in *Moody's Investors Service, Inc. v. Department of Revenue*.[201] There the court determined that *any* magazine qualified for the

1961 exemption, not just newsmagazines.[202] The earlier rationale was expanded but at base it was essentially the same. The court focused on the fleeting or transitory nature of information in a magazine, de-emphasizing the news aspect of the *Time* decision and therefore, ironically, broadening the category of transitory, and less "valuable," information.[203]

THE SERVICE OCCUPATION TAX ACT OF 1961

The Service Occupation Tax Act of 1961[204] was similar in most respects to the Retailers' Occupation Tax Act, but its purpose was to tax the sale of services rather than tangible personal property. A "sale of service" was defined as "any transaction except a retail sale of tangible personal property taxable under the Retailers' Occupation Tax Act . . . or under the Use Tax Act."[205] Similar language exempting newsprint and ink from the tax was included in the Service Occupation Tax Act;[206] indeed, as the court in *Time, Inc. v. Hulman* had noted,[207] the same exemptions applied to the services tax as applied to the Retailers' Occupation Tax Act.

The exception for newsprint and ink under the Service Occupation Tax Act had the effect, perhaps unanticipated, of exempting the "service" of printing, but only partly. Printers of newspapers and magazines were exempted, but not printers of "letterheads, forms, booklets, catalogs, brochures, circulars, briefs, and other varieties of printed matter." The exemption was, predictably, challenged as unconstitutional by printers in *Klein v. Hulman*.[208] The claim was partly based on a provision of the Illinois Constitution that required a tax statute to be "uniform as to the class upon which it operates."[209] The printers made the now-familiar argument that the business of printing was substantially similar regardless of whether the paper and ink were used for conveying news and information or for other purposes.[210] But this time the Illinois Supreme Court disagreed, concluding that there was a substantial difference between the *purpose* of conveying news and that of printing letterheads or catalogs.[211] The exemption for ink and newsprint used in the service of printing for the purpose of conveying news was therefore valid, and printers using ink and newsprint for other purposes were subject to the tax.[212]

The decision in *Klein* was, it seems, largely preordained by the decision in *Time*, even though different taxes and taxable activities were involved in the two cases. Both courts allowed a legislative exemption for newspapers and magazines. In the *Time* case it was from sales tax for the product and sales and use tax on the components that make up the product (ink and paper). The exemption was justified largely on the value of the publication — the conveyance of news that has transient value. Under this reasoning, it seems, books which have longer life spans would not be exempt. At the same time, under the *Klein* case printers of catalogs, circulars, forms, and perhaps even books were deemed subject to the service tax based largely on the purpose of the publisher — whether the publisher whose product was being printed intended to convey current information to the public or to serve essentially private interests. But the general consistency of the decisions does not resolve the more basic question of whether this manner of distinguishing media — based on its transient nature and value, or its purpose along those lines — is satisfactory or, instead, potentially invidious.[213] That is an issue to which we shall return in due course.

THE USE TAX ACT OF 1955

The Illinois use tax, like most use taxes, complemented and supplemented the sales tax by taxing goods purchased outside of the state (and thus free from sales tax) and consumed within the state. The 1955 Use Tax Act imposed a tax upon persons using "tangible personal property."[214] The Act provided that it was not applicable to any use of tangible personal property by a retailer of tangible personal property whose product would be taxable under the Retailers' Occupation Tax Act.[215] The use tax, therefore, operated in tandem with the occupation tax. In 1961, a proviso was added to the Use Tax Act, as it had been in the Service Occupation Tax Act and the Retailers' Occupation Tax Act, specifically exempting from taxation the "purchase, employment and transfer of such tangible personal property as newsprint and ink for the primary purpose of conveying news (with or without other information)."[216]

Although newsprint and ink were thus exempted from the use tax, and therefore the issues so laboriously — indeed painstakingly — fought out in the sales and service tax settings seemed safely resolved, the underlying "tangible personal property issue" could not be so easily avoided. It seemed, indeed, to have a life of its own. This time it arose in relation to machinery used in the publishing process, which was fully taxable under the use tax.[217] The use of machinery, of course, was fully taxable as a general matter under the broad terms of the use tax, and the application of the use tax to machinery employed in the publishing process was clear because no exception was made in the Use Tax Act for publishers. Likewise, no exemption for use or purchase of goods leading to taxable sale was available, because the subsequent sale was exempt from tax.

Once again the legislature tried to solve the problem. Once again it failed. In 1979 an amendment was enacted which purported to exempt from the use tax machinery used in the process of manufacturing goods and materials for sale at retail.[218] While the amendment, which applied to all machinery (not just printing equipment), appeared at first glance to embrace printing equipment used by newspapers, it contained a proviso that the covered machinery must be used in the production of "tangible personal property."[219] The Illinois Department of Revenue, far from chastened and by now impressively familiar with the nuances and intrigues of the complex taxing system, particularly as it applied to publishers, issued a regulation excluding printing machinery from the new exemption on the ground that newspapers and magazines were not tangible personal property, thus subjecting such machinery to the use tax.[220]

Predictably, the matter found its way to court. Two decisions in the same case were important in interpreting the application to the media of the Use Tax Act and the 1979 amendment. The first was *Chicago Tribune Co. v. Johnson*, decided by the Illinois Court of Appeals in 1983.[221] In the first *Johnson* case the *Tribune* asserted that several new printing presses they had purchased were exempt from the use tax due to the exemption for "machinery and equipment primarily [used] in the process of the manufacturing or assembling of tangible personal property for wholesale or retail sale."[222] The Revenue Department, of course, claimed that the resulting newspapers were not "tangible personal property" for sale under the meaning of the exception.[223] In response, the *Tribune* argued that the Use Tax Act should be treated *differently* from the Retailers' Occupation Tax Act, and therefore that an exemption under one should not determine taxability under the other, even though the operative "tangible personal property" language was identical. The Court of Appeals, however, found that the two acts were designed to be complementary,[224] and held that the newspaper's machinery was *not* exempt from use tax, citing legislative intent that newspapers were not to be considered tangible personal property.[225]

In an ingenious response, the newspaper made the further argument that the legislative rationale for the newspaper exemption from the sales tax was to prevent discrimination against newspapers, and that the same rationale should be used to exempt newspapers from the use tax.[226] But the difficulty with this argument, as the Court of Appeals noted, was that electronic media also used machinery to transmit their information and were *not* exempted. Therefore, no differing tax treatment resulted among media; instead, viewing the machinery use tax in isolation, all forms of media were equally subject to the use tax.[227] In the end, the *Chicago Tribune* was subject to use tax even under the 1979 amendment.[228]

The decision of the Court of Appeals was revisited in an appeal to the

Illinois Supreme Court in 1985. In *Chicago Tribune Co. v. Johnson*,[229] the Illinois Supreme Court reviewed the history of the Retailers' Occupation Tax Act and the Use Tax Act and the impact of both acts on the media.[230] The court also reviewed the 1961 amendment to the Retailers' Occupation Tax Act that had effectively exempted newspapers and periodicals from the tax.[231] Both the *Chicago Tribune* and the Department of Revenue agreed that a 1981 graphic arts amendment to both earlier tax acts had the effect of exempting printing presses and other machinery from both the sales and use, including machinery, taxes.[232] The issue, then, was only whether the *Chicago Tribune* was subject to use tax between 1979 and 1981.

The Illinois Supreme Court found clear legislative intent that the manufacturing-machinery exemption should *not* include printing presses.[233] Legislative debate from the graphic arts bill had demonstrated that prior to that act printing presses and media machinery were not considered exempted from the use tax.[234] The court also rejected the *Tribune's* constitutional challenges based on differential taxation. A dissenting judge argued that the words of the statute indicated that newspapers were not to be considered tangible personal property under the Retailers' Occupation Tax Act, but that newspaper printing presses were to be exempted under the Use Tax Act.[235] The dissent interpreted the graphic arts amendment as merely a "reaffirmation of existing legislation," to correct erroneous interpretations by the Revenue Department.[236] But the dissent was only that — a dissent.

By the time it was handed down, the Illinois Supreme Court's decision was only of narrow and limited practical consequence. The exemption issue had already been resolved for the future through the 1981 graphic arts amendment to the Use Tax Act, which purported to settle the debate for good. The amendment provided expressly that machinery used in the production of publications would not be subject to taxation under either the Retailers' Occupation Tax Act or the Use Tax Act.[237] Ironically, this meant, when the dust had once again settled, that print-based news was in a differentially advantageous position to broadcast and other media. Differential taxation in *some* form, it seems, was inescapable. And indeed this is one of the important lessons to be learned from this complex saga, though the lesson was hardly noticed at the time.

*Knowledge Taxation Under the Fourth Constitutional Convention:
Confronting Technological Change*
The complex and even Byzantine web of issues raised by the sales, services, and use tax acts serves as an appropriate background for the fourth constitutional convention and the coming era of technological explosion in com-

munications. The tax issues had, in all candor, proved close to intractable even in the relatively simpler environment of print and broadcast communication. One suspects that few would have imagined in 1919 that the single phrase "tangible personal property" could generate such a profusion of problems and complex of meanings. But if print and broadcast technology generated such complexity, the task of fitting simple and traditional terminology—whether "tangible personal property" or its more recent sibling, "nondiscrimination"—to the rapidly changing communications environment would seem doubly doomed. And the attempt itself would serve only to exacerbate an already-too-complex set of competing interests.

The 1970 Illinois Constitution contained identical provisions to the 1869 document with reference to the state's policy toward freedom of communication.[238] The definition and scope of the communications industry had changed drastically, however. The telecommunications industry, just beginning to emerge in the first half of the century, had revolutionized the processes of communications. The catalysts for the surge in technological development in the communications arena were the early developments in television and radio. But almost from the beginning of broadcast technology, communication by way of electronic messages had also begun to develop, becoming over time increasingly accessible to the public and therefore more popular. The new popularity created a burgeoning industry which the state, two decades into a new period of raising revenue, sought to regulate and tax. The result of this combination of factors was the Message Tax Act of 1945,[239] which laid the foundation for later tax bills affecting the telecommunications industry.

The message tax was imposed in addition to all other occupational, privilege, or municipal taxes in effect in the state.[240] The tax took the form of a three percent tax on gross receipts,[241] and was imposed on the transmission for consideration of messages. "Transmission of messages," in turn, was defined to include the provision of services or facilities for the transmission of messages.[242] The Act was sufficiently broad to cover not only the various means of message communications available at the time, but also new technologies such as cable, telephonic, microwave, and satellite communications that would develop much later. But even with the broad and inclusive definitional language, the Message Tax Act ultimately became anachronistic in view of rapid technological developments, and in any event its scope became unduly restrictive in light of the greatly increased potential for revenue afforded by new technologies of communication—and the state's insatiable appetite for it.

The legislature, therefore, turned its attention once again to the question and, in 1984, enacted a new and broadened tax, which was titled the Telecommunications Excise Tax Act and which appears to have superseded the Message Tax Act.[243] The Telecommunications Excise Tax Act imposed a higher rate of tax — five percent — and broadened the scope of the tax.[244] The most notable features of the tax concerned its greatly expanded scope, which the Act set forth in the following way:

> [I]n addition to the meaning ordinarily and popularly ascribed to it, [telecommunications] includes, without limitation, messages or information transmitted through use of local, toll and wide area telephone service; private line services; channel services; telegraph services; teletypewriter; computer exchange services; cellular mobile telecommunications service; specialized mobile radio; stationary two-way radio; paging service; or any other form of mobile and portable one-way or two-way communications; or any other transmission of messages or information by electronic or similar means, between or among points by wire, cable, fiber-optics, laser, microwave, radio, satellite or similar facilities.[245]

The excise tax targeted a new group by levying a tax on the gross charge paid for services by a consumer. Now the burden for at least some of the taxes would fall directly on the consumer. No consumer was safe under the law, either, as the five percent excise tax applied to interstate as well as intrastate communications. The former message tax had only applied to messages transmitted within the state and had therefore been limited in application. In contrast, the telecommunications excise tax could be applied to a very broad range of communications and to a broad range of consumers, making the act a lucrative venture for the state.

The constitutionality of the Excise Tax Act was challenged in 1987 in the case of *Goldberg v. Johnson*.[246] *Goldberg* was a class-action suit filed against the Illinois Department of Revenue seeking a declaration that Section 4 of the Act, which involved interstate communications, represented an unconstitutional taxation of interstate commerce.[247] After a lower court ruling that the section was unconstitutional, the case was appealed to the Illinois Supreme Court. The Illinois Supreme Court first determined that because the taxable event was the placement or receipt of an interstate telephone call, the tax applied to the retail purchase price.[248] Finding that the interstate telephone call constituted interstate commerce, the court concluded that the proper scrutiny of the tax would be under prevailing Commerce Clause holdings.[249] The court examined the issue according to the four-part test set forth in the United States Supreme Court decision in *Complete Auto Transit, Inc. v. Brady*,[250] and held that the tax was not an impermissible tax on interstate commerce.[251]

The Illinois telecommunications tax raises two points that deserve mention here, though they relate to issues that will be discussed in a broader setting in the next chapter. The first point is that the tax represents an early but clear example of the newly developing forms of knowledge taxation, a central feature of which is that the "knowledge" implications of the tax are buried in its wide and indiscriminate application. The tax does not simply fall on knowledge — recent and current published information. Instead, it falls on *all forms* of information and transmission, only some of which invoke the basic policies of the struggle against knowledge taxation. This characteristic of the tax implies the need for a different and more discrete approach to assessing the impact of a tax on the distribution of knowledge.

The second point concerns the issues raised by the new "forms" of taxation and, in the context of the Illinois history, is deeply ironic. It will be remembered that Illinois, in the end, exempted newspapers, magazines, and the like from virtually all forms of taxation on the ground, among others, of the need for equal treatment: because the transmission of information by radio and television broadcast did not fit within the definition of tangible personal property, they were not taxed; it would therefore be unfair and unequal to subject the print media to taxes not visited upon these "new," nontangible media. With the enactment of the telecommunications tax, however, the tables were turned, for by that tax the "new" media became subject to taxation under a rationale not dependent on the "tangibility" issue. Now it is the print media that remain exempt — and, it will no doubt soon be argued, unfairly and unequally so.

In addition to a statewide tax, the Illinois Municipal Code also granted municipalities the right to assess their own "message" taxes. Many municipalities adopted their own message and excise tax acts.[252] There has been little litigation concerning either the state or local excise taxes, and to date there have been no challenges based on the First Amendment. But the acts are recent in origin, and their impact on the communication of news and current information is not yet clear. As telecommunication becomes a more pervasive medium for the transmission of news, issues will surely arise concerning the taxation of that medium in the face of exemption of the print and broadcast media. Such questions are likely to make the complexity of the "tangible personal property" issue pale by comparison.

Local Ordinances Regulating Sellers or Vendors of Publications
Before concluding our discussion of taxation in Illinois during the twentieth century, we will turn to a brief and, indeed, sketchy review of selected

municipal taxes and regulation. The subject is relevant largely because it permits the picture of state and local taxation in Illinois to be filled out completely.

An interesting district court opinion from 1988 dealt with a local ordinance that banned the placement of news racks in certain areas.[253] In *Chicago Newspaper Publishers Ass'n v. City of Wheaton*,[254] the United States District Court for the Northern District of Illinois ruled that the local ordinance was unconstitutional. The court held that a public street is an important public forum, where the government's ability to restrict speech was at a minimum.[255] The licensing provisions were invalidated on the ground that they represented an unconstitutional prior restraint[256] and because they gave the city manager too much discretion on the placement and removal of the news racks.[257] The City of Wheaton had argued in support of its ban on residential news racks that there was an important interest in maintaining the "residential character" of a neighborhood, but the court dismissed the argument because it was unproven how the news racks would destroy the residential character of the neighborhood involved in the case.[258] The court also recognized that methods of news delivery have changed and that protection for newspapers is essential in that changing environment.[259]

Another district court case involving the validity of a local licensing ordinance banning newsstands was *Rubin v. City of Berwyn*.[260] There the plaintiff was denied a license and permit to operate newsstands in the city and brought suit in federal court.[261] Even though there were three other newsstands approved by the city, the city argued that Rubin's should be denied because he would serve motorists and highway users in violation of the ordinance.[262] Although the court acknowledged the city's interest in public safety, it ruled that the public safety justification had not been established.[263]

Two other cases warrant brief mention. In *Osborn v. Village of River Forest* the Illinois Supreme Court ruled that a local ordinance requiring the registration of hawkers and peddlers was unauthorized by state legislative grant.[264] The court interestingly avoided reaching the First Amendment issue by construing the ordinance to be beyond the power of the village.[265]

A final case was *City of Chicago v. Charles Rhine*.[266] The city of Chicago had prohibited the sale of any article except daily newspapers in the Loop and Wilson Avenue districts.[267] After finding that the city did have the power to pass the ordinance, the court had to address the fact that while newspaper distribution was allowed, magazine distribution was prohibited.[268] The court quickly dispatched the differential regulation argument, holding that the city's classification was reasonable and that the magazine sellers "had no inherent right to operate [their] business in or upon the streets of the city."[269] The court viewed the restriction as a mere regulation, not a suppression, and found that like businesses were being treated equally.[270]

Conclusion

The twentieth-century Illinois history leaves one, I suspect, a bit glassy-eyed. And that is the principal point of the narrative. The history is complex and subtle, indeed Byzantine, in character. The issues were not defined or fought in terms of large and sweeping principle. Rather, the knowledge tax questions followed an evolutionary course; they arose as technology changed the very meaning of formerly settled notions, such as "tangible personal property"; they occurred in the interstices of various tax schemes; and they were fought as skirmishes rather than full-scale battles.

Perhaps most importantly, the issues did not arise on the surface, but beneath it. By this I mean that the application of sales and service taxes to newspapers and periodicals was rarely placed in issue; the nineteenth-century pattern of exemption was largely followed. Instead, taxation was driven beneath the surface, to the sale of newsprint, ink, and paper, to the use of machinery, and to the "service" of printing itself. By this subterranean tax strategy the state succeeded in gathering revenue and at the same time compounding the already Byzantine quality of the enterprise.

In these respects both the politics of knowledge taxation in Illinois and the forms in which issues arose may foretell the future. The English struggle was broad-based and framed in general terms. This was also true, though to a lesser extent, in nineteenth-century America, where taxation schemes were crude, as was communications technology. But as the Illinois history illustrates, communication in the twentieth century is vastly more complex. Concerns about the burden or impact of a tax must be judged in light of the various print media and their distribution systems; in the broader context of other media such as radio, television, cable, computer, microwave, telecommunications, and satellite distribution, to name but some; and in view of the multiplication of activities engaged in by various media, any one or more of which might be made an incident of taxation.

The issues will therefore be more complex in the future, as will the politics. And the questions will often arise in unexpected ways, with statutes written for one purpose having unforeseen application to new developments. Questions about the function and value of affected communication technologies, such as cable transmission or computer data bases, will be difficult. Questions about differential burdens and discrimination, such as between satellite and telephone and cable distribution systems, will most likely prove intractable. It is against this background that we must reflect on the twentieth-century experience, particularly in Massachusetts and Illinois, and then turn our attention on an even broader scale to the present and the future.

The Illinois and Massachusetts Experiences: Reflections at the Dawn of a New Era

The Massachusetts history is instructive mostly by way of contrast with that of Illinois. Massachusetts seems to have learned its lesson early with the colonial taxes, and to have remembered it well. No state can be expected to have a perfectly clean record on the subject of knowledge taxation, particularly given the uncertainties in the very definition of the term, and Massachusetts is not an exception to this rule. Indeed, its experience with efforts at taxation, beginning with the colonial period and including the recent past, is one of the very longest. But its record in resisting the temptation once tendered, and doing so on the basis of a firm and entrenched, and even unwarrantedly broad, view of press freedom from taxation and regulation may know no equal.

This surely has something to do with the political culture and heritage of Massachusetts; it was never a "frontier" state like Illinois, and certainly never entertained the populist notion of creating a state and society out of nothing, writing on a clean political and legal slate. Perhaps as important, at least in more recent times, is the fact that Massachusetts has so far largely avoided—though not for long—the challenges to tax policy posed by the increasing complexity and technological character of communications. Massachusetts's appetite for revenue may have been more satiable. And its "press" may have been more politically powerful. Whatever the explanation, the state has so far managed to confine the knowledge tax issue to one bearing on the application of sales and related taxes to the established and largely print-medium press. In that relatively narrow setting taxation of knowledge has successfully been resisted in Massachusetts. But it will surely become increasingly difficult to cabin the knowledge tax issue within those untenably narrow confines.

The pattern of legislation involving taxation of knowledge in Illinois stands in bold relief when compared to Massachusetts. Beginning with a relatively libertarian, indeed even populist, attitude toward freedom of expression in the nineteenth century, when essentially no taxation was imposed on the printed word, we see a reversal of that trend in the twentieth century. The reversal was first manifested in legislative activity designed to safeguard reputation and protect public morals, followed by a regime of local, county-based, and state-level sales and use taxes that, at least initially, included the printed word in all forms within the tax base, almost as if no further thought had been given the matter.

The occasion for the sales, use, and retailers' taxes, of course, was the emergency presented by the Great Depression, which hit Illinois hard. And it was the calamity of the period that made the competing issue of taxing the printed word seem a less pressing cause for concern, for the public imperative was not simply increasing tax revenues but providing public relief for the poor and unemployed. Yet after the Depression was over, the same tax regimes were continued unabated and, for our purposes, in essentially unchanged form for many years. The interests of the press seem not to have spoken out until the century was more than half over.

But Illinois is instructive in another, and more important, respect, for when the time finally came to address knowledge taxation as an element of legislative policy, it did so quite explicitly and in a broad array of settings. This was apparent when the taxation issues arose in the sales and use tax areas, where the issue of exemption for publications was hard-fought and, ultimately, widely successful. Newspapers and, later, periodicals were broadly exempted from the sales tax and the use tax, including an exemption for raw material and, to some extent, for the machinery employed in the production of news publications. Illinois, too, began addressing the knowledge tax issues involved in new technologies of communication at an early stage, taxing messages first, and then addressing other forms of broadcast and related communication technologies. The issue of equal treatment, raised no doubt by the traditional media (print) in its self-interest, became an explicit part of the taxing equation.

But perhaps the most interesting, though perhaps not the most important, aspect of the Illinois history was its rationale for ultimately excluding newspapers from the sales and use tax system. The issue had arisen because of new technology; because, that is, other forms in which information and news were being transmitted, such as broadcasting, were not being taxed because they did not fit within the "tangible personal property" framework of the tax system. The legislature, therefore, "desir[ing] to prevent discrimination against newspapers and in favor of competing news-conveying agencies,"[271] granted them (and ultimately other news publications) an exemption. As the legislature put it:

> Whereas, . . . information conveyed by newspapers . . . can lose its value even before being read, if not read immediately; and
>
> Whereas, the value and purchase price of newspapers attaches to the news and other information contained therein, rather than to the tangible characteristics of such newspaper, and such information has only a fleeting value and, because of its transitory character, would be just as valuable if conveyed by media (such as radio and television) that convey the news without transferring any tangible personal property;
>
> *   *   *
>
> The purchase, employment and transfer of such tangible personal property as newsprint and ink for the primary purpose of conveying news (with or without other information) shall not be deemed to be a purchase, use or sale of tangible personal property.[272]

It is the rationale for the exemption, not the fact of exemption, that is important for purposes of our study of taxation of knowledge. According to the legislature, news was exempted because of its "lack" of value — its "fleeting" and "transitory character." Few state legislatures are likely to have been as explicit in stating the rationale. No court has recently expressed the knowledge tax concern in such terms. Indeed, the Supreme Court's approach has been quite the opposite, grounded firmly on preventing discrimination in the incidence of a tax that rests on considerations of importance, permanence, and the like. How, then, should we judge the rationale expressed in Illinois?

As a statement of sales tax policy, the Illinois legislature's explanation made some — though in the end precious little — sense. It was, after all, tangible personal property that was being taxed, and the assumption in the tax was that the property had some value. The product of newspapers was news, not paper, and its value disappeared once consumed, and even if not consumed it evaporated by the mere passage of time. The problem, however, is that the rationale does not distinguish newspapers from, for example, fruit, which loses value once consumed and spoils if not consumed. But few would argue that fruit is not tangible property. The rationale was destined from the beginning to cause problems in its application to future technology—and it did. How does one judge by such reasoning the taxability of computer disks and tapes, or of telephone transmission of data? As a statement of political expediency rather than tax policy, we might judge the legislature's explanation to be unexceptional. At least this was so in terms of the newspaper industry's short-term interests. But I doubt that many newspapers would choose to put the matter the same way. To exempt newspapers because they lack value seems somehow unfitting.

Finally, as a statement of First Amendment policy the legislature's exemption seems, at least at first blush, to turn the world on its head. If we take seriously the proposition that protection should, as a general matter, be given to those publications that are *most* important, the Illinois legislature's action did just the opposite. Books, works of poetry, music, and other forms of serious and lasting writing were subject to tax and not exempted because, by the legislature's criterion, they were too important; only news was exempted. It would strain the limits of the First Amendment to exempt only newspapers if "importance" or *a priori* "value" were the standard.

Yet if the stated rationale seems wrong, perhaps the error lies in its stating, not in its substance. It is indisputable that as a matter of historical practice the Illinois newspaper exemption fits comfortably into the pattern set in the struggle against knowledge taxes. For the object of that struggle has always been to protect the dissemination of news, beginning with the long English struggle against the stamp and ending with the bulk of our experience in this country. The problem is that even at the time of the English struggle, and certainly in the years that have followed, the basic rationale behind the objection to knowledge taxation has remained largely unarticulated.

Perhaps this is because the classic jurisprudence of the First Amendment, which has been shaped around the freedom to *speak*, not to know, has gotten in the way, permitting us to ignore the different but equally pressing problems that arise in the knowledge tax setting. Forgotten, therefore, has been the fact that "value" has many meanings and many contexts, and that the resistance to taxation of news in England was based on a quite specific idea of "value." Newspapers were the sole means of *mass* distribution of information to the common classes in society. Knowledge, *especially* knowledge about current affairs, was seen as a threat by the ruling and powerful classes, for to deprive the population at large of knowledge—accessible and affordable knowledge about current affairs—was to deny it a dangerous political tool by which to exert its will. The struggle for knowledge was not a struggle over books, political theory, poetry, music, or the like; it was not a struggle for the hearts and minds of the elite. It was instead a struggle for the facts that governed everyday life, for the source of power to act independently, to reach decisions free of the dominance of the Crown *and* the elite classes — free, indeed, of the political imperatives of the established order. Lest we think this simply an English phenomenon, we need only recall the same efforts at dominance of political will exercised by Virginia through knowledge taxes before and during the Civil War, or the ease with which the political imperative of war, and the irresistible allure of absolute conviction, facilitated the federal taxes during the same period.

Historically, then, freedom of news from taxation has been based on its primary value, not on its lack of value. But "value" here is not used in its intrinsic sense, but in its most basic political sense. Freedom of news from taxation flows directly from the fact that "news" *is* often commonplace and transitory — that its instrumental political and social value can be lost if not grasped quickly — and that it therefore needs greater, rather than lesser, protection from extinction by taxation because the threat is immediate. Its value lies in its availability to all, not just to a sophisticated few, and at a reasonable price which, given its low cost, can be easily increased through the expediency of taxation. Books last (at least those that are deserving); newspapers don't. Books can wait; news can't. Books can be borrowed, even handed down; news can't.

The policy expressed by the Illinois legislature was correct; at least it was of a piece with the history of enlightened policy in the taxation of knowledge. But the rationale was dead wrong. And it is the absence of a clear rationale for an otherwise correct policy that has, for Illinois, created confusion in addressing problems posed by new technologies of communication. As we will see in the next chapter, the confusion is not Illinois's alone.

Notes

1. Michael Schudson, *Discovering the News: A Social History of American Newspapers* 30 (1978).

2. This is not, of course, to say that the very same patterns of exaction and exemption are followed, nor that the "knowledge tax" issues were even perceived, much less addressed, in many of these new settings. Indeed, those issues were generally not perceived and are typically not perceived today. Rather, experience with many of the new forms of "exaction" has little to offer *because* of the absence of any reference to the "knowledge tax" kinds of questions, and therefore those forms

of "exaction" are primarily relevant as examples only of what was done in fact, and on this score I will allude with some frequency to such examples.

3. 3 Special Subcomm. on State Taxation of Interstate Commerce, *State Taxation of Interstate Commerce*, H.R. Rep. No. 256, 89th Cong., 1st Sess. 607–615, 617, 620, 894 (1965) [hereinafter *State Taxation*].

4. Herman C. McCloud, "Sales Tax and Use Tax: Historical Developments and Differing Features," 22 *Duq. L. Rev.* 823 (1984).

5. *State Taxation* at 609.

6. See, e.g., Hinson v. Lott, 75 U.S. (8 Wall.) 148 (1868) (Alabama liquor tax); Bowman v. Continental Oil Co., 256 U.S. 642 (1921) (gasoline tax).

7. Paul J. Hartman, *Federal Limitations on State and Local Taxation* 578 (1981).

8. *Id.*

9. See Helson v. Kentucky, 279 U.S. 245 (1929) (invalidating use tax on gasoline purchased outside the state but consumed primarily within the state, because the tax burdened interstate commerce); see also Real Silk Hosiery Mills v. City of Portland, 268 U.S. 325 (1925); Sonneborn Bros. v. Cureton, 262 U.S. 506 (1923); Crew Levick Co. v. Pennsylvania, 245 U.S. 292 (1917).

10. See William C. Warren & Milton R. Schlesinger, "Sales and Use Taxes: Interstate Commerce Pays Its Way," 38 *Colum. L. Rev.* 49, 57–58, 63–64 (1938).

11. *State Taxation* at 613–14.

12. *Id.*

13. John F. Due & John L. Mikesell, *Sales Taxation: State and Local Structure and Administration* 245 (1983).

14. Henneford v. Silas Mason Co., 300 U.S. 577 (1937).

15. *Id.* at 582–83.

16. See Due & Mikesell at 245.

17. See Jerome R. Hellerstein & Walter Hellerstein, *State and Local Taxation* 647 (4th ed. 1978); Todd F. Simon, "All the News That's Fit to Tax: First Amendment Limitations on State and Local Taxation of the Press," 21 *Wake Forest L. Rev.* 59, 87 (1985).

18. See *infra* notes 56–69 for a discussion of current exemption practices in the states.

19. 2 N.Y. Laws (Thompson 1939) ch. 60, § 424(1)(f) (tax on liquor sold or used within the state); § 284(2) (tax on motor fuel "held for use, distribution or sale within the state"); § 452 (tax on milk when at rest and sold within the state).

20. See *id.* ch. 60, at 620 (index of taxes).

21. N.Y. City Admin. Code (1937) ch. 929, §§ E41–221 to -238 (covering Dec. 10, 1934 to Dec. 31, 1935); §§ E41–239 to -257 (covering Jan. 1, 1936 to June 30, 1936); §§ E41–258 to -276 (covering July 1, 1936 to June 30, 1937); §§ E41–277 to -294 (covering July 1, 1937 to June 30, 1938).

22. *Id.*

23. Ohio Gen. Code Ann. § 5546 (Page, 1938).

24. See *id.* § 5546–26(1a).

25. See *id.* § 5546–2.

26. The definition, which was contained in the Tax Commission regulations

quoted in the text accompanying note 27, is ambiguous on this point. It could be interpreted to exempt *any* sales so long as the periodical met the definition of a newspaper or magazine and possessed a second-class mailing permit.

27. Tax Commission of Ohio, *Ohio Sales Tax Law Regulations and Special Rulings and Ohio Use Tax Law and Regulations* 37–38 (1937).

28. Colo. Stat. Ann. ch. 144, § 4(a) (1949 replacement volume of the 1935 Code); *id.* ch. 144, § 5.

29. *Id.* ch. 144, § 2(o).

30. *Id.* ch. 144, § 2(k); see also *id.* ch. 130, § 2.

31. *Id.* ch. 144, § 34.

32. *Id.* ch. 144, § 35(i).

33. Ariz. Code §§ 66–1001 to -1031 (Supp. 1952).

34. See Henneford v. Silas Mason Co., 300 U.S. 577 (1937).

35. Wash. Rev. Stat. Ann. tit. 54, § 8370–16, -19(c) (Remington 1932 & Supp. 1940).

36. Wash. Rev. Stat. Ann. tit. 3, § 8370–19(c) (Supp. 1943); § 8370–19(c) (Supp. 1945).

37. Wash. Rev. Stat. Ann. tit. 54, § 8370–31 (Remington 1932).

38. *Id.* § 8370–32.

39. *Id.* § 8370–78(a)-80(t) (one-fourth cent per gallon fuel oil tax); *id.* § 8370–82 (20 percent cigarette tax).

40. George W. Pepper & William D. Lewis, *Digest of Decisions & Encyclopedia of Pennsylvania Law, 1754–1898*, at 36915–16 (1905) (citing Acts of April 2, 1821, and May 4, 1841).

41. Pa. Stat. Ann. tit. 72, § 3282 (1949).

42. Pa. Stat. Ann. tit. 72, § 3407–101 to -702 (Supp. 1963).

43. *Id.* § 3406–101 to -602.

44. *Id.* § 3406–102(4)(j).

45. *Id.* § 3407–102(7)(k).

46. *Id.* § 3403.

47. *Id.* § 3403–203(v).

48. Pa. Stat. Ann. tit. 72, § 3403–1 to -605 (1964).

49. *Id.* § 3403–203(f).

50. *Id.* § 3403–203(h).

51. *Id.* § 3403–203(r).

52. *Id.* § 3403–203(t).

53. Pa. Stat. Ann. tit. 72, §§ 7101–10004 (1990).

54. *Id.* § 7204(33).

55. *Id.* § 7204(30).

56. See Laneco, Inc. v. Commonwealth, 520 A.2d 542, 543 (Pa. 1987).

57. N.C. Code § 105–164.13(28) (1991 Cum. Supp.).

58. Ala. Code § 40–23–62(20) (Supp. 1992).

59. Ariz. Code § 42–1310.01(26) (1990).

60. Idaho Code § 63–3622I (1989).

61. E.g., Mont. Code § 15–53–101(2) (1991).

62. See Chapter 7.

63. The failure to provide *any* form of exemption was rare. See, as an example of only partial exemption, the Louisiana tax invalidated on constitutional grounds in the *Grosjean* case. Grosjean v. American Press Co., 297 U.S. 233 (1936). The exemptions, when granted, were of course not uniform in scope. Some states exempted a broader range of publications than others, as reflected in the contrast between Ohio and Colorado. See *supra* text accompanying notes 22–32. Other states, such as Washington, exempted newspapers and periodicals from the sales tax but did not exempt paper and ink from the use tax.

64. Grosjean v. American Press Co., 297 U.S. 233 (1936).

65. See Chapter 4.

66. See Chapter 1.

67. See Chapter 1.

68. For a brilliant social history of the American newspaper, see Schudson, *supra* note 1.

69. See the later discussion of Illinois policy in this chapter.

70. See Chapter 4.

71. Resolve of July 23, 1928, Mass. Acts 565. The legislature requested the commission to recommend "such changes in such general laws as may appear desirable and expedient." There does not appear, at least in the Resolve, any motivation for convening the commission other than updating the laws.

72. An Act Concerning Hawkers and Pedlars, § 2, 1846 Mass. Acts 167. See also Chapter 4.

73. See Breard v. City of Alexandria, 341 U.S. 622 (1951).

74. See An Act Relating to Hawkers and Pedlers, § 3, 1929 Mass. Acts 398. This provision amended Mass. Gen. L. ch. 101, § 17 (1921), which had retained the exemption for books and pamphlets.

75. See generally Mass. Gen. L. ch. 101, § 17 (1921) for details of the licensing procedure.

76. Final Report of the Commission to Investigate the General Laws Relative to Hawkers and Pedlers . . . , Senate Doc. No. 5, at 6 (Mass. 1929), quoted in Commonwealth v. Anderson, 172 N.E. 114, 117 (Mass. 1930).

77. See An Act Relative to the Sale of Religious Publications, 1931 Mass. Acts 300 (approved May 4, 1931). Again there is no evidence of a reason for the amendment.

78. The constitutionality of such an exemption may be cast in doubt by the Supreme Court's recent decision in Arkansas Writers' Project, Inc. v. Ragland, 481 U.S. 221 (1987).

79. The ordinance is discussed in detail in Wulp v. Corcoran, 454 F.2d 826 (1st Cir. 1972).

80. *Id.*

81. The court analyzed Mass. Ann. Laws ch. 101, § 17 (Law Co-op. 1967), and determined that the licenses referred to in that section were "transient vendor" licenses. The court said that this statute did not prohibit localities from requiring local licenses for hawkers and vendors. In the end the court found it unnecessary to reach a conclusion on this statutory ground because the constitutional issue resolved the matter. See *Wulp*, 454 F.2d at 833, for a complete discussion of the statute.

82. *Id.* at 834 (quoting Strasser v. Doorley, 432 F.2d 567, 569 [1st Cir. 1970]).

83. See *supra* note 81 discussion about Mass. Ann. Laws, ch. 101. The court acknowledged that the fee aspect of the ordinance was probably invalid under the Massachusetts law, but concluded that this would not resolve the key issues of wearing a badge and registering. See *Wulp*, 454 F.2d at 833.

84. For the current law, see Mass. Gen. Laws Ann. ch. 101, § 17 (West 1988).

85. See Minneapolis Star & Tribune Co. v. Minnesota Comm'r of Revenue, 460 U.S. 575 (1983); Arkansas Writers' Project, Inc. v. Ragland, 481 U.S. 221 (1987); Leathers v. Medlock, 111 S. Ct. 1438 (1991), discussed in Chapter 9.

86. See S. 1093 (Mass. Senate Bill, 1979) (a bill further regulating private detectives) and S. 1308 (Mass. Senate Bill, 1979) (a bill to require financial disclosure from reporters at the General Court). For general descriptions of the bills, see Laurence Collins, "Reporters as Detectives," *Boston Sunday Globe*, Mar. 18, 1979, at 30.

87. Collins, *supra* note 86. This comment referred to the financial disclosure bill but seems to reflect his view toward both pieces of legislation.

88. Norman Lockman, "Reporter Licensing Urged Again," *Boston Globe*, Apr. 18, 1979, at 18.

89. Neither bill was designed to raise revenue. Although the bill to license investigative reporters did attempt to collect a licensing fee, this purpose was clearly secondary to the regulatory objective.

90. The Globe Spotlight Team, a special investigative reporting team, reported that an aide to Senator McKenna had been collecting over $14,000 in state pay while living in retirement on Cape Cod. McKenna himself denied that his motives were vindictive. See Collins, *supra* note 86; Lockman, *supra* note 88.

91. Lockman, *supra* note 88.

92. The *Globe* had an editorial against the bill (S. 1093) on March 19, 1979. "Reporters as Private Detectives," *Boston Globe*, Mar. 19, 1979, at 12.

93. *Id.* (quoting Mass. Const. pt. 1, art. XVI).

94. *Id.* This seems to be exactly what Senator McKenna intended his bill to achieve.

95. See Leslie C. Henderson, "Reporter Licensing," *Freedom of Information Center Report* (June 1981), for a more detailed analysis of this attempt to license investigative reporters.

96. See Lockman, *supra* note 88; Collins, *supra* note 86. See these articles for comments of other legislators. The *Globe* warned in its editorial that vigilance was necessary to protect rights like freedom of the press. See "Reporters as Private Detectives," *supra* note 92.

97. See generally Opinion of the Justices to the Senate, 392 N.E.2d 849 (Mass. 1979).

98. *Id.* at 852. In addition to the required disclosure there was a potential for civil penalties on the reporters. Both of these factors, the court argued, might have worked to discourage press coverage. *Id.*

99. *Id.* The court in this statement seemed to address directly the purposes behind the bill as it was proposed by Senator McKenna.

100. See Laurence Collins, "Bellotti Says Public Property Ban of Newspaper Vending Boxes Is Legal," *Boston Globe*, Dec. 22, 1985, at 40.

101. The *USA Today* vending racks are blue, white, and black. The three towns which attempted to license the machines were Norwood, Randolph, and Winchester. For more information on the situation in the individual towns, see Gannett Satellite Info. Network, Inc. v. Town of Norwood, 579 F. Supp. 108, 110–112 (D. Mass. 1984).

102. See *id.* at 115.

103. *Id.*

104. For details on background of the bill, see Collins, *supra* note 100. The bill was proposed by Rep. Christopher Hodgkins (D-Lee).

105. See 1985 Op. Mass. Att'y Gen., No. 5. The second purpose of the bill was described as "advanc[ing] aesthetic values by prohibiting an intrusive and unattractive format for expression." *Id.*

106. See Chapter 4, discussing Massachusetts taxation of the press in nineteenth century.

107. See 1985 Op. Mass. Att'y Gen., No. 5, for final analysis of the bill's constitutionality.

108. Collins, *supra* note 100.

109. *Id.*

110. *Id.* The *New York Times* had been one of the newspapers that had been involved in a controversy in Representative Hodgkins's hometown by placing racks in public places.

111. For background on the ordinance and the issue, see Peggy Hernandez, "Council Votes to Regulate Newspaper Vending Boxes," *Boston Globe*, Dec. 10, 1987, at 43.

112. *Id.*

113. *Id.*

114. *Id.*

115. See Chapter 9.

116. See generally, 1966 Mass. Acts ch. 14. The act includes all the exemptions originally allowed to the sales tax.

117. *Id.* The newspaper industry was one of several powerful lobbying groups which exerted pressure for exemptions from the new sales tax. The number of exemptions which were approved to the sales tax made it the narrowest one in the country. Several legislators have grumbled about the power of the press over the General Court. See Joan Vennochi, "Publishers Unify Against Tax Proposal," *Boston Globe*, June 8, 1990, at 27, for more information on the 1966 sales tax.

118. See 1966 Mass. Acts ch. 14 § 6(r)-(s). Section 6(r) exempted "[s]ales of materials, tools and fuel . . . which become an ingredient or component part of tangible personal property to be sold or which are consumed and used directly . . . in an industrial plant in the process of the manufacture of tangible personal property to be sold, including the publishing of a newspaper." Section 6(s) exempted "[s]ales of machinery, or replacement parts thereof, used directly . . . in an industrial plant in the manufacture, conversion or processing of tangible personal property to be sold, including the publishing of a newspaper."

119. The amendment changed the wording in Section 6(r) and (s). Section (r) now would read "used directly *and exclusively in*." Section (s) also added the words "and exclusively in." See 1971 Mass. Acts ch. 555, § 45. In a 1977 opinion, Houghton Mifflin Co. v. State Tax Comm'n, 370 N.E.2d 441 (Mass. 1977), the court, in a footnote, remarked, "[T]he amendment (of 1971) would represent an attempt to tax materials which are consumed and used in process of printing (such as reproduction proofs) unless those materials are consumed and used in the actual printing (ink and paper, for example). The result of such a change is to impose a sales tax on numerous products used in the manufacturing process." *Id.* at 444, n.5. This interpretation was not followed in the landmark opinion in Lowell Sun Publishing v. Comm'r of Revenue, 493 N.E.2d 192 (Mass. 1986).

120. *Lowell Sun*, 493 N.E.2d.

121. See *id.* at 195. For broader background, see *Lowell Sun* generally.

122. See *supra* note 119.

123. See 1990 Mass. Acts ch. 121 § 48. This bill replaced the words "including the publication of a newspaper" in ch. 64, § 6(r) and (s) with the words "excluding the publication of a newspaper."

124. See Mass. Comm'r of Revenue, Technical Info. Release 90–9 (Aug. 24, 1990), quoted in Globe Newspaper Co. v. Commissioner of Revenue, 571 N.E.2d 617 (Mass. 1991).

125. Some sources suggested that one purpose of this tax was retaliation toward the media for its criticism of legislative leaders. The *Boston Globe*, which would have paid one of the highest burdens of tax, had been very critical of Senate President William Bulger. See Gordon McKibben, "Globe Opens Fight on Newspaper Tax," *Boston Globe*, July 20, 1990, at 21, 22. Despite this speculation, nothing said by any legislator indicated that this tax was intended as revenge.

126. See M. E. Malone, "Many Sales Tax Exemptions Remain," *Boston Globe*, Jan. 13, 1990, at 8, for a description of different services that had required increased sales taxes. The commonwealth budget deficit left the General Court no choice but to look for many areas to increase or impose a sales tax.

127. For general information on the beginning of the lawsuit, see McKibben, *supra* note 125. See generally Brief for Plaintiff, Globe Newspaper Co. v. Commissioner of Revenue, 571 N.E.2d 617 (Mass. 1991) (Docket No. 5511).

128. See Brief for Plaintiff at 8, *Globe Newspaper Co.* (Docket No. 5511). The *Globe* argued that they were the only manufacturers who were not exempt from the sales tax on materials and that they were specifically excluded in the statute.

129. *Id.*

130. The Commissioner argued that because there were no magazines actually manufactured in Massachusetts there could be no benefit to magazines or injury to newspapers. Therefore, according to the Commissioner, there could be no discrimination in the distinction. For argument and citations, see Brief for Defendant at 50–52, *Globe Newspaper Co.* (Docket No. 5511).

131. See Minneapolis Star & Tribune Co. v. Minnesota Comm'r of Revenue, 460 U.S. 575 (1983), for background on these arguments. In the Commissioner's Brief, he elaborated on a complex series of computations that demonstrated how much less a newspaper would pay on this tax as compared to a retail sales tax. For

example, the *Boston Globe* itself would pay only $856,718 per year with the new tax structure, while a retail sales tax would cost the newspaper $4,619,218. The Commissioner pointed out that this was only 18.5 percent of the larger number. He reasoned that the disparity was sufficiently large to allow the courts to be sure that newspapers would benefit from the new tax structure. One of the problems in *Minneapolis Star* was that the Supreme Court did not want to engage in economic speculation because it might miscalculate. In the Massachusetts case, the Commissioner wanted to point out that the newspapers would certainly benefit. For elaboration of the argument, see Brief for Defendant at 9–14, *Globe Newspaper Co.* (Docket No. 5511).

132. See *Minneapolis Star*, 460 U.S. at 588. See also Reply Brief for Plaintiff at 8, *Globe Newspaper Co.* (Docket No. 5511).

133. See *supra* note 131 for discussion of the difference between the burden of an amended sales tax and the potential burden of a retail sales tax on newspapers.

134. See Vennochi, *supra* note 117, at 27–28.

135. *Id.*

136. Scott Himstead, the publisher, remarked that "[i]t would be quite difficult for a company to ride this out" and also said that the newspaper industry was feeling the same sluggishness as other businesses. *Id.*

137. See generally *Boston Globe* in April–July 1990 for its editorial position on increasing the sales tax.

138. See Vennochi, *supra* note 134, at 27–28, for brief discussion of the irony of this lawsuit. The *Globe*, of course, did not view the issue as one merely of tax policy and fairness, but rather as a freedom of the press issue. The *Globe* maintained that it paid its fair share of taxes, both state and local, but objected to the taxation differential.

139. For general description of this argument, see Brief for Plaintiff at 20–22, *Globe Newspaper Co.* (Docket No. 5511).

140. Bowe v. Secretary of the Commonwealth, 69 N.E.2d 115 (Mass. 1946).

141. See *Bowe*, 69 N.E.2d at 129. This case resolved the nineteenth-century debate over the extent of Article XVI. The court also remarked that "authors and publishers are entitled to a high degree of protection from legal accountability for what they write and publish."

142. See Brief for Plaintiff at 20, *Globe Newspaper Co.* (Docket No. 5511). For background on the McKenna bill, see above. See also Opinion of the Justices to the Senate, 392 N.E.2d 849 (Mass. 1979).

143. *Opinion of the Justices*, 392 N.E.2d at 825.

144. See Brief for Plaintiff at 21, *Globe Newspaper Co.* (Docket No. 5511), for details of the argument. The *Globe* contended that this interpretation of a "per se" rule would be consistent with Massachusetts history, which supported the view that *no* impositions or licenses on the press could be permitted.

145. See generally Globe Newspaper Co. v. Commissioner of Revenue, 571 N.E.2d 617 (Mass. 1991).

146. See *id.* at 621. This reflects language from *Minneapolis Star*, 460 U.S. 575, 589–590 (1983).

147. *Globe Newspaper Co.*, 571 N.E.2d at 621.

148. See *id.* at 621–22. This is consistent with the U.S. Supreme Court's analysis in *Minneapolis Star*, which also found any arguments of administrative burdens unpersuasive, comparing newspapers to vending machine sales which are taxed. See *Minneapolis Star*, 460 U.S. at 587, n.10.

149. *Globe Newspaper Co.*, 571 N.E.2d at 620. The court did not address the Commissioner's argument that newspapers were already different from other manufacturers in that newspapers were exempt from a retail sales tax, while other manufacturers' products were subject to a retail sales tax.

150. The decision did not foreclose newspapers from being made subject to the (greater) sales tax.

151. See *Boston Globe*, May 21, 1991, at 20.

152. *Id.*

153. *Id.*

154. See Randall P. Bezanson, "The Future First Amendment," 37 *S.D. L. Rev.* 11 (1992).

155. See Randall P. Bezanson, "The Right to Privacy Revisited: Privacy, News, and Social Change, 1890–1990," 80 *Cal. L. Rev.* 1133 (1992).

156. It is not surprising that turn-of-the-century Illinois law was active in welfare protection because this was a period of progressivism and populism in American history. This progressivism was especially strong in places like the Midwest. These two movements used laws to improve working conditions and restrict the freedom that business enjoyed during the Gilded Age of the late 1800s.

157. See Chapter 4.

158. General Corporation Act, § 105, 1919 Ill. Laws 312, 340.

159. *Id.*

160. *Id.* § 137 1919 Ill. Laws at 346. See Sales Tax Act, 1932 Ill. Laws 17.

161. Under the Act " 'Sale at retail' means any transfer of the ownership or title of tangible personal property to the consumer for use and not for purposes of resale in any form, for a monetary consideration. Transactions whereby the possession of the property is transferred but the seller retains the title as security for payment of the price shall be deemed to be sales." Sales Tax Act, § 1, 1932 Ill. Laws 17, 18.

162. Winter v. Barrett, 186 N.E. 113 (Ill. 1933).

163. "Governor Signs Sales Tax Bill; See Court Test," *Chi. Daily Trib.*, Mar. 23, 1933, at 7. "The ink on the bill had hardly dried before a group of about 150 determined merchants . . . met in a local hotel and decided to fight hard in the courts against collection of the tax." *Id.*

164. Retailers' Occupation Tax Act, § 2, 1933 Ill. Laws 924, 925.

165. See *infra* note 169 et seq.

166. *Id.*

167. See *supra* note 163.

168. Retailers' Occupation Tax Act, § 3(8), 1933 Ill. Laws at 926.

169. An Amendment to the Retailers' Occupation Tax Act, § 1, 1941 Ill. Laws 1079, 1080.

170. See *infra* notes 187 et seq. for discussion of whether the Retailers' Occupation Tax Act even covered newspapers as sales of tangible property.

171. Time, Inc. v. Hulman, 201 N.E.2d 374 (Ill. 1964).

172. *Id.* at 375.

173. Calumet Pub. Co. v. McKibben, No. 41 C 3507 (Cir. Ct. Cook Cty., Mar. 17, 1944); see Time, Inc. v. Hulman, 201 N.E.2d 374 (Ill. 1964).

174. Time, Inc. v. Hulman, 201 N.E.2d 374 (Ill. 1964).

175. *Id.* at 376; see *infra* text accompanying notes 187 et seq.

176. Act of July 25, 1945, § 2(a), 1945 Ill. Laws 1278, 1279 (amending sales tax provisions).

177. Village of South Holland v. Stein, 26 N.E.2d 868 (Ill. 1940). Both *Stein* and the *Kozul* case (*infra* note 179 and accompanying text) could be placed in a section on hawker and peddler taxes and licenses and not in this section on sales tax. However, I have left these cases here for the sake of continuity.

178. *Stein,* 26 N.E.2d at 871.

179. City of Blue Island v. Kozul, 41 N.E.2d 515 (Ill. 1942).

180. *Id.* at 517.

181. *Id.*

182. *Id.* at 518.

183. Grosjean v. American Press Co., 297 U.S. 233 (1936).

184. Near v. Minnesota, 283 U.S. 697 (1931).

185. *Kozul,* 41 N.E.2d at 519.

186. *Id.* at 519. The court stated, "The publishers and distributors of newspapers, magazines, pamphlets, circulars, books or other printed matter are not immune from the ordinary forms of taxation for the support of the government, but they can not be compelled to purchase, through a license fee or a license tax, the privilege freely granted by the constitution." *Id.*

187. The 1961 amendment specifically provided that "[t]he purchase, employment and transfer of such tangible personal property as newsprint and ink for the primary purpose of conveying news (with or without other information) shall not be deemed to be a purchase, use or sale of tangible personal property." Act of July 10, 1961, § 1, 1961 Ill. Laws 1743, 1744 (amending § 1 of Retailers' Occupation Tax Act).

188. *Id.* at 1743 (Introduction).

189. See *supra* notes 169–71.

190. *Id.*

191. Time, Inc. v. Hulman, 201 N.E.2d 374, 375 (Ill. 1964).

192. *Id.* at 376.

193. *Id.* at 376–77.

194. *Id.* at 377.

195. *Id.*

196. See *supra* note 187 for the text of the amendment, which referred to use of newsprint and ink "for the primary purpose of conveying news."

197. *Time, Inc. v. Hulman,* 201 N.E.2d at 378.

198. *Id.*

199. *Id.* at 378–79. The holding of this case might be undermined by the recent holding in *Leathers v. Medlock* 111 S. Ct. 1438 (1991). The Court was assuming that newspapers and magazines were so similar that an exemption for one and not the other would be unconstitutional. This assumption may not be valid today.

200. Time, Inc. v. Hulman, 201 N.E.2d at 379.

201. Moody's Investors Service, Inc. v. Department of Revenue, 445 N.E.2d 1331 (Ill. 1983).

202. *Id*. at 1336.

203. *Id*.

204. Service Occupation Tax Act, 1961 Ill. Laws 1745.

205. *Id*. § 2 1961 Ill. Laws at 1746.

206. *Id*.

207. Time, Inc. v. Hulman, 201 N.E.2d at 379.

208. Klein v. Hulman, 215 N.E.2d 268, 269 (Ill. 1966).

209. *Id*.

210. *Id*. at 270.

211. *Id*.

212. *Id*. at 270–71.

213. See, e.g., Minneapolis Star & Tribune Co. v. Minnesota Comm'r of Revenue, 460 U.S. 575 (1983); Arkansas Writers Project v. Ragland, 481 U.S. 221 (1987); and other cases addressing the permissible ways of taxing the media differently.

214. Use Tax Act, § 3, 1955 Ill. Laws 2027, 2029.

215. *Id*.

216. Act of July 10, 1961, § 2, 1961 Ill. Laws 1777, 1778.

217. For a brief review of the use tax, see Chicago Tribune Co. v. Johnson, 477 N.E.2d 482 (Ill. 1985).

218. Act of Sept. 22, 1979, § 1, Public Act 81–991, 1979 Ill. Laws 3636, 3636–37. The Act amended Section 3 of the original act to apply to manufacturing machinery. In addition, the amendment made the same changes to both the Retailers' Occupation Tax Act and the Service Occupation Tax Act.

The actual language read, "The tax imposed by this Act does not apply to the use of machinery and equipment primarily in the process of the manufacturing or assembling of tangible personal property for wholesale or retail sale or lease." *Id*.

219. *Id*.

220. Ill. Admin. Code tit. 86, § 130.330(b)(5) (1980).

221. Chicago Tribune Co. v. Johnson, 456 N.E.2d 356 (Ill. App. Ct. 1983).

222. *Id*. at 358.

223. *Id*.

224. *Id*. The newspaper knew that because they were excluded from the definition of tangible personal property under the Retailers' Occupation Tax Act, if the same construction were used in the Use Tax Act, they would not be able also to claim an exemption for equipment used in the production of tangible personal property.

225. *Id*. at 359–60.

226. *Id*. at 359.

227. *Id*. at 360. The court discussed at length the differing purposes of the Use Tax Act. The legislative exemption for newspapers from the Retailers' Occupation Tax Act was necessary, according to the court, because electronic media were not selling tangible property and therefore newspapers might be treated inequitably. *Id*.

228. The court also addressed the constitutional issue of differential taxation.

The opinion discussed Minneapolis Star & Tribune Co. v. Minnesota Comm'r of Revenue, 460 U.S. 575 (1983), and found that because the Illinois tax was generally applicable and *not* a special tax, the use tax did not violate the First Amendment. *Id.* Chicago Tribune Co. v. Johnson, 456 N.E.2d at 361.

229. Chicago Tribune Co. v. Johnson, 477 N.E.2d 482 (Ill. 1985).

230. *Id.* at 483–84.

231. *Id.* at 484. The 1961 amendment essentially held that newspapers and, later, periodicals were not tangible personal property.

232. *Id.* For the Graphic Arts Amendment, see Ill. Rev. Stat. ch. 120, para. 439.3 (1981).

233. Chicago Tribune Co. v. Johnson, 477 N.E.2d at 484–85.

234. *Id.* at 485.

235. *Id.* at 486–88. The dissent found it perfectly logical for the legislature to exempt all facets of the production of a newspaper from taxation.

236. *Id.* at 488.

237. Graphic Arts Amendment, Ill. Rev. Stat. ch. 120, para. 439.3 (1981).

238. Ill. Const. art. I, § 4.

239. Message Tax Act, 1945 Ill. Laws 1243.

240. See Adler v. Illinois Bell Telephone Co., 381 N.E.2d 294 (Ill. 1978), for an example of a local Chicago transmission of messages tax ordinance.

241. Message Tax Act, § 2, 1945 Ill. Laws at 1244.

242. Message Tax Act, § 1, 1945 Ill. Laws at 1244. The section reads, "the furnishing, for a consideration, of services or facilities (whether owned or leased), or both, to persons in connection with the transmission of messages where such persons do not, in turn, receive any consideration in connection therewith, but shall not include such furnishing of services or facilities to persons for the transmission of messages to the extent that any such services or facilities for the transmission of messages are furnished for a consideration, by such persons to other persons, for the transmission of messages." *Id.*

243. Telecommunications Excise Tax Act, Pub. Act 84–126, 1984 Ill. Laws 1444. Section 24 of the Act notes that much of the first section of the Message Tax Act is replaced with newer definitions of transmitting messages.

244. *Id.* § 2(c) 1984 Ill. Laws at 1445.

245. *Id.*

246. Goldberg v. Johnson, 512 N.E.2d 1262 (Ill. 1987).

247. Section 4 of the Telecommunications Excise Tax Act reads: "A tax is imposed upon the act or privilege of originating or receiving interstate telecommunications by a person in this State at the rate of 5% of the gross charge for such telecommunications purchased at retail from a retailer by such person. To prevent actual multistate taxation of the act or privilege that is subject to taxation under this paragraph, any taxpayer, upon proof that that taxpayer has paid a tax in another state on such event, shall be allowed a credit against the tax imposed in this Section 4 to the extent of the amount of such tax properly due and paid in such other state. However, such tax is not imposed on the act or privilege to the extent such act or privilege may not, under the Constitution and statutes of the United States, be made the subject of taxation by the State." 1984 Ill. Laws at 1447.

248. *Goldberg*, 512 N.E.2d at 1265.

249. *Id*. at 1266.

250. Complete Auto Transit, Inc. v. Brady, 430 U.S. 274, 287 (1977).

251. *Goldberg*, 512 N.E.2d at 1268. The court found that the telecommunications tax met all four parts of the *Complete Auto Transit, Inc. v. Brady* test. *Id*. at 1266–68.

252. A small amount of litigation has arisen out of local level enforcement of the state's municipal code version of these telecommunications taxes.

The applicability of the Chicago City Messages Tax Ordinance to interstate calls was at issue in *Concannon v. Illinois Bell Telephone Co.*, 501 N.E.2d 183 (Ill. 1986). The issue in *Concannon* was the applicability of the city ordinance to interstate as well as intrastate communications in light of the lack of any provision defining which types of communications were governed by the law. The statute stated only that it applied to "all persons engaged in the business of transmitting messages by means of electricity," without any references as to where the messages were transmitted. At the time of the ordinance's passage, federal constitutional law barred taxes on interstate revenues. Therefore, the court concluded, the city ordinance could not have been applied to interstate communication revenues and should not be construed as permitting such a tax.

The Illinois Municipal Code also allows for local administration of a version of the Excise Tax Act, entitled the Municipal Excise Tax Act, Ill. Pub. Act 84–126, ch. 24, para. 8–11–10 (1984). The municipal act functions in exactly the same manner as the state tax, but is administered by the individual municipalities rather than the state revenue department.

253. The ordinance regulated the placement of newspaper dispensing devices (news racks) on the city streets of Wheaton, Illinois. The actual regulation is reproduced in an appendix to the district court's opinion. The terms of the regulation involved distances from crosswalks, other machines, and emergency facilities, as well as an outright ban on vending machines in residential areas.

254. Chicago Newspaper Publishers Ass'n v. City of Wheaton, 697 F. Supp. 1464 (N.D. Ill. 1988).

255. *Id*. at 1466.

256. *Id*. at 1466–67.

257. *Id*. at 1467–68.

258. *Id*. at 1469–70. The court used close scrutiny in looking at the municipal reasons.

259. *Id*. at 1470.

260. Rubin v. City of Berwyn, 553 F. Supp. 476 (N.D. Ill. 1982).

261. *Id*. at 477.

262. *Id*. at 479.

263. *Id*. at 480–82.

264. Osborn v. Village of River Forest, 171 N.E.2d 579 (1961). The court held that the city was without power from the state to enact this ordinance.

265. *Id*. at 580–81.

266. City of Chicago v. Charles Rhine, 363 Ill. 619 (1936).

267. *Id*. at 620.

268. *Id*. at 622.

269. *Id*. at 624.

270. *Id*. at 626.

271. Act of July 10, 1961, 1961 Ill. Laws 1743 (amending Retailers' Occupation Tax Act of 1933).

272. *Id*. § 1, 1961 Ill. Laws at 1743–44.

7. Beyond the Traditional Setting: Knowledge Taxation in New Environments

As we have observed in the experience with taxation at the state level, the knowledge tax problem seems by mid-century to have assumed an almost docile, indeed anachronistic, quality in the conventional historical setting of sales and use taxation. But it had not disappeared. Indeed, the apparently settled exemption of newspapers from sales and use taxes by mid-century was more likely a reflection of the irrelevance of such taxes to a more complex economic and technological environment than a reflection of settled values in the arena of expression. If anything, the knowledge tax problem has arisen more dramatically in the twentieth century than before, but most often in a complex of new settings. And in the new settings the strands of history have become submerged or at least harder to discern and apply, thus affording an opportunity for the very kinds of mischief that have plagued knowledge taxes from the beginning.

My purpose in the following pages is to probe, albeit briefly, some of the new settings in which the knowledge tax problem has begun to take hold. The settings are varied, and I will not purport to address them all. Some have already been touched upon, including the "second wave" of sales and use taxation; the growth and maturity of new print methodologies which have made new media, such as "magazines," an effective substitute for the newspaper with increasing capacity for specialization and market segmentation; sophisticated (and largely print) distribution systems; and the emergence of over-the-air broadcasting, both radio and television. Others that have not yet been touched upon in any detail include cable, microwave, and satellite transmission, computer-based storage of information, and the expanding telecommunications technologies. All of these developments are influencing the production and assembly as well as the distribution stages of communication. Also relevant to the knowledge tax issue, although reserved for separate discussion in the next chapter, is the complex (some would say impenetrable) and increasingly anachronistic postal rate system.

The mere listing implies, by itself, the necessarily limited depth of the inquiry that follows, and the broad brush with which I will paint. My purpose, however, is not to explore the full depths and details of these topics, but rather to venture some thoughts about the way in which we must begin to draw connections from our past to our present. Our discussion will focus on the basic questions of definition: how can we tell when a knowledge tax problem exists; and how can we begin to address it when it does?

Some Preliminary and General Considerations

As we begin to explore the knowledge tax issues in present and future technological environments, it is important that we identify from the outset the general nature of the inquiry. Specifically, the knowledge tax issue will begin to unfold in two separate dimensions, one following the traditional framework explored up to this point but extending it to new technological developments, the other an altogether new, and still nascent, dimension of the knowledge tax problem.

The first dimension involves application of the traditional strands of knowledge tax inquiry in the increasingly complex environment of media diversity. The issues of knowledge taxation, for example, no longer simply involve the print media, or even the print and broadcast media, but instead the infinitely more complex and varied media spawned by computer-based, telephonic, and satellite technologies. And the issues must be addressed in an environment marked by diversity and fragmentation. The technologies of publication and distribution of information have permitted the emergence of many new forms within the established media. Audiences have been greatly fragmented, and the publication process has become increasingly segmented and specialized. Distribution systems, too, have become much more complex.

The application of tax policy in this new environment has likewise become more complex. The changes are most dramatically reflected in the sheer numbers of media to which tax policies apply, but the most important changes are occurring in the sometimes radical and sometimes subtle differences in form and function that are emerging within and among the various media. Our treatment of these changes will be illustrative, not exhaustive. It will represent a sampling of the new contexts in which taxation issues arise and the difficulties that courts and legislatures are having in addressing the knowledge tax problem in an infinitely more complicated environment.

It is the second dimension of change in the communication process, however, that presents the most challenging issues, for here tax policy will have to comprehend radical changes in the very meaning of the press and public communication. And this change will occur even in the most basic and traditional institutions. Technology is changing the very meaning of current and useful information—news, or information on "politics and political economy," as the People's Charter Union put it in 1849.[1] It is changing what we want, what we need, the form in which we receive it, and the use we make of it.

Let me illustrate the point in the familiar and seemingly comfortable setting of the newspaper. From the very beginning the newspaper or periodical has been seen as an institution devoted to the tasks of acquiring information, assembling, sorting, and selecting that which is to be published, and distributing it to the readers. Our conventional notions of the newspaper—and indeed our conventional notions of the press, whatever the medium—have been predicated on a single institution in which all three of these functions are performed. Our approach to the knowledge tax problem, too, has been based upon this institutional presupposition.

Such an institutionally centralized and coherent view of "news" has made it fairly easy to define the scope and limits of the knowledge tax problem, at least with respect to news or current information of public significance. The institutions involved in that enterprise, and therefore those with which we must be concerned in the knowledge tax context, have been a stable and easily identifiable group. As a result, taxation of the press has been allowed to unfold with a focus on "taxation," and without much concern about the meaning of "press."

But the situation has already begun to change, and the change is soon to evolve at an exponential rate. It is clear even today that newspapers are no longer unified institutions performing with ruthless independence and competitiveness the three functions of acquiring, selecting, and distributing information. In the acquiring stage, for example, newspapers today are increasingly relying on independent and specialized information gathering organizations. Many of these we call data bases, and at last estimate they number in the tens of thousands.[2] Vast stores of information are being assembled by independent entities whose business is strictly the acquisition of information for use by others, including news organizations. Newspapers, at the same time, are finding that the acquisition functions performed within their organizations can be restricted and more focused.

The selection and sorting of information, too, is changing. The power of selection, both of subject and of approach, is being distributed by news organizations to other organizations, as well as to individuals. The selection process, which we have come to call the editorial process, through which broadly useful current information has been filtered for dissemination to a mass audience, increasingly is being conducted at wholesale by the news organization with further judgments at retail being made by other independent organizations which combine and repackage news for delivery to increasingly segmented markets. And ultimately, with computer-based telecommunication capacities, power will be placed in the hands of the consumer, whose menu of options will span a full range of news products, and from which the consumer will be able to pick and choose in whole or in part.

Finally, the distribution system is likewise being transformed. The street-corner sale of newspapers and the subscription sale of newspapers and periodicals will likely account for an ever-decreasing proportion of total circulation. Printing technologies will give news organizations as well as other separate organizations the capacity to shape a publication in specific and discrete ways in response to increasingly segmented markets. And computer data bases and services will permit further repackaging and open up possibilities for truly decentralized electronic distribution at the level of the local community or, even, the home. In the field of law, for example, a significant proportion of the circulation of law journals and other periodicals already takes place through data bases rather than printed copies. The distribution of law journals by subscription is becoming problematic from an economic point of view; indeed publications are now beginning that will never appear in print, but only on the computer data bases from which users can draw on a selective basis. Newspapers are already in the beginning stages of such a transformation.

The point I am making in this overelaborate illustration is that we will have to find ways in the knowledge tax setting to confront these new forms of acquisition, assembly, and distribution of information, and indeed to confront new meanings of the concept of current and useful information for the body politic. We will have to address the tax policy issues in their application not only to the single and unified organizations of the "press" as we have always understood it, but also to new kinds of information and to specialized organizations that perform only part of the functions traditionally associated with "news" or the "press." I list below just a few of the questions that will have to be addressed in the future.

- How, for example, will we address the knowledge tax issue in its application to Mead Data, a company whose services include Nexis, a data base devoted to storing a quite remarkable breadth of information drawn from a variety of sources, including newspapers and magazines published throughout the country?
- Is assembled data, standing alone, an essential part of the information on which society relies for its knowledge, and does its taxation raise First Amendment and knowledge tax issues?
- Does the searching and retrieval of information from data bases serve in our time the same function as the penny newspaper did in the nineteenth century?
- How do we address the taxation questions as they apply to services such as Prodigy, or to other services that specialize in the repackaging and redistribution of news and information?
- How will the knowledge tax problem be addressed in its application to the "common carriers" of information, such as AT&T, which may prove to be a central distribution link in an increasingly decentralized communications environment?
- Is there, once again, a danger that taxation may become an instrument of censorship or control on the forms of communication by which people receive information about politics and political economy, including science, culture, and the arts?

The point of these questions is, I hope, by now obvious: not only will we need to deal, in the first dimension of the knowledge tax problem, with an increasingly diverse and complex set of *conventional* news organizations; we will also, and perhaps more significantly, have to deal with entities, and even individuals, that are involved in but one aspect of a process the totality of which constitutes the traditional function of news. How do their functions relate to the knowledge tax issues? Finally, we will have to explore issues raised by *new forms* of taxation, forms that do not look like traditional taxes and that are imbedded in an infinitely more complex communication environment.

Our discussion of the implications of technology for knowledge taxation will focus largely on recent judicial decisions. The discussion will be illustrative rather than exhaustive, but it will hopefully demonstrate the types of problems likely to arise in the near future and the range of issues that will have to be addressed in formulating an approach to the knowledge tax issues. We will begin with a discussion of issues arising in the broadcast and cable setting, turning thereafter to the telecommunications and computer-software environments.

Taxation of Broadcast and Cable

As one might expect, given cable television's dramatic growth over the last twenty years, many of the new forms of knowledge tax have arisen in the cable and broadcast setting. The most prominent and recent, although far from the most challenging, case is *Leathers v. Medlock*,[3] decided by the United State Supreme Court and discussed at some length in a subsequent chapter.[4] The *Leathers* case involved a challenge to an Arkansas sales tax that was imposed on cable television subscriptions, but which exempted scrambled satellite reception. The Arkansas Supreme Court had held that the exemption for scrambled satellite broadcasts violated the First Amendment because it discriminated among taxpayers within the same (cable) medium.[5] Justifications based upon revenue objectives, administration of the tax, and encouraging the provision of cable service to rural communities were deemed insufficiently important to survive constitutional challenge. At the same time, the Arkansas Supreme Court concluded that a tax imposed on both scrambled satellite and cable television, but not on newspapers and magazines, was constitutional, because under such a scheme there would be no discrimination within a given medium, and it was permissible to impose differential taxes between separate media.

The United States Supreme Court reversed the first part of the Arkansas Supreme Court decision, holding that all of the distinctions within the relevant Arkansas sales tax scheme were constitutional, including the differential taxation of cable television when compared to satellite broadcast television. For present purposes, two things are notable about the Supreme Court's decision. First, the Court left wide flexibility to the states in making judgments about taxation among media, and, with respect to the newer cable medium, the Court provided states broad flexibility to make distinctions within a medium. Little was said by the Court about the kinds of justification needed to support such discrimination, but it seems clear that considerations of administration of the tax as well as encouragement of service to rural areas accounted for the Arkansas scheme.

The second and perhaps more notable observation to be made about the *Leathers* case is that the Court, essentially without discussion or explanation, accepted cable television as a medium fully protected by the First Amendment. As we shall see, courts in other contexts have drawn fairly explicit distinctions between cable transmission, which is often viewed as a common carrier of information and not as a producer or "full" speaker under the Speech and Press Clauses, and broadcast transmission, which enjoys full First Amendment status.

A case decided at about the same time as the Arkansas Supreme Court case was *Oklahoma Broadcasters Association v. Oklahoma Tax Commission*,[6] which also involved distinctions between media, but at a further level of specificity and complexity. The Oklahoma sales tax at issue in the case differentiated between print and broadcast media in a number of respects. One tax provision levied a sales tax on licensing agreements involving·the broadcast media, but exempted similar agreements entered into by radio stations and newspapers. The net effect, of course, was to impose the tax largely on television broadcasting and not on radio broadcasting, and likewise to provide a relatively narrow print media exemption only for newspapers. Another provision imposed a sales tax on radio and television advertising, but newspapers, periodicals, and billboards were exempted from the tax. Finally, Oklahoma imposed a two percent sales tax on the purchase of broadcast equipment by broadcasters, but exempted machinery used in the production of newspapers.

The Oklahoma Supreme Court made relatively short shrift of the statute in a decision which followed the *Minneapolis Star* case but preceded the *Leathers* decision. The court applied strict scrutiny in judging the constitutionality of the different classifications drawn in the tax statute, and struck them all down as unconstitutional. This was an obvious result given that under strict scrutiny neither revenue justifications nor the protection or encouragement of specific media through differential taxation are constitutionally permissible objectives. The court found that there was no "special characteristic" of the favored or disfavored media that warranted the discrimination.[7] In view of the subsequent *Leathers* decision, the Oklahoma Supreme Court's invalidation of the statute may, today, be questionable. But the case is interesting not so much because of its result, but because it illustrates the various levels of detail and forms of transaction that can be employed in the tax setting, including taxes on machinery and equipment, advertising, and licensing agreements.

Another illustration of the types of activity that can be made the subject of taxation is provided by a California decision titled *City of Alameda v. Premier Communications Network, Inc.*[8] The *Alameda* case involved a local business license tax on television subscription service. Premier Communications challenged the tax under the First Amendment, and the California Court of Appeals invalidated it on the ground that the tax was both a unique *form* of license tax not applicable to other businesses and was more burdensome in amount than other forms of tax applied to business generally. Whether the tax would have been viewed differently were it structured as a sales tax imposed on subscribers is unclear. The *Minneapolis Star* decision would suggest that, unless the different or unique form of a license tax were *necessary* in the television subscription service setting, a more common and generally applicable form of tax, such as a sales tax, would be required. Little discussion of the potentially different nature of subscription services and the resulting appropriateness of a license tax in that setting was provided in the opinion, though one would have hoped that such issues might have been addressed.

They were addressed, although in a somewhat different context, in a Pennsylvania decision titled *Suburban Cable TV Co. v. Commonwealth*.[9] In the *Suburban* case the State Revenue Board had ruled that cable television systems were not exempt from capital stock or sales and use taxes, although other media, such as newspapers, were exempt under the general exemptions provided for manufacturing. While the court held that cable stations were entitled to a processing exemption from the capital stock, sales and use taxes, it held that cable stations were not entitled to manufacturing exemptions from those taxes. In language reminiscent of the "tangible personal property" debate in Illinois,[10] the court concluded "that electrical signals and microwaves [do] not constitute a product but rather only the means by which such broadcasting occurs," and that "broadcasting essentially is the transmission of information rather than the manufacture of information."[11] The opposite conclusion was reached in an Ohio case, *Warner Cable Communications, Inc. v. Limbach*.[12]

The Virginia Supreme Court went one step further in *Chesterfield CableVision, Inc. v. County of Chesterfield*,[13] a case that involved a county license tax imposed on all businesses, including cable companies, but from which television broadcasting stations and service were exempted.[14] The county ordinance specifically listed "supplier[s] of cable TV" as a business subject to the tax.[15] The Virginia Supreme Court responded to the cable company's argument that it was engaged in television broadcasting, and thus exempt, by stating that "CATV systems do not in fact broadcast or rebroadcast. Broadcasters select the programs to be viewed; CATV systems simply carry, without editing, whatever programs they receive."[16] The court thus treated cable companies under the ordinance as common carriers, much like telephone companies. The cable company's argument to the contrary was not in the least bolstered by resort to the First Amendment, as the Virginia Supreme Court held that cable distribution was sufficiently different from broadcasting — for the reasons given above — to fully warrant the distinction, which in any event raised no significant First Amendment problems.

Finally, distinctions between subscription television services and franchise cable television services were examined in an Illinois case titled *Satellink of Chicago, Inc. v. City of Chicago*.[17] There a municipal tax was made applicable to subscription television services but not to franchised television services. The court applied strict scrutiny to the distinction and, on equal protection grounds, struck the tax down as unconstitutional because no compelling and nonrevenue-related interest justified the differing treatment. The argument had been made that unlike subscription television services, franchise cable television services were subject to a separate franchise fee imposed by the city. The court did not consider this to be an adequate reason to justify the distinction or offset the differing tax treatment; the strict scrutiny applied by the court, combined with a reluctance to inquire into effect, left analysis of the argument essentially stillborn.

The court's analysis seems quite clearly wrong, or at least historically unwarranted. All taxes on knowledge are not invalid; the hard task is distinguishing the good from the bad. Strict scrutiny forecloses that inquiry from the outset by effectively making the circumstances of a tax irrelevant. And discrimination in a tax can provide no easy solution, either, for in most settings today it cannot be escaped. At the very least, one can say that the argument ignored by the court is a hard one to avoid, for the effect of the court's decision invalidating the exemption of franchised cable services is to leave (by virtue of the franchise fee) differential taxation between the franchised cable business and subscription services. This is a paradox that simply cannot be escaped, and strict scrutiny falls far short of an intellectually satisfying means of addressing the paradox.

The lesson to be learned from these cases, and from many others not mentioned, is twofold. First, it should be clear even from this brief discussion of illustrative cases that the incidence of sales, use, franchise, licensing, and other forms of taxation in the new environments of subscription, cable, broadcasting, and other services is complex and does not lend itself to simplistic or categorical analysis. This is particularly so if the analysis focuses largely on purpose, with the measure of constitutional scrutiny substituting for the need to address hard questions, and with the questions of economic effect and burden being cast aside.

The second observation is that, even in these relatively straightforward and now more conventional technological settings, distinctions in the underlying character of the medium are lurking beneath the surface and occasionally emerge. The courts, perhaps understandably, have been reluctant in their decisions to make much of such factors as whether a medium is involved in the production and/or selection, as well as distribution, of information. When such distinctions do arise they are offered cautiously and are firmly grounded in the terminology of the tax statutes, not in considerations relevant to First Amendment analysis. We are, thus, left wondering whether—and, if so, how—the fact that a medium produces and selects its programming rather than merely distributes it should be relevant for First Amendment purposes, much less in relation to the knowledge tax question. While these are issues that remain largely unexplored in the cases just discussed—and indeed in virtually all of the cases involving taxation of new technologies—they are more difficult to ignore as we turn to the relatively few cases arising in the telecommunications and computer settings.

Taxation of Telecommunication and Computer Technology

The telecommunication and computer areas are still rapidly developing, and so, consequently, is the legal treatment of taxation visited upon them. An illustration of the issues that can arise in the telecommunications setting is given by the recent, and post-*Leathers*, case of *Bosworth v. Pledger*,[18] which arose in Arkansas, an apparent hotbed of knowledge taxation. The case involved, once again, the Arkansas sales tax which taxed regular long-distance service, but exempted WATS. The Arkansas Supreme Court considered the case as one raising First Amendment issues, although it did not elaborate on the basis for this conclusion. Instead, following the *Leathers* case, the court sustained the tax exemption for WATS against First Amendment challenge on the ground that there was a reasonable basis, grounded principally in the differences among users of such services, for the differential tax treatment.

The court observed that WATS was principally purchased by high-volume telephone users—even today a doubtful proposition—and that most of those high-volume users were likely to be businesses. Given Arkansas's history of providing exemptions in order to encourage business and commercial development in the state, the exemption for WATS was sustained as serving an economic development objective—an objective which, notably, had essentially nothing to do with any First Amendment interests that were at stake. Indeed, in accepting the rationale the court seems, *sub silentio*, at least, to have adopted the proposition that common carrier-type information transmission services, such as basic telephone service and WATS, are different and differently protected enterprises under the First Amendment. There may well be good reasons for this conclusion, and even good reasons that relate directly to the presence or absence of knowledge tax issues, but they went largely unexplored in the case.

Perhaps the most obvious way in which telecommunications now relates to the distribution of public information is through computer data bases, computer software, and the like. Interestingly enough, taxation issues have begun to arise in this field, although they have only *just* begun. And, perhaps predictably, the issue has often boiled down to a tax-specific and definitional one: whether computer software and computer-based information is "tangible personal property" as that term and its variants are employed in the state sales, use, and related tax structures.

The tangible personal property issue was at the center of the controversy in a case titled *Chittenden Trust Co. v. King*,[19] which arose in Vermont. The Vermont use tax was construed by the Tax Department of that state to apply to the purchase of computer software by a business. The use tax in Vermont applied to the use of all tangible personal property within the state, purchased at retail, and not otherwise subject to the sales tax. The Vermont Supreme Court held that computer software was taxable because it was tangible; computer software, the court stated, "can be seen, weighed, measured and touched, and is not a right or credit."[20] The court reached this conclusion by analogy to films, videotapes, books, cassettes, and records, which had been held subject to the tax because they constituted tangible personal property, and which, like computer software, were capable of storing and later displaying or transmitting their contents.[21]

These functional qualities, however, seem not in the end to have been determinative, as the court stated that had the business obtained the software by telephonic transmission, rather than by purchase of a physical tape, the tax could have been avoided. This conclusion seems quite clearly inconsistent with the earlier reasoning. In any event, it vividly illustrates the limitation of reasoning by analogy, particularly in the increasingly complex field of communication, where questions of value and function are more important than form.

A similar insistence on the literal and physical "tangibility" of a tape was expressed by the Maryland Court of Appeals in a relatively contemporaneous case, *Comptroller of the Treasury v. Equitable Trust Co.*[22] There the court held that even though the information on a computer tape was intangible, and in the case of "canned" programs represented "existing, prepackaged programs of general application"[23] and "a reproduction of the product of intellectual effort,"[24] the fact remained that the tape or physical medium on which the information was maintained *was* tangible, just as a record is tangible quite independent of the "intangible" information or artistic material computer tapes or records contain. The reasoning, of course, is not only narrowly and technically couched in tax considerations; it also is reminiscent of the treatment in Illinois of the tangibility of newspapers. There, it will be recalled, the decision went the other way, with newspapers being exempt from taxation on the ground that their sole value was information, which was intangible, and that information was not transformed into a taxable piece of tangible personal property by its manifestation on a physical sheet of paper.[25]

In view of this, it is not surprising that the same approach has been taken to the tangibility of computer programs in Illinois. In *First National Bank v. Department of Revenue*,[26] the Illinois Supreme Court held that computer software was intangible and thus not subject to sales and use tax. The court reasoned that computer tapes acquired by a business were simply a "means of programming its computer so that it could perform functions the bank needed to have performed."[27] As the court had earlier said with respect to newspapers, it said in the computer setting that "it is not the tapes which are the substance of the transaction, it is the information."[28] It seems obvious that, at least as a matter of knowledge taxation and the First Amendment, the definitional question of tangibility should not be the beginning and end of analysis. Indeed, the question should have no bearing whatsoever on the knowledge tax issue.

Looking Forward

This brief survey of cases provides little more than a glimpse of the issues that are certain to be posed as we address knowledge tax issues in the new and rapidly changing technological environment. But it provides some guidance and a simple, but important, lesson. The lesson is this: the knowledge tax inquiry requires, *before* consideration of such issues as discrimination, differential taxation, tangibility, and the like, that we come to grips with the nature of the medium being taxed and the role it plays in the system of expression and in the availability of information to members of the society. These issues of value and function, not of form, are admittedly difficult to address under the best of circumstances. We may now be at too early a stage of evolution in the media of communication to fully comprehend the role that various technologies play, much less their future significance in the overall scheme of distribution of information. But the uncertainties of prediction should not excuse an utter failure to address them in any degree. The alternative to addressing them is wholesale resort to the technical meaning of language in the tax statutes and to reasoning by inadequate, and perhaps even anachronistic, analogy, thus leaving the issues entirely and conclusively to legislative determination without any measure of First Amendment scrutiny. This is a result that cannot be justified even in view of our imperfect understanding of new technologies and their future.

The inadequacies of our current approaches in meeting the challenges posed by knowledge taxation in today's technological environment lead me to offer a number of conclusions about the past *and* the future.

1. *Tangibility*. Any approach to tax policy in publication and communication settings will become increasingly dependent on notions of "value" divorced from the idea of tangibility. The very concept of "tangible" products as incidents of taxation is untenable in today's world, where both the creation of information for distribution as well as its transportation to recipients are physically evanescent. The same, of course, is true for knowledge taxes, for the future incidence of taxation of knowledge will most often be visited upon transactions involving "pure" information rather than on physical products. In the tax setting, such exactions will increasingly take the forms of "service," "telecommunication," and value-added or use taxes, rather than conventional sales taxes. Perhaps more importantly, "exactions" are likely to take new forms, such as government-regulated user or access fees or publicly conferred market — and pricing — power.

2. *Pricing and the Private Market*. The pricing of products in the private market has always had a significant impact on the availability of information to the body politic, and, as a general rule, private pricing systems, even those that are regulated by government, have not been viewed as part of the

knowledge tax equation. Perhaps this limited approach has been mistaken for some time; at the very least it seems ripe for reexamination in view of technological change. For example, in the past, telephone charges—even their taxation—have not been seen as raising a knowledge tax issue, no doubt because the telephone has historically been used for private, not public, communication. This is obviously no longer the case, for the telephone system carries vast quantities of information destined for publication to the consumer. Much of that information is the raw material of later news publications. Some of it is the transmission of news to decentralized printing facilities. And increasingly that information is being forwarded directly, or through intermediary data bases, to the consumer.

The pricing of the information and access to it by the consumer are often directly influenced by government as well as by pure market forces. There are many possible incidents of taxation throughout the stream or flow of information. Equally important, however, are other and subtler forms of government "exaction." Copyright and intellectual property protections afford producers and data-base repackagers of information significant—and government-assisted—market power. And government is deeply involved in the regulation and pricing of telephone, microwave, and satellite transmissions. In these and other ways government involvement already has a fundamental impact, reflected in price and in the very structure of the market, on access to information by citizens. I am not arguing that market pricing should be incorporated directly into the knowledge tax inquiry, but I am suggesting that "market" price is built upon many hidden incidents of government involvement, and that it would therefore be as artificial to completely ignore the pricing system as it would be to incorporate it wholesale into the knowledge tax inquiry.

3. *The Complex Information Environment.* Finally, and perhaps most importantly, it must be recognized that the very nature of information distribution in today's world is experiencing radical change. We no longer have discrete products or organizational entities that specialize in providing current information on "politics and political economy." Instead we have vast flows or streams of information, some current and some historical, some political and some private, some assembled or synthesized and some in the rawest of form. Increasingly the use to which the information is put is dependent on each particular user rather than on the inherent quality of the information itself.

Yet the knowledge tax question, historically, has not concerned *all* information, but rather certain types of information committed to certain, largely instrumental and democratic, uses. As we judge taxation, pricing, fees, and other and new forms of indirect government exaction, it will become increasingly important that we keep the underlying purposes of the struggle against knowledge taxation in mind, and that we craft a more discrete approach to our scrutiny of such "taxes" with those purposes in mind. We must, in short, judge government's role through taxation or otherwise by its *effect* on broad availability throughout society of diverse information and views on subjects of "politics and political economy."

A final point should be made in light of the likely *increase* in the quantity and complexity of government involvement in the new communication environment. The knowledge taxation problem originated in the crucible of newly developed technologies of communication. It was the threat posed by the new technology of the printing press that first led the Crown to act. It can also be said that resort to knowledge taxation has often corresponded with the emergence of new forms of communication, such as the penny press in the mid-nineteenth century or broadcasting in this century. For in the uncertainties they produce, new technologies provide the occasion for taxation, reinforced by the temptation to control. It is worth remembering how the king in Mr. Collet's tale responded to the new art of writing. "I should," he said, "be surrounded with plots."[29]

Notes

1. See Collet Dobson Collet, *History of Taxes on Knowledge: Their Origin and Repeal* at 45 (facsimile reprint 1971) (1933).

2. See Randall P. Bezanson, "The Right to Privacy Revisited: Privacy, News, and Social Change, 1890–1990," 80 *Cal. L. Rev.* 1133, 1155–56 (1992).

3. Leathers v. Medlock, 111 S. Ct. 1438 (1991).

4. See Chapter 9.

5. Medlock v. Pledger, 785 S.W.2d 202 (Ark. 1990).

6. Oklahoma Broadcasters Ass'n v. Oklahoma Tax Comm'n, 789 P.2d 1312 (Okla. 1990).

7. *Id.* at 1316–17.

8. City of Alameda v. Premier Communications Network, Inc., 202 Cal. Rptr. 684 (Cal. Ct. App.), *cert. denied*, 469 U.S. 1073 (1984).

9. Suburban Cable TV Co. v. Commonwealth, 570 A.2d 601 (Pa. Commw. Ct. 1990).

10. See Chapter 6.

11. *Suburban Cable*, 570 A.2d at 607–8 (quoting Golden Triangle Broadcasting, Inc. v. Pittsburgh, 377 A.2d 839, 846–47 [Pa. Commw. Ct. 1977], *aff'd*, 397 A.2d 1147 [Pa. 1979]).

12. Warner Cable Communications, Inc. v. Limbach, 587 N.E.2d 369 (Ohio Ct. App. 1990).

13. Chesterfield CableVision, Inc. v. County of Chesterfield, 401 S.E.2d 678 (Va. 1991).

14. *Id*. at 679.

15. *Id*.

16. *Id*. at 680.

17. Satellink of Chicago, Inc. v. City of Chicago, 523 N.E.2d 13 (Ill. App. Ct. 1988).

18. Bosworth v. Pledger, 810 S.W.2d 918 (Ark.), *cert. denied*, 112 S. Ct. 617 (1991).

19. Chittenden Trust Co. v. King, 465 A.2d 1100 (Vt. 1983).

20. *Id*. at 1101.

21. *Id*. at 1102.

22. Comptroller of the Treasury v. Equitable Trust Co., 464 A.2d 248 (Md. 1983).

23. *Id*. at 250.

24. *Id*. at 261.

25. See Chapter 6.

26. First Nat'l Bank v. Department of Revenue, 421 N.E.2d 175 (Ill. 1981).

27. *Id*. at 178.

28. *Id*. at 179; see also John Wei-Ching Kuo, "Sales/Use Taxation of Software: An Issue of Tangibility," 2 *High Tech. L.J.* 125 (1987); David C. Tunick & Dan S. Schechter, "State Taxation of Computer Programs: Tangible or Intangible?," 63 *Taxes* 54 (1985).

29. See Collet at 1.

8. The Postal System

Introduction

The knowledge tax struggle in England concerned the stamp, paper, and advertising taxes. These three broadly defined fields of exaction comprehended the totality of the English knowledge tax problems, but they contained within them — particularly with the stamp — the directly related "exactions" for use of the postal system. The American experience, as we shall see, followed a different course, largely because unlike England the origins of knowledge taxation occurred not in 1712 as the postal systems and related print and transportation technologies were developing, but in the eighteenth and nineteenth centuries when publishing and distribution systems (crude as they originally were) had already taken hold and the postal system possessed an independent institutional identity. As a consequence, perhaps, the knowledge tax policies, including peddler, sales, paper and ink, and other taxes, arose independent of the "separate" postal system in America, and they continue to do so today. But the basic knowledge tax issues are the same and, as we will see, so are the questions of free expression, broad dissemination of information, differential exactions, and policy, politics, and economics. Our separate treatment of these issues in this book reflects, on the one hand, their inextricability from the phenomenon of knowledge taxation, and, on the other hand, the fact that in America the inextricable has been extricated.

In the following pages we will deal separately and fairly briefly with the postal system and the postal rate structure. It is not my intention to plow any new historical ground. Indeed, drawing heavily on the able work of others, most notably Wayne Fuller,[1] Richard Kielbowicz,[2] Daniel Roper,[3] Alan Sorkin,[4] and a few others cited throughout the text, my limited purpose will be to trace the evolution of the rate structure, especially as it concerns newspapers and periodicals, focusing on the various shifts in policy that have occurred over the past 250 or so years and, most importantly, the reasons underlying those shifts. We will begin with a chronological history of the postal system, placing principal emphasis on events that bear most directly on the knowledge tax question. Following the historical account, we will step back and reflect in more general terms on the patterns that emerge from the accumulated record of experience, relating them to the sometimes parallel, sometimes conflicting, historical record in the setting of direct forms of taxation on which we have focused so far.

A Concise History of the Postal System and the Rates of Postage

COLONIAL ORIGINS

Postal systems are ancient in origin, beginning almost with the written word. The American system therefore had many antecedents, both in England and in other times and places. As a general matter, postal systems have arisen from and been shaped around practical needs. So it was in America, where the beginnings of the postal system emerged from practical necessity. And the necessity was *not* communication among the Colonies, or within them, but from England.

The "system" for delivery of letters in the early 1600s was at best casual. It was also, as Fuller reports, "completely unpredictable."[5] It began with letters brought on ships from England simply being dropped at the coffeehouses in various ports. Delivery was dependent on the willingness of customers and travelers to take them to their ultimate destination.[6] This crude system was followed by various localized and rudimentary[7] efforts to regularize delivery, either with a small fee for the deliverer[8] or a penalty for noncooperativeness.[9]

With the growth and geographic dispersion of the population of the Colonies, localized systems proved inadequate,[10] and demand for a general system of internal postage increased. This resulted in the establishment by Britain of a single postal service for the Colonies in 1691, when Thomas Neale was awarded a twenty-one-year monopoly on postal service throughout the Colonies.[11] Although Maryland and Virginia refused to join the system, the Neale post office nevertheless began operating in 1693.[12] Andrew Hamilton was its first postmaster general.[13] But the service lasted only four years, dragged under, according to Fuller, by high rates, inadequate revenue, and lack of uniformity.[14] The failure of the first system, and particularly the problems occasioned by the absence of a uniform rate structure, led the British government in 1707 to purchase Neale's system (then owned by Hamilton's successor and son, John) and take control of postal services in the Colonies.[15] The British proceeded to abolish the colonial rates in favor of an empire-wide system based on the number of sheets in a letter and the distance it was sent.[16] Profit was also a motive; the new postal system was established to help finance Queen Anne's War. Virginians called it "taxation without representation" and refused to comply; resistance was felt elsewhere, as well.[17]

All that began to change, however, with the appointment of Benjamin Franklin as Philadelphia's postmaster in 1739.[18] Like many other postmasters of his day, Franklin was both a newspaper editor and a postmaster, a combination that allowed him to circumvent a general ban on sending papers through the mails.[19] By holding both positions, an editor-postmaster could simultaneously obtain mail privileges for his paper and deny his competitors that service.[20] But obtaining such a competitive advantage apparently was not the only, or perhaps even the principal, reason Franklin sought the position of postmaster.[21] Franklin, it seems, also saw in the post office the potential "to better colonial life, to speed communications among men with scientific and philosophical interests, to enhance the position of Philadelphia as the hub of the colonies, and possibly even to strengthen the ties among the colonies."[22] And so, in 1753, Franklin became one of two deputy postmasters general for the American colonies,[23] and he quickly increased the efficiency of delivery on existing routes and established new routes.[24]

One of the early problems Franklin confronted, a problem that would persist in one form or another to the present, was that of newspapers and the post. Despite the policy against mailing newspapers, Franklin recognized that their delivery was in fact so common that newspapers had "become extremely burthensome to the Riders."[25] The post office, of course, was absorbing the costs of their delivery, printers were having trouble collecting from distant subscribers, and some riders charged their own "exorbitant" rates for newspaper delivery.[26] In view of these problems, Franklin reversed the policy and permitted newspapers to be delivered in the mails. The terms were generous, with a fixed rate dependent only on the distance of delivery.[27] In a way that was on many subsequent occasions to illustrate the direct link between postal policy and the press,[28] newspaper circulation soared, both in terms of coverage area and copies sold,[29] and the postal system soon showed its first profits, boosted by the initiation of regular mail service between England and the Colonies in 1755.[30]

Peace and prosperity were not to last long, however. The colonists persisted in their complaints against the high letter rates, following the adoption of the Stamp Act in 1765.[31] As discussed in an earlier chapter, the House of Commons, mindful that Franklin's postal system had operated at a profit, saw no difference between a stamp tax and the existing postal system, even though — as Franklin noted in testimony before a committee of Parliament at the time — postage, unlike a tax, represented a payment for service rendered, "as it compels no person to send letters by it."[32] Thus a postal system — even a profitable one established by Parliament to generate revenue without the consent of the colonists — was not taxation without representation, in Franklin's view.[33]

Ironically, it was Parliament's view that prevailed in the Colonies, yet as Fuller rightly observed, niceties aside, Americans "came to regard postage as a tax and the Post Office as an instrument of British tyranny."[34] Colonial dislike for the British postal system took the form of efforts to undermine and circumvent it.[35] In January 1774 the British dismissed Franklin,[36] and soon thereafter events took a rapid turn for the worse, as the colonists moved to abandon the British system altogether.

Less than a year after Franklin's dismissal, William Goddard (whose newspaper, the *Pennsylvania Chronicle*, had been banned from the mails as seditious by a Loyalist postmaster) established an independent postal system, which he named the Constitutional Post.[37] The Second Continental Congress established a post office in 1775, getting an immediate head start by absorbing Goddard's system, and Franklin became its first postmaster general.[38] The new postal system proved vital to the colonists during the American Revolution; the mails carried letters to and from soldiers and families and the government and its armies.[39] Because letters from soldiers and congressmen were delivered free of charge, the system proved unprofitable. But the importance of mail delivery was clear, and so the system was subsidized heavily by Congress.[40] With matters of war to concern them, the Congress and other government officials took no action concerning postal policies toward newspapers until 1782, when a detailed postal law was adopted.[41]

After the Revolution: Beginnings of the Federal Postal System

Following the Revolution, America's first postal law, known as the Ordinance of 1782, was enacted. It was relatively short-lived, partly, it seems, due to an inability to enforce rates.[42] The first postal system was replaced by the new Congress shortly after the ratification of the Constitution. A new national postal system was established, newspapers were officially admitted to the mails,[43] and uniform rate zones for newspapers were set.[44]

The terms on which newspapers were admitted were advantageous—indeed, remarkably so. A paper could be sent up to one hundred miles for a penny; delivery beyond one hundred miles cost one and a half cents. But publishers did not pay postage directly; postmasters were left with the burden of collecting from the subscribers.[45] Letter rates were significantly higher; they ranged from six cents per sheet for delivery of up to thirty miles to twenty-five cents per sheet for delivery beyond 450 miles. Thus, as Kielbowicz observed, sending a four-page letter 450 miles cost one dollar; sending a newspaper the same distance cost one and a half cents.[46]

The politics behind the early newspaper rate structure were interesting. The driving force, it seems, was not simply the papers, but rather the rural (and non-newspaper) interests, with whom the large urban papers no doubt joined in what would later prove to be a wavering and occasionally unholy alliance. The principal argument made in Congress was that newspaper rates based on distance would leave residents of outlying areas uninformed about affairs in the nation's capital. "Newspapers contained general information, and ought to come to the subscribers in all parts of the Union on the same terms," said one member of Congress.[47] Other legislators said the widest diffusion of information would check a badly run federal government and would safeguard the people's civil liberties.[48] But ignorance or naïveté also played a part, for Congress, according to Fuller, "had no notion of how successful [the subsidy for newspapers] would be, of how many newspapers it would spawn, of how quickly the cost of transporting newspapers would outrun the ability of letter postage to pay for that transportation."[49] The winners, in short, were *both* knowledge *and* the large metropolitan papers.

Lined up in opposition to a flat rate for newspapers without regard to distance of delivery were many members of Congress who feared a uniform rate "would pit big-city newspapers against their smaller rural counterparts."[50] For them, it was important that postal policy protect rural printers from urban competition. As Fuller expressed it, in the late eighteenth century (and thereafter to the present), "[t]he little newspapers in rural America, whose offices so often bulged with government documents, were the special darlings of Congress, whose policies were deliberately designed to foster them and make them competitive with city newspapers. It was to protect them against the encroachments of the urban press that Congress set the postage rate a half-cent higher on interstate newspapers going more than 100 miles."[51]

The urban papers already enjoyed the advantage of being closer to the news (local affairs merited little attention, even in small-town papers); they also were the source of much of the information the local papers reported anyway. Members of Congress who opposed a uniform rate understandably feared that readers in outlying areas would choose a less expensive and more timely big-city paper over a more expensive local product that merely reprinted the same stories as the urban press.[52] Not surprisingly, a compromise — the one-hundred-mile standard, with a relatively slight increase in cost for papers sent beyond that distance — resulted.

It was, however, an imperfect and ultimately unstable compromise, and the politics of news caused its revision in due course. But it was revision only; subsidy of news had become a permanent fixture. After the War of 1812 elimination of the subsidy was impossible, for "[b]y that time the press had become too powerful and the people too anxious to have their newspapers for the government to alter the policy."[53]

EARLY NINETEENTH-CENTURY EXPANSION

> The expression "diffusion of knowledge" . . . had a special meaning for nineteenth-century Americans. It implied "mass communication," as the jargon of contemporary America would have it, but it meant more precisely the dissemination of political information among the mass of Americans for the special purpose of making self-government possible.[54]

As the nation expanded westward, the postal service followed. By 1812, according to Daniel Roper, the federal mail service covered more than fifty thousand miles of post roads and was operating at a surplus.[55] At first the government used the profits to support other government activities; but in 1823 Postmaster General John McLean began the practice of applying virtually all postal revenues to improving the system.[56] The number of post offices soon soared, from 4,498 in 1823 to 7,651 in 1828.[57] With so many offices and routes and so much money at stake, it is not surprising that, in 1836, Congress again captured postal profits in the general revenues supporting the government.[58]

In 1838 railway transportation of the mails began, with rates set at no more than twenty-five percent of the rates paid for stagecoach delivery.[59] Although the use of railroads was designed to trim costs, the expense of establishing such service, the costs of stagecoach delivery, continuing illegal private competition, and high postage rates that discouraged use of the system combined to bring an end to postal profits.[60] Letter rates had remained essentially steady since 1792 notwithstanding the fact that transportation costs (over that entire period) had dropped considerably.[61]

The high letter rates encouraged people to avoid the mail, and sure enough, Americans increasingly used friends and acquaintances to carry letters, thus skirting the postal system.[62] Not surprisingly, both political and economic pressures mounted, and a cheap-postage movement developed. Supporters of the movement argued that cutting rates would reduce the incentive to find alternative means of delivery and would increase the volume of mail and postal revenues; like supply-side economists, they argued that charging less would generate more income. Such arguments, Roper reported, led to an 1845 law that set a rate of five cents for a letter weighing less than one-half an ounce and traveling less than three hundred miles; a greater distance increased the rate to ten cents.[63]

The newspaper subsidy being firmly entrenched, with newspaper rates already less than delivery costs, it is nevertheless remarkable that the cut in letter rates was also accompanied by a reduction in the cost of sending newspapers.[64] Here, too, the idea that lower rates would lead to greater volume and greater revenues was crucial. Kielbowicz quotes one leader in the cheap-postage movement asserting that "[i]f anything can make the newspaper postage pay for itself, it will be the multiplication of newspapers, as it is well known that a great reduction of cost of individual articles is produced by the great number required."[65]

The appeal for lower newspaper rates was also based on broader principle, according to Kielbowicz. Reduced rates, it was said, would "eliminate inequities in acquiring public information" and, through the broadened distribution of news, "bind the nation."[66] A group of Boston publishers complained that any law "which renders the access to knowledge more difficult or expensive directly *increases the power of the few, and diminishes the influence of the many*, and thus tends to weaken the foundation of our Government."[67] In a similar vein, a petition to Congress from a group of Williams College students sought free postal delivery of printed matter as a means of "spread[ing] literature" and disseminating "knowledge among the lower classes."[68] Other supporters of free newspaper postage read the First Amendment "as imposing an affirmative obligation on government to foster — not merely refrain from interfering with — a free press."[69]

But those who opposed a reduction in (or elimination of) newspaper rates argued that a reduction would hurt postal operations and increase the burden on letter writers as "underwriters" of the press.[70] Perhaps more tellingly, given the politics of news, a reduction was seen as a threat to the survival of small-town newspapers and a step toward domination of the news by the large metropolitan press.[71] Kielbowicz reports that the opponents prevailed narrowly in one of the first votes on the matter: the Senate in 1832 killed a motion to abolish newspaper postage.[72] But the margin was just one vote.[73]

The arguments over reduced rates for newspapers continued, however, assisted now by the newspapers' political power. And this time the metropolitan and rural newspapers joined together. "Congress' solicitude," according to historian Wayne Fuller, "was largely a tribute to [newspapers'] political power," particularly the country papers, most of which "supported a political party with passion."[74] The debate eventually produced two newspaper-related provisions in the Postal Reform Act of 1845. One retained the existing maximum newspaper rate of one and a half cents, but it also provided a slightly higher rate for newspapers greater than 1,900 square inches in size: two and a half cents for the first ounce and one cent for each additional ounce.[75] Considerably more controversial but ultimately more lasting and significant was a second provision: free delivery of a newspaper within thirty miles of its place of publication.[76]

Initially, the idea of free delivery of newspapers to nearby readers was supported in urban areas and opposed in more rural parts of the nation, although with time the politics would change. And economics was at the center of both politics and change, according to Kielbowicz's able account. One Alabama legislator called the proposal "a New England bill," because virtually all people in that region would receive a newspaper for free under the proposal; the same was true of only a quarter of Southerners or Westerners, he claimed.[77] But Northeasterners responded that the North paid nearly two million dollars per year to the postal system — twice what the South contributed — while expenses in the regions were roughly equal.[78] Furthermore, according to Kielbowicz, "[r]egardless of its unequal benefits, free circulation within 30 miles [would enhance] the competitive edge of local publications, protecting a community's outlets for news, opinion and culture. [But an] across-the-board reduction in newspaper postage, as proposed by some, would have brought city papers into direct competition with the country press."[79]

The provision in the 1845 Postal Reform Act which set different rates depending on the size of the newspaper was less controversial than the free-delivery exception for local papers, but it was also of some consequence, for it protected standard newspapers but increased the rates charged to the "satanic" press, cheap literary journals disliked by the editors of their more conventional counterparts, as well as the "mammoth weeklies and monthlies" that took full advantage of the low rates.[80] Perhaps more importantly, debate over both provisions of the 1845 act displayed, among both citizens and lawmakers, "mounting dissatisfaction with having letter writers subsidize newspaper postage."[81] In 1850, according to Kielbowicz, newspaper postage averaged sixteen cents per pound, whereas letter postage averaged $3.16 per pound.[82] One commentator called "manufacturers of newspapers . . . [a] privileged class . . . [enjoying] the proceeds of a tax on the writers and receivers of letters."[83] While such a "tax" was not without its supporters, the problem was with its imposition on letter writers alone. Said John Niles, a senator and former postmaster general: "If the public interest requires that printed matter should be transmitted in the public mail, at a charge greatly below the actual cost, then the additional charge should be borne by the public equally like all other public burdens."[84]

In the end the reduced newspaper rates and the free local delivery exemption were enacted. But in just two years the screws were tightened. In 1847 the government perfected its monopoly on the mails by enacting penalties for delivery outside the system.[85] More significantly, the privilege of free delivery of newspapers within thirty miles of the place of publication was also eliminated.[86] These and other reforms made the mails self-sufficient again by 1848.[87] But Congress, according to Kielbowicz, was immediately "flooded . . . with petitions calling for lower transient postage, a restoration of free local conveyance, or both,"[88] and the uneasy compromise over newspaper rates remained unstable—largely on political, not economic, grounds—and letter postage rates remained too high. Further change was in the offing.

The 1851 Act and Its Nineteenth-Century Progeny

The 1851 Postal Act and the 1852 act that followed were perhaps the most important in the nineteenth century. Rate reform was the principal subject, and public policy was once again mixed in with partisan politics, regional protectionism, rural and urban conflict, and of course the economic self-interest of newspapers. The 1845 victory had not sated the postal reformers' appetite; they pushed for and obtained a further letter-rate reduction in the 1851 act. The new basic rate of three cents for letters sent not more than three thousand miles would help bring back postal deficits that would endure for the next sixty years.[89]

Most important for our purposes, however, was the fact that the 1851 law restored free local circulation for weekly newspapers—now on a county-wide basis.[90] This time the Southern and rural interests, previously aligned with the metropolitan papers, lined up firmly behind the change. Without such a provision to protect rural newspapers from urban competition, said a North Carolina representative,

> poisoned sentiments of the cities, concentrated in their papers, with all the aggravations of such a moral and political cesspool, will invade the simple, pure, conservative atmosphere of the country, and, meeting with no antidote in a rural press, will contaminate and ultimately destroy that purity of sentiment and purpose, which is the only true conservatism. . . . We desire our country papers for our country opinions, our provincial politics, the organs of our conservative doctrines, and to assert the truth, uninfluenced by the morbid influences of city associations.[91]

To such sentiments were also added "southern fears that urban newspapers were likely to be filled with northern ideas."[92]

Other legislators, according to Fuller, advanced the more moderate argument that free local circulation did nothing more than offset the advantages of large-scale and low postage already possessed by big-city papers. Such sentiment, combined with the political influence of the rural press,[93] eventually prevailed, though the zone of free delivery was limited to the county in which the newspaper was published.[94] This provision, coupled with advances in technology, ended up giving rural papers with telegraph equipment an edge over their urban counterparts, for, as one opponent observed, "[b]y the time city papers reached the country . . . local publications already had received and printed important national and international news."[95]

Beyond the county of publication, the 1851 law established complicated, short-lived postal zones, which set quarterly rates for weekly newspapers at five to thirty cents per copy, depending on the distance of delivery.[96] But within a year this system was swept aside, and news "was to go cheaper than ever."[97] Congress abandoned the zones in favor of a nationwide rate, described by Fuller as "breathtaking in its generosity,"[98] of one cent for any newspaper weighing three ounces or less; each extra ounce added another cent to the cost of delivery. For papers that paid in advance, the rate was cut in half.[99] Free in-county delivery was retained and half-cent rates were established for in-state delivery of papers weighing one and a half ounces or less.[100] Debate on these changes was relatively calm. The weight limit was great enough to include virtually all newspapers (though low enough, it appears, to exclude the undesirable "mammoth weeklies"), and the result was that one provision — the flat rate — encouraged nationwide circulation, even as another — free in-county circulation — protected local interests.[101]

But perhaps the most important development, begun in 1852, was the elimination of "the sixty-year-old postage discrimination between newspapers and periodicals,"[102] and ultimately the welcoming of books into the mails. And with these developments the "diffusion of knowledge had become dissemination of *information* . . . [which was] much more encompassing" than political intelligence.[103]

Postal Delivery of Books and Magazines

Congress's action in 1851 was the beginning of the end of confusion over the mailing of books. The original 1792 postal act had not mentioned books at all, but a law passed seven years later effectively banned many books from the mail based on their weight.[104] Those books that were carried went at letter rates or as pamphlets.[105] But Postmaster General R. J. Meigs, Jr., attempted to halt even that practice in 1823 when, as Kielbowicz reports, he told postmasters not to deliver any books. Books, according to Meigs, did not convey timely information, and they burdened carriers, damaged letters and newspapers, and could be carried by freight companies instead.[106] From the vantage point of mail carriage, books were like any other form of commercial product — "blocks of wood," as Meigs put it. Their quality as instruments for the dissemination of knowledge seemed lost on him.[107] A subsequent postmaster general reaffirmed Meigs's action a decade later.[108]

But Congress poked a significant loophole in the ban in 1845. A postal law of that year made formal the previously informal practice of mail contractors carrying books and other merchandise "outside the mails."[109] And six years later, in the 1851 Postal Act, Congress admitted books to the mails outright, though not, according to Kielbowicz, for cultural or educational reasons, but rather because the rapidly expanding use of railroads for mail transport mitigated concern about their weight and bulk.[110] The first rate structure allowed books weighing no more than thirty-two ounces to be sent up to five hundred miles for one cent per ounce; the rate increased to five cents per ounce beyond 3,500 miles.[111] In 1852 an even simpler and more generous book rate was adopted: a book weighing less than four pounds could be sent up to three thousand miles for one cent per ounce; delivery over a greater distance cost two cents per ounce.[112]

The changes of 1851 and 1852, though significant, did not clear up all confusion, because the many kinds of printed materials—books, newspapers, magazines, and advertising circulars, for example—were subject to different rates. Schuyler Colfax, the Congressman from Indiana who was at the center of the federal knowledge taxes discussed in Chapter 3, observed that a postmaster had three hundred rates from which to choose when determining the cost of mailing a particular item.[113] Postmasters had struggled for decades, for example, to distinguish magazines from newspapers.[114] According to Kielbowicz's account, some based that distinction on content. For example, Attorney General John Mason in 1845 suggested that a newspaper could not be defined by its form, but rather as "*a publication communicating to the public intelligence of passing events.*"[115] Such a definition reflected a view that timely news was more important and more deserving of government subsidy than other information. That view was clearly what Congress had in mind from the beginning of the postal system,[116] and it is a view reflected throughout the history of knowledge taxation. But while in accord with congressional intent, the definition was difficult to apply.[117] Postal regulations reflected the confusion: the 1847 edition of those rules required that a newspaper be published at least monthly and convey "intelligence of passing events," that is, news; but the definition of a magazine acknowledged that magazines, too, contained news.[118]

Confused postmasters were not the only advocates of reform. Magazines for years had pressed for a uniform rate for periodicals. But their efforts had been interrupted by the 1851 postal law, which replaced a flat magazine rate (adopted in 1845) with a complicated system based on delivery distance and weight. Even the postmaster general questioned this system, as well as any distinction between newspapers and magazines. Kielbowicz quotes the following passage from the *1851 Report of the Postmaster General*:

It is difficult to assign a sufficient reason for charging upon such periodicals as the reviews, the numerous magazines, and theological, medical, and law journals, more than three times the amount of postage charged for the same distance on an equal weight of newspapers. Such periodicals are less ephemeral than the ordinary newspapers, and certainly not less beneficial in their influence. The same rates of postage, according to their weight, would be just and equitable, would simplify the accounts of the Department, and relieve it from the perplexing and often invidious duty of discriminating between different publications, and declaring one a newspaper and the other not a newspaper, in cases where little difference can be perceived.[119]

The result was 1852 legislation that set uniform rates for magazines and newspapers without regard to distance of delivery.[120] Magazines, like newspapers, could be mailed at a rate of one cent for the first three ounces and a penny more for each additional ounce.[121] But it would take Congress another eleven years to move from uniformity of rates to a single category for periodicals.

Postal Reform During the Civil War

Legislation of 1863 cut the three hundred categories of mail to three classes: correspondence, periodicals, and everything else.[122] Kielbowicz reports that the Senate passed the bill without debate; the House likewise gave it swift approval.[123] The result was a lowering of the basic newspaper rate to 0.38 cent and an increase in the weight limit to four ounces. Distance of delivery became largely irrelevant, though weeklies retained free in-county circulation.[124] But some magazines still were not treated quite as kindly as newspapers; though weekly journals enjoyed newspaper rates, the rate on periodicals published less frequently than every week was one cent per copy, or more than twice the basic newspaper rate.[125]

The year 1863 brought another major change in the postal system: the advent of free city delivery.[126] This massive undertaking was to a significant extent made possible by Southern secession; had the Confederate States not left the Union, thus allowing the federal government to suspend hundreds of unproductive routes throughout the South, city free delivery likely would have had to wait. But they had left the Union and therefore, according to Fuller, "Congress met with only a minimum of opposition when it authorized the postmaster general to establish free delivery service wherever he thought necessary and raised the postage [on intracity mail] to two cents to help pay for the new service. Two years later, . . . Congress took away his discretionary power and ordered . . . free delivery in every city with more than 50,000 residents."[127]

With these final changes, the basic features of the postal system, features that would persist from the end of the Civil War well into the twentieth century, were at last set. The nation had a "flat-rate postage system" with free city delivery, and use of the system, particularly for letters as well as for such services as registered delivery and money orders, was becoming widespread.[128] The system included — indeed subsidized — newspaper, periodical, and book distribution. And the end of the Civil War also restored another fixture of the modern postal system: a deficit. As mail routes through the Confederate States reopened, followed by the initiation of thousands of additional routes through the Rockies, the postal service once again went into debt.[129]

Of equal importance, by 1865 the outlines of the modern print-based communication industry, and particularly the basic structure of the daily and periodical press, were established. And those outlines were significantly shaped by the postal system. A deeply interdependent relationship between government and the press had been forged.

Private Competition in the Nineteenth Century

The middle of the nineteenth century brought increasingly rapid delivery of all kinds of mail, including news, by rail and steamboat. But such service was available only on select routes, and private carriers soon began efforts to fill the gaps in the government's system.[130] According to Kielbowicz's account, newspapers were particularly fond of private carriers; some delivery companies carried the papers (as well as messages between editors and reporters) at no charge in exchange for free advertising.[131] At least one postmaster general sought to put such services out of business; he ordered the arrest of an owner of the *New Orleans Crescent City* "for using public post roads to transport private mails."[132] But express service nevertheless flourished during the Mexican War, because the government could not afford to provide a competing service to carry war reports from Texas to the cities in the East. Kielbowicz reports the development of joint enterprises, with newspapers combining to share news and establish a system of riders, boats, rail delivery, and telegraph lines.[133] Not surprisingly, competing newspapers objected; one in New Orleans complained that a rival paper, which received market reports from Europe via a private express, gave its readers an advantage in America's commodities markets.[134]

Although then-Postmaster General Johnson was sympathetic, his concern about private carrier systems would soon be irrelevant, as telegraph lines pushed west and south, soon to replace express mail routes as carriers of unpublished information.[135] This new technology, Johnson realized, was a far greater threat to his monopoly than private carriers. He and some members of Congress therefore pushed for government control of the telegraph system.[136] But opponents, including of course the president of Western Union, argued that America's private telegraph system, begun in 1844, was by 1883 far more efficient than the "socialized" telegraphs of Europe.[137] Fuller quotes an editorial in the *New York Post* predicting years earlier in 1846 that a government-owned telegraph "would suffer as all enterprizes [sic] suffer, which are taken out of the hands of individuals. It would cost more; it would be less punctual; there would be less anxiety to obtain custom[ers] by efforts to accommodate the public."[138] The argument was made once again and the effort met with success. Government control of the telegraph system was rejected, and the press once again demonstrated its political power.[139]

Bulk Rates: The Floodgates Open

The postal law of 1863 had sought to combat one other obstacle to postal efficiency: bad debt on newspapers and periodicals. It will be recalled that postmasters had for years been saddled with the burden of collecting postage from the subscribers; only in 1863 did Congress begin to require prepayment on newspapers and periodicals at either the post office where they were mailed or the office of delivery.[140] But as late as 1874, according to Fuller, when the system should have been collecting more than $2,000,000 for delivery of periodicals, the department was in fact receiving only $800,000.[141] The problem, of course, was with the option given: most collection was to occur upon delivery to the reader's post office. Fuller recounts one local postmaster's explanation of the problem: "A man comes in for his newspaper; he has not the money to pay the quarter's postage, or he cannot make the change, or I cannot make it, and I violate the law and let him have the paper for several weeks without paying the postage. He is a friend of mine; I do not want to make him angry."[142]

The obvious and simple solution was to collect the postage prior to mailing. But publishers were not the least bit interested in doing so, either as an alternative under the existing system or as an element of reform.[143] And while they did not ultimately succeed in maintaining the old collection system, they exacted their pound of political flesh and got what would ultimately turn out to be worth much more. Under the terms of the compromise eventually reached in Congress, postal authorities and publishers agreed to a series of laws enacted between 1874 and 1885 that provided low bulk rates and registration of newspapers and magazines with the publishers' local postmasters. Fuller described the solution as follows:

> Reflecting both the government's old policy of diffusing knowledge and the power of the press, Congress established an astonishingly low tariff for this bulk mail. At first the postage was set at two cents per pound, and when this seemed too high it was changed in 1885 to one cent. This made it possible to send approximately eight papers for what it had previously cost to mail two. To obtain these rates, however, a publication had to be published at stated intervals — four times [per] year at least. . . . It also had to be published for the

dissemination of information of a public character or to be "devoted to literature, the sciences, arts, or some special industry."[144]

Not surprisingly, this plan greatly improved collection of payment for second-class postage. But efficiency was not the only argument at work here: Congress also sought a freer flow of information as one means of "Americanizing" immigrants, and the postal service was "referred to again and again as the great educator of the nation . . . not only of political affairs but of science, literature, art, and industry as well.[145]

Other consequences, some intended, some not, but each important, flowed from the compromise. And each reflected the clear connection between postal policy and structural developments in the publication industry. Fuller reports that the new bulk rate opened the door for journals "plainly" devoted to advertising, and because the law allowed the sending of unsolicited sample copies at bulk rates, magazines were able to obtain huge "subscription" lists and thus boost their advertising rates.[146] Similarly, according to Fuller, new postal laws fostered a huge increase in sales of paperback books. An 1874 statute allowed publishers of paperbacks to obtain bulk rates by merely showing that the "books" were "without board, cloth, leather, or other substantial binding," that they had literary merit, and that adequate subscription lists existed.[147] And many of these books went not directly to individual subscribers, but rather to book dealers not served by postal express companies.[148] Such "books," combined with new magazines, pushed the total weight of second-class mail from less than 70 million pounds in 1881 to 315 million pounds in 1895.[149]

In these (as well as other) respects the original purpose of diffusing political knowledge was broadened. It was, said Fuller, "[l]ike many such policies . . . nobly conceived, selfishly used, . . . defended with specious arguments. . . . [and] successful beyond all expectation."[150] Postal policies, especially those pertaining to the press, served the political, social, and ultimately the business and economic interests of the country, creating what Roper described as "a national market for standard brands of merchandise"[151] — as well, of course, as information.

THE TWENTIETH CENTURY

Rural Free Delivery: The Floodgates Widen
As the volume of second-class mail exploded, Congress turned its attention to another subject that would expand the volume even more: free mail de-

livery to rural areas. The politics were popular, and therefore smart, even if the economics were not. In the fray, not surprisingly, were the newspapers which strongly supported the extension of free mail service to America's farmers. The publishers, of course, realized that with free in-county circulation (for local weeklies) already established, only the absence of daily delivery was deterring rural residents from subscribing.[152] And sure enough, as rural free delivery opened across the country, newspaper sales "boomed so spectacularly," according to Fuller, "that a writer in the *Editor and Publisher* was convinced that daily newspapers had 'never had such a boom in circulation as they have since the rural free delivery was established.'"[153]

For the postal system, however, the economics of the matter were, in a word, grim. Combined with the rising volume of second-class matter to urban areas, the increase in mail to rural areas sent postal deficits soaring. Fuller recounts President Theodore Roosevelt's speech to Congress in 1901, in which Roosevelt reported that second-class matter constituted sixty percent of the mail's total volume by weight but contributed only four percent of total revenues, or only $4.3 million of the system's $111.6 million in operating costs. But Congress did nothing about the huge postal deficit until 1909, when Fuller again reports President Taft warning Congress that the system was losing $63,000,000 annually on second-class mail alone.[154]

Congress finally paid attention and the result was a new rate structure for magazines, which often were carried far greater distances than newspapers and therefore cost the system more money. Magazines were to pay one cent per pound for their educational content and four cents per pound of advertising.[155] Predictably, publishers were less than pleased with the idea. In a style of reasoning familiar even to this day, they argued that their advertising created a profit for the postal system by stimulating first-class mail-order business, and they blamed the costs of rural free delivery and postal inefficiency for the rising debt.[156] The magazine publishers also envied their counterparts in the newspaper business, who were exempted from the rate increase.[157]

It was not until 1918 that Congress passed a wartime measure raising second-class rates to one and a half cents per educational pound and more for each advertising pound (the exact amount depended on distance of delivery). But now the protests of the publishers were muffled by the imperatives of war. Enactment of the new rates marked the first time postage rates had been permanently increased since the establishment of the system in the 1790s, and it ended more than a century of efforts to diffuse knowledge by cutting the postage rate on printed matter.[158] But as Fuller put it, such efforts, though at times used for private gain, had "contributed immeasurably to the democratic process and made Americans as a whole perhaps the best informed people in the world in the nineteenth century."[159] And those efforts succeeded, said one postmaster, because the postal system's facilities

> made possible the cheap publication of newspapers [and later other publications] by placing upon all periodical popular reading matter the lowest rate of postage ever known in a civilized land. In no other country have the masses ever before enjoyed such an inestimable intellectual privilege, and no money expended by the Government in any of its multiform agencies has ever conferred such enormous advantages.[160]

Changing Technologies for Delivery

The first postage rate increase in 1918 did not mark the end of government efforts to diffuse knowledge. Indeed, as Fuller observed, "from that time to 1970, during which information became so abundant that the bad threatened to drive out the good, newspapers and magazines were still carried through the mails at a fraction of their cost."[161] But with the end of westward expansion, increasing use of private carriers for parcels and newspapers, and the advent of radio and television, demands for improved mail service became less frequent, less pressing, and less central to public policy in an expanding regulatory world.[162] Congress, therefore, turned its attention to other matters and to other ways to spend tax dollars; for their part, postal authorities turned to new technologies to make the mails cheaper and speedier.

The first technology to which postal authorities turned was rail. The rate paid to the railroads for carrying mail had remained basically stable from 1870 to 1912. Only after 1916, according to Alan Sorkin, did a combination of rate changes and improvements in railroad efficiency change the situation. In that year legislation was enacted that required the postal service to pay the railroads on the basis of volume carried, not weight. The reduction in cost was significant: in 1919 the postal department paid eight million dollars less for rail service than it had in 1916, even though the volume of mail carried by rail had increased substantially.[163]

The next focus of the postal authorities' attention was the use of air service. Airmail was initiated in 1919 by the establishment of a route between Cleveland and Chicago; the rate was set at twenty-four cents per ounce.[164] The new service expanded quickly. By 1923, according to Sorkin, airmail delivery had reduced the time for transporting mail from New York to San Francisco from one hundred hours to thirty-two hours. Airmail service was begun on a nationwide and continuous basis in 1924.[165]

Despite such technological advances, the postal system continued to operate at a deficit, as it has almost constantly in this century. But the deficit came increasingly to attract Congress's attention. Indeed, the focus on the deficit became so imperative that Sorkin attributes virtually all rate increases since 1945 to the growing imperative of trimming the deficits.[166] And deficit reduction became a euphemism, also, for subsidies. Thus "public service" subsidies, which directed tax revenues to support the costs of certain designated postal functions, were established by the Postal Policy Act of 1958. Even this strategy was imperfect, however, as at the same time that more parts of the postal system were given public service subsidies, thus serving in political (though not economic) terms to reduce the operating deficit, other parts continued to lose money.[167] This occurred, moreover, in the face of an increase in mail volume of 130 percent between 1945 and 1970[168] and a doubling of first-class rates.[169] The increase in volume, according to Fuller, simply overwhelmed the system, and this was due in part to the dismantling of the rail-delivery system of the 1930s. By 1969, the routes served by rail were only one-quarter of the distance that had been served at their zenith.[170]

To deal with a system that was losing money hand over fist even as both demand and its prices soared, postal authorities returned to the same system used prior to the Civil War: centralized distribution. The end of the Civil War and the spread of railroads had led to a shift away from central post offices in favor of a rail-based system. In the 1930s, however, postal authorities decided that they could save money if they quit sorting the mail aboard postal trains.[171] Only after central post offices with huge staffs were developed to sort the mail did the post office recapture some modicum of efficiency. But by then salary costs were an obstacle to cutting postal deficits. And the system was susceptible to collapse: in October 1966 the Chicago post office all but shut down for nearly three weeks because of an increase in volume and overtime restrictions.[172]

Reorganization

As a result of the Chicago disaster, a Commission on Postal Organization was established. In its 1968 report the Commission made a radical proposal: the post office should be transformed into a government corporation. The Postal Reorganization Act established that corporation, the U.S. Postal Service, in 1971.[173] But the Commission wanted more than a change in the system's name; it also, as Fuller put it, "declared that the Post Office was no longer needed as an instrument of government policy to support American politicians, newspaper and magazine publishers, and the transportation system."[174] Rather, said the Commission, "today the Post Office is a business. Like all economic functions it should be supported by revenues [from] users. The market should determine what resources are to be allocated to the postal service."[175]

While some members of Congress weren't fully convinced, according to Fuller, and persisted in making the well-worn (and usually successful) argument that without legislative control rural constituents (including newspapers) would be hurt, Congress nevertheless relented, giving up much of its authority over the system.[176] In place of the former postal system, an eleven-member board of governors was established to oversee the Postal Service, with a chief executive officer, who bore the traditional title of postmaster general, reporting to it. Congressional control was largely limited to the enactment of postal legislation (a constitutional authority) and to authorizing postal subsidies. The rate-making activities of the board of governors were to be overseen by a separate organization, the Postal Rate Commission.[177]

The theory of the new system was that mail should bear its full costs, but in politics, especially perhaps the politics of postage, theory and practice rarely coincide. Congress sought to cushion the blow in the Reorganization Act by requiring that higher rates on certain classes of mail be phased in.[178] Initially, adjustment periods of ten years for second- and third-class mailings by charitable organizations and libraries, and of five years for newspapers, books, and magazines, were required. But Congress later extended the five-year adjustment period to eight, and the ten-year period to sixteen.[179] As a consequence the higher rates would not fully affect newspaper publishers until 1979, and charitable organizations until 1987.[180] While the extended phasing period was not, according to the Senate Committee on Post Office and Civil Service, designed to undermine "the intent of the Postal Reorganization Act that over a period of time each class of mail shall provide revenues equal at least to its attributable cost," the Committee believed that the shorter adjustment periods would cause "substantial changes in the publishing industry" and would threaten "the Nation's basic educational, information and literary services."[181] The prospect of a three hundred percent rate increase for second-class publications between 1971 and 1975 was a cause of great concern,[182] as the Postal Service in 1974 held "a *de facto* monopoly over the distribution of magazines and many newspapers."[183] With the full support and encouragement of the press, Congress approved the extended protection, at a cost to the treasury of $753.7 million.[184]

Knowledge Subsidies Today

The end of the extended protection periods did not, however, witness a final end to congressional subsidization of knowledge distribution through the independent Postal Service. To this day, Congress continues to appropriate funds annually in the form of subsidies for reduced rates charged newspaper and magazine publishers and nonprofit groups.[185] The subsidies, which Sorkin describes as greater than the appropriations Congress formerly made to the Post Office Department,[186] are a direct result of the current four-class rate structure, with its across-the-board distinction between two kinds of mail: regular-rate and reduced-rate.[187] Reduced-rate materials consist primarily of in-county second-class mail[188] and second-class and third-class mail sent by nonprofit organizations.[189] In theory, "regular" rates are to reflect "postal costs attributable to that class or type plus that portion of all other costs of the Postal Service reasonably assignable to that class or type."[190] In contrast, "reduced" rates are limited to the "postal costs attributable to such class of mail or kind of mailer (excluding any other costs of the Postal Service)."[191] Through the Reorganization Act Congress thus committed, Sorkin concludes, to subsidize, or fully fund, the reduced rates for second-class mail sent by local publishers and nonprofit organizations — forever.[192]

Taxpayer subsidies for the diffusion of knowledge thus survived postal reorganization, and became a permanent part of the postal system's enabling legislation. The kinds of mail subsidized at reduced rates were limited in 1986 to in-county second-class materials, nonprofit bulk mail, and library-rate mail.[193] Interestingly, there seems to have been no debate on this provision, most likely because it was a small part of the massive Comprehensive Omnibus Budget Reconciliation Act. But comments made on other occasions clearly suggested that Congress, while no longer able to control postal rates, was unwilling (or politically unable) to live with a system in which the rates charged reflect the full cost.[194] Indeed, it seems likely that further hidden subsidies of much second-class mail — particularly newspapers and periodicals, but also catalogs and the like — continue today in the interstices of the rate structure because of inadequate attribution of full costs within the pricing structure.[195]

Current Classifications of Mail

Let us conclude this account with a snapshot of today's rate structure. Under current law, mail is broken down into four basic classes.[196] The first class, subject to certain limitations on size and weight,[197] includes sealed material, most handwritten or typewritten material, bills, and other mail that the sender designates first-class.[198]

Second-class mail—which consists mostly of newspapers and other periodicals—has "long enjoyed the most favorable postage rates," provided as a way of "encouraging public dissemination of information and ideas."[199] Second-class mail must meet one of two sets of rather complex criteria. Under the first, a second-class publication must: (1) be "issued at stated intervals and at least quarterly"; (2) have a "known office of publication"; and (3) be "formed on printed sheets by some process other than stencil, mimeograph, or hectograph."[200] It must also, with the exception noted below, contain "information of a public character, or devoted to literature, the sciences, art, or some special industry" and have a "legitimate list of subscribers" who pay more than a nominal amount.[201] But the last two requirements need not be met by, *inter alia*, schools, trade unions, churches, and public educational broadcasters.[202]

A second and alternative set of criteria provides second-class rates for publications that: (1) are at least twenty-four pages in length; (2) are "issued at stated intervals and at least quarterly"; (3) are not primarily a form of advertising for a single business; (4) do not consist of more than seventy-five percent advertising; (5) have a known office of publication; and (6) are requested by at least fifty percent of those who receive it.[203]

A further advantage is also given to second-class mail that is mailed in, and addressed for delivery within, the county of publication.[204] Echoing the nineteenth-century privileges extended to local newspapers, the advantageous rates are restricted to small publications with less than a 10,000-copy paid circulation, or with more than one-half of the paid circulation in the county of mailing.[205]

For our purposes, third-class mail consists of any material weighing less than sixteen ounces which does not fit within any of the other classes.[206] Thus, for example, if less than half of a publication's mailed circulation is to paid subscribers, the higher third-class rate will apply.[207] Also defined as third-class matter are unsolicited religious or political materials[208] and the various forms of bulk mail.[209]

The final category consists of fourth-class mail, which includes all other items weighing more than sixteen ounces.[210] Parcel post is the principal constituent, although the fourth class also includes certain types of "special" mail, such as books, films, recordings, educational charts and printed music, and library mail, which includes interlibrary loans and books sent by a publisher to a school or library.[211]

Postal Rates and the Taxation of Knowledge

This history of the postal system has been intentionally — and of necessity — brief, focusing on the system's evolution and the many stages through which it has passed, as well as on the basic shape of the rate structure as it has affected, in particular, the distribution of news, periodicals, and books. But while brief, the history provides a basis upon which we can identify general themes and relate them to the knowledge tax question. We will begin with the postal system's distinct and largely separate development in America, turning then to the various twists and turns of postal policy and rate structure over the past two hundred years and exploring their relationship to technological advances in printing and distribution systems. Finally, we will turn our attention to the future, exploring, in that setting, the likelihood that the postal system will play a rapidly diminishing role in the knowledge tax equation as new technologies such as computer-based communication and telephonic, electronic, and satellite distribution make the dissemination of the preprinted word increasingly anachronistic. With these developments the postal system may become anachronistic, too.

We begin with the past. In a real sense the development of the postal system in America was set on its own separate course from the very beginning. Unlike in England, where the "knowledge taxes" found their origin in quite explicit efforts to control information by the Crown and Parliament, the "taxation" question arose in America at a time when the "postal system" was fast developing and possessed an independent, quite benign, and democratically important identity. Thus effectively partitioned in the American mind, the postal system has remained, to a quite remarkable extent, separate ever since from any issues of knowledge taxation or, for that matter, from most concerns about freedom of the press. The reasons for this, I suspect, are also to be found in the formative colonial experiences with taxation by England, and with the different sorts of issues, such as taxation without representation, that those early colonial taxes raised. The focus of attention was on taxes, as such, not on postage or the mails. More broadly democratic and egalitarian values took root in America; values that permitted the postal system to be seen as a "public" good rather than a source of revenue, as an enterprise to be fostered in the interest of democratic participation rather than as a freestanding agency of abstract, even foreign, origin with the real capacity to control information needed by the body politic.

Whatever the combination of reasons, it is striking that the knowledge tax issue has almost never been raised in the postal setting; indeed, the postal system has not really been viewed, in the American political psyche, as connected with knowledge taxation at all. This would be understandable were postal rates to have represented nothing more than a charge for the actual cost of delivery, even though by a government monopoly. But this has never been the case; subsidies and preferences have been the norm, not the exception. It is as if an issue significantly forged (in eighteenth- and nineteenth-century England) in the combination of taxation and postage was permanently split in two, with the two components rarely, if ever, intersecting again. The consequence, of course, is that postal rates and the very structure of the postal system have evolved in a world of their own, freed in significant respects from the constraints that might have been imposed were knowledge tax issues to have been more explicitly broached; freed, at least, for partisan politics and economic self-interest, as well as democratic principle, to hold sway.

This is borne out throughout the two hundred years of the postal service. It is manifested both in large-scale structural changes and also in relatively discrete aspects of the rate structure. Over the course of its history the postal system has changed from a free (and subsidized) means of communication for all citizens, to one that charged full price and turned a profit; to a self-supporting, but still very public and democratic, institution whose policies quite explicitly subsidized the distribution of knowledge in the form of current information broadly disseminated as news, and whose policies were often wrought with partisan influence, economic self-interest, and subsidy; and, finally, to one that is now being transformed, in large part, into a private (yet government-sponsored) participant in a competitive market. As recounted in the previous pages, the shifts in structure and policy had vast implications for the distribution of current information on public matters throughout the country, whether in relation to fostering the distribution of newspapers, discouraging the development of magazines, protecting local newspapers from urban, regional, and national media, or until this century discouraging the distribution of books as contrasted with periodicals.

Many of these implications were foreseen; others were not. But they occurred with what often seems to have been but a whimper of protest about the consequences thus visited; with little attention to the purposes that, from the beginning, have animated the very idea of freedom from knowledge taxation. The knowledge tax issue seems to have had no bearing whatsoever. It was, as Benjamin Franklin had earlier put it in a very different context, "postage," not "taxation," that was involved.[212] This attitude, however artificial, served as an effective cover under which government policy could be forged free of scrutiny and, more importantly, in which the press, or certain quarters of it, could become actively engaged in promoting its self-interest in the political process.

Equally interesting — perhaps even *more* interesting — observations can be made about the rate structure. There the government was allowed to draw distinctions and create preferential policies that would at the very least have raised serious questions if addressed from the knowledge tax perspective. This occurred almost from the beginning with the patterns of partisan subsidy and patronage effected, most often, through franking privileges. These steps were often taken in the open; they became part of the habit of partisan struggles. The same things, of course, occurred in England, but as often as not they were hidden under the surface of the "administration" of the taxes.

While the explicit manifestations of partisanship soon passed, they were followed by a system of preferential policies for certain publications or types of publications. Lines were drawn in the rate structure between large publications and small ones; between dailies and weeklies; between "legitimate" papers and the "satanic" press or the massive weeklies; between newspapers and magazines and books; between local publications and state, regional, or national ones. Indeed, the system became so complex, with as many as three hundred different rates at its apex, that it nearly fell of its own weight.

But even in the simpler rate environment of the present day such distinctions remain; were they to be addressed today as knowledge tax questions they might not, in view of some of the Supreme Court's recent decisions,[213] survive constitutional scrutiny. Preferences (that is, lower rates) exist, for example, for nonprofit and religious organizations; for newspapers and periodicals produced and mailed locally; for books; and for newspapers that receive subscription revenues, but not for many news-papers that do not (irrespective of the actual content). These and other incidents of the rate structure would face daunting scrutiny in light of the Court's nondeferential attitude toward discrimination and differential taxa-tion.

It may be true that, in the main, the policies subserved by the postal rate structure are consistent with the objectives of broad dissemination of information to the body politic. And this may have implications both for our understanding of history and for the approach we should craft to the knowledge tax question under the First Amendment.[214] But there are also some notable exceptions to this generally benign view. One suspects, for example, that the same presumption could not be so generously entertained on the question of encouraging diversity of information. The politics of postage best served the interests of large publishers and the more estab-lished forms of communication. However one reads the record — benignly or not — and whatever part of it one focuses on, it is abundantly clear that discrimination and differential rates and policies were the norm, not the exception.

Yet the more interesting historical point is the one with which we began. In America the postal system seems to have become, from its inception, a law unto itself, cordoned off effectively at its very beginning from the knowledge tax *and First Amendment* issues that its policies ines-capably raised. This, too, is a lesson history teaches about knowledge taxation, particularly in its translation to America, for it is a quality perhaps unique to the American mind that two aspects of the same phenomenon can be effectively isolated one from the other, especially in our legalized culture. And it is a quality of the American political faith in democracy that that which would be obvious were a foreign agency involved is effectively obscured in the comforting mists of self-government.

Technology is the final strand that the history of the postal system discloses, for technology has quite clearly affected (and has been affected by) the evolution of the system; it will even more clearly influence the future. When the system began, the technology of printing had far out-paced the technology of distribution. The postal system began as a rela-tively crude means of transporting information — slow, cumbersome, and expensive. Over the next two hundred years, and indeed until very recently, change in the system has largely been a function of improved distribution, or transportation, technology. First came the telegraph, a technology over which the postal system initially sought monopoly control. Then came trains and their implications for increased speed, new modes of sorting and sending, and new economies of mailing and delivery. As technology continued to expand — ultimately to air transportation — the publishers of information began to shape their publications around it, both in terms of size and weight and, more obviously, in terms of mode of distribution. They began also to develop their own independent distribution systems, first through train and truck transportation and then through distributed or decentralized production facilities. The postal system adapted — often too late — to these changes; as a consequence, ever-increasing proportions of printed information escaped the postal system altogether with the formation of local, regional, and even national distribution systems that did not rely on the mails. This left the smallest and the weakest, or the just-emerging, publishers subject to the postal system, and the strongest ones increasingly independent of it. Perhaps the best illustration of this is to be found in the now-developing technologies for transmitting information.

Beginning, perhaps, in the middle of the twentieth century, the technologies of publication began once again to develop at a rapid pace and, most importantly, they began to catch up and even merge with the fast-developing technologies of distribution. This all occurred in the caldron of computer, telecommunications, satellite, and related technologies. Creation of information increasingly coincided with, indeed even became part of, its transmission; and distribution itself, assisted by the power of the computer to select, sort, and reorganize, became part of the creative process.[215] Most importantly for the postal system, the separation between the publication of a physical product — words on paper — and its distribution began to evaporate. As information became increasingly technological, the postal system stood still, devoted to the carriage of physical objects.

It has been said on more than one occasion that if you just leave a problem alone for long enough, it will go away. Perhaps that, too, is a lesson to be learned about the postal system and knowledge taxation. Over its long history, postal regulations have commonly discriminated in rates based on the content of publications, the fact of local publication and/or distribution, and the form of publication (newspaper versus magazine versus book), and have exerted significant influence on the technologies of publication as well as the distribution systems. Notwithstanding the potential knowledge tax implications of these and other features of the postal system and its rate structure over the past two hundred years — implications that have gone unscrutinized for the most part — now is probably not the time to try to fix them, for many of them will soon be irrelevant. Indeed, as a carrier of physical objects the postal system is probably already irrelevant to most daily news; its rates simply don't matter because they don't affect many publishers or customers.

Instead of the postal system, our attention today and in the future should be directed to the private sector, both regulated and unregulated, for it is with the telephone companies, with AT&T, with commercial and public satellites, with microwave transmission facilities, with computer data bases and networks, that the knowledge tax issues belong. These technological gateways and the organizations that control them are the postal systems of the future. Through access policies, copyright and intellectual property interests, and pricing practices, they will deeply influence the availability of information in usable form to the body politic. The knowledge tax problem will become partially transformed from a government exaction question into a regulated or purely private market pricing question. The interests in broad dissemination and availability of diverse sources of information on "politics and political economy" will remain the same. But the struggle may no longer be one *against* government involvement, a shibboleth that even the Supreme Court has taken too seriously.[216] It may, instead, become a struggle *for* it.

Notes

1. Wayne E. Fuller, *The American Mail* (1972).

2. Richard F. Kielbowicz, *News in the Mail: The Press, Post Office, and Public Information, 1700–1860s* (1989).

3. Daniel C. Roper, *The United States Post Office* (1917).

4. Alan L. Sorkin, *The Economics of the Postal System* (1980).

5. Fuller at 13.

6. *Id.*

7. The Dutch established a similar system at New Amsterdam in 1652. Fuller at 14.

8. *Id.* at 13–14.

9. In 1657 the Virginia Assembly passed a law requiring each plantation owner to deliver mail to the next plantation; failure to do so could cost the owner a fine "of one hogshead of tobacco." Roper at 17. Massachusetts established the first formal prices for postage about a decade later. Letter carriers were to be paid threepence a mile for their services, and innkeepers could charge no more than certain fixed amounts for oats and hay for the carrier's horse. Fuller at 15.

10. The Colonies' first postal route was established in 1672, when the governor of New York initiated monthly mail delivery between New York and Boston. Roper at 17. The service was short-lived. *Id.* at 18. Some ten years later, in 1683, a

mail service from Philadelphia was begun by William Penn, with rates of twopence for letters to Chester, threepence for letters to the falls of the Delaware River, and sixpence for letters to Maryland. Fuller at 15. The rates reported by Roper are a bit different. Roper at 19.

11. Fuller at 18; Roper at 20.

12. Fuller at 18–19.

13. Roper at 21.

14. Because each colony set its own rates, sending a letter from New York to Boston cost 12 pence, but sending a letter from Boston to New York cost only ninepence. Fuller at 20. Predictably, letters continued to travel outside the mails, thus cutting into Neale's revenues (which fell well short of the costs). *Id.*

15. Roper at 24; Fuller at 20–21.

16. Fuller at 22. For example, the basic letter rate was fourpence for 60 miles, with increased rates for longer distances. Roper at 27.

17. Fuller at 22–24. Taking advantage of a loophole that provided free postage for any letter accompanying or pertaining to merchandise, the crafty Virginians claimed that all their letters were in that category. As a result, the British did not attempt to establish a postal service in Virginia until 1732. British efforts in the North were in part more successful, and mail on the Boston, New York, and Philadelphia routes arrived on regular schedules. But colonists continued to object to rates and to send letters outside the mails whenever they had the chance. *Id.*

18. *Id.* at 24. Roper reports the date of Franklin's appointment as 1737. Roper at 26.

19. Fuller says simply, "newspapers were not allowed in the mails," but says that becoming an editor-postmaster provided a way around this ban. Fuller at 25. But another historian, Richard Kielbowicz, goes further: he says some printers arranged with postmasters ("if they were not postmasters themselves") for unofficial delivery at something less than letter rates and concludes that newspapers "probably" could be sent at the full letter rates. Kielbowicz also implies that, because "colonial postmasters emulated their counterparts in England," they may have allowed the franking of newspapers, an accepted practice in England. Kielbowicz at 17.

20. Fuller at 25.

21. In fact, Franklin at first admitted a competing paper to the mails free of charge (but he later closed the mail to his rival after the two editors fought over which had first planned to publish a particular magazine). Kielbowicz at 16.

22. Fuller at 25.

23. Kielbowicz at 17.

24. Fuller at 26–27.

25. Kielbowicz at 17. The passage appeared in a 1758 circular from Franklin to colonial postmasters, quoted in Ruth L. Butler, *Doctor Franklin, Postmaster General* 58 (1928).

26. *Id.*

27. According to Kielbowicz, the carriers received 80 percent of the assessment, and the postmasters kept a 20 percent commission. The plan (at least in theory) equalized printers' access to the postal system and eliminated the practice of

some riders of charging additional fees; it also gave printers collection agents, because postmasters, having an incentive to do so, would collect subscription fees. Kielbowicz at 17–18.

28. See *infra* notes 48, 52, 73–87, 100, 126–28, 149.

29. By 1762, the *New-York Mercury* claimed readers in "'ev'ry Town and Country Village' in Connecticut, Rhode Island, and New Jersey." Fuller at 29. And the number of colonial newspapers grew from 20 in 1763 to 38 in 1775. Alan L. Sorkin, *The Economics of the Postal System* 2 (1980).

30. Fuller at 27.

31. *Id.* at 30; see also Chapter 2.

32. John Phillip Reid, *Constitutional History of the American Revolution: The Authority to Tax* 175 (1987).

33. Fuller at 30–31.

34. *Id.* at 32.

35. Colonists sought to undermine the postal system by abusing the merchandise exception, by forcing ship captains to leave incoming mail at coffeehouses rather than post offices, and by paying carriers directly to deliver mail outside the official system. *Id.*

36. Roper at 35; Fuller at 34.

37. Kielbowicz at 21.

38. Fuller at 33–34; Kielbowicz at 22.

39. Fuller at 35.

40. *Id.* at 36.

41. Kielbowicz at 23.

42. In respect to the press, the Ordinance of 1782 authorized the licensing of postal riders to deliver newspapers at rates fixed by the postmaster general. The resulting practice, however, was that the rates were negotiated directly between printers and riders. *Id.* at 23. As was true in so many other respects, as well, the federal government under the Articles of Confederation seemed to lack sufficient authority or, as likely, sufficient will to give force and effect to the law's provisions. Roper at 42; Fuller at 42.

43. Fuller at 46.

44. Act of Feb. 20, 1792, 1 Stat. 235.

45. Kielbowicz at 34.

46. *Id.*

47. Shearjashub Bourne of Mass., quoted in *Annals of Cong.*, 2d Cong., 1st Sess. 285 (1791), quoted in Kielbowicz at 33.

48. Kielbowicz at 33.

49. Fuller at 118.

50. Kielbowicz at 33.

51. Fuller at 113.

52. Kielbowicz at 34. Of course, the increased cost of delivering a newspaper a greater distance also was a factor, but this appears to have been a secondary concern. *Id.* at 33.

53. Fuller at 120.

54. *Id.* at 109.

55. Roper at 48.

56. *Id.* at 50.

57. *Id.* at 51.

58. *Id.* at 57.

59. *Id.* at 59–60.

60. *Id.* at 60.

61. For example, sending a letter from New York City to Troy, New York, cost 18.5 cents, but a barrel of flour could be sent the same distance for only 12.5 cents. Sorkin at 5; Fuller at 61.

62. Fuller at 61–62.

63. Roper at 63; Kielbowicz at 84.

64. Roper at 67–68.

65. Joshua Leavitt, *Cheap Postage* 41 (1848), quoted in Kielbowicz at 83.

66. Kielbowicz at 59.

67. H.R. Doc. No. 106, 22d Cong., 1st Sess. 2 (1832) (emphasis in original), in Kielbowicz at 59.

68. H.R. Record Group 233, file 22A-G16.3, National Archives, in Kielbowicz at 59.

69. Kielbowicz at 59–60.

70. *Id.* at 59.

71. *Id.*

72. *Id.* at 61.

73. *Id.*

74. Fuller at 115.

75. Kielbowicz at 84.

76. *Id.*

77. *Cong. Globe*, 28th Cong., 2d Sess. appendix, 339–40 (Feb. 24, 1845), quoted in Kielbowicz at 84.

78. H.R. Rep. No. 483, 28th Cong., 1st Sess., at 15 (1844), quoted in Kielbowicz at 84.

79. Kielbowicz at 84. There is evidence indicating widespread circulation of urban newspapers. According to Kielbowicz, for example, Boston publishers in 1832 said their city's mails carried 1,275,000 newspapers annually; 750,000 of those papers traveled more than 100 miles to reach their destinations. And papers in more than a dozen cities aimed special editions at rural readers. *Id.* at 62.

80. *Id.* at 85.

81. *Id.*

82. 1850 Postmaster Gen. Ann. Rep. 409, quoted in Kielbowicz at 108.

83. L. Bacon, "The New Post Office Law," *New Englander*, Oct. 1845, at 540, quoted in Kielbowicz at 85.

84. *Cong. Globe*, 28th Cong., 2d Sess. appendix, 210 (Jan. 16, 1845), quoted in Kielbowicz at 85.

85. Act of Mar. 3, 1847, 9 Stat. 202; Roper at 65.

86. Kielbowicz at 86.

87. Roper at 67.

88. Kielbowicz at 86.

89. Roper at 67.

90. Act of Mar. 3, 1851, 10 Stat. 39.

91. Rep. Abraham W. Venable, D-N.C., in *Cong. Globe*, 31st Cong., 2d Sess. 74 (Dec. 18, 1850), quoted in Kielbowicz at 86–87.

92. Fuller at 113.

93. *Id*. at 115.

94. Kielbowicz at 87.

95. *Id*. at 87.

96. *Id*. at 88.

97. Fuller at 122.

98. *Id*.

99. *Id*.

100. *Id*.; Kielbowicz at 89.

101. Kielbowicz at 90.

102. Fuller at 125.

103. *Id*. at 134.

104. Act of Feb. 20, 1792, 1 Stat. 235, 238; 1 Stat. 734, 738–40.

105. Kielbowicz at 132–33.

106. Letter from R. J. Meigs, Jr., Postmaster Gen., to Sen. Montfort Stokes, Chmn., Comm'n on Post Offices and Post Roads (Feb. 21, 1823), reprinted in *American State Papers*, 17th Cong., 2d Sess. 112 (1823). Quoted in Kielbowicz at 133.

107. *Id*.

108. *Id*. at 133.

109. Postal Act of 1845, 5 Stat. 737; Kielbowicz at 134.

110. Kielbowicz at 134.

111. *Id*.

112. Fuller at 125–26.

113. See *Cong. Globe*, 37th Cong., 2d Sess. 494 (1862).

114. See Kielbowicz at 122–24.

115. 4 Op. Att'y Gen. 410, quoted in Kielbowicz at 130 (emphasis in original).

116. See Kielbowicz at 121.

117. *Id*. at 130.

118. 1847 Postal Laws and Regulations 24–25, quoted in Kielbowicz at 137, n.53.

119. 1851 Postmaster Gen. Report, reprinted in S. Exec. Docs., 31st Cong., 2d Sess., at 428 (1851), quoted in Kielbowicz at 131.

120. Kielbowicz at 131.

121. Fuller at 125.

122. Act of Mar. 3, 1863, 12 Stat. 705.

123. Kielbowicz at 92.

124. *Id*.

125. *Id*. at 132.

126. Fuller at 71.

127. *Id*. at 71.

128. *Id*.; Sorkin at 6.

129. Fuller at 71–72.

130. Kielbowicz at 170.

131. *Id.*

132. *Id.* at 171.

133. *Id.* at 172.

134. *New Orleans Tropic*, May 8, 1846, quoted in Kielbowicz at 172.

135. Kielbowicz at 172.

136. Fuller at 173–74.

137. Norwin Green, "The Government and the Telegraph," 137 *N. Am. Rev.* 16 (1883), quoted in Sorkin at 8.

138. Fuller at 174.

139. Sorkin at 8–9.

140. Fuller at 131.

141. *Id.*

142. *Id.* at 132.

143. *Id.*

144. *Id.* at 133.

145. *Id.* at 134.

146. *Id.* at 135.

147. *Id.* at 136, 138.

148. *Id.* at 135–36.

149. *Id.* at 137.

150. *Id.* at 146.

151. Roper at 180.

152. Not surprisingly, more than 100 newspapers joined the pro-RFD parade soon after it formed in 1891. Fuller at 139.

153. *Id.* at 139–40.

154. *Id.* at 141–43.

155. *Id.* at 143.

156. *Id.* at 144.

157. See Fuller at 144. Because the classification of a publication as a periodical or newspaper was made by the postmaster general, who possessed certain discretion in charging the higher rate, publishers claimed that the executive branch could drive some publications out of business. But Fuller reports that some newspaper editors muted their criticism when rates were increased for their "exposé-filled, muckraking competition." Said the *Boston Herald* in 1911: "The magazines have been having a glorious time in the past decade. . . . [T]hey have unveiled graft; they have impugned motives; they have lambasted leaders and derided dynasties; and they have set up a spartan standard of honesty and a heroic code of patriotic ethics. . . . Now the shoe is on the other foot; and the common man is grinning at the preachers, patriots and purists who appear to be much the same predatory patriots the 'interests' and 'trusts' were alleged to be. . . . The magazines are getting for a penny something that costs the Government nine pennies." Fuller at 144. But such arguments were not enough to defeat the magazine subsidy.

158. Fuller at 146.

159. *Id.* at 146–47.

160. *Id.* at 147 (address by Postmaster T. L. James).

161. *Id.* at 147.
162. *Id.* at 333.
163. Sorkin at 11; Fuller at 187.
164. Sorkin at 11.
165. *Id.*
166. *Id.* at 12.
167. *Id.*
168. *Id.* at 13; Fuller at 334.
169. Fuller at 336–37.
170. *Id.* at 335.
171. *Id.*
172. *Id.* at 335–36; Sorkin at 14.
173. Sorkin at 14.
174. Fuller at 337.
175. Postal Commission Rep., quoted in Fuller at 338.
176. Fuller at 341–42.
177. Sorkin at 25–26.
178. Postal Reorganization Act, 39 U.S.C.A. § 3626 (West 1980).
179. Pub. L. No. 93–328 (1974).
180. S. Rep. No. 765, 93d Cong., 2d Sess. 1 (1974).
181. *Id.* at 4.
182. *Id.* at 5.
183. *Id.* at 4.
184. H. R. Rep. No. 1084, 93d Cong., 2d Sess. 16 (1974).
185. See 39 U.S.C.A. § 2401(c) (Supp. 1992) (authorizing appropriations to compensate Postal Service for, *inter alia*, second-class in-county publications, non-profit bulk mail, and various items sent to or from libraries and schools); see also Treasury, Postal Service and General Government Appropriations Act, Pub. L. No. 102–141, tit. II, 105 Stat. 834, 842 (1991) (allocating $470 million to Postal Service "for revenue forgone on free and reduced rate mail"). The Congress also provides free mail service to certain diplomats, 39 U.S.C.A. § 3217 (West 1980 & Supp. 1992), the blind or other handicapped persons, *id.* §§ 3403–4, and for ballots sent in by Americans overseas, *id.* § 3406. Until 1983 Congress reimbursed the Postal Service "for public service costs incurred by it in providing a maximum degree of effective and regular postal service nationwide, in communities where post offices may not be deemed self-sustaining." 39 U.S.C.A. § 2401(b) (Supp. 1992). And Congress directly funded the transitional costs of the Post Office Department's conversion to the Postal Service. Sorkin at 38–39.
186. Sorkin at 39.
187. 39 U.S.C.A. § 3626(i)(1) (Supp. 1992). Reduced-rate mail was formerly known as "preferred-rate" mail. See, e.g., former 39 U.S.C.A. § 4358(a), which was rescinded by the Postal Reorganization Act but appears in the appendix to the 1980 edition of 39 U.S.C.A. at 467. And Sorkin, for some reason, refers to "favored-rate" mail. Sorkin at 40–41.
188. 39 C.F.R. § 3001, App. A, § 200.0211 (1991).
189. *Id.* at App. A., §§ 200.0212, 300.0212; see also Sorkin at 41.

190. 39 U.S.C.A. § 3622(b)(3) (West 1980).

191. 39 U.S.C.A. § 3626(a)(2) (Supp. 1992).

192. Sorkin at 41.

193. Comprehensive Omnibus Budget Reconciliation Act, Pub. L. No. 99–272, § 15102(b), 100 Stat. 82, 330 (1986). This section now appears as 39 U.S.C. § 3626(a); its adoption eliminated the now-expired schedule for phased rate increases that were in § 3626(a) under the Postal Reorganization Act. See 39 U.S.C.A. § 3626(a) (Supp. 1992).

194. For example, when elimination of postal subsidies was proposed in 1985 by the Reagan Administration—a step that would have shifted the burden of reduced rates from taxpayers to regular-rate mailers—Mickey Leland, chairman of the House Subcommittee on Postal Operations and Services, said administration officials were "swinging their budget ax at whatever nonmilitary targets they can find." *Impact of the President's 1986 Budget on U.S. Postal Service: Hearings Before the Subcomm. on Postal Operations and Services of the House Comm'n on Post Office and Civil Service*, 99th Cong., 1st Sess. 1 (1985). Leland defended the in-county privilege as "designed to help newspapers in rural areas and small towns provide the vitally needed information and communications needs [sic] of those areas." *Id.* at 2. Another legislator, California's Mervyn Dymally, asked: "What will happen if Congress does not appropriate the funding necessary to sustain preferred mailing rates at the level that [nonprofit] mailers rightfully have planned on for many years? Recording for the Blind, Inc., which provides blind students with taped books and materials critical to their education, would incur additional expenses equal to seven percent of RFB's budget. And who will pay for the reduced service to these blind students? Without the education [that] helps blind students become productive, independent citizens, the American taxpayer will pay in the long run. The Salvation Army would incur additional postage costs of $2.6 million annually. Who will pay if the Salvation Army raises less funds to assist the poor and the needy? The American taxpayer will pay in the long run." 131 Cong. Rec. E 2387 (1985). And beneficiaries of the reduced rates, of course, were likewise opposed to removal of their taxpayer subsidy. Coleman Hoyt, an official with the Direct Marketing Association, told Leland's panel: "This nation's charitable institutions and enterprises benefit all the citizens and have traditionally been supported in their use of the mails by the citizens through general tax revenues. It makes no sense at all to shift this national tax burden from all taxpayers to a selected group who happen to be mailers." *Impact of the President's 1986 Budget, supra*, at 28. The 1986 budget law and subsequent congressional funding of postal subsidies indicate that Congress agreed. The subsidization of knowledge diffusion continues.

195. See James C. Miller III & Roger Sherman, "Has the 1970 Act Been Fair to Mailers?" in *Perspectives in Postal Service Issues* 53 (1980).

196. 39 C.F.R. § 3001, App. A.

197. *Id.* App. A, § 100.03.

198. *Id.* App. A, § 100.011.

199. Elizabeth Gorman, "The First Amendment and the Postal Service's Subscriber Requirement: Constitutional Problems with Denying Equal Access to the Postal System," 21 *U. Rich. L. Rev.* 541 (1987).

200. 39 C.F.R. § 3001, App. A, § 200.01.
201. *Id.* App. A, §§ 200.0104 and 200.0105.
202. *Id.* App. A, § 200.0106.
203. *Id.* App. A, § 200.0110.
204. *Id.* App. A, § 200.0211.
205. *Id.* App. A, § 200.02111.
206. *Id.* App. A, § 300.01.
207. Gorman at 542–43.
208. *Id.* at 543.
209. 39 C.F.R. § 3001, App. A., § 300.021.
210. *Id.* App. A, § 400.010
211. *Id.* App. A, §§ 400.020–400.022.
212. See Reid at 175. "The Post Office," Franklin said in his testimony before the House of Commons on the Stamp Act question, "is not so much a tax as a regulation, as it compels no person to send letters by it." *Id.*
213. See Chapter 9 for a discussion of the Court's recent decisions.
214. See Chapter 9.
215. See Office of Technology Assessment, *Science, Technology, and the First Amendment*, Special Report, (1988); M. Ethan Katsh, *The Electronic Media and the Transformation of Law* (1989); Symposium, "Media at the Millenium," 5 *Media Stud. J.* 1 (1991); Ithiel De S. Pool, *Technologies of Freedom* (1983).
216. See Chapter 9.

9. Developing Doctrine in the Supreme Court: Some Lessons from History

History does not provide solutions to current problems, nor does it even tell us with certainty where potential mistakes lie. Times change, by which we mean that economic, social, and cultural conditions and values, among others, evolve and take on meaning in their own context. Through history, however, we can attempt to capture the conditions and values of the past and, having given them definition, more clearly identify the values that fit our day and their application to contemporary predicaments.

So it is with freedom of the press, and particularly with the problem of taxation. It is important that we understand the past, even if we do not choose to draw upon it for answers. If we do not do so, the value of continuity as an element of change will be lost, and we will be forced to forge a path without the moorings and perspective of history. There is, in all candor, some risk that this is precisely what is happening with the Supreme Court's emerging jurisprudence of government taxation of knowledge. In its trilogy of recent opinions[1] the Court has announced broad-ranging although not entirely consistent principles, and has crafted a system of rules and presumptions whose roots in the historical experience of the press and the people are ambiguous, at best.

We will begin our inquiry into the Supreme Court's developing First Amendment jurisprudence with a fairly detailed discussion of the *Minneapolis Star & Tribune*[2] case, the Court's first opinion dealing directly, and broadly, with knowledge taxation. We will then turn to the 1991 Supreme Court decision in *Leathers v. Medlock*,[3] a decision that extends and clarifies — some would say contradicts — the *Minneapolis Star* decision. Our discussion will focus not only on legal rules, but also on the perspectives that history might shed on the issues addressed by the Court, and on the general themes through which history can provide guidance in future cases and varied settings. Finally, we will turn to the *Arkansas Writers' Project, Inc. v. Ragland*[4] decision as we attempt in conclusion to draw the seemingly disparate strands of the Court's trilogy together.

Knowledge Taxes and Freedom of the Press:
The *Minneapolis Star & Tribune* Case

The Supreme Court's first effort to identify broad principles of freedom of the press in the knowledge tax area occurred in its 1983 decision in *Minneapolis Star & Tribune Co. v. Minnesota Commissioner of Revenue*.[5] The *Minneapolis Star* case involved a challenge by the Minnesota Star and Tribune Company to a 1971 Minnesota law that imposed a four percent use tax on the cost of paper and ink products consumed in the production of a publication.[6] The paper and ink tax was part of a general system of sales and use taxes begun in 1967.[7] The sales tax had been imposed in varying amounts since that year,[8] and from the beginning retail sales of periodical publications were exempted.[9] Concomitant with enactment of the sales tax, a use tax was enacted for the "privilege of using, storing or consuming in Minnesota tangible personal property."[10] As originally enacted, the use tax, like the sales tax, exempted from taxation goods such as paper and ink used in the production of a publication and acquired in another state.[11] Until the use tax statute was amended in 1971, therefore, the *Star and Tribune*, as well as all other newspapers and periodical publications, were specifically exempted from the sales and use taxes in Minnesota.

For reasons that are not entirely clear, although they surely made for interesting politics, the advantaged status of periodical publications — including most notably newspapers — came to an end in 1971. The expedient was the use tax, not the sales tax. In that year, the use tax component of the sales and use tax scheme was amended to impose a use tax on "the cost of paper and ink products used or consumed in producing a publication."[12] The sales tax exemption was maintained, and the use tax rate was the same as that for the general sales tax. The economic effect of the amendment was to bring the tax burden on the previously exempted publishers closer to that otherwise imposed, although the effective cost of the tax was lower because its incidence was on the cost of materials used in production rather than on the retail price of the finished product.[13]

The asserted, although somewhat tautological and unrevealing, purpose of the 1971 amendment was to enact a substitute for the sales tax, which could otherwise have been imposed on the publications at the point of sale.[14] The use tax was used, according to the State, because of its simplicity of collection in comparison to the relatively more cumbersome collection of sales tax on a multitude of small transactions.[15] The Supreme Court, interestingly, refused to credit this argument in light of the fact that the hybrid use tax mechanism applied only to publications, while many other equally small transactions were not exempt from the sales tax. But the Court's treatment of the issue was, as we shall see, cursory at best and of questionable relevance, as well, for the significance of the Court's refusal to accept the State's asserted purpose is not clear from the Court's opinion.[16]

In response to the State's argument that its choice was one of selecting the most effective and practicable means of collection and administration of the tax, the Court stated that "[i]f the real goal of this tax is to duplicate the sales tax, it is difficult to see why the State did not achieve that goal by the obvious and effective expedient of applying the sales tax."[17] Like the State's justification, this, too, is little more than a tautology, a rejection of the State's argument by ignoring it, and in any event it misses the more basic question: Why did the legislature decide to impose *any* tax on publications, given their history of exemption from tax?

The State argued, of course, that its purpose was straightforward — raising revenue — and that the choice of a use tax was, if anything, advantageous to publishers. On the question of purpose, the Court simply ignored the subject, although at various points in the opinion the Court was careful not to infer any improper or censorial motivation underlying the tax scheme.[18] Purpose, it seems, was not a subject that the Court was eager to probe; indeed, for all practical purposes, the Court treated it as irrelevant. And perhaps rightly so in the circumstances, for a state's decision to increase revenue by eliminating a voluntary exemption, even for publications, is hard to negate.

On the question of economic effect — that is, on the State's claims that the cost of the use tax was, if anything, lower for the affected publications — the Court simply chose to avoid the question on the ground "that courts as institutions are poorly equipped to evaluate with precision the relative burdens of various methods of taxation."[19] As three justices noted, this is surely an overstatement if not, indeed, simply wrong in terms of the Court's longstanding practices in tax cases.[20] More significantly, the Court's disavowal wholly disables a state from tendering any justification for a form of tax other than a sales tax, even if, as Minnesota argued, the economic burden of the tax is lighter in use tax form than it would be in sales tax form. As the Court explained, "even without actually imposing an extra burden on the press, the government might be able to achieve censorial effects."[21] This would prove to be the critical factor in the Court's analysis, and we shall return to it after discussing the other challenged provision of the Minnesota tax.

In 1974, three years after the use tax had been extended to publications, the Minnesota legislature amended the use tax statute to exclude from taxation the first $100,000 of taxable paper and ink products used in any calendar year for the production of a publication.[22] The effect of this amendment was to grant a $4,000 tax credit to all affected taxpayers. While seemingly plain and almost self-explanatory on its face, the amendment was characterized quite differently in the Supreme Court's majority opinion, on the one hand, and in the dissenting opinion of Justices White and Rehnquist, on the other.

Justice O'Connor, writing for the majority, purported to avoid questions of legislative purpose, as she had before, but then proceeded to construct a purpose from the economic effect of the amendment, notwithstanding the Court's earlier disavowal of its ability to undertake such a venture. As Justice O'Connor put it for the Court, "Minnesota's ink and paper tax violates the First Amendment . . . because it targets a small group of newspapers. The effect of the $100,000.00 exemption enacted in 1974 is that only a handful of publishers pay any tax at all, and even fewer pay any significant amount of tax."[23] The tax accordingly singled out a part of the press, a result deemed violative of the First Amendment because "the tax begins to resemble more a penalty for a few of the largest newspapers than an attempt to favor struggling smaller enterprises."[24] Why this is so is hardly apparent from the opinion, for the Court rejected the State's claimed purpose of tax equity on the remarkable ground that the State had not "grant[ed] benefits to small businesses in general."[25] This line of argument hardly disposes of the State's claimed purpose on its merits, whether on the facts of the case or as a general principle. Indeed, it reflects the Court's willingness to probe the forbidden domain of a tax's effect, but only so far, and no further. The Court's rejection of "equity" considerations (favoring small and diverse publications) also flies in the face of common, if not almost universal, experience with the most benign and unobjectionable forms of taxation throughout the long history of knowledge taxation.[26]

In dissent Justices Rehnquist and White characterized the $100,000 exemption differently, although not necessarily more fully. Noting that the effect of the exemption was to give a $4,000 credit to all taxpayers, large and small alike, they did not view the exemption as itself creating a legislative subcategory within the use tax structure. Rather, they looked to the motive and effect of the tax in light of its incidence, recognizing on the one hand that very few newspapers in fact ended up with a tax liability, but on the other hand that the exemption was facially neutral, benefited all papers, and therefore the constitutional infirmity, if any, must relate to the specific purposes or economic consequences of the amended scheme. In this they seemed closer to the mark than the majority, and their reasoning led them easily to the tenable conclusion that the basis for the exemption was rational, perhaps even beneficial to small papers, and its economic impact, like that of the underlying use tax itself, was to lighten the relative burden on the press as compared to other taxpayers.[27] But their view did not prevail, and in the end Justice Rehnquist, the lone dissenter, and Justice White, the skeptic in partial concurrence, were left tilting at the windmills of the majority's opinion.

POLITICAL AGNOSTICISM AND ITS RELATION TO FREEDOM OF THE PRESS

While the vagaries of the Minnesota tax are interesting and complex, and while the Court's analysis of the tax may be subject to dispute, we must, of necessity, take the Court at its word for the present, and turn our attention to the *constitutional* basis for the decision. The Court assumed that the tax represented a singling out of the press — a differential treatment which, in this instance, represented a special tax burden imposed on a part of the press. A tax that singles out the press, the Court held, is constitutionally suspect.[28]

The case actually involved a number of forms of singling out, two of which will principally occupy our attention: a differential tax imposed on the (print) press in a *form* not applicable to other similarly situated taxpayers (the use tax itself); and a differential tax that fell unevenly, in effect,[29] on a subgroup of the press (small publishers whose tax revenues would be less than the level of credit allowed, versus large publishers). With respect to each of these, singling out resulted in the imposition of a differential burden — a tax different in form imposed on the press — as well as the conferral of a differential benefit — a lower rate or level of tax for the press.

Notwithstanding the apparent differences among these various forms of singling out, the Court embraced them all within a single constitutional rule. As the Court expressed it: "Differential taxation of the press . . . places such a burden on the interests protected by the First Amendment that we cannot countenance such treatment unless the State asserts a counterbalancing interest of compelling importance that it cannot achieve without differential taxation."[30] Differential taxation was the nub of the problem; the constitutional violation was the unjustified singling out of the press in the *form* of taxation, whether for the conferral of a benefit or the imposition of a burden.

This, of course, is merely to state the conclusion without the reasons. For the reasons why differential taxation of the press is constitutionally unacceptable in the absence of special justification, we must look to other portions of the opinion. That examination discloses four stated reasons.

1. The First Amendment was historically intended to prohibit such taxation in the absence of special justification. As the Court put it, "[t]here is substantial evidence that differential taxation of the press would have troubled the Framers of the First Amendment."[31]

2. By imposing a tax that exacts a differentially higher cost on the press, government can deter or censor content through the power to destroy by taxation. A requirement that taxes be imposed alike on the press as the public represents a political safeguard against motivation or threat.[32]

3. A tax with differential impact on only some elements of the press "begins to resemble . . . a penalty for a few of the largest newspapers," and provides an opportunity for government suppression aimed at specific content.[33]

4. A tax which "single[s] out the press for a different method of taxation [in which] . . . the burden on the press [is] lighter than that on other businesses . . . threatens the press . . . with the possibility of subsequent differentially *more burdensome* treatment."[34]

Each of these expressed grounds shares a common theme: that singling out the press will affect the conduct of the press and what it will publish. Direct government censorship as well as deterrence and self-censorship are the consequences that the singling out rule is designed to avoid.

But the Court's opinion is not entirely forthcoming in explaining precisely how singling out the press in the form of taxation will yield one or more of these consequences; how the various forms of singling out addressed in the case will lead to the same result; and how the ultimate consequence of self-censorship through deterrence relates to the central principles underlying the First Amendment guarantee of freedom of the press in the knowledge tax setting. Indeed, the opinion is hardly forthcoming at all, and the reason, perhaps, is that the Court's logic, and its history, is flawed.

The Singling Out Principle
We shall, at any rate, explore the questions in a more forthcoming way. And in doing so, we will focus on two specific questions. First, what is the

relationship between the singling out rule and the central value reflected in the free press guarantee, freedom of editorial judgment? Second, how can the principle underlying the singling out rule be harmonized with the Court's seemingly indiscriminate application of the rule to the various kinds of singling out addressed in the Court's opinion?[35] We shall explore, in short, how, if at all, the Court's result can be reconciled with the historical background of knowledge taxation. If it can, it will be for reasons very different from those supplied by the Court.

The reason first cited by the Court to support condemnation of differential taxation of the press was historical. The Court stated that "differential taxation of the press would have troubled the Framers of the First Amendment."[36] Even as a general proposition the statement is overbroad, at best; the historical record, as we have seen, falls well short of a universal condemnation of differential taxation.[37] When applied to the particular setting of a use tax applied to newspapers in lieu of a higher sales tax, with no evidence of any but benign motivation, moreover, the statement seems almost openly defiant of historical experience, and the historical record bearing on the meaning of the First Amendment is far from clear.[38] From the earliest times the basic evil of taxing speech or religion was its censorial purpose and effect.[39] In the absence of any showing of purpose or historically based reason for excusing that showing, history alone would not warrant a constitutional standard that indiscriminately condemned all forms of differential taxation.[40]

This is not to say that the effect of a tax was historically unimportant, for the invalidity of a differential tax whose effect is not to censor but rather to significantly restrict the broad availability of current information and diverse opinion to the populace, even though its purpose is benign, may find rich historical support.[41] It is noteworthy, however, that the Court did not even discuss effect problems at all; nor, it appears, was there any evidence in the record to support the proposition that the Minnesota tax had any censorial or inhibiting effect.[42] Quite the contrary, in fact, seems to have been the case. By the Court's own statement the effect of the tax was a matter that lay beyond judicial competence. Yet effect is most likely at the heart of the historical argument relied upon by the Court,[43] for the questions of deterrence and self-censorship concern "effect" at least as much as, and (in view of the English history) perhaps more than, "purpose."

Similarly, the Court's companion statements that apart from history the constitutional problem with differential taxation is what such taxation means in terms of illicit government purpose cannot justify the conclusion reached in the case, for the standard applied by the Court requires no showing of purpose, nor does the opinion explain why such a showing is not required if illicit purpose is really the chief evil at which the Court's rule is directed. And apart from the Court's few and ill-advised references to purpose — all constructed from the face of the statute or, more disturbingly, from the Court's implicit view of its *effect*, and all disputable even on that thin record — nothing is really made of purpose in the opinion.

The third and final argument made in support of the rule against differential taxation of the press is that the very possibility that such taxes may be permitted, even though only in limited circumstances, poses a risk that additional and more burdensome taxes will be attempted. The safest protection against that threat is the majoritarian principle that taxes or regulations imposed on the press be imposed on the public as well, assuring a political safeguard against the press being isolated in the political arena.[44] This is a principle deeply rooted in constitutional jurisprudence,[45] and one with important application to the Minnesota case and to the constitutional approach to differential taxation of the press. How the principle applies in the context of differential taxation of the press and the reasons supporting its application, however, are far from self-evident on the face of the Court's opinion. The Court presents us not with an answer, but with a puzzle. If purpose and effect are not preconditions to making a differential tax constitutionally suspect, when and why will a tax pose dangers that call for special majoritarian protection from the political process?

Political Agnosticism and the Majoritarian Political Process

One might begin the search for an answer to the puzzle by examining in detail the precise character of the tax, and in particular the specific types and magnitude of the differential burdens or benefits imposed by it and the particular firms subject to it. But such an approach will not take one very far, for little information on these issues is provided in the opinion; notably, the Court refused to consider them.[46] Indeed, perhaps the most important insight is that the Court seems to have considered such questions *constitutionally* irrelevant.

At first blush, it is difficult to make sense of this result, as one would think that a tax on the press whose form is identical to that generally applied, but whose substance (rate, methodology) is differential when applied to the press, would call for the same inquiry engaged in by the Court. One would think, in other words, that a sales tax applied to newspapers as to all retail sales, but at a higher rate for newspapers, would be treated with as much constitutional suspicion as the Minnesota scheme of applying a use tax to newspapers and a sales tax to other retail sales. But on reflection it is clear that this is not the case, that the two situations are viewed differently by the Court; and this is clear *because of* the Court's refusal to inquire into effect.

The reason the Court refused to consider issues concerning the economic burden or comparability of the Minnesota tax was not, it seems, because it was differential in rate, but rather because it was differential in *form*. As a consequence, differential effects in the incidence of the tax were irrelevant. The effect of the tax is by definition irrelevant (or at best a subsidiary question to be addressed only if differences in form are inescapable) if form is determinative. The Court's conclusion suggests that *form is constitutionally significant* in and of itself, quite apart from questions of equality or comparability in effect.[47] Left for a future day are cases in which form must *necessarily* be different, or in which *form* is the same, but the incidence of a tax is differential.[48]

The conclusive weight placed on form provides an important element of the Court's approach; indeed, it provides the only analytically complete explanation for the decision. A concern only with economic impact in the context of a unique form of tax imposed on the press would reflect a predominant interest in purpose or specific censorship, which the Court disavows. A concern focused on equality as an end in itself under the First Amendment, which might explain the decision, though not without much more development, would not only lead to insuperable problems of adjudication, but would suggest an egalitarianism that is inconsistent with historical experience with knowledge taxation and anathema to the competitive assumptions of free expression. In contrast, an interest in form rather than effect shifts the focus away from equality as such and toward an inquiry into the central purposes of freedom of the press and their relationship to the *forms* of the political system and the relationship of the press to the partisan, democratic political process.

The central concern of the free press guarantee, established and confirmed in an extended line of cases, is editorial freedom: government may not censor or directly influence the editorial judgments made about what to publish and when to publish, except within a narrow band of circumstances.[49] The primary, if not the exclusive, reason for this freedom is protection of the press's ability to serve as a check on centers of political and economic power, a function served by the press's need to formulate judgments free from coercion or inducement, and by the freedom to disseminate broadly information upon which the governed can act.[50]

The Court's prior taxation decisions have largely related to purposeful censorship. This was the basis for the Court's earlier decision in *Grosjean v. American Press Co.*;[51] a facially benign statute arose in a context that made impossible any other conclusion but that the political system was attempting to exact specific retribution for prior editorial judgments and to influence specific editorial judgments in the future. The Court's unequivocal distinction of the *Grosjean* case in the *Minneapolis Star* opinion[52] suggests, on the one hand, that censorship was not at issue in Minnesota but, on the other hand, that its absence did not avoid all constitutional concerns arising from statutes that formally single out the press. Instead, the Court's concern with forms of the political process and with editorial freedom in the absence of specific proof of legislative purpose or effect suggests that the remaining concerns relate to the *general* relationship of the press to the political system. This is a concern that lies at the heart of the knowledge tax problem.

Editorial freedom of the press connotes a degree of disengagement from the concrete political process; it requires the government's relationship with the press to be at arm's length — to be neutral, as I have previously suggested.[53] The Court's reason for making constitutionally suspect any formal singling out of the press was to protect the political neutrality of the press as an institution committed to the process of reasoned and open inquiry, and which serves also as a check on the political process.[54] The Constitution, of course, does not require or permit the government to require that the press be politically detached, neutral, or agnostic, but it does prevent the government from undermining the press's capacity to assume that posture by forcing it unnecessarily to engage actively in the political process in order to protect its own self-interest or by making it susceptible, even tacitly, to the preferences of the political system.[55] Such submission to the partisan political will was, of course and not coincidentally, the very object of the taxes that were exacted on the press in seventeenth-century England.

Neutrality and Editorial Freedom

The role of the press under the First Amendment is safeguarded by editorial freedom. Editorial freedom connotes both freedom in choice of material and freedom in the opportunity to publish. As historical experience in

England and America confirms,[56] a newspaper which must be actively engaged in the political process in its own self-interest is less likely freely to exercise editorial judgment if specific economic and political interest are constantly at stake, and if it must devote part of its energies to the political process in specific and personal terms.[57] Under such circumstances the political process may, itself, become part of the calculus of editorial judgment.[58] Direct political self-interest is likely to color the judgment of what is important as *news*, and to undermine the press's commitment to open and reasoned inquiry.

The concept of safeguarding the press's neutrality or agnosticism as a means of assuring editorial independence is of recent vintage in the jurisprudence of freedom of the press.[59] Its origins are far from recent, however, in other settings. Academic freedom is predicated on the same idea — independence of thought and inquiry is a necessary instrument for the advancement of knowledge.[60] As a corollary to academic freedom, tenure is the means employed to disengage the scholar from concerns of the moment, whether political, ideological, or economic, in order to permit honest intellectual thought. Equal protection doctrine, in its imposition of heavy scrutiny on racial classifications, for example, is predicated largely on a companion idea that requiring of *all persons* that which might otherwise be visited only upon a discrete few imposes a powerful practical constraint on the ability of the political process invidiously to discriminate.[61] With greater generality of legislative application comes a greater measure of certainty that political isolation of those with certain beliefs or racial characteristics will not occur, and a corresponding measure of confidence that the political process has been disengaged from consideration of belief or race.[62] In the case of the press, this result removes the press's compulsion to be a participant in rather than an observer of the political process.

Perhaps the closest analogy in constitutional doctrine is found in the religion guarantees, and particularly in the Establishment Clause. In general, the religion guarantees assure freedom of religious thought as well as its organized practice by presumptively foreclosing government actions which advance or burden religion or single out any particular religious sect for conferral of a benefit or imposition of a burden.[63] A corollary principle of nonentanglement is designed to assure the independence of religious institutions from indirect influence resulting from specific, direct, and self-interested engagement in the political process.[64]

Like the singling out rule of the *Minneapolis Star* case, the nonentanglement rule is a necessary corollary to prohibition of direct or overt government regulation of religious institutions. For the press as for religious institutions, fostering a degree of disengagement from the political process safeguards against the more subtle and less concrete, but no less systematic and real, consequences that would follow from an interrelationship requiring dependence rather than independence, and partisanship rather than agnosticism.[65]

But singling out in the tax setting can take many forms, and the Court's concern seemed centered on only one — the imposition of a tax unique in nature, or distinct in *form* from that applied to other taxpayers. Singling out, for example, can also occur by exemption or by the imposition of different rates of taxation within a generally applicable tax, and this singling out would seem to require, as well, partisan engagement by the press. This leaves us with the question: How do we justify a special rule of nondiscrimination when the tax differs in *form* rather than in rate?

The difference between different rates and different *forms* of tax, it appears, lies in the majoritarian process. The imposition of a different rate within a generally applied tax requires that the differential treatment be explicit. It is more likely, as a consequence, to have been a product of open political judgment, with less advantaged interests able to express their view and, perhaps more importantly, with the press able to measure clearly its position against the objective benchmark of rates applied to others. Moreover, assuming that differential rates, and especially specific exemptions from tax, are *not* presumptively invalid — a view that the historical experience overwhelmingly supports — drawing distinctions among rates of tax in the open environment of a single tax scheme may well lead to more thorough and candid consideration of the relevant public policies, including the benign if not desirable ones of *encouraging* the broad availability of current information or assisting the presentation of diverse views through conscious use of differential rates.

Singling out the press through a unique *form* of exaction, in contrast, takes place in isolation. The unique form need not be, and often will not be, part of the general political compromise reflected in the context of a broadly applicable tax. The distinct form of tax, therefore, need be neither open nor explicit, and the political check provided by direct comparison of one taxpayer's situation with another is, as the *Minneapolis Star* case illustrated, undermined. Differential forms of tax, therefore, subject the press to the political system in different and concrete continuing terms and require active involvement or entanglement in that system. The press cannot rely on the open majoritarian process to protect its interests, or at least to make explicit the policies pursued on its behalf or against it. A rule that defers less to the majoritarian legislative process, like the rule of *Minneapolis Star*, is therefore warranted when differences of *form* are involved.

Whether or not one agrees with the Court's distinction based on the *form* of a tax rather than its rate, the animating principle seems plain: the press should be enabled, to the extent practically consistent with its general amenability to taxation, to maintain a posture of neutrality or agnosticism in the protection of its noneditorial interests in the partisan political process. To draw from the late Professor Bickel's observations in decrying the politicization of academic institutions:

> An institution politically involved . . . could hardly avoid committing its largely human resources to that end; it would try to induce and finally to compel its members to devote themselves to the attainment of the end to which the institution is committed. That is the death not merely of diversity and exchange of ideas, but of free inquiry altogether. . . . Loss of intellectual quality, and ultimately of content, would follow.[66]

As the Supreme Court saw it, intuitively to be sure, the Minnesota paper and ink tax, both in its form as a hybrid use tax rather than a sales tax, and to a lesser degree through the use tax credit imbedded in that different form of tax, compelled the direct engagement of the affected newspapers in the political arena to protect their economic self-interest. The Court indicated, though with less elaboration than might have been desired, that this occurred largely *because* the form of the tax was different than that applied to other, similarly situated taxpayers, even though its purpose was benign and its effect probably beneficial.

The State's justifications for the different form of tax were, accordingly, constitutionally irrelevant. They were not improper; indeed, they were perfectly logical. But they were irrelevant, for the pertinent constitutional question was not whether reasons existed for departing from a consistent form of tax. Rather, the constitutional question was whether, apart from permissible policy reasons, the form employed *had* to be different. If a different form was not necessary, its use would present the risk, if not the likelihood, that the affected papers would be isolated in the political system, that their position would not be open, but hidden, and as a consequence that the press would have to direct their energies to their political self-interest. They could not seek shelter against political choices in the broader majoritarian process — the broader constituency of taxpayers whose interests would equally be affected were they subject to the same form of tax.

"That is the death not merely of diversity and exchange of ideas, but of free inquiry altogether."[67]

CONCLUSIONS AND IMPLICATIONS

The general principle underlying the *Minneapolis Star & Tribune* decision is one of political agnosticism or neutrality, not nondiscrimination, as such. More specifically, freedom of the press requires that in its actions affecting the press the government act in a way that protects an arm's-length, or disengaged, relationship with the press in order to safeguard the exercise of editorial judgment free of direct influence by the political process. This general principle can, in turn, be broken down into three rules, or propositions, based on the specific facts of the *Minneapolis Star* case.

First, by using a distinct *method* or *form* for taxation of the press, government symbolizes the press's concrete and unique stake in the outcome of the political process. This may cause the press to consider its political interests as part of its calculus of editorial judgment. This concern would account for the Court's distrust of different *forms*, as opposed to different levels, of taxation, and would likewise justify an equal concern with differentially lower as well as higher taxes on the press.

Second, a differential tax on the press, although broadly applied to all elements of the press, may at some level pose a risk of financial dependence of the press on government, just as the English taxes imposed on the press in the eighteenth century were often calculated to ensure obedience of the press through subsidy, special privileges, and bribes.[68] A rule that forecloses higher levels of taxation on the press than on other like-situated taxpayers would largely avoid this danger.

Third, a tax imposed only on some elements of the press may, by analogy to the concept of government neutrality toward religion, represent a form of endorsement, even though it is not so intended, thereby imposing "coercive pressure upon [particular elements of the press] . . . to conform to the prevailing official approved" mode of operation.[69] This third form of differential taxation would appear to have particular relevance to the challenged use tax exemption, as its effect may have been reasonably perceived as endorsing or encouraging those smaller papers that were exempted.

It is on this third and final point, however, that further reflection in light of historical evidence is needed. While a presumption (though not a conclusive one) against the imposition of a unique form of exaction on the press alone, and a presumption against a differentially higher rate of taxation of the press, may find support in the historical experience, as either would raise concerns about broad accessibility to diverse information, a presumption against differential rates of exaction *within or among* the press finds considerably less support in historical experience and does not, as a generally applied rule, necessarily serve accessibility and diversity interests. It seems likely, for example, that a statute that is benign in purpose and that provides a reduced burden of exaction for small, new, or alternative publications, or even for the principal media through which current information is obtained by the populace, would serve the interests in accessibility and diversity rather than disserve them.[70]

We should be careful, in other words, not to erect an indiscriminate presumption against all differential exactions for fear that legitimate ones might be foreclosed. But we should also understand that avoiding that result will require — at least in the absence of differential *forms* of taxation — that our analysis embrace issues of effect more thoroughly than the Supreme Court has so far been willing to do.

By now I have attributed much to the Minnesota tax case that is not evident on the face of the opinion — perhaps too much. But the rule established by the Court, combined with the history and reasoning the Court chose to disclose, seems to lead inexorably to the general view I have outlined. Were the case dealing only with purposeful discrimination, or were it more limited in the species of discrimination condemned, I would be less confident that any general view of freedom of the press underlay the opinion. The breadth of the prohibition on singling out, however, combined with the unimportance of purpose and the focus on the form rather than the purpose or effect of legislation, suggests that the principle at work in the decision transcends the particular circumstances of the case and transcends as well the equally important but much more limited concerns about purposeful censorship. And in important respects the principle transcends history, as well.

If anything, my view about the general relationship between the singling out rule and freedom of the press is confirmed by an examination of the rule's specific operation, for the opinion makes constitutionally suspect the singling out of the press as a whole, or of any part of the press, and it equally condemns singling out for conferral of a benefit as well as imposition of a burden. A rule that transcends these differences is difficult to explain except by reference to a concern with *form* rather than substance or rate of taxation. Such a concern, moreover, seems best explained by an interest in the press's general relationship to the political system — a relationship in which disengagement or agnosticism protects and fosters the independence of free editorial judgment and serves the interests of broad availability of information from diverse, privately controlled quarters that the historic struggle against knowledge taxes reflected. It is perhaps not coincidental that a relationship of political detachment is an important part — but a part only — of the historic struggle for press freedom.

That relationship was further probed, and with mixed results, in the two succeeding cases, to which we shall turn. The *Minneapolis Star* decision, open-textured as it was, represented an important beginning for the Court. But it was a beginning only, and much remained to be explored in the complex area of knowledge taxation under the First Amendment.

Knowledge Taxation Revisited in a Larger Framework: *Leathers v. Medlock*

The questions left open in the wake of the *Minneapolis Star* decision — questions about the meaning and scope of the decision, its application to different rates rather than different forms of taxation, and its application in settings beyond the news and print media — were addressed eight years later in *Leathers v. Medlock*.[71] In the intervening years between 1983 and 1991, the Court decided another tax case which was grounded on purposeful discrimination. The 1987 decision in *Arkansas Writers' Project, Inc., v. Ragland*[72] seemed at the time to be unremarkable in its outcome and its rationale. We shall have more to say about the *Ragland* decision later, for in hindsight it will prove to be highly instructive and anything but unremarkable. But in the interregnum between 1983 and 1991 it raised few eyebrows and appeared to fit easily into conventional First Amendment doctrine and the tidy, if analytically obscure, rules of *Minneapolis Star*.

Ironically the *Leathers* case, like *Ragland*, arose in Arkansas. It involved questions which seemed, to many, to have been resolved in *Minneapolis Star* — questions of differential taxation and singling out — although as we shall see these questions arose in the very different context of a single tax structure, rather than a unique *form* of tax imposed on knowledge. *Leathers* also involved the broader issue of taxation of different media of communication, which the Court in *Minneapolis Star* had touched on only lightly and in the expansiveness of dicta. Given the many types of differential tax challenged in *Leathers*, and the seemingly inflexible rules against discrimination that the Court had articulated eight years earlier in the *Minneapolis Star* case, it was no doubt of considerable surprise to many that the Court, in language as expansive as *Minneapolis Star*, sustained the Arkansas tax in the face of First Amendment challenge.

It was a changing Court in 1991 with, most notably, Justices Powell and Brennan retired, but the author of the *Leathers* decision, Justice O'Connor, had also authored the *Minneapolis Star* decision. Perhaps more importantly, it was a Court that may by then have better understood and foreseen the broad consequences of the rigid rules of *Minneapolis Star*. Unfortunately, it was not a Court that saw history more clearly. Discrimination remained the sole focus of the Court's analysis. The only difference was whether, as in *Minneapolis Star*, an improper purpose was presumed from the fact alone of discrimination, or whether, as in *Leathers*, specific proof of improper purpose must be shown as a necessary precondition to unconstitutionality. This was an important difference, to be sure, but in the broader setting of knowledge taxation, with its principal historical focus on access to broad and diverse information by the populace (a focus premised heavily on effect rather than purpose), it should hardly have been decisive.

The Arkansas Tax

Before turning to a comparison of the *Leathers* and *Minneapolis Star* cases, we should first turn to the precise tax that was challenged in *Leathers* and the specific issues that were presented. Interestingly, the *Leathers* case did not involve taxation of the "press" as such, at least not in its traditional form, nor did it principally involve the print medium. Perhaps most notably, *Leathers* did not involve different *forms* of tax imposed on expression. Instead, it involved taxation of cable television and concerned the constitutionality of specific exemptions, both within the cable medium (if we can so characterize it) and in contrast to the exemption of other, largely print, media.

Like most states, Arkansas imposed a sales tax, which it called a "gross receipts tax," on sales of tangible personal property and on some services. The state tax rate was four percent, to which a one percent county tax (on the same tax base) was added, and a one-half to one percent city tax was authorized, though not required.[73] All sales of newspapers were exempt from the tax, as were subscription sales of magazines.[74] Also untaxed, prior to 1987, were cable and broadcast television and radio, although their freedom from taxation was not by exemption but by virtue of the fact that their product was deemed not to be "tangible personal property."[75]

In 1987 the gross receipts tax was broadened to include receipts from sales of some, although not all, services. Among the services made subject to the gross receipts tax was cable television,[76] but receipt of cable service by scrambled satellite (through a dish on the viewer's property) was not included as a taxed service.[77] In 1988, after an Arkansas chancery court had invalidated the satellite exclusion—on the authority of *Minneapolis Star*—the exclusion was eliminated and all subscription-based or pay-per-view distribution of television and radio was made subject to the tax.[78] The earlier exclusion remained at issue in the Supreme Court, however, as a refund claim for previous years was still outstanding.

The questions presented for the Court's decision, therefore, were twofold:

1. The constitutionality of subjecting cable and satellite distribution of information to taxation, but exempting newspaper and subscription magazine sales from the tax.
2. The constitutionality of excluding satellite distribution of cable service from a tax imposed on all other forms of cable distribution.

The issues, in short, were the treatment of differential taxation among media (print versus cable) and differential taxation within a nonprint medium which is not exclusively or even primarily devoted to news.

The answers given by the Court were the same; both challenged tax provisions were upheld. According to the Court's opinion, differential taxation, as long as its proven purpose is not to censor ideas or viewpoints, is permissible; indeed, such differential taxation "does not implicate the First Amendment" at all.[79] And the differences between the Minnesota statute invalidated in *Minneapolis Star* and the Arkansas statute sustained in *Leathers*—intramedium versus intermedia discrimination, and discrimination among news media versus non-news media—appeared by the Court's opinion to be decisive, even if not wholly persuasive.

THE COURT'S RATIONALE

The Court began its analysis of the issues by distinguishing the *Minneapolis Star* and *Ragland* cases. With respect to *Minneapolis Star*, the Court, speaking through the author of that opinion, Justice O'Connor, stated that the Minnesota tax had "singled out the press . . . a single constituency . . . for special treatment."[80] By this simple statement, the Court effectively recast *Minneapolis Star* as a decision focused on the press, not on expression generally, and one whose rationale rested on the press's role in the political system[81] rather than on the more general issue of taxation of knowledge.

This recasting of *Minneapolis Star* was accomplished by the Court with barely a blush, notwithstanding the Court's broad-ranging and numerous references in the *Minneapolis Star* opinion to the general knowledge tax question and to the seemingly identical discrimination between large and small publishers within the same medium;[82] indeed, notwithstanding, as well, the Court's own failure to supply a definition of "press" that excluded cable television and radio.

On the issue of discrimination among taxpayers within a medium, the Court explained that the Minnesota tax — through its use tax credit — had targeted a "small group of newspapers,"[83] a group so narrowly defined that the tax "resemble[d] a penalty"[84] rather than an "attempt to favor struggling smaller enterprises."[85] The apparently similar discrimination among cable services, upheld in *Leathers*, was thus distinguished. But there is a certain inconsistency between this explanation of *Minneapolis Star*, in which purpose was effectively treated as nondecisive because it was presumed to be improper from the fact of discrimination alone without any specific proof (or even a suggestion to that effect by the Court[86]), and the remainder of the *Leathers* decision, in which it was held that constitutional infirmity was dependent on *proof* of illicit purpose. The Minnesota exemption for small papers would seem easily to pass muster under the *Leathers* decision, for by the Court's own admission nothing existed in the Minnesota statute to negate a benign purpose of easing the burden on small and diverse papers, much less to prove an illicit one.[87] If illicit purpose was the problem in *Minneapolis Star*, then surely we deserve a better and more complete explanation of its basis in the record, and a better explanation of why it shouldn't have equally been a problem in *Leathers*.

If the Court's effort to distinguish *Minneapolis Star* was creative, although not wholly persuasive, the Court's treatment of the *Ragland* decision was at least brief. *Ragland* was cursorily dismissed as fitting neatly with the reconfigured "narrow targeting" rationale of *Minneapolis Star*. The Arkansas provision challenged in *Ragland*, which exempted "religious, professional, trade and sports magazines,"[88] represented a "narrow targeting of individual members" of the press.[89] Because only a few Arkansas magazines paid the tax — and therefore, one must assume, illicit purpose can be presumed — the statute "suffered from the same type of discrimination identified in [*Minneapolis Star*]."[90] If the explanation sounds a bit lean, that's because it is. Surely something more than numerical disparity is required to satisfy the *Leathers* requirement that illicit purpose be proved, especially in view of the fact that under *Leathers* "proper" purpose is presumed, and the reason for the satellite cable exclusion challenged in *Leathers* seems much more evanescent than the reason for the Minnesota credit.

As if this were not quite enough, the Court added, almost as an afterthought, the observation that "the basis on which the tax [in *Ragland*] differentiated among magazines depended entirely on their content."[91] The difficulty with this explanation is that, later in the *Leathers* opinion, the Court made a point of emphasizing that suppression of viewpoint or particular ideas, not content, was the essence of a constitutional violation, and that illicit purpose directed at "particular ideas" must be proven, and proven by the challenger.[92] No showing of improper purpose, much less one based on viewpoint, was required (much less demonstrated) in *Ragland*, as the analytical framework applied in that case — presuming unconstitutionality from a distinction falling along content lines, though no illicit purpose was shown — placed the burden of proving purpose on the State, not, as in *Leathers*, on the person challenging the statute.

But in the end all of these careful and subtle, if not altogether successful, distinctions drawn by the Court between *Leathers*, on the one hand, and *Minneapolis Star* and *Ragland*, on the other, came to naught. And the deed was done by the Court's own pen, for the Court framed its conclusion in *Leathers* in terms that literally swept the former decisions aside. "[D]ifferential taxation of speakers, *even members of the press*," the Court said, "does not implicate the First Amendment unless the tax is directed at, or presents the danger of suppressing, particular ideas."[93] And the burden of proving that a tax is directed at particular ideas, or presents a danger of suppressing them, rests squarely on the shoulders of the person challenging the act.[94] Viewed fairly, such a showing under such a standard could not be made in *either* the *Minneapolis Star* or *Ragland* cases. So much, it seems, for the special rules applicable to the press. So much, as well, for the explanations and distinctions based on targeting and content. So much, finally, for distinctions based on differential taxation among, rather than within, particular media.

The explanation for the Court's quite remarkable conclusion in *Leathers v. Medlock*, as well as its implications, must be found, if at all, in the logic and reason of the opinion itself, to which we now turn. We turn to it briefly, however, for there is little developed reasoning to be found. There is simply a conclusion, stated as if self-evident and not requiring explication.

The first step taken by the Court in explaining its decision was to observe that the Arkansas tax was of general applicability. It applied, that is, to the full range of covered goods and services, including expression. The point is made briefly and almost as an introductory aside; little is made of it. But it is an important point, more important than the attention given it, and important for reasons not expressed by the Court but critical, as I shall explain, to the knowledge tax question. For it is in the generally applicable nature of the Arkansas tax that a distinction between it and the Minnesota use tax challenged in *Minneapolis Star* exists.

In *Minneapolis Star* the challenged tax was a unique use tax imposed in lieu of an otherwise generally applicable sales tax, and the challenged use tax was applicable only to newspapers. In *Minneapolis Star*, therefore, the Court was addressing the constitutionality of a tax the *form* of which, though not the impact of which, singled out the press. *Leathers*, in contrast, involved the constitutionality of an exemption scheme within a single, generally applicable tax.[95] The *form* of tax was the same; the rates were different (and lower). This distinction can—indeed I think it does, as I have already mentioned and as I shall explain more fully later[96]—supply an adequate explanation for the different analyses of the Minnesota and the Arkansas tax schemes. It cannot do so, however, without further development of the reason that the distinction should be decisive on the knowledge tax question. But the Court supplies none.[97] Indeed, it gives little, if any, weight to the distinction between differences in the *form* of a tax and in the rate of taxation.

Beyond this, and beyond the rather conclusory statements that the Arkansas tax challenged in *Leathers* is not purposefully discriminatory in a way that penalizes a few for their "particular ideas"[98] or that targets speakers based on the content of their speech,[99] the Court supplied no explanation for its decision, just a conclusion. Discrimination based on viewpoint or particular ideas, the Court said, was the danger and the sole source of First Amendment violation.[100] One searches in vain for an explanation of why viewpoint discrimination is improper in the tax setting, though in all fairness to the Court the reason may have been considered self-evident and well established in First Amendment doctrine. More importantly, there is no explanation why *no other* forms of discrimination are troublesome. It is as if the Court wrote the entire history of knowledge taxation out of the Constitution without so much as a word of explanation. It did so unadvisedly and, I suspect, unsuccessfully, for the issue will present itself again if the history of knowledge taxation is a guide.

While it is indisputable that knowledge taxes have been used as a mechanism for censorship—for keeping specific ideas from being published—it is equally clear that history has proved this method ineffective, indeed futile, from the beginning.[101] Taxation is simply too blunt-edged for this purpose. Censorship, therefore, is perhaps the least important part of the history of knowledge taxation. But differential taxes and differential burdens have, throughout history, caused the unequal distribution of knowledge, or choked its availability from some sources to some groups. This is not always the result, and the *Minneapolis Star* case erred, as I have stated previously, by appearing to condemn differential taxation too broadly. But a rule that differential taxation presents essentially *no* First Amendment problem absent proven censorship errs equally at the other extreme.

The important theme to be drawn from history is not one of censorship of particular ideas, but of limitation of access through differential exaction to some kinds of information by some kinds of people, or more generally one of denial of access to *all* knowledge by *all* people through the weight of economic exaction. Taxation can serve as a useful expedient to this end by increasing the price of knowledge[102] or distributing economic and competitive advantages.[103] The struggle against knowledge taxes was most importantly a struggle, not *against* specific censorship, but *for* access by the populace to diverse and useful information. Taxation is effective at limiting access and stifling diversity; it is less effective as a means of censorship. This is perhaps the most important insight yielded by history. It is the insight ignored by the Court in *Leathers v. Medlock*.

Knowledge Taxation and the Constitution: *Minneapolis Star*, *Ragland*, *Leathers*, and Beyond

If the Court's efforts to distinguish *Minneapolis Star* and *Ragland* in the *Leathers* case were somewhat disingenuous, they may nevertheless have led to a proper result; they may even have yielded an approach to the knowledge tax question that is truer to the historical experience. So the Court would claim—and, quite frankly, with some justification. To understand why this is so, we must examine the three cases in terms of the broader history of knowledge taxation. That examination leads to some interesting conclusions.

As I have previously indicated,[104] the *Minneapolis Star* decision, when viewed in light of the history of knowledge taxation, was probably correct in the final analysis, but for the wrong reasons. The most questionable aspect of the decision was the unconstitutionality of the small newspaper exemption—actually a tax credit within the use tax structure. For the Court, discrimination among papers was enough to justify invalidating the exemption, but we can question the conclusion that any discrimination existed at all. The tax applied to all papers; all papers got the benefit of the tax credit. The discrimination, if that be an apt term, was "in effect" alone; the bigger the paper's circulation, the greater the tax bill. The credit simply allowed some to escape any tax liability.

The more important point, however, is that even if we accept the Court's characterization of the tax credit as "discrimination," the historical experience suggests quite plainly that discrimination itself should not be enough; that discrimination was a feature of virtually all knowledge taxes, both the good and the bad; and that the better inquiry is whether the discrimination has the effect of limiting access to knowledge and restricting its diversity. On the latter question, the Minnesota exemption, standing alone, increased access and facilitated greater diversity. The Court's focus on discrimination as an evil in and of itself, and the Court's requirement that any discrimination be justified by compelling interests unrelated to revenue-based or administrative needs, had the effect of disguising the more important underlying questions of access and diversity.

But while the exemption issue in *Minneapolis Star*, when viewed in isolation, may have been incorrectly decided, the ultimate conclusion reached on the use tax (or at least the heightened scrutiny applied to it) may, from a historical perspective, have been warranted. This is not because of discrimination in the tax scheme, as such, nor because newspapers were subject to a tax, but rather because the tax to which papers were subject (and from which the small papers were "exempted") was unnecessarily different *in form* from the tax applicable to all other taxpayers. The tax in Minnesota was a unique use tax imposed as an alternative to a sales tax, and it was applicable in that form to a narrow category of publications. Because the form of the tax was different, there was less assurance that it would be imposed in a like fashion and like amount on newspapers as on other taxpayers.[105] It thus partook, in its character, of the English stamp and advertising taxes, though less so of the paper tax, which applied more broadly. It is interesting to note in this connection that the stamp and advertising taxes were the first of the English taxes to be repealed, and that the case against the more broadly applicable paper tax was the most difficult one to make on principle, according to Collet.[106]

As with the English taxes that bore down uniquely on publications and thereby isolated their situation from that applicable to other taxpayers, thus presenting a problem overcome only when the struggle against the knowledge taxes was joined with the Anti-Corn Law and Charter movements, so also the different structure or form of the Minnesota tax permitted the legislature to exact a higher tax on the papers while disguising that fact in a distinct form that made comparison difficult. This, in turn, had the effect of isolating the Minnesota papers politically, requiring them to devote attention to the political process in a special way. They could not seek comfort in the legislature's inability to exact a higher tax on them without that fact being obvious. Nor could the papers seek broader support in the political process, as Collet and his colleagues had done with the Charter Movement and later with the agitation against the bread, hop, window, and other taxes.[107]

It was therefore the different *form* of tax, and the political detachment available in a broader constituency that the papers would have to sacrifice in protecting their financial interests, that was troublesome, and ultimately unconstitutional, in the *Minneapolis Star* case. Discrimination in *form*, not in incidence or amount, rightly yielded the more exacting scrutiny applied by the Court. This, of course, reflects a relatively narrow reading of the *Minneapolis Star* decision, but it is one at which the Court in *Leathers* hinted, although tersely and less than explicitly, when it said: "[T]he general applicability of any burdensome tax law helps to ensure that it will be met with widespread opposition. When such a law applies only to a single constituency, however, it is insulated from this political constraint."[108]

This understanding of *Minneapolis Star* affords a distinction that explains more cogently than did the Court the reasons that the decision in *Leathers* was, as a general matter, correct. The *Leathers* case involved a single tax structure — indeed, a single and straightforward sales tax. The issues in the case involved the exemption of newspapers, subscription magazine sales, and satellite cable. The discrimination reflected in the exemptions was open and obvious; its impact could be measured against the rate applied to all nonexempt taxpayers, including media and nonmedia interests alike. Under such circumstances, discrimination itself is not determinative.

If discrimination should not be our principal guide — and it should not — the questions suggested by history are twofold. The first question is whether the discrimination was motivated by an aversion to particular ideas. Did it, in short, constitute an attempt at censorship? To this question the Court in *Leathers* supplied a perfectly appropriate answer. No evidence existed that the structure of the exemptions would induce self-censorship, nor did the structure imply the likelihood of censorial purpose. No direct evidence of illicit motive was offered. While the exemption for newspapers was, in a most general sense, content-based — predominantly news content versus entertainment content — neither did this content distinction suggest any likely illicit purpose. Indeed, from a historical perspective it implied precisely the opposite, as it was in the interests of dissemination of current information — news — more than any other that the English struggle was fought.

The second question that bears on history involves the effect of the Arkansas tax, and specifically its consequences for access and diversity. We can couch this issue in terms of discrimination among taxpayers, although we need not do so. On this issue the important fact is that the discrimination in *Leathers* did not involve the *form of tax*, but rather the rate within a single tax. Those who were exempted, and those not exempted, were not therefore subject to the political system in isolation from other taxpayers. With respect to the specific exemptions for newspapers, subscription magazines, and satellite cable, the Court quite rightly concluded that these "discriminations" were benign. Indeed, if the exemptions had any systematic consequences they served to increase access by the populace to the most important general information (newspapers) and made available to rural viewers a service (cable) available to urban ones, but without tax. Access was not limited, and diversity was not narrowed; if anything, both were encouraged by the structure of the exemptions.

The important point about the *Leathers* case, however, lies in the distinction it draws in terms of principle and constitutional standard. Because *Leathers* involved only an exemption, not a differential *form* of tax, the Court could justifiably be less concerned about improper motive and about subjecting knowledge to penalizing tax burdens. The rate applied to all taxpayers was effectively the ceiling; the issue was exemptions from that rate. The danger of higher taxation inherent in an exemption was limited because the rate structure, itself, would provide protection from singling out knowledge for a special burden — something not present when the *form* of tax is different. And the danger of favoritism was limited because the exemptions were open and explicit; not, as in Minnesota, disguised in a separate form of tax. The press, therefore, was not isolated and would not have to devote its energies as concretely to the political system in order to protect its interests.

It is for this reason that the Court was correct in distinguishing *Minneapolis Star*, and was equally correct in not exacting the same high level of scrutiny in the *Leathers* case. One might have hoped, however, that the

Court would have gone beyond discussion of purpose and acknowledged that more than censorship is involved when knowledge is taxed. The impact of a tax on access to knowledge and on diversity — its effect — is also at stake when knowledge is subject to taxation.

Finally, we should turn our attention to the *Ragland* case, for while it was generally viewed as unremarkable at the time it was decided, it is actually the most instructive and problematic of the trilogy of cases decided by the Court. *Ragland*, like *Leathers*, involved a single sales tax — indeed, the same underlying tax structure involved in *Leathers*. The challenged exemption was for religious, sports, and other special interest magazines. The exemption did, to be sure, constitute discrimination, and discrimination based on content. Indeed, the content-based distinction between general interest magazines and those directed to special interests, such as sports or religion, was perhaps sufficiently specific to warrant a certain amount of scrutiny. It was clearly more content-oriented than the generic distinction between cable television and newspapers in *Leathers*.

But the distinction did not warrant the disabling scrutiny applied by the Court. The discrimination was not based on viewpoint. It was manifested as an exemption from a single form of tax and thus open and undisguised. In view of these facts, the focus should not have been restricted to purpose but should have concerned effect. The issue, in other words, should have been whether the facilitation of religious, professional, trade, and sports magazines had the effect of encouraging or suppressing access to knowledge, and whether the exemption facilitated or penalized greater diversity in the marketplace of knowledge.

On this point the conclusion is surely debatable. One could question, with the support of empirical fact, whether increased diversity would result from the exemption, for example, of professional, trade and sports magazines. If demand for such publications is (as I suspect) relatively inelastic, and if those types of periodicals would exist without the exemption, then the exemption would best be viewed, as the Court implied, as an emblem of government support — as a subsidy justified by agreement with or special support for the content or ideas, not one justified by need.

This inquiry, it should be noted, is based on effect, not purpose. And the "effect" case may not have been provable in *Ragland*. If not, the question becomes whether the underlying presumption should be against the exemptions or in their favor. The Court followed the former rule. History, I think, suggests the latter one. For my part I doubt that such narrowly framed exemptions within a generally applicable and nonoppressive tax have much, if any, negative impact on access to nonexempt publications, which in any event could still be subject to the tax in the absence of the exemptions.[109] I also doubt that such exemptions would affect the relative competitive position of traditional publications directed to general audiences. This is especially so when the nonexempt publications are the large and traditional ones, which have established market presence and financial strength. Indeed, exemptions of this kind directed to narrow or special interest publications will often serve to promote diversity.[110]

Let us assume, however, a slightly altered set of facts under which, *unlike* the Arkansas tax in *Ragland*, the exemption for specialized periodicals was *not* also accompanied by an exemption for newspapers. In such circumstances one might take a further step in view of history. The central knowledge tax question has always been access by the general populace to the basic daily information upon which actions could be taken and decisions, political and otherwise, could be made. In view of this overriding principle, exemption of religious magazines, for example, but *not* of newspapers — the principal means (with television) by which most people receive the news of the day — could be seen as distorting the priorities, and rewarding narrow rather than general information or sophisticated rather than general readership. While such an exemption scheme could not, in fairness, be viewed as limiting access and diversity, and it might often be promotive of the latter,[111] its exclusion of the most important medium of information, combined with the conferral of content-based exclusions not clearly restricted to fledgling, diverse, or minority publications, would justify placing a special burden of persuasion on the State, a burden that could be met only by proffering a reason specifically related to the nonexclusion of newspapers.[112]

This, in effect, is what the Court did in *Ragland*, and with historical warrant, but it did so by judging discrimination in the unrealistically narrow analytical confines of discrimination between religious or sports magazines on the one hand, and other nonexempt *magazines* on the other hand. And the Court enforced its presumption by imposing a standard of justification (strict scrutiny) that was unduly harsh and historically unwarranted. One wonders whether the result[113] would have been different were the standard of justification to have been more forgiving and, in addition, were the effect question to have been judged in the larger context of the exemption for newspapers that was also granted by the Arkansas statute. The distorting consequences of the Arkansas exemption for special interest magazines seem less evident when viewed from this more general perspective.

In any event, one might well reach the conclusion, based on the principal aims of the struggle against taxation of knowledge, that had the Arkansas tax *not* exempted newspapers, the reasoning in *Ragland* and the result in *Leathers* might have been different. And perhaps they should have been, for the history of taxation of knowledge is the history of people's struggle for access to the general and daily information necessary for existence in a free and organized society. As the People's Charter Union put it, "if we are asked why we cannot be satisfied with the elegant and polite literature which may be had cheaply, we reply that we can no longer exist upon the earth without information on the subjects of politics and political economy."[114] We might only wish that, in approaching the knowledge tax issue in *Minneapolis Star*, *Ragland*, and *Leathers*, the Court had been more attentive to that history and the animating purposes it implies.

Notes

1. Leathers v. Medlock, 111 S. Ct. 1438 (1991); Arkansas Writers' Project, Inc. v. Ragland, 481 U.S. 221 (1987); Minneapolis Star & Tribune Co. v. Minnesota Comm'r of Revenue, 460 U.S. 575 (1983).

2. 460 U.S. 575 (1983).

3. 111 S. Ct. 1438 (1991).

4. 481 U.S. 221 (1987).

5. 460 U.S. 575 (1983). Much of the following discussion is drawn from Randall P. Bezanson, "Political Agnosticism, Editorial Freedom, and Government Neutrality Toward the Press," 72 *Iowa L. Rev.* 1359 (1987).

6. 460 U.S. at 577; Minn. Stat. §§ 297A.14, 297A.25(1)(i) (1982) (amended). Between 1967, when the use tax was originally enacted as a companion to the Minnesota sales tax (Minn. Stat. § 297A.14 [1982] [use tax], Minn. Stat. § 297A.02 [1982] [sales tax]), and 1971, periodical publications were exempted from sales and use taxes. Minn. Stat. § 297A.25(l)(i) (1982).

7. See Minn. Code of Agency Rules, Tax S. & U. 300 (1979).

8. See Minn. Stat. Ann. § 297A.02 (West 1991) (providing current rate of six percent and citing prior changes in sales tax rate).

9. Minn. Stat. § 297A.25(l)(i) (1982).

10. Minn. Stat. §§ 297A.14, 297A.24 (1982). The use tax supported the sales tax by eliminating any tax incentive for Minnesota residents to acquire goods in other states in order to avoid the sales tax.

11. Minn. Stat. § 297A.25(1)(i) (1982).

12. 1971 Minn. Laws 2561, 2565; Minn. Stat. §§ 297A.14, 297A.25(l)(i) (1982).

13. There is considerable — and interesting — interchange between the majority and Justice Rehnquist, in dissent, on the burden of the use tax as contrasted with

a sales tax at the same rate. Compare 460 U.S. at 591 n.14 with 460 U.S. at 597–98 (Rehnquist, J., dissenting). The interchange concerns the relationship between paper and ink costs subject to the use tax and the retail price charged for a paper (exclusive, that is, of advertising revenue, for example). The debate illustrates that calculation of the relative tax burdens of sales and use taxes is a bit more complicated than might at first appear, but it establishes little else. The majority does not really dispute Justice Rehnquist's analysis as applied to the *Star & Tribune*, nor does the majority claim that the actual burden is incapable of fairly straightforward calculation in each case. Indeed, the majority's principal point is that the calculation is essentially irrelevant, for the Court states that the tax would be equally unconstitutional whether the burden is greater or lesser. 460 U.S. at 588, 590 n.13.

14. 460 U.S. at 586–87. It is noteworthy that the 1971 amendment applied the use tax to all paper and ink products used in producing a publication, not just to those purchased in another state. The statute, therefore, was a hybrid combining, in effect, a substitute sales tax and a complementary use tax for products purchased out of state.

15. *Id.*; Minneapolis Star & Tribune Co. v. Commissioner of Revenue, 314 N.W.2d 201, 207 (Minn. 1981).

16. The Court ultimately concluded that the Minnesota Legislature's motives were not improper, and suitable public purposes may have been served by application of a use tax, but that motive and purpose were not decisive — or even relevant — if the State could not demonstrate the impossibility of applying a nondifferential *form* of tax. See 460 U.S. at 590 n.13, 592–93.

17. 460 U.S. at 587–88.

18. 460 U.S. at 592–93.

19. 460 U.S. at 589.

20. See 460 U.S. at 594–96 (White, J., concurring in part and dissenting in part); 460 U.S. at 600–601 (Rehnquist, J., dissenting).

21. 460 U.S. at 588.

22. Act of May 24, 1973, ch. 650, art. XIII, § 1, 1973 Minn. Laws 1606, 1637; Minn. Stat. § 297A.14 (1982).

23. 460 U.S. at 591.

24. 460 U.S. at 592.

25. *Id.*

26. See Chapters 1, 4, 5.

27. 460 U.S. at 597–98, 601–3 (Rehnquist, J., dissenting). Justice White concurred in the majority's invalidation of the use tax exemption, dissenting only to the invalidation of the underlying use tax. 460 U.S. at 593.

28. 460 U.S. at 593–94.

29. The use tax exemption did not, in reality, "fall unevenly" since all publishers got the advantage of a $4,000 credit, but it yielded, in effect, or perhaps more accurately in appearance, a large population of publishers that owed no net tax after the credit, and a small population of larger publishers who owed tax. Whether the disparity between one publisher that owes no tax because of the exemption and another that owes $100,000 is significantly different, and constitutionally worse, than between a publisher that owes $4,000 and another that owes $104,000, in the

absence of an exemption, is unclear from the Court's opinion—perhaps because it is, in fact, unclear.

30. 460 U.S. at 586.

31. 460 U.S. at 583–84.

32. 460 U.S. at 585.

33. 460 U.S. at 592.

34. 460 U.S. at 588.

35. It should be noted that a number of issues lie beneath the surface of the Court's formulation, although they will not be addressed here. For example, the Minnesota tax case involved the singling out of newspapers and periodical publications—a term itself subject to varied definitions—for treatment distinct from other forms of print communication such as books, as well as other forms of nonprint communication such as broadcasting, cable transmission, telephone communication, and the like. Moreover, the Court seems to have been referring in its singling out concept to regulations with differential impact on various components of the print medium—newspapers as opposed to magazines, books, and the like—within a given market. The Court did not seem concerned about differential imposition of a tax on weekly newspapers on the one hand, and weekly collections of essays or research papers on scientific research on the other hand. The potential relevance of these and other forms of singling out is left unaddressed in the opinion. Rather, the Court restricted its discussion to differential burdens or benefits visited upon the print news media which are not applicable to all other businesses subject to the tax, including nonprint news enterprises.

36. 460 U.S. at 583.

37. Likewise, in most tax and regulatory environments, forms of regulation will have to be different in order that they be nondifferential. For instance, would a five percent sales tax on the "sales" of a broadcaster—advertising—be the same as a similar tax on the retail price of a newspaper? Would it make a difference if the newspaper had no advertising and instead—much like the *Progressive*—relied heavily on contributions? How is one to compare a three percent gross subscription tax on a cable operator with a five percent sales tax on a newspaper? These and other problems will not disappear merely by ignoring them, but if one attaches *constitutional* importance to the Court's refusal to address them, the manner in which they will and inevitably must be addressed in the future is placed in a new light.

38. Indeed, the historical record related directly to the First Amendment and its free press guarantee is, on the question of taxation of the press, slim. See Chapter 2. The Court cites only a few statements contemporaneous with the Bill of Rights (see 460 U.S. at 583–85), the principal one made by Richard Henry Lee, which is ambiguous, at best, on the types of taxes that might be prohibited by press freedom, and the reasons for such prohibition. Richard Henry Lee, "Observations Leading to a Fair Examination of the System of Government," Letter 4, reprinted in 1 Bernard Schwartz, *The Bill of Rights: A Documentary History* 474 (1971).

39. Given the paucity of material bearing directly on the purposes of the Free Press Clause with respect to taxation (as distinguished from licensing) and the open-textured words in the text, the principal sources of historical material from which generally perceived concerns and cultural traditions can be ascertained are the

English and Colonial experiences. Here there is a large amount of material rich with implications that three of the principal problems posed by taxes on the press were purposeful censorship (which did not work effectively), making the press politically and financially dependent on the government and therefore susceptible to influence, subsidy, and bribes, and the constriction through economic burden of the broad availability of diverse information on current events to the public. See Chapters 1–4; Frederick S. Siebert, *Freedom of the Press in England, 1476–1776*, at 305–55 (1952); Clyde A. Duniway, *The Development of Freedom of the Press in Massachusetts* (Franklin ed. 1969)(1906); Collet Dobson Collet, *History of the Taxes on Knowledge: Their Origin and Repeal* (facsimile reprint 1971)(1933); 2 T. May, *The Constitutional History of England, 1760–1860*, at 102–245 (1880); William Wickwar, *The Struggle for the Freedom of the Press, 1819–1832*, at 28–32, 49–82 (Johnson reprint 1972)(1928). The major historical works on the meaning of the First Amendment hardly touch on the taxation issue, focusing instead on the principal point of discussion and controversy at the time of the Constitution and ratification of the Bill of Rights — seditious libel. See, e.g., Leonard W. Levy, *Emergence of a Free Press* (1985); David A. Anderson, "The Origins of the Press Clause," 30 *UCLA L. Rev.* 455 (1983).

40. Indeed, the Court itself acknowledged that at least one form of differential tax — a lower rate for the press — might not be constitutionally suspect. 460 U.S. at 590 n.13. On this issue, Justice Blackmun refused to concur. 460 U.S. at 577.

41. See Chapters 1–4; Siebert; Duniway; Collet; *Pennsylvania and the Federal Constitution* 181 (Historical Society of Pa. 1888).

42. 460 U.S. at 580, 588–91, nn.12, 14; 460 U.S. at 596 (White, J., concurring in part and dissenting in part).

43. 460 U.S. at 588, 592.

44. 460 U.S. at 585.

45. See *infra* notes 49–53 and accompanying text.

46. 460 U.S. 587–90.

47. The Court stated: "We would be hesitant to fashion a rule that automatically allowed the state to single out the press for a different *method* of taxation as long as the effective burden was no different than or the burden on the press was lighter than that on other businesses." 460 U.S. at 588 (emphasis supplied). The Court's emphasis on *method* or *form* of tax is also clear from its statement that a tax lighter in burden but nondifferential in form would not be constitutionally suspect. 460 U.S. 590 n.13.

48. This is a subject taken up in the discussion of the *Leathers* case, which follows.

49. See Nebraska Press Ass'n v. Stuart, 427 U.S. 539 (1976); New York Times Co. v. United States, 403 U.S. 713 (1971); Near v. Minnesota, 283 U.S. 697 (1931).

50. See cases cited in note 49, *supra*; Vincent Blasi, "The Checking Value in First Amendment Theory," 1977 *Am. B. Found. Res. J.* 521; Potter S. Stewart, "'Or of the Press,'" 26 *Hastings L.J.* 631 (1975).

51. Grosjean v. American Press Co., 297 U.S. 233 (1936).

52. 460 U.S. 579–80.

53. Randall P. Bezanson, "The New Free Press Guarantee," 63 *Va. L. Rev.* 731,

751–65 (1977); Randall P. Bezanson, *"Herbert v. Lando*, Editorial Judgment, and Freedom of the Press: An Essay," 1978 *U. Ill. L.F.* 619–23.

54. See authorities cited note 53 *supra*.

55. See Siebert at 322, 335–36; May at 213–15; Chapters 1–4.

56. See Chapter 8 concerning experience with postal prerogatives, bribes, subsidies, and purposeful exemptions.

57. *Id.*; see W. Van Alstyne, "The Hazards to the Press of Claiming a 'Preferred Position,'" 28 *Hastings L.J.* 761 (1977).

58. Siebert at 322, 335–36.

59. See *supra* notes 50, 53, 57.

60. See Sweezy v. New Hampshire, 354 U.S. 234, 261–63 (1957) (Frankfurter, J., concurring); "Developments in the Law — Academic Freedom," 81 *Harv. L. Rev.* 1045, 1048 (1968).

61. Palmore v. Sidoti, 80 L. Ed. 2d 421, 431–33 (1984); Hunter v. Erickson, 393 U.S. 385, 391–94 (1969); Loving v. Virginia, 388 U.S. 1, 10–11 (1967).

62. See Regents of the Univ. of California v. Bakke, 438 U.S. 265, 292–95 (1978); Hunter v. Erickson, 393 U.S. 385, 391–94 (1969); Loving v. Virginia, 388 U.S. 1, 10–11 (1967).

63. Larkin v. Grendel's Den, Inc., 103 S. Ct. 505 (1982); Walz v. Tax Comm'n, 397 U.S. 664 (1970); Everson v. Board of Educ., 330 U.S. 1 (1947).

64. Larkin v. Grendel's Den, Inc., 103 S. Ct. 505, 512 (1982); Lemon v. Kurtzman, 403 U.S. 602, 613–14 (1971).

65. See Walz v. Tax Comm'n, 397 U.S. 664 (1970); Board of Educ. v. Allen, 392 U.S. 236, 249 (1968) (Harlan, J., concurring); P. Kurland, *Religion and the Law* 112 (1962); J. Choper, "The Religion Clauses of the First Amendment: Reconciling the Conflict," 41 *U. Pitt. L. Rev.* 673 (1980).

66. A. Bickel, *The Morality of Consent* 130–31 (1975).

67. *Id.*

68. See Chapter 1.

69. Wallace v. Jaffree, 472 U.S. 38, 69–70 (1985) (O'Connor, J., concurring in the judgment) (quoting Lynch v. Donnelly, 415 U.S. 668, 688 [1984]).

70. See Chapter 6 for examples of differential levels of tax that served interests of broad dissemination of diverse information.

71. 111 S. Ct. 1438 (1991).

72. 481 U.S. 221 (1987).

73. Ark. Code Ann. §§ 26–52–301, 302 (1987 & Supp. 1989) (state); *Id.* §§ 26–74–307, 26–74–222 (county); Ark. Code Ann. § 26–75–307 (1987) (cities).

74. Ark. Code Ann. §§ 26–52–401(4), (14) (Supp. 1989); Revenue Policy Statement 1988–1 (March 10, 1988).

75. Ark. Code Ann. § 26–52–301 (1987).

76. Radio is also transmitted by cable and was a service included in the 1987 tax act. 1987 Ark. Acts, No. 769, § 1.

77. *Id.*

78. 1989 Ark. Acts, No. 769, § 1. Of course, over-the-air television and radio were not taxed, as people do not pay for them.

79. 111 S. Ct. at 1447.

80. 111 S. Ct. at 1443.

81. For a discussion of this view, see Bezanson, *supra* note 5.

82. 460 U.S. at 578–80; see also Bezanson, *supra* note 5.

83. 111 S. Ct. at 1443.

84. *Id.*

85. *Id.*, quoting *Minneapolis Star*, 460 U.S. at 592.

86. The Court quite explicitly stated that it harbored no suspicions that the purpose was illicit. 460 U.S. at 592.

87. See *Minneapolis Star*, 460 U.S. at 592–93.

88. 111 S. Ct. at 1443.

89. *Id.*

90. *Id.*

91. *Id.*

92. *Id.* at 1447.

93. *Id.* (emphasis supplied).

94. *Id.* at 1446.

95. See Bezanson, *supra* note 5.

96. *Id.*

97. The Court did say in *Leathers*, though tersely and without elaboration, "that the general applicability of any burdensome tax law helps to assure that it will be met with widespread opposition. When such a law applies only to a single constituency, however, it is insulated from this political constraint." 111 S. Ct. at 1443.

98. *Id.* at 1445. The Court noted — indeed emphasized — that more than a few cable operators were subject to the tax, and the exempt group of satellite sellers was small in number and proportion. *Id.* at 1444.

99. The Court noted that material distributed by satellite (exempted) was essentially the same as that distributed by conventional cable, and therefore content was not involved. *Id.* But the Court was — quite understandably, it seems — silent on the newspaper exemption, for the same explanation would not work in that setting if content, as opposed to viewpoint, were the issue. It was not, of course. *Id.* at 1443–44.

100. *Id.* at 1443.

101. See Chapter 2 for a discussion of the experience in England with the use of taxation as a means of censorship.

102. See Chapter 2 for a discussion of the impact of taxes on the affordability of news to the general population — as well as the habit, developed in response, of "lending" or "renting" newspapers to escape the stamp.

103. Perhaps the best illustration of the impact of taxation on competition, and therefore on diversity, was the advantage given the London dailies over the rural papers with the elimination of the stamp, thus affording the London papers free postage in rural areas. What appeared to be a situation of nondiscrimination was, in reality, discriminatory in favor of the London papers, which required use of the mails to reach the rural areas, and against the rural papers, which did not require posting in their local areas. The lesson to be drawn from this illustration is that discrimination ought not to be a determinative test, even when it can be safely

judged, and that in any event a rule of nondiscrimination does not effectively safeguard the objective of equal treatment, much less the other interests involved in the taxation of knowledge.

104. See Bezanson, *supra* note 5.

105. The judgment of equal tax burden distributed among taxpayers could not be made simply by reference to the rate exacted in a single tax, but rather was disguised by the different structure of the use tax when compared to the sales tax.

106. Collet at 68–74, 132–33, 136, 150, 162–65, 179–89.

107. See Chapter 1.

108. 111 S. Ct. at 1443.

109. It should be noted, however, that while couched in terms of specialized audiences and interests, grounds for suspicion about its narrow impact and benign effect exist, as all but three—perhaps all but one—in-state magazines were exempted from tax under the challenged provision. 481 U.S. at 229 n.4.

110. This was true, for example, before repeal of the stamp in England, when the London newspapers were subject to postage in their distribution to rural areas, but the local papers, which did not require posting, were not, and therefore were able to thrive. See Chapter 2.

111. *Id.*

112. Such a justification could, of course, be promotion of diversity, as the State of Minnesota might more successfully have argued in *Minneapolis Star.*

113. The remedy required by the Supreme Court (subject to proceedings on remand) seems to have been to extend the exemption to all magazines, though it is not clear whether the Court meant this to include only magazines printed and published within the state and sold by subscription, and not out-of-state non-subscription sales, as well as sales of other "publications." See Arkansas Writers' Project, Inc. v. Ragland, 481 U.S. 221 (1987).

114. Collet at 42.

10. The Perspectives of History

In the *Minneapolis Star*, *Ragland*, and *Leathers* cases, the Supreme Court has begun what will surely be a continuing and evolving inquiry into the knowledge tax problem. At this early stage, the Court's opinions have focused on the complex relationship between taxation of knowledge and the problems of censorship and direct government influence on publication. Both problems are deeply rooted in historical experience. From the very beginning, taxation has been used as an instrument of government control of the press, both by direct censorship of publication and through creation of an environment of dependence on government caused by economic instability. Neither concern, however, reflects the full measure of historical experience with knowledge taxation, and in this respect the Court's approach remains incomplete. It does not reflect the remaining, and most basic, concern with broad availability of diverse information.

The principal rules of the *Minneapolis Star*, *Ragland*, and *Leathers* cases are that the evils of taxation of the press are censorship and direct government influence over publication, and that the remedy should take the doctrinal form of a rule against discrimination in the incidence or administration of taxes.[1] The difficulty with an approach based on these central premises is that logic informed by history defies the necessary relationship between taxation and censorship, or at least that the relationship defines the whole of the problem. While discrimination may be a problem associated with taxation of the press, it is not the main problem, and it is surely not an efficient and complete way to approach the larger issue of taxation. The history of taxation of knowledge is a long and rich one. It yields many conclusions. Those conclusions emerge from the history we have surveyed.

Taxation of knowledge found its genesis in ignorance and in the desire to perpetuate it. In the seventeenth century information was becoming a source of power: power to the Crown if information could be controlled; power to the populace if it could be obtained. Licensing was, at first, the chosen and effective means to perpetuate ignorance and control knowledge. But licensing and its associated instruments proved unworkable because they were cumbersome and, more importantly, too direct and effective, and therefore too obvious and ultimately politically untenable.

Thus with the demise of licensing and other direct means of censorship and control came taxation of knowledge as a conscious governmental policy toward the regulation of information. As an alternative to licensing, taxation proved expedient and even profitable. But its initial objective was censorship and specific control of published information, and this objective proved illusory. Taxation was inefficient as a means of censorship because it was blunt-edged. For censorship discrete and targeted means are needed, and taxation proved poorly adapted to that task. It was inexpedient because taxation was politically sensitive, both to its victims and, perhaps as importantly, to its friends, for the taxes usually fell equally on friend as well as foe. And the foes, with little to lose and their survival at stake, often proved more creative in escaping the tax by clever ploy or simply by disobedience.

But taxation as an instrument of government policy proved useful, though in ways other than censorship. It became an effective tool for protecting the established and loyal press — even the loyal, but safely conventional, opposition — and thus took its proud place in the armament of subsidy, bribery, and privilege used by the party in power to influence the press. This occurred frequently in England, but also in the United States, where in early times postal and other privileges were judiciously meted out, and in the Civil War, where a "price" in loyalty was exacted for the privilege of publishing free of confiscatory tax.

Taxation proved useful, as well, in generally dampening the spread of information through simple economic force. Particularly in England the availability of news to the common person was very dependent on price and affordability. Taxation proved an effective means of keeping the number of papers low, the circulation limited, and the price high; it thus served its objective of keeping much information from the hands of the masses. The competitive edge afforded by low rates of tax has also been consciously employed in America, again during the Civil War and also in the current century as new technologies of communication have arisen. Through taxation classes of publication — urban versus rural, daily versus periodical, news versus essay or political tract, cable versus broadcast, for example — were favored or disfavored, depending on the climate of the time. Thus the form of publication was influenced, not discretely and often not intentionally but nevertheless in important and lasting structural ways.

And taxation achieved another, although less obvious, purpose. It established a system of government presence in publication — an apparatus, for lack of a better word — through which *particularized* discretion could be employed, yet hidden. In other words, what taxation did not permit to be accomplished directly — specific censorship and control — was nevertheless facilitated by indirection. Even tax statutes (one might be inclined to say *particularly* tax statutes) confer discretion both explicitly and, more importantly, in the subtleties and ambiguities of imperfect language. Instances of the lenient or unforgiving hand of the tax commissioner abound in England as well, it seems, as in this country. In England favored papers were often relieved of burdensome taxes, while unfavored ones were not. This was also true — no doubt it remains so today — in America, where the imposition of tax depended on such terms as "resident," "information of general concern," "tangible personal property," or, in a more mundane but contemporary setting, on the aesthetic and safety considerations involved in licensing and taxing newspaper vending machines.

The impact of knowledge taxes was not always predictable, of course. Indeed, a strand that consistently runs throughout the history is that of unintended consequences. Sometimes, despite the clearest of purposes, the taxes hit hardest those intended to be helped. On other occasions the taxes forced unanticipated changes in publication or distribution which found the disfavored publishers suddenly prospering and competing effectively with established publishers.

Finally, knowledge taxes have proved most effective in influencing the *form* of publication. In England it was, at various times, the pamphlets, the cheap weeklies, or the rural papers that were discouraged through the stamp, the paper tax, and the advertising tax. This pattern was less evident in America, where the economics of publishing were much more advanced at the very beginning. Here it has been another pattern — that of new media of communication — that has prevailed. Taxes have been used in America — mostly in this century — to discourage or encourage new media. More frequently their use has been to discourage new media, either because they are new and therefore threaten the established order and entrenched interests, or because of the fear of the unknown coupled with government's predictable tendency to dampen change and establish regulatory footholds. And as in England, the established media are often active participants in such efforts. In this area taxation in America has blossomed beyond the narrow confines of publication itself, finding its way into the increasingly varied world of distribution of information — whether by news rack, telephone and telegraph, computer and satellite transmission, or cable and telephonic distribution. It is only logical that taxation should find its greatest power in the structural aspects of communication, for the instrument of taxation itself is well-adapted to categorical distinctions such as those between newspapers and magazines and books, print media and broadcasting, transmission by wire and transmission by satellite, and the like.

These, then, are some of the strands that are woven through the history of knowledge taxation. They suggest that censorship is not the principle burden of knowledge taxes; that unintended results are as important as intended ones; that structural impact is as significant as particularized impact; and, most importantly, that understanding and assessing a tax on knowledge is an enterprise that should be focused as much on effect as on purpose — indeed, even more on effect than on purpose. Purposes are rarely clear, and they are even more rarely, it seems, accomplished efficiently in the medium of taxation.

What, then, are the conclusions to be drawn from the history of taxation of knowledge? At the risk of oversimplification, I would suggest that they fall into two general areas. The first and most fundamental conclusion involves the underlying values from which the aversion and resistance to knowledge taxes emerged. The second and less fundamental but more instrumental conclusion concerns the particular ways in which these values were offended by government through taxation, and the resulting specific safeguards that ought to surround any legal rules whose principal objective is protection of the basic values. The second conclusion, while important, is secondary, and lacks meaning — just as the rules it generates would lack purpose — without the framework of the first. The Supreme Court's error, in my judgment, is of this sort. The rules created by the Court may not, in the end, be wrong, but they are incomplete and for that reason escape criticism, for they are only rules and lack the context or definition of basic purpose.

We will turn, then, first to the subject of basic value. The broad landscape of our experience with taxation of knowledge, both in Great Britain and in America, is marred throughout with examples of corruption, abuse, and a wide variety of forms of taxation.[2] Curiously, throughout this varied experience the term "knowledge tax" has persisted, notwithstanding the significant differences between the Stamp Act of 1712, the colonial tax, and the more recent sales taxes, and despite the greatly differing surrounding circumstances, such as confiscatory levels of tax, maladministered taxes, the use of taxation to protect entrenched interests or to buy control through bribery or patronage, or the outright and explicitly purposeful imposition of a tax directed at a specific newspaper. It is as if the term "knowledge tax" is more than just a handy reference, but is instead a manifestation of a broader concept whose scope comprehends all these varied forms and settings. And so, it appears, it is.

What is the meaning of the concept of "knowledge tax," and what values or purposes does it reflect? The answer, manifested not only in what was said from time to time, but more importantly in what was implicit in the continued struggle against taxation despite changes in climate, is that the concept of "knowledge tax" reflects two interrelated and underlying values: the value of broad diffusion of knowledge, irrespective of the purpose behind any impediment to it; and the value of preserving individual choice across the spectrum of possible interests or points of view. Put differently, the values that animated the struggle against taxation of the press were universal education and pluralism. On reflection, these basic values should not be surprising, as they are central social values in both Great Britain and, even more so, in America.

These values were perhaps never better nor more effectively expressed than in an appeal written by the People's Charter Union in January 1849, concerning repeal of the English newspaper stamp. The episode is fully recorded by Collet,[3] who reports the letter as follows:

> We are told that Englishmen are too ignorant to be entrusted with that franchise which is now nearly universal in Western Europe; we demand, then, that ignorance should no longer be compulsory. It is not always easy to know who are our real friends; but we think we are safe in denouncing as our enemies all those who desire to perpetuate our ignorance. By the penny stamp not only are we debarred from the expression of our thoughts and feelings, but it is made impossible for men of education or of capital to employ themselves in instructing us, as the price of their publication would be enhanced by the stamp to an amount which we cannot pay. A cheap *stamped* newspaper cannot be a good one. And if we are asked why we cannot be satisfied with the elegant and polite literature which may be had cheaply, we reply that we can no longer exist upon the earth without information on the subjects of politics and political economy. . . . If compelled to leave the country of our birth [for jobs], we would fain know in what land our labor is in demand, and not, as too many have done, strew with our bones an inhospitable soil. . . . And we say to those who are within the pale of the Constitution, "if you cannot give us this knowledge, at least do not prevent us from seeking it ourselves; to tax the light of knowledge was ever a crime—see that you commit not the crime of perpetuating that tax." Those who should do so would brand themselves indelibly as the willful oppressors of the poor, and would be justly responsible for all the inevitable results of ignorance.

If such a part exists in England, we feel assured that you, sir [Mr. Cobden, author of a budget proposal to the exchequer on behalf of the Liverpool Financial Reform Association], would scorn to be their leader. Were you, as your enemies assert, a mere free trader, you could not for a moment support a tax which is a *differential duty* in favor of the rich against the poor.

According to Collet, Mr. Cobden was not only impressed by the appeal, he was convinced, and thereafter took up the cause. Collet asserts that the "address and Mr. Cobden's reply were the basis of the whole of the subsequent agitation; leading to the repeal of the taxes on knowledge of England."[4]

If the core values underlying the concept of knowledge taxes are broad diffusion of knowledge and the preservation of individual choice, what impact do these values have on the rules or standards by which taxation of the press should be viewed? The first and most obvious impact is felt in relation to the concept of discrimination (or, in its recent formulation, singling out).[5] What limitations, if any, should apply to our assessment of a tax that discriminates against certain newspapers, for example, or treats certain types of publication differently from others? We might venture the following general conclusions, among others:

First, if a tax is imposed on a particular paper or group of papers and no others, if there are other papers that would be taxed were the tax to apply generally, *and* if the reason for taxing only the affected papers relates to editorial position or particular substantive content, the problem is not, truly, a knowledge tax problem. Instead, it is a problem of direct censorship under the guise of taxation, and it should be prohibited because it represents censorship, not because it represents taxation. This is the way the Supreme Court approached the *Grosjean* case, and it did so correctly, in my view.[6] It helps little to formulate such a problem as a knowledge tax question; indeed, such an approach may do more harm than good, as it may have done in the recent *Leathers* decision.[7] It may result in a doctrine that unduly restricts our approach to taxation itself by allowing concern with censorship to preempt a rightful concern with taxes that do not censor but which, for example, unnecessarily constrict broad diffusion of knowledge.

Second, a tax imposed on some, or most, papers, but not on all, or on some forms of publication, but not all, should not be presumptively forbidden by that fact alone. Discrimination in the imposition as well as the incidence of taxes has been a norm in the history of knowledge taxes. In some instances improper consequences have followed. In others, they have not. The fact of the matter, put simply, is that *non*discrimination in taxation can be as potentially harmful to the interests of diversity and broad access as is discrimination. And in any event nondiscrimination may be an illusory standard, because of the impossibility of its accomplishment in today's communication environment.

When faced with a discriminatory tax, the question should be, at least initially, whether the discrimination has the effect of reducing or encouraging the broad dissemination of knowledge and the availability of individual choice of diverse material. It is perfectly plausible—*and historically precedented*—that some papers, or some periodicals, should be encouraged through the assistance of lower taxation, or by exemption from taxation. It is possible, in other words, for a tax to be levied in permissible amount, along with other like transactions, and for some fledgling papers or periodicals to be subject to a lesser burden for the purpose of fostering the very diversity they bring, and in order not to foreclose people from receiving them because of price.

Third, broad dissemination of knowledge and diversity of material can, of course, be effectively inhibited by exactions that compromise the press's independence and, as both history and the *Minneapolis Star* case illustrate, discrimination can be an effective instrument in achieving this end. But not all forms of discrimination lead to this conclusion, and it can be achieved without discrimination, as well.

The necessary condition for press freedom is a degree of independence of the press from the partisan political process. Knowledge taxes that are imposed specially on the press (or part of it), or that are imposed in special and unique *form* on the press, are problematical precisely because they are unlikely to be based openly on broad and general concerns of government policy, but rather on concerns specifically related to the conduct of the press, and because taxes unique in *form* imposed upon the press do not reflect a political determination about their impact on a larger body politic, and thus can too easily be used to disguise improperly motivated (or simply arbitrary) differential exactions. In contrast, differential rates imposed within a general tax scheme cannot so easily be concealed and are therefore more likely to reflect open and explicit (and therefore examinable) policy choices concerning general public ends, including the desirability of encouraging the expression of diverse views or the need to safeguard the broad availability of important information.

The point is a subtle one, but it is particularly critical to an analysis of knowledge taxation in the more complex environment of pervasive government regulation and the developing technologies of communication. It is in these settings that the opportunities for taxation and regulation greatly expand as a result of rapid growth in communication, fragmentation of markets, diversity of content, and decentralization of control in the communication industry.

It is for this reason that the Court in the *Minneapolis Star* case focused on the unique *form* of a tax, rather than its discriminatory character alone, in establishing a presumption against constitutionality. The Court's rule — that a tax which is uniquely imposed, *in form*, on the press or some part of it, or a tax that is uniquely burdensome when compared to other taxes imposed on nonpublication activity, should for that reason be presumed unconstitutional, with the government bearing a heavy burden to overcome the presumption — is sound and consistent with historical experience. It should also be recognized, however, that such taxes are rare.

But it is important to note that a rule imposing special scrutiny on taxes that differ in *form* falls short of a broadly applicable presumption against any tax that falls differently on the press than on other objects, and this is especially so with a tax that applies differentially to various media or publications within its scope. Apart from taxes that are unique *in form* and economic burden, there is insufficient basis in history or common experience to impose such a heavy presumption against constitutionality based only on the fact of discrimination, as discrimination in the incidence or amount of a tax, as such, is not the heart of the knowledge tax problem.[8] Instead, the problem occasioned by knowledge taxes is discrimination in the availability of important and diverse information to the body politic, and this type of discrimination has but a tenuous, and often a converse, relationship to discrimination in the incidence or amount of a tax. Discrimination, to be sure, may be a device in the tax setting for censorship or, more likely, for constricting rather than fostering the diffusion of knowledge and the availability of choice; but discrimination may equally be an instrument for achieving broad diffusion of knowledge and preserving or fostering pluralism.[9]

Fourth, discrimination among media poses the same problems for an approach to knowledge taxes as does discrimination within a medium, except the problems are even more complex, and an approach based on a discrimination concept grounded on the incidence or the form of a tax is even more ill-fitting. Aside from the often impenetrable difficulties of administering a discrimination principle in the multimedia context,[10] it is far from obvious that the use of different tax levels, or even tax structures, for magazines or books, as opposed to daily newspapers, produces undesirable effects. Such effects may occur, to be sure, but their likelihood is far from evident from the fact of discrimination, itself. Our experience abounds with examples of such discrimination, many of which we may not find offensive or, at least, describable with the pejorative label of "knowledge tax." When we purchase books or magazines, we usually pay sales tax; for newspapers, most of us do not. Cable operators pay franchise taxes based on revenue; broadcasters do not. The broadcast industry is directly regulated (at least at this moment); the print media are not. Public broadcasting is tax-supported; commercial broadcasting is not.

Are these examples of discrimination—and there are many, many more—impermissible? I would suggest that they are not self-evidently so, at least on the basis of our concepts of knowledge taxation, even though they represent instances of differential incidence, rates, and even *forms* of taxation which, according to the Supreme Court, should bear a heavy presumption against constitutionality. Some such examples may involve improper taxation, others may not, but discrimination does not afford a helpful, and certainly not a decisive, standard for judgment.

The reason that a principle of discrimination is not decisive across media of communication is that the pertinent question is not simply equal treatment, but whether the purpose and effect of the departure from equality is conducive to, rather than destructive of, broad dissemination of knowledge and preservation of pluralism and choice, and whether differences in the form of exaction are necessary, either as a purely practical matter or as a means of encouraging diversity. It may be consistent with these values to exempt newspapers, the historic medium of broad dissemination of current information, from an otherwise reasonable tax imposed on magazines or books, because such an exemption could be conducive to the broadest, most diverse, and practical dissemination of knowledge on "politics and political economy." This, after all, was the basis upon which the penny stamp was ultimately resisted in England, as the People's Charter Union put it in 1849:

> A cheap *stamped* newspaper cannot be a good one. And if we are asked why we cannot be satisfied with the elegant and polite literature which may be had cheaply, we reply that we can no longer exist on the earth without information on the subjects of politics and political economy. . . . And we say to those who are within the pale of the Constitution, "if you cannot give us this knowledge, at least do not prevent us from seeking it ourselves; to tax the light of knowledge was ever a crime."[11]

Discrimination, in short, is neither good nor bad when it comes to taxation. Rather, "it depends," and we should focus our attention on whether and why "it depends" rather than on the fact of discrimination itself.

*   *   *

Finally, our approach to knowledge taxation must address, as approaches based on censorship and discrimination completely fail to address, the central questions posed by *any* form of tax. Any form of taxation of expression presents a difficult question in light of our notions of liberty because taxation itself exacts a price on expression and therefore inevitably contracts its availability. And it is equally of note that the contraction of availability will most often occur at the margin — with the least established publisher, or the least popular idea. While it may seem ironic at first blush, it seems clear on reflection that the central perspective afforded by history is that it is often the nondiscriminatory, generally applicable taxes that present the greatest threat to the free dissemination of knowledge and the availability of individual choice, and this is particularly so, from a historical perspective, with knowledge on matters of current public interest.[12] The ultimate dismantling of the English taxes resulted, in the end, from persistent opposition even after the obnoxious features of the original duties were eliminated. In large part this was because taxation itself, *especially* when exacted in broad and general form, favors the established media and chokes diversity.

This is not to say that all taxes should be deemed forbidden, no matter what the level or justification, for such a conclusion would not be dictated by experience.[13] It is to say, however, that the first and most important question that should be addressed in *any* case involving taxation is the amount of a tax and its effect on the availability of information of diverse character. This question — that is, the question of "effect" — is the one abjured by the Supreme Court in the *Minneapolis Star* case, and it is worth repeating that the Court's focus on discrimination was the very reason the Court was able to avoid it.

If history suggests anything, it is that a broadly applicable and nondiscriminatory tax should be treated with every bit as much suspicion as a discriminatory one, and that such a tax may well be unconstitutional even if not ill-motivated or confiscatory, as long as the demonstrated effect of the tax is materially to constrict the broad availability of information and diverse views. In this connection, it is worth repeating once again the moral of Mr. Collet's story: "When the King of the Tonga Isles, in the Pacific Ocean, was initiated by Mr. Marriner, the missionary, into the mysteries of the art of writing, he was alarmed at the idea of his subjects learning to read: 'I should,' he said, 'be surrounded with plots.'"[14] The value, as well as the travail, of freedom of expression has been its availability throughout all parts of a society.

If the general observations recounted above accurately reflect the broad strands of our experience with knowledge taxes, the outlines of a general approach to judging the propriety of knowledge taxes can be stated. The first step is a definitional one. It is necessary to determine at the outset whether the problem posed by a tax is best viewed as a knowledge tax issue or, instead, as an instance of censorship under the guise of taxation. If the purpose is to censor a particular viewpoint or subject matter, the tax ought to be addressed from the standpoint of censorship, not taxation. If the purpose is benign, or if the tax is intended to encourage and expand communication, the matter should be addressed as a knowledge tax problem.

Once the definitional inquiry is concluded and it has been determined that the relevant question is the permissibility of taxation rather than censorship, the focus of inquiry should turn to the effect of the tax. By effect I mean the size, incidence, and practical consequences of a tax on the publications subject to it, as well as on those not subject to it. The object of such an inquiry is to ascertain the type of publications and information affected by the tax ("polite and elegant" or focused on "politics and political economy," as the People's Charter Union put it); whether the disputed tax will broaden or narrow the reach or availability of publications affected by it; and whether the tax will encourage or deter, in whole or in part, the amount and diversity of expression available to the public. This inquiry will place in appropriate context the judgments that must be made about the tax itself, as well as the justifications for, and consequences of, any disparities in its form or its incidence. It will also disclose potential disparities that are not apparent on the face of the tax provisions, an issue which, history teaches us, is *at least* as important as the formal terms of a tax, if not more so.[15]

Only after the effect of the tax is understood should one look to discrimination in its form or application, for one cannot make soundly based judgments about discrimination without regard to the effect of the tax. Against the background of effect, the discriminations in application of a tax can be judged, and the judgments will be of two general types. First, if the effect of the tax is not to constrict availability and diversity of information significantly, either directly, or indirectly by serving the economic self-interest of dominant media in order to preserve their advantaged competitive position, or to politically isolate the press, it should be permitted so long as the revenue-related purpose is benign and the revenue advantages, in view of revenue objectives sought by government in other nonpublication settings, outweigh any slight effect on distribution and diversity. Of course, if such a tax also contains exemptions that foster additional distribution or diversity, it ought not, for those reasons, to be condemned, although we should view such provisions, in light of our experience, with a healthy measure of skepticism.

The second type of inquiry involves assessment of a tax that does have significant effects on availability of information, its diversity, or on structural features of the communication marketplace, but that is nevertheless grounded on benign revenue-related objectives. Such a tax might well be viewed with suspicion, but not with such a level of suspicion that further analysis is, as a practical matter, excused. The reason for mandating additional exploration is that some such taxes may not violate the concepts underlying forbidden knowledge taxes. It is possible that an entirely revenue-related tax may have a meaningful impact on distribution of information, but that it may also include exemptions that are intended to, or do in fact, encourage broader distribution of publications whose distribution is currently too limited, that encourage dissemination of information of general importance and practical usefulness to all segments of society, or that encourage the distribution of publications that enhance a measure of diversity found lacking in the marketplace.[16] Such taxes should not be deemed impermissible without assessing the trade-off they reflect and measuring the advantages of increased dissemination and diversity in certain quarters against the loss of distribution or diversity in others. While one might require fairly stringent proof to justify such a tax, particularly in view of the historically well-founded suspicion of governmental *and publisher* motives in the context of news, it will not do for a court to erect such an insurmountable legal barrier to inquiry that neither the issues of effect nor of justification can ever be probed.

Two examples of such a potentially justifiable tax come readily to mind, one from the recent past, one from the more distant past. The recent illustration is the tax credit feature of the Minnesota use tax, which was stricken in the *Minneapolis Star* case.[17] That case, it will be recalled, involved a hybrid use tax imposed as a substitute for a sales tax, but at a lower cost than a sales tax. The use tax provisions exempted, through a credit available to all papers, small papers below a threshold level of sales, and thereby also exempted a class of special purpose publications that would otherwise have fallen within the operative definition of taxed publications. The benign and revenue-related purposes of the tax were unimpeached. The Supreme Court's decision striking the tax was based on two premises, both challengeable: that inquiry into the effect of the tax was unnecessary; and that the discrimination between the large and small papers in the incidence of the tax required a special justification that could not be satisfied by either a good faith showing of revenue purposes or a demonstration that the exemptions were intended to, and in fact did, encourage greater and more diverse dissemination of information.

It is impossible to venture firm conclusions about the *Minneapolis Star* case because of the absence of evidence about the effect of the tax, both on availability of the *Star* and on other exempted publications, and because of the decisive factor of the tax's unique form. It seems clear, however, that from the perspective of the history of knowledge taxes the unconstitutionality of the exemption, or credit, feature of the tax is far from self-evident. The impact on the *Star*'s circulation, which we can presume existed, might well have been offset by the revenue justifications and the concomitant increase in circulation — or even survival[18] — of other and more diverse papers. And in view of the historical experience, a tax that imposes a larger burden on the major and established (and politically influential) publishers should not, *by that fact alone*, be deemed invalid. Striking a balance among such considerations cannot be escaped unless we are willing, as the Court was rightly not, to conclude that *any* level of tax that affects distribution is *per se* forbidden.

The second example serves to amplify the difficulties raised by the *Minneapolis Star* case. By the Act of 1836[19] the British stamp was reduced to one penny, with an associated right of free postage without additional charge — a right that was of value only to those papers using the post. The purpose of the Act, as a general matter, was by then effectively purged of the prior history of government control (although some other non-taxing provisions which would be relevant to a *full* consideration of the Act and its effect retained this specter[20]), and revenue justifications accounted for the decision to stop short of complete repeal. It is clear that the Act had the effect of broadening the distribution of news, and even more so the diversity of available information and opinion, by reducing the cost of papers to all citizens. Yet the postal prerogative also had the effect of retaining and increasing the distribution of the principal London daily and weekly papers in the rural areas — a fact of some concern to the provincial papers that didn't use the post but paid the tax. Are we to assess the 1836 tax without exploring its effect — and exploring it much more than I have here? Are we to be satisfied by a conclusion that the tax was impermissible because the postal prerogative discriminated in favor of the urban papers that relied on rural distribution for a large part of their circulation?

If we are to be satisfied by such limited reasoning, how would we judge the constitutionality of the later complete repeal of the stamp, which forced the leading London papers (among other things) to pay postage, and therefore gave the smaller urban papers and the local provincial press a real competitive edge? How are we to judge a decision to eliminate the stamp but maintain the paper tax in order to assure needed revenue, when the consequences of the paper tax were highly uneven? Should such a paper tax be deemed improper because, while nondiscriminatory on its face, it affected only publishers that used taxed paper, or advantaged those papers that chose to compress the news into fewer sheets?[21] Or was it proper because the repeal was neutral according to its literal terms, although discriminatory in effect? If, in response to such questions, we answer that such acts should not necessarily be deemed forbidden knowledge taxes because the effect of some of them were, on balance, positive — because they resulted in a net increase in dissemination and diversity of information — then we should not adopt a mode of analysis that forecloses such reasoning from the very beginning.

Let me, finally, respond to one criticism that is certain to be leveled against the approach I have outlined. The criticism is this: by recommending an approach based upon effect, grounded in the constitutional value of broad dissemination of useful and practical current information, particularly to those who can least afford it, I am proposing something akin to a redistribution of knowledge based on wealth, or a test which countenances, and indeed rewards, an effective subsidy by those best able to purchase knowledge on behalf of those least able to obtain it. The charge, it seems to me, is quite correct, and I plead guilty to it. It is not, however, a decisive one, nor is the approach of *my* making. It is instead the approach reflected in the history of knowledge taxation.

Knowledge is common property. In a free and democratic country dependent ultimately on the consent of the governed, the broad diffusion of knowledge is the most basic premise upon which we have cast our fate. To paraphrase the appeal of the People's Charter Union in 1849, if ignorance is the evil that undermines democracy and freedom, then we must find a means by which "ignorance should no longer be compulsory."[22] To some, the very idea of knowledge as common property is, and will always be, folly; so too the idea that we all have a stake in realizing it, even by redistributive means. But the very core of free expression, of individual liberty, of democratic self-government, and of course the very history of knowledge taxation, foreclose us as a *constitutional* matter from entertaining such a view. Knowledge *is* common property. This is the lesson of history. It is a lesson yet to be learned, and therefore yet to be taught, by the United States Supreme Court.

In characterizing and criticizing the Supreme Court's current efforts to develop a jurisprudence of taxation of the press, I am mindful of the concern that history ought not to be seen as the fixed definitional source of constitutional principle or doctrine. History reveals, but it does not substitute for independent reasoning in light of current values and contemporary social and political conditions. The history of knowledge taxes cannot, therefore, be the exclusive source of constitutional reasoning, any more than the subjective intentions of a committee convened two hundred years ago should bind us today.[23] The history of knowledge taxation in England and America does not establish either constitutional values or doctrine. But that history does shed light that permits us to see our current problems within a larger perspective as we formulate our constitutional values and develop concrete doctrines that protect and foster those values. The revelation of *this* history — the light it sheds — is that the values of broad dissemination of information and diversity of opinion will serve us well as guides, and that if we heed their guidance our approach to judging the limits of taxation of knowledge will be both different and broader than the one we are now using.

Notes

1. See Chapter 9; Randall P. Bezanson, "Political Agnosticism, Editorial Freedom, and Government Neutrality Toward the Press," 72 *Iowa L. Rev.* 1359 (1987).

2. See particularly Chapters 1 and 4.

3. See Collet Dobson Collet, *History of the Taxes on Knowledge: Their Origin and Repeal*, 42–46 (facsimile reprint 1971) (1933).

4. *Id.*

5. Minneapolis Star & Tribune Co. v. Minnesota Comm'r of Revenue, 460 U.S. 575 (1983).

6. Grosjean v. American Press Co., 297 U.S. 233 (1936).

7. Leathers v. Medlock, 111 S. Ct. 1438 (1991).

8. See Bezanson, *supra* note 1.

9. One of the most obvious examples is public broadcasting in the United States, which is clearly the product of intended discrimination through the provision of public funding.

10. For example, how are we to compare "equivalence" in taxation of newspapers, periodicals, books, leaflets, broadcast television and radio, cable transmission, data-base companies, computer-based reassemblers or repackagers of publications, and the various transmission media, ranging from news racks to telecommunications to satellite, to name only a few possibilities?

11. Collet at 45.

12. This seems to be the clearest and most obvious lesson to be drawn from the Stamp Act of 1712, as well as of the subsequent enactments designed to perfect the general applicability of the stamp duty once the unanticipated loopholes were discovered. See Chapter 1.

13. See Chapter 1 (1836 act reducing the newspaper tax to one penny; retention of paper tax); Chapter 3 (federal paper tax); Chapter 6 (sales taxes).

14. Collet at 1.

15. The English history is, of course, replete with evidence of actual administration designed to achieve censorial ends that the statute itself did not, and perhaps could not, make explicit, and of taxes that produced very different results from those intended. See Chapter 1.

16. A contemporary example would be the imposition of local cable franchise fees, or taxes, coupled with the requirement that local access channels be provided free of charge. Other examples might include public broadcasting, or in the future publicly accessible data bases and services. For other historical examples, see Chapter 6.

17. Minneapolis Star & Tribune Co. v. Minnesota Comm'r of Revenue, 460 U.S. 575 (1983).

18. This is particularly true with a use tax, the cost of which must be borne as part of the publication costs rather than as an add-on to the price paid by the consumer, for the tax burden cannot be passed through to the buyer as a simple add-on to the stated retail price.

19. An Act to Reduce the Duties on Newspapers, etc., 6 & 7 Will. 4, ch. 76 (1836).

20. See Chapter 9.

21. The practice of compressing news into fewer sheets was common in England, and at least one paper was published on cloth to escape the paper tax (the experiment was not successful). See H. R. Fox Bourne, *English Newspapers*, vol. 1 (1887) (reissued 1966); Chapter 1.

22. See Collet at 42–46.

23. See the elegant essay, "Parchment Matters: A Meditation on the Constitution as Text," by H. Jefferson Powell, in 71 *Iowa L. Rev.* 1427–35 (1986).

Selected Bibliography

Anderson, David A., "The Origins of the Press Clause," 30 *UCLA L. Rev.* 455 (1983).

Andrews, Alexander, *History of British Journalism* (London: Richard Bentley 1859) (republished 1968).

Aristocrotis [pseud.], "The Government of Nature Delineated, or an Exact Picture of the New Federal Constitution" (Carlisle 1788), reprinted in 3 *The Complete Anti-Federalist* at 204 (Herbert J. Storing ed., 1981).

Bezanson, Randall P., "The Future First Amendment," 37 *S.D. L. Rev.* 11 (1992).

——, "*Herbert v. Lando*, Editorial Judgment, and Freedom of the Press: An Essay," 1978 *U. Ill. L. F.* 619.

——, "The New Free Press Guarantee," 63 *Va. L. Rev.* 731 (1977).

——, "Political Agnosticism, Editorial Freedom, and Government Neutrality Toward the Press," 72 *Iowa L. Rev.* 1359 (1987).

——, "The Right to Privacy Revisited: Privacy, News, and Social Change, 1890–1990," 80 *Cal. L. Rev.* 1133 (1992).

Bickel, Alexander M., *The Morality of Consent* (1975).

Blasi, Vincent, "The Checking Value in First Amendment Theory," 1977 *Am. B. Found. Res. J.* 521.

Botein, Stephen, "'Meer Mechanics' and an Open Press: The Business and Political Strategies of Colonial American Printers," in 9 *Persp. in Am. Hist.* 127 (1975).

——, "Printers and the American Revolution," in *The Press and the American Revolution* 11 (Bernard Bailyn & John B. Heuch eds., 1980).

Bourne, H. R. Fox, *English Newspapers*, vol. 1 (reissued 1966) (1887).

Bryson, William H., *A Bibliography of Virginia Legal History Before 1900* (1979).

Butler, Ruth L., *Doctor Franklin, Postmaster General* (1928).

Cappon, Lester J., *Virginia Newspapers, 1821–1935* (1936).

Centinel [Samuel Bryan], Letter 2 to the People of Pennsylvania (1787), reprinted in 2 *The Complete Anti-Federalist* at 146 (Herbert J. Storing ed., 1981).

——, Letter 8 to the People of Pennsylvania (Dec. 29, 1787), reprinted in 2 *The Complete Anti-Federalist* at 177–79 (Herbert J. Storing ed., 1981).

Chicago Daily Tribune, Mar. 23, 1933, at 7.

Choper, Jesse H., "The Religion Clauses of the First Amendment: Reconciling the Conflict," 41 *U. Pitt. L. Rev.* 673 (1980).

Cincinnatus [Richard Henry Lee or Arthur Lee], Letter 1 to James Wilson, (*New York Journal*, Nov. 1, 1787), reprinted in 6 *The Complete Anti-Federalist* at 7–10 (Herbert J. Storing ed., 1981).

Clyde, William M., *Struggle for Freedom of the Press* (1934).

Collet, Collet Dobson, *History of the Taxes on Knowledge: Their Origin and Repeal* (facsimile reprint 1971) (1933).

Collins, Laurence, "Bellotti Says Public Property Ban of Newspaper Vending Boxes Is Illegal," *Boston Globe*, Dec. 22, 1985, at 40.

———, "Reporters as Detectives," *Boston Globe* (Sun.), Mar. 18, 1979, at 30.

The Complete Anti-Federalist (Herbert J. Storing ed., 1981).

Crane, R. S., & F. B. Kaye, *A Census of British Newspapers and Periodicals, 1620–1800* (1927).

Cushing, William, Letter from William Cushing, C.J., to John Adams (Feb. 18, 1789), reprinted in *Mass. L. Q.*, Oct. 1942, at 12.

Debates in the Federal Convention of 1787 Which Framed the Constitution of the United States of America (Gaillard Hunt & James B. Scott eds., 1987).

"Developments in the Law — Academic Freedom," 81 *Harv. L. Rev.* 1045 (1968).

Documentary History of the Ratification of the Constitution (M. Jensen ed., 1976).

Due, John F., & John L. Mikesell, *Sales Taxation: State and Local Structure and Administration* (1983).

Duniway, Clyde A., *The Development of Freedom of the Press in Massachusetts* (Franklin ed., 1969) (1906).

Editorial, "Reporters as Private Detectives," *Boston Globe*, Mar. 19, 1979, at 12.

Editorial, *Boston Globe*, May 21, 1991, at 20.

The Era of the American Revolution (Richard B. Morris ed., 1939).

Fahrner, Alvin A., "William Smith: Governor in Two Wars," in *The Governors of Virginia, 1860–1978*, at 28 (Edward Younger & James Tice Moore eds., 1982).

A Farmer [Thomas Cogswell], Essay 1 (*Freeman's Oracle and New Hampshire Advertiser*, Jan. 11, 1788), reprinted in 4 *The Complete Anti-Federalist* at 206–7 (Herbert J. Storing ed., 1981).

The Federal and State Constitutions, Colonial Charters, and Other Organic Laws (F. Thorpe ed., U. S. Gov't Printing Off. 1909).

Federal Farmer [Richard Henry Lee], "Observations Leading to a Fair Examination of the System of Government Proposed by the Late Convention; And to Several Essential and Necessary Alterations in It," Letter 4 (Oct. 12, 1787), reprinted in 2 *The Complete Anti-Federalist* at 250 (Herbert J. Storing ed., 1981).

———, "Observations Leading to a Fair Examination of the System of Government Proposed by the Late Convention; And to Several Essential and Necessary Alterations in It," Letter 16 (Jan. 20, 1788), reprinted in 2 *The Complete Anti-Federalist* at 329–30 (Herbert J. Storing ed., 1981).

A Federal Republican, "A Review of the Constitution . . . " (1787), reprinted in 3 *The Complete Anti-Federalist* at 81 (Herbert J. Storing ed., 1981).

The Federalist No. 84 (Alexander Hamilton) (Benjamin F. Wright ed., 1966).

Frank, Joseph, *The Beginnings of the English Newspaper, 1620–1660* (1961).

Fuller, Wayne E., *The American Mail* (1972).

Gerald, J. Edward, *The Press and the Constitution, 1931–1947* (1968).

Gorman, Elizabeth, "The First Amendment and the Postal Service's Subscriber Requirement: Constitutional Problems with Denying Equal Access to the Postal System," 21 *U. Rich. L. Rev.* 541 (1987).

The Governors of Virginia, 1860–1978 (Edward Younger & James Tice Moore eds., 1982).

Hamburger, Philip, "The Development of the Law of Seditious Libel and the Control of the Press," 37 *Stan. L. Rev.* 661 (1985).

Hanson, Laurence, *Government and the Press* (1936).

Harris, Michael, "The Structure, Ownership and Control of the Press, 1620–1780," in *Newspaper History from the Seventeenth Century to the Present Day* (George Boyce, et al. eds., 1978).

Hartman, Paul J., *Federal Limitations on State and Local Taxation* (1981).

Hellerstein, Jerome R., & Walter Hellerstein, *State and Local Taxation* (4th ed. 1978).

Henderson, Leslie C., "Reporter Licensing," *Freedom of Information Center Report* (June 1981).

Herd, Harold, *March of Journalism* (1952).

Hernandez, Peggy, "Council Votes to Regulate Newspaper Vending Boxes," *Boston Globe*, Dec. 10, 1987, at 43.

Historical Society of Pa., *Pennsylvania and the Federal Constitution* (1888).

Holmes, O. W., Jr., *Touched with Fire: The Civil War Letters and Diary of Oliver Wendell Holmes, Jr.* (Mark DeWolfe Howe ed., 1946).

Howison, Robert R., *History of Virginia* (1848).

Hyneman, Charles S., & Donald S. Lutz, *American Political Writing During the Founding Era, 1760–1805* (1983).

Katsh, M. Ethan, *The Electronic Media and the Transformation of Law* (1989).

Kielbowicz, Richard F., *News in the Mail: The Press, Post Office, and Public Information, 1700–1860s* (1989).

Kuo, John Wei-Ching, "Sales/Use Taxation of Software: An Issue of Tangibility," 2 *High Tech. L.J.* 125 (1987).

Kurland, Philip B., *Religion and the Law* (1962).

Leavitt, Joshua, *Cheap Postage* (1848).

Leder, Lawrence H., *America 1603–1789: Prelude to a Nation* (1978).

Lee, Richard Henry, "Observations Leading to a Fair Examination of the System of Government, Letter 4," reprinted in 1 Bernard Schwartz, *The Bill of Rights: A Documentary History* 474 (1971).

Lee, William, *Daniel DeFoe: His Life and Recently Discovered Writings*, vol. 1 (photo. reprint 1968) (London, 1869).

Levy, Leonard W., *Emergence of a Free Press* (1985).

———, *Freedom of the Press from Zenger to Jefferson* (Leonard W. Levy ed., 1966).

———, *Judgments: Essays on American Constitutional History* (1972).

———, "On the Origins of the Free Press Clause," 32 *UCLA L. Rev.* 177 (1984).

Lewis, Lawrence, *The Advertisements of the Spectator* (1909).

Lockman, Norman, "Reporter Licensing Urged Again," *Boston Globe*, Apr. 18, 1979, at 18.

Lowe, Richard G., "Francis Harrison Pierpont: Wartime Unionist, Reconstruction Moderate," in *The Governors of Virginia, 1860–1978*, at 36 (Edward Younger & James Tice Moore eds., 1982).

Malone, M. E., "Many Sales Tax Exemptions Remain," *Boston Globe*, Jan. 13, 1990, at 8.

Marshall, John A., *American Bastille* (16th ed. 1875).

May, T., *The Constitutional History of England, 1760–1860* (1880).

McCloud, Herman C., "Sales Tax and Use Tax: Historical Developments and Differing Features," 22 *Duq. L. Rev.* 823 (1984).

McKibben, Gordon, "Globe Opens Fight on Newspaper Tax," *Boston Globe*, July 20, 1990, at 21.

"Media at the Millenium," 5 *Media Stud. J.* 1 (1991).

Miller, James C., III, & Roger Sherman, "Has the 1970 Act Been Fair to Mailers?" in Sherman, Roger, ed., *Perspectives in Postal Service Issues* (1980).

Miller, John C., *Origins of the American Revolution* (1943).

Miller, Samuel, *A Brief Retrospect of the Eighteenth Century* (1803).

Morison, Stanley, *The English Newspaper, 1622–1932* (1932).

Morton, Richard L., *History of Virginia* (1924).

Nelson, Harold L., *Freedom of the Press from Hamilton to the Warren Court* (1967).

New York Times, Jan. 19, 1862, at 4; Jan. 20, 1862, at 5; Jan. 22, 1862, at 1; Feb. 11, 1862, at 4; Mar. 4, 1862, at 4; Mar. 5, 1862, at 4.

Newspaper History from the Seventeenth Century to the Present Day (George Boyce, et al. eds., 1978).

North, Simon N., *History and Present Condition of the Newspaper and Periodical Press of the United States* (1884).

O'Brien, Connor Cruise, *The Great Melody: A Thematic Biography of Edmund Burke* (1992).

"Observations Leading to a Fair Examination of the System of Government Proposed by the Late Convention; And to Essential and Necessary Alterations in It," Letter 4 (Oct. 12, 1787), reprinted in 2 *The Complete Anti-Federalist* at 250 (Herbert J. Storing ed., 1981).

Office of Technology Assessment, *Science, Technology, and the First Amendment*, Special Report (1988).

An Old Whig [pseud.], Essay 3 ([Philadelphia] *Independent Gazetter* 1787), reprinted in 3 *The Complete Anti-Federalist* at 27–28 (Herbert J. Storing ed., 1981).

Pennsylvania Antifederalist [William Findley (?)], *Independent Gazetteer*, Nov. 6, 1787, reprinted in 3 *The Complete Anti-Federalist* at 93 (Herbert J. Storing ed., 1981).

Pepper, George W., & William D. Lewis, *Digest of Decisions & Encyclopedia of Pennsylvania Law, 1754–1898* (1905).

A Plebeian [Melancton Smith], Address (New York 1788), reprinted in 6 *The Complete Anti-Federalist* at 145 (Herbert J. Storing ed., 1981).

Pomerantz, Sidney I., "The Patriot Newspaper and the American Revolution," in *The Era of the American Revolution* (Richard B. Morris ed., 1939).

Pool, Ithiel De Sola, *Technologies of Freedom* (1983).

Powell, H. Jefferson, "Parchment Matters: A Meditation on the Constitution as Text," 71 *Iowa L. Rev.* 1427 (1986).

The Press and the American Revolution (Bernard Bailyn & John B. Heuch eds., 1980).

Price, J. M., "A Note on the Circulation of the London Press, 1704–1714," 31 *Bull. Inst. Hist. Res.* 219 (1958).

Ramsay, David, "The History of the American Revolution" (1789), reprinted in 2 Hyneman, Charles S., & Donald S. Lutz, *American Political Writing, 1760–1805* (1983).

Read, Donald, *Press and People, 1790–1850* (1961).

Reid, John Phillip, *Constitutional History of the American Revolution: The Authority to Tax* (1987).

Richards, Benjamin A., "Historic Rationale of the Speech-and-Press Clause of the First Amendment," 21 *U. Fla. L. Rev.* 203 (1968).

Roper, Daniel C., *The United States Post Office* (1917).

Rutland, Robert A., *The Ordeal of the Constitution: The Anti-federalists and the Ratification Struggle of 1787–1788* (1966).

Salmon, Lucy M., *Newspaper and Authority* (1923).

Schlesinger, Arthur M., *Prelude to Independence* (1958).

Schudson, Michael, *Discovering the News: A Social History of American Newspapers* (1978).

Schwartz, Bernard, *The Bill of Rights: A Documentary History* (1971).

Sherman, Roger, ed., *Perspectives on Postal Service Issues* (1980).

Siebert, Frederick S., *Freedom of the Press in England, 1476–1776* (1952).

Simon, Todd F., "All the News That's Fit to Tax: First Amendment Limitations on State and Local Taxation of the Press," 21 *Wake Forest L. Rev.* 59 (1985).

Smith, A. D., *The Development of Rates of Postage* (1917).

Smith, Culver H., *The Press, Politics, and Patronage: The American Government's Use of Newspapers, 1789–1875* (1977).

Smith, Jeffery A., *Printers and Press Freedom: The Ideology of Early American Journalism* (1988).

Snyder, Henry L., *The Circulation of Newspapers in the Reign of Queen Anne* (1968).

Sorkin, Alan L., *The Economics of the Postal System* (1980).

Special Subcomm. on State Taxation of Interstate Commerce, *State Taxation of Interstate Commerce*, H.R. Rep. No. 256, 89th Cong., 1st Sess. (1965).

Stewart, Potter S., "'Or of the Press,'" 26 *Hastings L.J.* 631 (1975).

Stewart, William, "Lennox and the Taxes on Knowledge," 15 *Scot. Hist. Rev.* 322 (1918).

Teeter, Dwight L., Jr., & Don R. LeDuc, *Law of Mass Communications* (7th ed. 1992).

Thomas, Isaiah, *The History of Printing in America* (Weathervane Books 1970) (1874).

Thompson, Mack, "Massachusetts and New York Stamp Acts," 26 *Wm. & Mary Q.* 253 (3d ser. 1969).

Tunick, David C., & Dan S. Schechter, "State Taxation of Computer Programs: Tangible or Intangible?" 63 *Taxes* 54 (1985).

Van Alstyne, William W., "The Hazards to the Press of Claiming a 'Preferred Position,'" 28 *Hastings L.J.* 761 (1977).

Veeder, Van V., "The History and Theory of the Law of Defamation," 3 *Col. L. Rev.* 546 (1903).

——, *Selected Essays in Anglo-American Legal History*, vol. 3 (1909).

Vennochi, Joan, "Publishers Unify Against Tax Proposal," *Boston Globe*, June 8, 1990, at 27.

Warren, William C., & Milton R. Schlesinger, "Sales and Use Taxes: Interstate Commerce Pays Its Way," 38 *Colum. L. Rev.* 49 (1938).

Whipple, Leon, *The Story of Civil Liberty in the United States* (1927).

Wickwar, William H., *The Struggle for the Freedom of the Press, 1819–1832* (Johnson reprint 1972) (1928).

Williamson, Hugh, "Remarks on the New Plan of Government" (1788), reprinted in Bernard Schwartz, *The Bill of Rights: A Documentary History* 551 (1971).

Table of Cases

Index

This book has been set in Linotron Galliard. Galliard was designed for Mergenthaler in 1978 by Matthew Carter. Galliard retains many of the features of a sixteenth-century typeface cut by Robert Granjon but has some modifications that give it a more contemporary look.

Printed on acid-free paper.